FESTIVE CULTURE IN GERMANY AND EUROPE FROM THE SIXTEENTH TO THE TWENTIETH CENTURY

Front Cover: The Picture was taken from the holdings of the National Szechenyi Library, Budapest, Hungary.

FESTIVE CULTURE IN GERMANY AND EUROPE FROM THE SIXTEENTH TO THE TWENTIETH CENTURY

Edited by
Karin Friedrich

The Edwin Mellen Press
Lewiston•Queenston•Lampeter

Library of Congress Cataloging-in-Publication Data

Friedrich, Karin
  Festive Culture in Germany and Europe from the Sixteenth to the Twentieth Century

ISBN 0-7734-7769-1   (hard)

A CIP catalog record for this book is available from the British Library.

Copyright © 2000 Karin Friedrich

All rights reserved. For information contact

The Edwin Mellen Press
Box 450
Lewiston, New York
USA 14092-0450

The Edwin Mellen Press
Box 67
Queenston, Ontario
CANADA L0S 1L0

The Edwin Mellen Press, Ltd.
Lampeter, Ceredigion, Wales
UNITED KINGDOM SA48 8LT

Printed in the United States of America

CONTENTS

List of Illustrations — vii
Foreword — ix
Acknowledgements — xv

Part I: Popular Festivals and Power

1. Introduction — 1
   Karin Friedrich
2. Election Festivals, Power and Society in Sixteenth-Century Burgundy — 17
   Mack P. Holt
3. *Trionfi* of the Holy Dead: The Relic Festivals of Baroque Bavaria — 31
   Trevor Johnson
4. Peace Festivals and the Culture of Memory in Early Modern South German Cities — 57
   Claire Gantet
5. The Politicization of Traditional Festivals in Germany, 1815–48 — 73
   James Brophy
6. Wine Festivals in Contemporary France: Reshaping Power through Time in Burgundy — 107
   Marion Demossier

Part II: Monarchic, Dynastic and Court Festivals

1. Habsburg Festivals in the Early Modern Period — 123
   Karl Vocelka
2. Four Weddings and a Funeral: Festival Forms and Dynastic Consolidation in Ducal Lorraine 1563–1624 — 137
   Kate Currey
3. The Petrine Year: Anniversaries and Festivals in the Reign of Peter I (1682–1725) — 149
   Lindsey Hughes
4. The Transformation of Ceremonial: Ducal Weddings in Brunswick, c. 1760–1800 — 169
   Thomas Biskup
5. The 1896 Millennial Festivities in Hungary: An Exercise in Patriotic and Dynastic Propaganda — 187
   Tom Barcsay

6. Province versus Metropolis: The Instrumentalized Myth of
   Archduke John of Styria (1782–1859) 213
   Dieter Binder

Part III: Military, National and Patriotic Festivals

1. Early Modern Tournaments and their Relationship to Warfare:
   France and the Empire Compared 233
   Helen Watanabe O'Kelly

2. Rituals of the 'Nations in Arms': Military Festivals in
   Germany and France (1871–1914) 245
   Jakob Vogel

3. War in Mind: Celebrations and War Enthusiasm in the Rhineland, 1913 265
   Ute Schneider

4. Celebrating the Republic without Republicans:
   The *Reichsverfassungstag* in Berlin, 1929–32 281
   Pamela Swett

5. The Nation Honours the Dead: Remembrance Days for the Fallen
   in the Weimar Republic and the Third Reich 303
   Sabine Behrenbeck

6. Celebrating Christmas in the Third Reich and GDR: Political
   Instrumentalization and Cultural Continuity under the
   German Dictatorships 323
   Corey Ross

7. The King's Right Hand: A Hungarian National-Religious Holiday and
   the Conflict between the Communist Party and the
   Catholic Church (1945–48) 343
   Árpád v. Klimó

Index 363

LIST OF ILLUSTRATIONS

(between pp. 186–87)

1. Peter I and Catherine sailing in St Petersburg: from an engraving by A. Zubov, 1716.
2. The 1896 Hungarian Millennial Procession passes in front of the Supreme Court building: 'the imposing building forms a gigantic background [...] the group depicted on this photograph is reminiscent of a wonderful dream which the world has never seen before' (from *Das Huldigungs-Banderium vom 8ten Juni 1896 verewigt in Wort und Bild unter der Redaktion Stanislaus Tumárisz*, ed. Julius Laurencic, Budapest, 1896).
3. Survey map of the routes taken by the messengers of the German Gymnasts' Movement on 16–18 October 1913 (from *Deutsche Turn-Zeitung*, Leipzig, 1913, p. 742).
4. Konsum (German state department store) advertisement: 'Konsum prepares for Christmas'; the caption below reads 'Our rich array of goods is the result of our workers' hard work for the victory of socialism!' (Leipzig: VEB Graphische Werkstätten, 1958, reproduced from *Deutsches Historisches Museum Magazin*, 5, 1995, 14, p. 35).
5. Woman and children gazing at a Christmas tree and what we are to understand to be a portrait of their fallen husband and father (from *Deutsche Kriegsweihnacht*, 1944, p. 123). This Nazi publication appeared annually during the war years.

FOREWORD

Margaret McGowan

When Jean Jacquot inaugurated the scholarly study of *fêtes* in the early 1950s,[1] he was aware of the rich vistas he was opening up. Interpreting *fêtes* very broadly, he foresaw major areas of artistic and historical endeavour. He recognized the importance of ritual, of beliefs and tradition, the role of the arts in society, the interaction of festival with politics and social concerns, and the philosophical and religious foundations on which many celebrations were predicated. And yet, in attempting to map the incidence of festivals across Renaissance Europe, he could hardly have anticipated the vast academic industry which was to develop.

The simplest definition of festival — a manifestation through which a society or group makes plain its consciousness of its own identity and its determination to preserve that identity — calls forth an immense range of celebratory activities. If the location of festivals is considered, we need to evoke courts and churches, urban space which accommodated carnivals, princely entries and civic ceremonies such as the Lord Mayor shows; colleges where Jesuits displayed their ingenious inventions; and village greens where the annual cycle of feasts was enjoyed. If the participants are considered, multiple performers of diverse ranks appear: the élite at court whose lives — in peacetime — were defined by ritual and ceremony, and who — at times of war — displayed their prowess in splendour on the battlefield; the burghers and citizens who forked out the money required to welcome their prince with due honours and spectacle; the urban populace who watched and cheered the cortège; and the rural poor (together with their urban fellows) whose relaxation was to stare in awe at the sight of the Body of Christ as it was carried through the streets and who danced and got drunk on feast days. Festivals involved the whole of society.

The tenacity of festival traditions, their varied forms and their ubiquity in all societies, have raised fundamental questions about how we interpret the past. Sometimes records of these spectacles survive in abundance; sometimes there are

---

1 Jean Jacquot, *Les Fêtes de la Renaissance*, 3 vols, Paris, 1956–75.

only a few crumbs of information left in the archives. Diaries, official records and descriptions tell prejudiced tales about performances and their reception. How is the historian, the musicologist, the anthropologist, the scholar interested in the theatre and in art history to assess these complex events long gone? How can we reconstruct festivals that, for their full understanding, require a knowledge of the precise historical, social and political context, and an interdisciplinary approach which appreciates both the independent role of the individual arts (music, painting, dancing, poetry and philosophy) and the ways in which they were harmonized together to produce particular effects?

Festivals transformed the arts because their organizers demanded the best that their contemporaries could manage. They called forth the skills of engineers to create the ambitious machines that walked the streets or metamorphosed the stage. They inspired poets to devise new myths and to find values in old ones; musicians to invent compositions which reminded audiences of familiar tunes but which also put them in touch with novel ways of combining sound; choreographers to startle dancers and spectators with complicated steps and rare figures. From such inspiration came the creation of new forms — the *ballet de cour* and opera.

Politics and festivals have always been closely connected. Princes used court entertainments to project enhanced images of themselves, believing that the more lavish the spectacle the greater was the prestige. They supported the extravagant inventions of artists, who recognized that their own status depended on being able to compete successfully with artists from other courts. Such rivalry conditioned the nature of court festivals, which became ever more spectacular. But festivals also provided the terrain on which arguments might be fought out, whether in chivalric display or in other forms of *divertissement*. Thus, Catherine de' Medici had her Catholic sons fight victoriously against Protestant nobles in the armed combat arranged as part of the celebrations devised for the wedding of Marguerite de Valois and Henri de Navarre in 1572; Catholics and Protestants again sought dominance in celebrations in Bavaria in 1693, when different festival traditions (church feast days and motifs and forms from Roman Triumphs) interacted; or interpretation of these events can still align historians on different sides of the arguments, as in Vogel's confrontation with George Mosse in the discussion of military festivals in Germany at the beginning of the twentieth century. In these cases, hold on power was fragile and social harmony was at risk, with rifts and

Foreword   xi

tensions threatening just below the surface. For the time of the entertainment, at least, it seemed possible to reinforce the power of the prevailing authorities.

And yet the issue of control remained a major preoccupation. At courts, despite petty squabbles over precedence and worries about individual status, the problem barely surfaced in a situation where shows were organized by an élite for whom the performance was an extension (perhaps a heightening) of their everyday lives. Court entertainment confirmed and supplied an intensified awareness of accepted values, rituals and hierarchies. Control became more problematic, however, at times when princes made their entries into the towns of their realm. Although the solidarity between the prince and the urban authorities was the *raison d'être* of the exercise, the urban population present in force and passively gazing on the procession, puzzling over the monuments that had been erected for the occasion, were a possible threat to civil peace. Their potential eruption and their unpredictability had been demonstrated more than once at carnival times and even on church feast days when inflammatory sermons had encouraged them to break out.

Over time, changes in the politics of festival are perceptible. Before the mid-eighteenth century, when festivals in Europe were chiefly organized and controlled by the court or the Church, their established authority was expressed and reinforced by the splendour of their shows, the ingenuity of their design and the quality of artistic performance. As is demonstrated in this book, after 1770 festivals were no longer the privilege of the court. They had become events belonging to the general public. The populace, passive spectators of yesteryear, were now full participants in the ceremonies. Festivals had acquired new functions. The prince lost his aura and had given way to the state as the focal point of festival occasions. The symbolism of the nation had ousted images of sovereign power in order to display social and political harmony and stability; subjects became citizens; private festival space virtually disappeared.

This book, arranged thematically and broadly chronologically, charts modifications made to festival traditions by successive generations, especially from the late seventeenth century. The principal focus is Germany, and each chapter documents the gradual politicization of festivals. France provided some early examples of festivals as active components of government, and the national celebrations following the French Revolution undoubtedly influenced the content and pattern of festivals throughout Germany where, increasingly, public representation of power invaded popular culture. The role played by the armed forces in popular celebrations became more marked: for instance, the Kaiser's ceremonial parades (introduced from 1878) showed the ruler and the army side by side for all to see, representing together the unifying bond of the German national state.

Two conditions were necessary for the political seizure of festival traditions to be efficacious. First, it was essential to choose festival forms that were deeply rooted in popular custom and experience, so that the mysterious chords of familiar ritual could sound as everyone, from all ranks of society, participated in the new manifestations. Secondly (from the early nineteenth century), preparation for the reception of new political ideas needed to have been made by the many associations which had sprung up and whose members read, debated and assimilated current political discourses. Perhaps the most positive use of festival in all its possible manifestations was the series of millennial celebrations in Hungary (1896). Imitating the rest of Europe in the scale, length and expense of the festivities to celebrate the coming of Árpád and his chieftains and the founding of their country (c. AD 900), Hungary, although still a state of many nations, contrived to reconcile warring factions, to erect monuments and bridges, to start the magnificent parliament building and to establish schools. King Franz Joseph was given a role at the centre of the celebrations. Endorsing the general theme of progress, he visited exhibitions, attended the opera, was present at numerous masses and admired costume parades, surrounded everywhere by cheering crowds.

In Germany, by the 1930s, the importance for the authorities of securing a monopoly on political space shaped the form of festivals. These became vehicles of persuasion, ways of getting the people to believe in a confident and united nation. By the time Hitler came to power, the whole festival apparatus was ready for his exploitation. Martyrs to the National Socialist cause were honoured like saints, and their sacrifice was turned into a triumph celebrating the party's assumption of power, which was made manifest in processions, chants and increasing mass hysteria.

Despite the political annexation of festivals, however, it should be noted that they spawned many ambiguities and contradictions. In the period 1648–60, the

200 peace festivals in south German cities reconstructed the realities of war in order to bury the memory of the experience. Messages regarding war in festivals were, in fact, rarely straightforward. Celebrations in the Rhineland in 1913, for instance, projected a romanticized idea of war which was then used to justify increases in expenditure on arms in preparation for another conflict — the Great War. Carnival saw the spectacle of the world turned upside down, championed free speech and liberal governance and, at the same time, reinforced the structures it consciously sought to satirize, while local festivals which were established to dissipate tensions and to integrate the community frequently ended in strife.

The historical myths that were the stuff of festival themes were volatile and were deployed with considerable flexibility both by the organizers of celebrations and by the historians who subsequently tried to reconstruct them. The personal legacy of Archduke John of Austria, for example, has been 'marketed' by historians to defend their own particular view of history or to advance their ideological objectives. Thus the Archduke appears as Styrian leader devoted to his country, as promoter of the needs of the peasantry, as loyal to the federal government and as strong supporter of a common Austrian fatherland. Each strand demonstrates the richness but also the haphazardness of political analogues. Similarly, there were attempts, under the Communists in Hungary, to replace St Stephen's Day with a 'Peasants' Day'; or, under the Third Reich and the German Democratic Republic, to secularize Christmas using the traditional celebrations for propaganda purposes against the West. Such re-shapings of religious traditions were doomed to failure.

As festivals became Europeanized and increasingly politicized, broad themes and similar forms were common across national borders. To detect distinctiveness, it will be necessary to continue to study individual festivals in their precise contexts, or to examine clusters of symbols applied in a particular place at a specific time. Peter the Great imposed his individual stamp on the development and direction of festivals in Russia by modifying tradition, inserting new priorities, reducing the role of the Church and introducing significant military dimensions closely related to the image he wished to project of his country and of himself. And yet, in his vast territory, the great mass of the population remained indifferent to — even unaware of — the changes. None the less, political masters in the nineteenth and twentieth centuries continued to exploit the potentialities of festival. Progressively, forms of celebration have collapsed into multifaceted spectacles where separate ingredients from long-established traditions are welded together — processions, songs, feasting, displays of physical prowess in theatrical contexts. Despite the ironing-out, and the universalization, public expectation remains. There is the excitement of sharing experience in an expressly heightened atmosphere; the emotions generated by music and movement; and the satisfaction of knowing how to read the symbols and understand the images. Festival touches deep human instincts which relate to origin and community; it brings back the past and comfortably assures its permanence; its secure role in society offers perennial challenges to the historian and reader alike.

ACKNOWLEDGEMENTS

This book benefits from the co-operation of several scholars specializing in the field of festival culture in Europe, some of whom contributed to the conference 'Feste Feiern wie sie fallen': Festivals in Germany and Europe, organized in London in 1997. I would like to thank the sponsors of the conference and of this publication, without whose support the completion of this volume would not have been possible. The German History Society funded its 1997 'Regional Conference' with particular generosity. I would like to thank Professor Anthony Nicholls and Professor Mary Fulbrook for their encouragement during the conference preparations. I am greatly indebted to the British Academy, which granted a considerable sum from its conference fund. Without this financial help the conference would not have had such an international profile, since it gave me the chance to invite scholars from several European countries and from North America. The German Historical Institute in London and its Director, Professor Peter Wende, showed great kindness and interest in the event by covering the travel and accommodation expenses of a German participant in the conference. I am very grateful to Dr Emil Brix, Director of the Austrian Cultural Institute, who showed his support by accommodating three Austrian scholars in the Institute and by chairing a conference session. I would also like to thank the Royal Historical Society for funding several research students, thus enabling them to attend the conference, and the Isobel Thornley Bequest Fund and Pat Crimmin for their generosity in supporting the publication of this book. Last, but not least, I owe a great debt to my own institution, the School of Slavonic and East European Studies (SSEES), and its Director, Professor Michael Branch, whose office not only helped me with the complex logistics of the conference but also contributed generously to the cost of publication. I received kind support for this project from Dr Robert Oresko, Professor Margaret McGowan, Dr Marion Demossier, Dr Robert Frost and Dr Philip Mansel and the Society for Court Studies. My thanks also go to Dr John Pritchard and Mrs Iona Williams of Edwin Mellen Press, as well as to the copy-editor, John Andrew.

Karin Friedrich *SSEES, University College London*
September 1999

PART I
POPULAR FESTIVALS AND POWER

INTRODUCTION

Karin Friedrich

In 1990, Manfred Hettling and Paul Nolte criticized the 'impressionist haphazardness' in the presentation of cultural history through case-studies.[1] At first sight, a book on festival culture in Europe, spanning five centuries, might fall into this category. Yet the following eighteen papers, which result from the 'Annual Regional Conference of the German History Society' in the United Kingdom, held at the School of Slavonic and East European Studies in April 1997, follow a coherent set of themes and issues. Far from offering a random collection of interesting but unconnected examples, this book puts a clear emphasis on German festival culture, albeit within a comparative European context, including festivals from the sixteenth to the twentieth centuries, from France and Germany, Burgundy and Lorraine, to Austria, Hungary and Russia. Since the 1980s, festival culture in Germany has been a growing field of study — mainly concentrated on the nineteenth century — but most contributions examine the social or political meaning of festivals, in order to support or contest the theory of a German *Sonderweg*, the 'exceptionalism' of the development of society and government in Germany.[2] Yet neither festivals with a national or

---

1 Paul Nolte and Manfred Hettling (eds), *Bürgerliche Feste. Symbolische Formen politischen Handelns im 19. Jahrhundert*, Göttingen, 1993, p. 12.
2 Dieter Düding, Paul Friedemann and Paul Münch (eds), *Öffentliche Festkultur. Politische Feste in Deutschland von der Aufklärung bis zum Ersten Weltkrieg*, Hamburg, 1988; Nolte and Hettling (eds), *Bürgerliche Feste*; James Brophy, 'Carnival and Citizenship: The Politics

nationalist agenda, nor the large field of political festivals organized by the German bourgeoisie or the labour movement — both of which have been thoroughly studied[3] — have paid much attention to cross-national comparisons. In contrast to scholarship on the European Renaissance, historians of modern German festival culture have only recently begun to analyse the subject with an eye for general European patterns, as shown in the works by Charlotte Tacke, Jakob Vogel, Étienne François, Michael Mitterauer and Emil Brix.[4] By mixing case-studies from Eastern and Western Europe across five centuries, the present volume hopes to add a new dimension to the analysis of festival culture. It also consciously aims at breaking down barriers between national traditions and chronological borders — often enhanced by existing academic divisions between the early modern and modern periods — in order to improve the communication within festival scholarship.

No less a figure than Jean-Jacques Rousseau was one of the first to study popular festival culture in the second half of the eighteenth century, when he

---

of Carnival Culture in the Prussian Rhineland, 1823–1848', *Journal of Social History*, 1997, pp. 72–104; Elaine G. Spencer, 'Regimenting Revelry: Rhenish Carnival in the Early Nineteenth Century', *Central European History*, 28, 1995, 4; Jonathan Sperber, 'Festivals of Unity in the German Revolution of 1848–9', *Past and Present*, 136, 1992, pp. 114–38, to name just a few examples.

3 See most contributions in Düding et al. (eds), *Öffentliche Festkultur*, especially Leo Haupt on the festivals to mark the reconstruction of Cologne Cathedral (pp. 191–211) and by Rainer Noltenius on the Schiller festivals (pp. 237–57); Nolte and Hettling (eds), *Bürgerliche Feste*; and several contributions in Étienne François, Hannes Siegrist and Jakob Vogel (eds.), *Nation und Emotion: Deutschland und Frankreich im Vergleich, 19. und 20. Jahrhundert*, Göttingen, 1995. On working-class festivals: Klaus Tenfelde, 'Mining Festivals in the Nineteenth Century', *Journal of Contemporary History*, 12, 1978, pp. 377–412; Gerhard A. Ritter (ed.), *Arbeiterkultur*, Königstein, 1979; Lynn Abrams, *Workers' Culture in Imperial Germany: Leisure and Recreation in the Rhineland and Westphalia*, New York, 1992.

4 Charlotte Tacke, *Denkmal im sozialen Raum: Nationale Symbole in Deutschland und Frankreich im 19. Jahrhundert*, Göttingen, 1995; Michael Mitterauer, 'Anniversarium und Jubiläum. Zur Entstehung und Entwicklung öffentlicher Gedenktage', in Emil Brix and Hannes Stekl (eds), *Der Kampf um das Gedächtnis. Öffentliche Gedenktage in Mitteleuropa*, Vienna, Cologne and Weimar, 1996; François et al. (eds), *Nation und Emotion*, and contributions in the present volume below.

proclaimed that the greatest value of festivals was the emotional creativity they produced among the mass of the people participating: 'Plant a pike in the middle of a market place and crown it with some flowers, assemble the people and you have a festival. Even better: give the spectacle an audience, turn the spectators into actors, and make them discover themselves in each other and love each other, so they will be even more united.'[5] It is not hard to see how such instructions appealed to the organizers of revolutionary festivals in the years following the events of 1789. What is crucial, however, in this early definition of popular festivals, is the advice that festivals have to be strategically organized, assembled, 'planted'. Spontaneity needs a managerial framework and an agenda which is usually dictated by power relationships.

This book attempts to modify and redirect the almost exclusive focus of social and cultural historians on the 'grass-roots', which was first guided by the *Annales* tradition and influenced by several seminal studies by Mona Ozouf, Robert Darnton, Peter Burke and others,[6] who ascribed to festivals the importance of spontaneity and the carnivalesque and stressed the importance of the world turned 'upside-down'. This approach relies strongly on Emil Durkheim's definition of festivals as 'sur-réalité', which interrupts everyday life and celebrates the suspension or even inversion of the well-known social, political and hierarchical order of a community.[7] Thus benefiting from anthropological influences, the analysis of mentality and behaviour, festivals and the ritualistic celebration of memory, especially in the early modern period, have remained the domain of the

---

5   Quoted in Paul Hugger (ed.), *Stadt und Fest. Zur Geschichte und Gegenwart europäischer Festkultur*, Stuttgart, 1987, p. 12 (my translation — K. F.).

6   Emmanuel Le Roy Ladurie, *Carnival in Romans*, London, 1980; Mona Ozouf, *Festivals and the French Revolution*, Cambridge, MA, 1988; Peter Burke, *Popular Culture in Early Modern Europe*, London, 1978; Robert Scribner, 'Reformation, Carnival and the World Upside Down', in Ingrid Bátori (ed.), *Städtische Gesellschaft und Reformation*, Stuttgart, 1980, pp. 234–64; Robert Darnton, *The Great Cat Massacre and Other Episodes in French Cultural History*, London, 1984; Lynn Hunt (ed.), *The New Cultural History*, Berkeley, CA and London, 1989.

7   Hugger (ed.), *Stadt und Fest*, pp. 14–16. See also J. Assmann (ed.), *Das Fest und das Heilige. Religiöse Kontrapunkte zur Alltagswelt*, Gütersloh, 1991, and W. Gebhardt, *Fest, Feier und Alltag. Über die gesellschaftliche Wirklichkeit des Menschen und ihre Deutung*, Frankfurt, 1987.

history of popular culture and social history from below.[8] In contrast, new trends in court studies, or the history of institutional culture, offer as yet largely unexplored venues, or are restricted to specialized publications.[9] Thus this collection tries to challenge and modify in several respects the way festivals in Germany and Europe have been studied over the last twenty years.

The contributors to this volume are concerned with the context provided by power relationships and the interaction between 'below' and 'above', reflected in popular festivals as well as in official, government-organized, institutionalized ceremonies, expressed in 'festival management'. The success of festivals and their impact on society depends on the way themes, symbols, identities, values, time and traditional social habits are organized. The core themes which structure this book have been chosen to reflect three groups of festivals for which the cultural context of institutions plays a major role: the reflection of power relationships (social, political, economic) in popular festivals; festivals in a monarchic and dynastic context; and military and national festival culture.

For most festivals, the involvement of the whole community in the preparation of the event was itself a constituent part of the festival, influencing identities, shaping intentions, sharpening conflicts, but also resolving existing tensions. The first section in this book focuses as much on power struggles within local political structures as on the ability of festivals to create political and communal cohesion

---

[8] Robert Scribner and Trevor Johnson (eds), *Popular Religion in Germany and Central Europe, 1400–1800*, London, 1996; Richard van Dülmen and Norbert Schindler (eds), *Volkskultur. Zur Wiederentdeckung des vergessenen Alltags, vom 16. bis zum 20. Jahrhundert*, Frankfurt am Main, 1984, with articles by Robert Scribner and Roger Chartier. See also Michael Maurer, 'Feste und Feiern als historischer Forschungsgegenstand', *Historische Zeitschrift*, 253, 1991, pp. 101–30, and U. Schultz (ed.), *Das Fest. Eine Kulturgeschichte von der Aufklärung bis zur Gegenwart*, Munich, 1988.

[9] Helen Watanabe O'Kelly and Anne Simon, *Festivals and Ceremonies: A Bibliography of Festival Books Relating to Court, Civic and Religious Festivals in Europe, 1500–1800* (forthcoming, October 1999); Ronnie Mulryne and Margaret Shewring (eds.), *Italian Renaissance Festivals and their European Influence*, New York and Lampeter, 1992; Iain Fenlon, *Lepanto: The Arts of Celebration in Renaissance Venice*, Cambridge, 1987; Mara Wade, *Triumphus Nuptialis Danicus: German Court Culture and Denmark*, New York, 1996; Sara Smart, *Doppelte Freude der Musen: Court Festivities in Brunswick-Wolfenbüttel, 1642–1700*, Wiesbaden, 1989.

Introduction   5

— in a sixteenth-century Burgundian village (Mack Holt), in a small seventeenth-century Bavarian town (Trevor Johnson), in several south-German cities after the Thirty Years War (Claire Gantet), in the Prussian-occupied Rhineland of the Vormärz period (James Brophy), and a wine-growing village in 1990s Burgundy (Marion Demossier). In all festivals presented under this first heading, the process of 'purging', healing and strengthening the community through festive rituals, be they connected with a political election, a pilgrimage, peace festivals, carnival, or associated with local wine-production, is the central theme.[10] The threat, however, that festivals can have a destructive rather than a conciliatory effect on society, is ubiquitous; for laughter, cheering, popular religious piety, the triumph of peace and civic values over disorder and chaos, can easily be inverted. Joyful cheers can turn into derision and mockery, piety into fanaticism, a meticulously planned pageant into a disorderly and threatening crowd, an evening of drinking at a harvest festival can decline into political cabal and jealousy, a dance into a brawl. Folklore and popular tradition, which often consciously create a mythical golden age — of peace before the Thirty Years War, or of social equality in a strictly hierarchical society — can acquire new political meanings by turning against the original intentions of the festival organizers. This potential ambivalence of popular festivals in the context of local or wider power relations is always lurking.

Cultural misunderstandings are often deliberate and have a purpose. Popular festivals usually follow cycles and seasons, or are attached to religious feast days, and are therefore deeply traditional. Especially in the early modern period, festivals confirmed and asserted existing social or political hierarchies, allegiances, laws and a certain order.[11] But behind this façade of recurring ritual, social and political shifts sometimes happen clandestinely, as in Vormärz Cologne and Bonn, where state censorship of political societies and newspapers turned popular festivals into informal channels of political protest, an instrument of political education and a maturing democratic will. The official imposition of a

---

10 Alain Corbin, Noëlle Gérôme and Danielle Tartakowsky (eds), *Les Usages politiques des fêtes aux XIX–XX siècles*, Paris, 1990, p. 11. Corbin speaks of a 'fonction propitiatoire ou conjuratoire' of festivals, in the form of ritual exorcism, denunciation and conciliation within a community.

11 Nolte and Hettling (eds), *Bürgerliche Feste*, p. 19.

political agenda, however, does not always work, as was demonstrated over a decade ago by Mona Ozouf, who explained the failure of the French revolutionary powers to create a new republican festival culture by means of the inability of the revolutionaries to tune in to local and religious traditions.[12]

The politicization of popular festivals never followed a linear chronology or a progressive development. As both Marion Demossier and Jim Brophy illustrate, 'tradition' and 'modernity' do not form a clear dichotomy: the social changes which affected 1990s Burgundy did not have the power fundamentally to alter the content and meaning of traditional wine-festivals; while the revolutionary demands of pre-1848 student associations were masked in the costumes of medieval Germany, in a festive invention of tradition. Similarly, mass participation in public festivals was not restricted to the 'modern age' of mass politics, as Mack Holt's analysis of early modern election rites demonstrates. The allegedly modern 'commodification of politics' (Brophy) through material culture and consumption, which accompanied nineteenth-century anti-Prussian protests in Germany, is also present in the boost given to the local economy in the shape of early modern religious tourism during pilgrimages in the Bavarian town of Kemnath (Johnson). The growth of public space, as a result of the — often only temporary — politicization of festivals is indeed not an invention of modernity with a clearly identifiable starting-point (such as the French Revolution), but links the late medieval and the modern world.[13]

Dynastic and royal festivals during the Renaissance have been the particular focus of interdisciplinary studies since the 1950s.[14] More recently the growing

---

12   Ozouf, *Festivals and the French Revolution*, p. 218.
13   This stands in contradiction to Jürgen Habermas's teleological model of the bourgeois public space only emerging in the late eighteenth and early nineteenth centuries; Habermas himself addressed such criticism in *Strukturwandel der Öffentlichkeit: Untersuchung zu einer Kategorie der bürgerlichen Gesellschaft*, Frankfurt, 1990, Introduction.
14   See footnote 9; also Jean Jacquot, *Les Fêtes de la Renaissance*, 3 vols (Paris, 1956–75); Richard Alewyn and Karl Sälzle, *Das große Welttheater. Die Epoche der höfischen Feste*, Hamburg, 1959; Roy Strong, *Art and Power: Renaissance Festivals 1450–1650*, Woodbridge, 1984; Roy Strong and Stephen Orgel (eds.), *The King's Arcadia — Inigo Jones and the Theatre of the Stuart Court*, London, 1973; Margaret McGowan (ed.), *Le Ballet comique, 1581, by Balthazar de Beaujoyeulx, facsimile edition* (= Renaissance Triumphs and Magnificences, 6), Bigharton, NY, 1982; Jennifer Woodward, *The Theatre of Death: The*

Introduction 7

interest in court culture has produced a series of works on this topic right across Europe. As in the first section on popular festivals, the main issue here also concerns the role of the public sphere: did a 'closed' court culture with its *pompes funèbres*, weddings, entries, embassies and so on have an impact beyond its own restricted sphere? Is it true that monarchic and dynastic ceremonies only became an instrument of communication with the mass of the people in the 'bourgeois age' of the nineteenth century, when such celebrations acquired an anachronistic and formulaic character?[15]

Michael Mitterauer has emphasized the importance of dynastic festivals and anniversaries for Protestant courts, for example in post-Reformation Germany, where after the reduction or abolition of traditional religious holidays new secular ceremonies in honour of the territorial prince were instituted and often merged with older church festivals.[16] This also happened outside Germany, as Lindsey Hughes demonstrates in her piece on Peter the Great. It indicates that certain festivals instigated and organized by the ruling house addressed a larger audience than the princely family, courtiers, ministers and the nobility. On the other hand, historians have noted that in the age of mass politics and a public mass culture, towards the end of the nineteenth century, the bourgeois (and therefore relatively exclusive) character of festivals in Europe was pushed aside in favour of a revived monarchic and dynastic ceremonial, as for the Kaiser's birthday, the inauguration of the reconstructed Marienburg castle in 1902, the carefully staged anniversaries of the victory at Sedan, or the 1813 Battle of Leipzig.[17] The assertion by Hettling and Nolte, however, that during the nineteenth century the gap between historical reality and festive inventions of history widened, and that ceremonies gained in

---

Ritual Management of Royal Funerals in Renaissance England. 1570–1625, London, 1997; Pierre Béhar, *Image et spectacle: Actes du XXXIIe colloque internationale d'études humanistes du Centre d'Études Supérieures de la Renaissance*, Tours, 1989.

15 Düding et al. (eds), *Öffentliche Festkultur*, pp. 11-15.
16 Michael Mitterauer, 'Anniversarium und Jubiläum', pp. 60–61. Similarly Hugger, in Hugger (ed.), *Stadt und Fest*, p. 24, mentions the mockery of the prince in the person of 'prince carnival'.
17 Nolte and Hettling (eds), *Bürgerliche Feste*, pp. 23–24; see also Ute Schneider, *Politische Festkultur im 19. Jahrhundert: die Rheinprovinz von der französischen Zeit bis zum Ende des Ersten Weltkrieges, 1806–1918*, Essen, 1995.

utopian quality, is questionable. As Karl Vocelka indicates in his programmatic text on Habsburg festivals, dynastic ceremonies in the sixteenth and seventeenth centuries followed the 'invented traditions' of ancient mythology and Christian symbolism with as great a sense of purpose and 'modernity' — reflected in elaborate architecture and mechanical apparatus — as did the jubilees staged for Kaiser Franz Joseph.[18] Moreover, Utopia and the assertion of reality must not be contradictory principles in creating effective festival agendas. James van Gelderen, in his research on Bolshevik festivals, draws conclusions similar to those of Vocelka: the utopian message of the revolutionary mass celebrations, which were staged by the avant-garde of Russian artists and theatre directors, took on a life of itself through the involvement of the masses in preparing the events, who themselves acquired a central role in the revolutionary events. Nevertheless, despite their modernity and revolutionary message, these festivals were deeply influenced by traditional festive forms, such as elements of Orthodox liturgy, the pomp of tsarist ceremonies and early working-class culture.[19]

The display of power through festivals and ceremonies, organized for the public and with the public, always formed an active ingredient of government. As Kate Currey shows convincingly with the example of the court at Nancy, festival forms were closely associated with specific messages, and rulers borrowed from each other's festival models and traditions, such as church ceremonies, the didactic character of Jesuit theatre plays, ballets, royal funerals and chivalric spectacles. Thus border regions, such as Lorraine, situated between the ceremonial conventions of German territorial courts and French royal traditions, functioned as conveyor-belts for these festival cultures.

The communication of changing festive forms was rapid and far-reaching. By attacking the powerful position of the Orthodox patriarchy in Muscovy and its religious festival traditions, Peter the Great not only substituted saints' days and monastic ceremonies with a more ruler-centred, secular and military agenda, but

---

18 Andrea Blöchl, 'Die Kaisergedenktage. Die Feste und Feiern zu den Regierungsjubiläen und runden Geburtstagen Kaiser Franz Josephs', in Brix and Stekl (eds.), *Der Kampf um das Gedächtnis* (see note 4 above), p. 138, points at the historical and allegorical plays performed at such occasions.
19 James van Gelderen, *Bolshevik Festivals, 1917–1920*, Berkeley, CA and London, 1993, pp. 4–8.

Introduction 9

also destroyed the great authority and power of a rival institution, the patriarchy. Festival culture yet again reflected political agendas and created a new ruler–subject relationship, although in contrast to German dynastic and civic festivals in the eighteenth century, Petrine festival culture did not succeed in involving a wider public sphere, as the mass of the people in the countryside continued to celebrate their saints' days as before. Several festival forms have been invented by, and created for, the exclusive use of the court, such as the *ballet de cour*, the opera and, as Helen Watanabe O'Kelly shows in her contribution to the section on military festivals, the tournament, when it lost its purely military preparatory role in the course of the seventeenth century. Yet research on court festivals raises the problem of the reliability of source materials. Thomas Biskup touches upon an important question when he queries the modern perception which reduces the meaning of court festivals to dynastic propaganda. Of course, official descriptions of such events usually stress the harmony between ruler and subjects, glossing over any existing conflicts. Formulaic glorification and exaggeration were part of the language used to report court ceremonial. Yet the modern idea, prevalent since the Enlightenment, that Baroque court festivals consisted of eye-catching but meaningless ornamental displays is challenged by Biskup's analysis of the changing character of ducal weddings in late eighteenth-century Brunswick.

Following the ubiquitous French model of festal court culture, the eighteenth-century rulers of smaller German territories depicted themselves as patrons of the arts and sciences, as well as ambitious commanders over a plucky army, whose upkeep usually went beyond their modest means. In Brunswick, it took a change of ruler to introduce more sober economic thinking, which was reflected in the change of the agenda for court festivals. In contrast to earlier events, the wedding of 1790 introduced a dynastic successor conscious of his civic duties, choosing a public festival as a medium of conveying his new political message. Instead of abolishing monarchic festivals, as the French Enlightenment thinkers had recommended, German court ceremonies were reformed into patriotic festivals which enabled the people to identify with the ruler in his role of a paternalistic benefactor. The active participation of the public was now consciously sought. The court opened its gates to the urban streets and alleys.

A century later, rulers still applied this approach, as Tom Barcsay demonstrates in his study of the 1896 millennial festivities in Budapest. The re-invention of

Emperor Franz Joseph as national Hungarian hero, alongside mythical figures such as Árpád and the Hungarian national saint St Stephen, elevated the traditional monarchic festival and its sacral atmosphere of dynastic power to a new level by including the whole nation and its fictitious, glorified history, led by a plebiscitary king — here the Emperor. This focus on the Habsburg dynasty's wise ruler over a multi-national Empire was unique in nineteenth-century Europe, and clearly relied more on historical myth than reality: hence, the *Banderium* marching past the Emperor dressed in the (imagined) style of the medieval Hungarian nobility. Once again, however, this festal display demonstrates the coalescence of historical fiction with modern technology and a conscious show of modernity — similar to Bolshevik multi-media shows, early modern *apparate delle feste* (Vocelka), or seventeenth-century fireworks (Gantet) — here reflected in the use of early cinematic shows, an exhibition of turn-of-the-century machinery, and the planning of 'millennial' schools, railway stations, theatres and museums. The festival was extended in the form of a political welfare programme for the people and thus entered the public sphere.

In a contrast to the 'nationalization' of monarchic festivals which happened in the metropoles of Budapest and Vienna, Dieter Binder contributes an interesting glimpse of the 'regionalization' or even 'provincialization' of a dynastic festival tradition with the example of Archduke John of Styria (1782–1859). Educated in the spirit of the Enlightenment under the supervision of his father, Leopold of Tuscany (Emperor Leopold II, 1790–92), John was impressed by the libertine traditions of the Helvetic confederation and the patriotic peasant movement in Tyrol under Andreas Hofer. The political idea he promoted as *Reichsverweser* during the 1848 revolutions was that of a united Germany, including Austria. A landowner in Styria, he enjoyed great popularity in the province, married a commoner, propagated new agrarian and industrial techniques, and was an important patron of the arts and sciences in Graz. In Styria, his image as 'the king of the Alps' remained a powerful focus of local identity, although he advanced to a figure of German-Aryan unity during the Nazi period. After 1945, in numerous festivals in his honour, John returned to his role of a provincial hero, embodying the powerful notion of a conservative bourgeois Styrian *Heimat*, in clear opposition to the Viennese metropolis and its leftist political activism, lending local political governors authority and the opportunity of identification with

Introduction

John's historical image. As Hettling and Nolte emphasized, however, the bourgeois creation of local identities in no way excludes a parallel national identity, expressed not least in the simultaneous flying of the local, provincial and national colours.[20]

These examples demonstrate that there cannot be a strict division between modern dynastic, popular and national festivals. The effective use of time and space, pageantry, operatic and architectural elements, the *'géstion de la mémoire'*,[21] which build a network of historical references and values into monarchic and court festivities, are also present in the mass events of imperial power at the end of the nineteenth century. Under the last heading, several authors attempt the re-evaluation of the two most essential elements of national and military festivals: ritual and propaganda. Again, one of the first theoretical writings summarizing the objective of national festivals stems from the pen of Rousseau, in his 1771 treatise on the constitution of Poland:

> All three legislators of ancient times [Moses, Lycurgus and Numa] [...] sought ties that would bind the citizens to the fatherland and to one another. All three found what they were looking for in distinctive usages, in religious ceremonies that invariably were in essence exclusive and national, in games that brought the citizens together frequently, in exercises that caused them to grow in vigour and strength and developed their pride and self-esteem; and in public spectacles that, by keeping them reminded of their forefathers' deeds and hardships and virtues and triumphs, stirred their hearts, set them on fire with the spirit of emulation, and tied them tightly to the fatherland.[22]

From early modern patriotic and chivalric displays to the *Gesamtkunstwerk* of Nazi parades, mass spectacles and communist rallies, festival organizers clearly followed this advice to respond to the need to link (often traditional) ritualistic forms with propagandistic messages. By presenting historical mythology with a national or patriotic content, such festivals do not just intend to recreate or 'invent' traditions, but express a moral imperative: they show the virtues a nation (united and in arms) had in the past and — even more important — ought to have in the future. The contributions by Tom Barcsay, Jakob Vogel, Ute Schneider,

---

20 Nolte and Hettling (eds), *Bürgerliche Feste*, p. 28.
21 Corbin, *Les usages politiques*, p. 11.
22 Jean-Jacques Rousseau, *The Government of Poland*, translated and with an introduction by Wilmoore Kendall, Indianapolis, IN and New York, 1972, p. 8.

Sabine Behrenbeck, and Árpád v. Klimó all demonstrate with fascinating detail the crucial role of historical symbolism. But, as James van Gelderen stresses, historical and political festival propaganda are not just cynical instruments of mass manipulation by the government or official institutions. Ideas that initiate festivals can change when they are celebrated and enter into a dialogue between their creators and the festival participants.[23] Therefore we have to abandon the much explored dichotomy between festivals 'by the people' versus festivals 'for the people'. Similarly, ritual elements often detach themselves from their original context: Helen Watanabe O'Kelly observes the progressive division between the military training aspect of late medieval tournaments, and their aesthetic, symbolic, social and political role at early modern courts in France and Germany. Considering that even in the 1830s, tournaments belonged to the regular programme of court pageantry in Berlin and Vienna — not as 'historicizing' amusement, but as reflection of chivalric values demanded of the nobility[24] — chivalric ritual formed an inherent part of European festival culture.

If we follow van Gelderen's definition of festive ritual as 'heratic, hermetic symbols used for compact communication and a unanimous interpretation among spectators',[25] Jakob Vogel's piece on French and German military festivals before the First World War critically tests this unanimity of the 'collective discourse' during Kaiser-parades, Sedan-day celebrations, troop inspections and other events linking the army, the people and the monarchy. Just as Styrian local identity, which produced the myth of Archduke John (Binder), posed no serious threat to Austrian national identity after 1945, Bavarian or other particular identities were no obstacle to the establishment of a united imperial German army in the federal Germany after 1871, at least in the long term. Here, as well as in France, where the Third Republic slowly undermined the strength of the Napoleonic cult with a more civic approach to the celebration of the army, ritual became an independent agent. Reflecting the relationship between the civic, political, social sphere and the army, as well as the historical role of rulership, the central role of the Kaiser in German ceremonies (to the exclusion of parliamentary representatives) starkly

---

23 Gelderen, *Bolshevik Festivals, 1917–1920*, p. 9.
24 Nolte and Hettling (eds), *Bürgerliche Feste*, p. 23.
25 Gelderen, *Bolshevik Festivals, 1917–1920*, p. 11.

contrasted with the ritualistic re-invention of the French president as a quasi-monarch commanding a republican army. Both German and French military festivals, however, appealed to the public, to the conscious acceptance of military duties and virtues by all male subjects and citizens. The emotional investment through theatrical, musical and religious elements in this 'European militarization process' (Vogel) cannot fail to remind the reader of certain festival patterns and continuities present in the festive public sphere created in Baroque and Enlightenment spectacles (Johnson, Gantet, Curry, Biskup).

Unlike nineteenth-century bourgeois festivals at the time of the Frankfurt parliament, the national and military ceremonies on the eve of the First World War mobilized masses for the 'nation in arms'. This is the topic of Ute Schneider's examination of the centenary celebrations of the Battle of Leipzig in the Rhineland, which during the Napoleonic wars had been allied to France and therefore found itself on the losing side in 1813. A century later, the authorities faced the awkward task of commemorating these events in a national festival of triumph over the 'hereditary' French enemy. The government's main desire during the 1913 festival was to persuade parliament to accept higher taxes and the Army Bill. Although neither Schneider nor Vogel consider this policy as an active preparation for war, it formed part of a wider mobilization of society's psychological, economic and physical readiness for armed conflict, even winning over former opponents of high military expenditure, such as the Social Democrats.

It is intriguing how successfully the German imperial tradition won popular approval for its festival culture, whereas the bourgeois festival tradition of the earlier nineteenth century fell into oblivion and could not be resurrected by the republican government after the First World War. Yet the massive presence of the public sphere is no guarantee for the success of a democratic political culture. This becomes obvious when we consider the failure of a republican festival vision during the Weimar period. Pamela Swett's account of Weimar's attempt to celebrate Constitution Day demonstrates that even the most sophisticated instrumentalization of history and ritual 'from above' has no impact if there is no input or acceptance 'from below' — a lesson Peter the Great had refused to learn when faced with the obstinacy of the people to his more secular festivals and holidays (Hughes).

The task of reconstituting unity within Weimar German society was blighted by public opposition to the very symbols of the new state and by the growing radicalism of alternative displays among radical left- and right-wing groups. A comparison with the Nazi Party's skills to mobilize society in ceremonies and mass spectacles on a hitherto unseen scale shows that, according to Sabine Behrenbeck, it was not Weimar's failure to rally emotional support in festive events, but Hitler's successful response to a quasi-religious yearning for public ritual which helped the latter to seize control. Demonstrating that the Weimar governments were wrongly accused of neglecting public ritual, Behrenbeck returns to the ambivalent quality of festive ceremonies, and their power to stabilize as well as to destabilize the public, political and social order. Using the form of a popular *pompe funèbre* for the Nazi martyrs of the Hitler putsch of 1923, the annual commemoration of the Party's dead turned into a pilgrimage whose participants were encouraged to sacrifice, being assured salvation and resurrection through the eternal memory of the nationalist-socialist *Volk*. Tapping into religious ritual — something Hitler consciously borrowed from Bolshevik festivals as well as from the pomp of the imperial tradition, which was still familiar to many people in the 1930s — the Nazis applied the old trick of putting customary symbols into a new political and social context. The same strategy was applied to religious festivals celebrated in the private sphere of the family, as Corey Ross shows in his comparison of the political agenda officially imposed on Christmas celebrations in Nazi Germany and the German Democratic Republic — this time, however, without much success. Even the most sophisticated festivals and public rituals meet resistance or apathy when their repressive and disciplining purpose becomes too apparent.

This is also true for the last contribution, by Árpád v. Klimó, on the conflict between the Hungarian Communist Party and the Church over a religious holiday celebrating the country's national saint, St Stephen. While the 1896 millennial festivities concentrated on Hungarian myths of origin and dynastic continuity, in post-1945 Hungary the relic of St Stephen's right hand became the symbol of a church-backed resistance to the appropriation of Hungary's traditions and historical myths by the Communist Party, until the show-trial of Cardinal Mindszenty and other clergymen put an end to the most successful anti-Communist mass demonstrations in the country's Stalinist period. Communist

Introduction

counter-festivals, in the form of Sports Days and Peasants' Days, although attracting large audiences, never produced the genuine atmosphere of national and religious identification with Hungarian history as did St Stephen's Day, which was only revived in the days of *glasnost'* in 1988.

Not all contributions address the political agenda of festivals, but all examples demonstrate the crucial role of power relationships, between festival organizers, participants, festival agendas and programmes. Unlike Barcsay, Binder and v. Klimó, who clearly focus on the usage of historical mythology in festivals, Swett, Schneider and Ross concentrate on the function of symbols in a wider cultural and socio-political context, while Holt, Demossier, Gantet, Johnson, Brophy and Behrenbeck attribute the power of the festivals they examine mainly to ritualistic elements. The receptiveness of the public sphere, which exists even in the most exclusive court ceremonies, religious celebrations, seasonal and life-cycle festivals, plays a crucial role at any time in history. Almost all case-studies show that festivals cannot survive if they are not publicly accepted and believed to be legitimate, whether justified by religious customs, a stable political and social hierarchy, or the belief in myths and deliberate anachronisms, cultural symbols and rituals without which social life would be meaningless. The means, techniques and the scale of mass participation, as well as the relationship to religion — all of this has changed the quality, form and content of festivals from the early modern to the modern period. But even today the anthropological basis is largely unchanged: the mythic, symbolic and ritualistic aspects of festivals remain the most powerful ingredients.

ELECTION FESTIVALS, POWER AND SOCIETY IN SIXTEENTH-CENTURY BURGUNDY

Mack P. Holt

The study of elections in the pre-modern world, that is, before they became firmly connected to ideas of popular democracy and representative government, is still a largely unexplored subject. A few singular studies stand out for their rarity, but on the whole very little work has been done on elections prior to the mid-seventeenth century.[1] And while a great deal of work has been done on pre-modern political festivals and rituals — particularly by the so-called Kantorowicz school in the United States, primarily Ralph Giesey and his many students — none of it has focused on elections.[2] What I propose to do in this chapter is to focus on one example of pre-modern elections: the annual mayoral elections in the Burgundian

---

1 One such exception is Mark Kishlansky, *Parliamentary Selection: Social and Political Choice in Early Modern England*, Cambridge, 1986.
2 See, for example, Ernst Kantorowicz, *The King's Two Bodies*, Princeton, NJ, 1975; Ralph E. Giesey, *The Royal Funeral Ceremony in Renaissance France*, Geneva, 1960; idem, *The Juristic Basis of Dynastic Right to the French Throne*, Philadelphia, PA, 1961; Sarah Hanley, *The Lit de justice of the Kings of France: Constitutional Ideology in Legend, Ritual, and Discourse*, Princeton, NJ, 1983; Richard A. Jackson, *Vive le Roi! A History of the French Coronation from Charles V to Charles X*, Chapel Hill, NC, 1984; and Lawrence M. Bryant, *The King and the City in the Parisian Royal Entry Ceremony: Politics, Ritual, and Art in the Renaissance*, Geneva, 1986.

capital of Dijon in the sixteenth century (though I shall glance back to the fifteenth century and forward to the seventeenth century at various points). An implicit argument running throughout the chapter is that these annual elections were not just about power, whether the political power of the élites who supervised the elections and controlled the candidates, or the empowerment of the people who made up the electorate; the elections were also about building social ties and communal bonds. Unlike modern elections, whose function and result are explicitly designed to generate political division, pre-modern elections were supposed to engender social harmony and community. That these elections were so spectacularly successful in joining together these political and social functions in the sixteenth century helps explain why the French crown in its absolutist mode ultimately suppressed them in the seventeenth century, with mayors of Dijon no longer elected by the people but appointed directly by the king. Thus, by combining political power with social harmony — in effect linking together the body politic and the body social — municipal elections in Dijon had created a strong political voice that threatened royal authority during the Wars of Religion, as the experience of the Catholic League made clear. No wonder that Henri IV, Louis XIII, and Louis XIV made explicit efforts to take away election powers in the seventeenth century. A secondary argument is that in a pre-democratic age these elections had none of the connotations of representative government of modern elections; as such they were less a means to an end than an end in themselves. What mattered most was the event — really series of events — that surrounded these annual rituals each June; in fact, it was the festivals themselves that were of primary importance to contemporaries. To focus just on outcomes and results of the elections is a limited and presentist way of looking at them. A third aspect about early modern elections, as both Peter Burke and Keith Thomas have reminded us, is that they were also *jours de fête*.[3] This link was especially strong in Dijon, where the elections were held in conjunction with the feast of

---

3   See Peter Burke, *Popular Culture in Early Modern Europe*, New York, 1978, pp. 196–97; idem, *The Historical Anthropology of Early Modern Italy*, Cambridge, 1987, ch. 6 and 13; and Keith Thomas, 'Social Differences in England, 1500–1750', lecture delivered at the Newberry Library, Chicago, IL, 10 April 1989.

Saint John the Baptist, the annual midsummer festival in June that culminated with feasting, dancing and the traditional bonfires. Thus, in order to appreciate the reality of early modern elections for sixteenth-century Burgundians we shall have to jettison our modern democratic values and replace them with an understanding of carnival.

The rituals and festivities surrounding the Dijon elections had been relatively unchanged since Hugues IV, duke of Burgundy, first granted the charter to the commune of Dijon in 1235 with the right to elect its own mayor.[4] In mid-June every year the outgoing mayor would turn over his official symbols of office — especially a manuscript copy of the gospel of St John decorated with two gilded crucifixes — to an appointed 'keeper of the gospels' (*garde des évangiles*) in a public ceremony in the cemetery of the abbey of St Bénigne. Then in the days leading up to election day — always 21 June unless this fell on a Sunday — the candidate or candidates for mayor would canvass in the parishes with a barrel of wine and occasionally even meat, fish and cherries. This produced a distinctly sociable form of campaigning, with every adult male who was a head of household being eligible to participate in the elections. Not surprisingly, this form of canvassing was frowned upon by the local Parlement, and the court made efforts to suppress it for over a century, without success. At six o'clock in the morning on 21 June — midsummer's eve — the outgoing mayor and aldermen on the city council (*échevins*) gathered in the Jacobin convent in the parish of Notre-Dame to record the 'voices' of the heads of household in the city. Dignitaries such as the governor, lieutenant-general, and a president from the *Chambre de comptes* went first, followed by all twenty outgoing aldermen. Then, organized by parish, all the adult males of Dijon trooped into the convent one by one to declare orally and publicly their 'voice' for the candidate of their choice. When all the 'voices' had been heard and the votes were tabulated, which could take all day in years of a heavy turnout, the candidate with the 'plurality of voices' was declared the winner. The new mayor-elect then led everyone who had cast a 'voice' in the election — not just his own supporters — back to his house, where he hosted them with food and drink in yet another rite of sociability and commensality. The

---

4   Archives municipales de Dijon (AMD), B 12, cote 31 (carton), November 1235.

celebratory meal symbolized neatly how the community was all of one accord as they shared bread together at the end of the day.

Two days later, on 23 June, the eve of the feast of St John the Baptist, the mayor-elect would select the twenty aldermen who would serve with him on the city council in the coming year, at least six of whom had to be chosen from among the outgoing aldermen. That night the entire city participated in the traditional ritual of the St John the Baptist bonfire, around which people of all classes mixed together, sang and danced. Traditionally the new mayor-elect would be given the honour of lighting the bonfire, always held in the plaza opposite the parish church of St-Jean. And it was also customary for all the inhabitants to take a few ashes or coals from the communal bonfire back to their own hearths for good luck throughout the year, yet another visible symbol of the social harmony surrounding these festivities. The following day — the feast-day itself, 24 June — the mayor-elect would be formally presented with the gospel of St John, the mayor's symbol of office and authority, by the 'keeper of the gospels' in the parish church of Notre-Dame. Then the mayor and newly chosen aldermen would all swear their oaths of office before the high altar, with one hand on the gospel of St John, while the priest of the parish stood before them holding the consecrated Host in his hand. After a communal Mass, the feasting of this important feast-day would begin. As a sign of his gratitude the newly elected mayor traditionally provided each of the seven parishes of Dijon with a barrel of wine, a dozen loaves of bread, a ham and a basket of cherries to serve as the foundation of their celebratory feast.[5] The enfolding together of political, religious and social rituals is very clear and intentional, and for contemporaries it was impossible to separate out the function of the transfer of political power with

---

5   Examples of the format of the election procedure show how rigidly this pattern was followed from the mid-fifteenth century to the mid-seventeenth century. See AMD, B 11, cote 2, 24 June 1446; B 168, fol. 283, 16 June 1514; B 196, 35^r–38^r, 23 July 1558; B 210, fols. 1–13^v, 21–24 June 1572; and B 12, cote 44, anonymous seventeenth-century copy. Also, see Joseph Garnier and Ernest Champeux, *Chartes de communes et d'affranchissements en Bourgogne*, Dijon, 1918, pp. 312–30. For the celebration of the feast-day itself, see Arnold van Gennep, *Manuel de folklore français contemporain*, part 1, vol. 4: *Cycle de mai, cycle de Saint Jean et cycle de Saint Pierre*, Paris, 1949.

Election Festivals, Power and Society in Sixteenth-Century Burgundy 21

the function of social harmony and cohesiveness so evident in many of the rituals. Thus, on the four days between 21 and 24 June each year, the inhabitants of the city of Dijon witnessed and participated in a series of rituals and festivals that explicitly bound together the body politic, the body social and the body of Christ. That these rituals were so consciously constructed to emphasize social harmony and community, however, only underscores how quotidian social tensions and rifts in the body social and body politic actually were in the pre-modern world. In the remainder of this chapter I wish to focus on several examples of tension and disorder that emerged during the rituals and festivals themselves, not just to illustrate how often and how commonly they occurred, but also to show how the festivals worked to try to ameliorate such tensions and rifts in the body social.

Several elections in the first half of the sixteenth century illustrate how the ritual of voting itself could lead to disorder and division. In 1528, for example, just as the voting was about to begin, the official record of the elections kept by the municipal secretary notes that 'several wine-growers [*vignerons*] and others of the lower classes [*menu peuple*], all inhabitants of this city, being at the said place in great number, began to cry in a loud voice the following words: Sayve! Sayve! And others in even greater number replied with these words: Bierne! Bierne!' Thus, a spontaneous demonstration erupted with the supporters of the two leading candidates — Pierre Sayve, seigneur de Flavignerot, and Jean Noel, sieur de Bierne — trying to out-shout each other. This outbreak of noise interrupted the usual decorum in the Jacobin convent and outraged the notables present, including the two candidates. Bierne, who was the incumbent mayor at the time, attempted to stop his own supporters, but was totally unsuccessful, so much so that they surrounded him, hoisted him upon their shoulders and began carrying him around the chamber to the continued shouts of 'Bierne! Bierne!' When order was finally restored, however, and the voting finally completed, it was the other candidate, Pierre Sayve, who was elected mayor. Despite losing the election, the demonstration of the wine-growers and artisans showed they took participation in the ritual of the event seriously, even constructing their own festive rituals to add to the proceedings.[6]

---

6   AMD, B 172, fols. 109^r–112^v, 22 June 1528 (quotation on fols. 110^v–111^r).

The following year's election provided even more disruption and controversy. When the proceedings began early in the morning on 21 June 1529, the mayor Pierre Sayve urged all those assembled to avoid any 'noisy demonstration or tumult'. Things seemed to be going smoothly as the all the notables and outgoing aldermen cast their votes without incident. After sixteen inhabitants had cast their 'voices', however, the voting had to stop because of all the pushing and shoving to get to the front of the line, led by the wine-growers and artisans. Sayve then cried out that if they wanted to vote in the election, they would have to do so in a quiet and orderly fashion 'without starting any demonstration'. He then ordered two armed sergeants to supervise the crowd so the voting could continue. But at this point, one Denis Marquet, a wine-grower, 'spoke up and told Monsieur Pierre Sayve that he did not have to wait [to hear all the votes given], since each of them wanted him to be re-elected mayor.' The group of three- to four hundred wine-growers and artisans then began shouting Sayve's name once more, hoisted him on their shoulders and carried him out of the convent to his own house for the traditional ritual of food and drink. The secretary recording these events, named Pierre Fenovier, notes that he was prepared to follow everyone else out of the convent to join in the feast, when he was stopped by twenty or so wine-growers, masons, and other artisans, who demanded to have their 'voices' recorded for another candidate named Tabourot. The secretary responded that since all the notables had left the convent, he no longer had any power to record their votes and that the election was over. The poor secretary was then surrounded by the group of wine-growers and artisans, who declared that the election was 'improper [*mal fait*]' if he would not record their 'voices'. Fearing some bodily harm, he managed to escape their entreaties and fled to the home of the re-elected mayor, Pierre Sayve. Shortly thereafter, however, he reports that all twenty of those wine-growers and artisans who had insisted he record their votes also turned up at the mayors house and joined in the festivities with Sayve's supporters 'all joined together [...] [where] they wined and dined in the accustomed manner, and all told there were more than six hundred people there, such that the two courtyards of the said house were completely packed with people, and not one of them said

Election Festivals, Power and Society in Sixteenth-Century Burgundy   23

anything more against the election'.[7] Once more, it is clear that the lower classes took their participation in the election seriously and wanted to insure that their proper 'voices' were recorded correctly as tradition dictated. Although they were willing to go on record as opposing the majority's choice, indicating some discord in the body politic, they eventually joined in the communal food and drink without further protest, showing that at least there was no rift in the body social.

Other demonstrations and disruptions of this sort were very common prior to the outbreak of the Wars of Religion in 1562. In 1545 a disturbance similar to those already described, with supporters of rival candidates trying to out-shout each other at the polling place, resulted in the postponement of the election for two days. Trying to seize the initiative, the magistrates of the Parlement attempted to prevent such comportment of the masses in future. 'Because some wine-growers and mechanics come to the elections for mayor in order to go drinking afterwards in the home of the one who is elected more than for any other reason', noted the register of the Parlement in June 1545, 'it has been deliberated [...] that the elected mayor as well as anyone else will henceforth be prohibited from giving either food or drink to the said wine-growers and aforementioned men on the day of the said election, under penalty of an arbitrary fine'.[8] This was obviously a serious blow to all those who took part in the elections, though it would clearly have spared the winning candidate each year a considerable expense. The wine-growers and artisans appealed to the Parlement of Burgundy, however, claiming that they had no right to alter or amend the rituals associated with the election itself. The Parlement, ever vigilant to maintain order on election day, was reluctant to grant their appeal, though the celebratory meal did eventually return the following year. More seriously, when the newly elected mayor in June 1558 decided not to make the customary donation of wine, bread, ham and cherries to each of the seven parishes on the feast-day of St John the Baptist (24 June), the day he took his oath of office, the people complained to the Parlement again. Their suit was upheld, and Parlement decreed that 'the wine-growers, labourers, and other inhabitants of Dijon [having remonstrated] [...]

---

7   AMD, B 173, fols. 43^r–45^v, 21 June 1529 (quotations on fols. 44^v and 45^v).
8   AMD, B 183, fols. 1^r–7^v, 20–22 June 1545 (quotation on fols. 4^v–5^r).

after the confirmation of the oath sworn by the elected mayor of Dijon on the feast-day of St John the Baptist, they have always had the right of taking and having from the said elected mayor as a sign of his gratitude seven barrels of wine, seven dozen loaves of bread, seven hams and seven baskets of cherries [that is, one for each of the seven parishes of the city], a right that they have always customarily had in former times. Thus, by decree of this court [of Parlement] it has been ordered that all the said items be collected and dispersed to each of the seven parishes'. Thus, not only did the wine-growers convince the Parlement, and ultimately the city fathers, that their celebratory feast was a 'right [*droit*]' protected by the court, they insured that the divisions of the election on 21 June would still ultimately end in community and harmony on the feast-day of St John the Baptist on 24 June.

A very different kind of discord threatened the election festivals with the advent of the Reformation. As so much of the ritual— from polling site, to swearing in, to the feast-day celebration itself — was explicitly tied to Catholic rituals and liturgy, the emergence of Protestantism was perceived by most Dijon Catholics as a serious threat to the enfolding together of the body social, the body politic and the body of Christ. Since I have already written elsewhere in some detail about the election of 1561, when a Protestant candidate made a serious attempt to win the mayoral election outright, I will not describe it at length here.[9] Suffice it to say that by 1561 a significant Protestant community of between 500 and 600 people had emerged in Dijon, out of a total population of around 10,000.[10] Not yet protected by the Edict of Toleration of January 1562, Dijon's Huguenots sought legal protection under the guise of a Protestant mayoral candidate in the June 1561 election, a president in the *Chambre des comptes* named Antoine Brocard. This was also in the wake of an extended period of

---

9   Mack P. Holt, 'Wine, Community and Reformation in Sixteenth-Century Burgundy', *Past and Present*, 1993 (February), 138, pp. 58–93; and idem., 'Popular Political Culture and Mayoral Elections in Sixteenth-Century Dijon', in Mack P. Holt (ed.), *Society and Institutions in Early Modern France*, Athens, GA, 1991, pp. 98–116.

10   The most realistic estimate of the size of the Protestant community in Dijon in the mid-sixteenth century is that of Jean Richard, 'Les Quêtes de l'église Notre-Dame et la diffusion du protestantisme à Dijon vers 1562', *Annales de Bourgogne*, 32, 1960, pp. 183–89.

Election Festivals, Power and Society in Sixteenth-Century Burgundy   25

Huguenot political pressure in many towns all over France, resulting in a *coup d'état* and seizure of control of several of them in the period 1560–62: notably Orléans and Rouen in the north and Lyon, Montauban, and Nîmes in the south. While there had been no attempted *coup* by the Huguenots in Dijon, they attempted to wrest control of the city hall via the mayoral election in June 1561. In response, an ultra-Catholic candidate, Bénigne Martin, who was also a former mayor, organized the wine-growers of the city to turn out in record numbers to support him and defeat the Protestant Brocard. The result was the highest turnout ever recorded in Dijon: nearly 500 male heads of household, or roughly one out of every four eligible voters. The Catholic Martin gained 322 'voices', or 65 per cent of the vote. The margin of victory was clearly the wine-growers' votes, who made up 203 of Martin's 322 votes, or nearly 60 per cent of the winner's total.[11] The Catholic Martin was re-elected mayor each year for the next five years, and the foundation of his support remained the wine-growers of the city. In 1564 and 1565, for example, the wine-growers made up more than half the total number of voters as well as more than half of those who supported Martin. And their support was absolute in those years, as all 267 wine-growers who voted in the election of 1564 and all 161 wine-growers who voted in the election of 1565 voted for Martin. Moreover, if the number of wine-growers who participated in these elections is compared to their total numbers on the tax rolls, it is clear that the wine-growers were the only occupational group in the city of which more than half regularly participated in the annual elections for mayor. While it is true that the élites of Dijon mobilized the voters to turn out by campaigning in the parishes with barrels of wine and baskets of food, as well as promising them a good feed on election night at the home of the winner, it is equally clear that motivations for voting increased significantly when the threat of Protestantism endangered the body politic and the body social as well as the body of Christ. Thus, the elections of the 1560s proved to be both a means of civic division as well as a means of communal supplication to combat the threat of Protestantism within their midst. The year 1561 proved to be a watershed in Dijon, as from that point forward pressure mounted against the Huguenots in the city and their numbers declined

---

11   AMD, B 199, fols. 1^r–10^r, 21 June 1561.

through emigration and abjuration. Ironically, as the successive peace edicts of the Wars of Religion commenced in 1562 to guarantee the legal rights of Protestants to exist, their ability to do so plummeted dramatically in Burgundy.[12]

While all the examples of election rituals I have discussed so far have focused on political or religious differences, it was the everyday social tensions in a hierarchical society that were always most likely to lead to division and disrupt the stability of the body social. One such example occurred in 1527. In the bonfire celebrations in the Place St-Jean of 23 June — two days after the election and the day before the swearing in of the new mayor on the feast-day of St John the Baptist the next day — a young draper asked the fiancée of a nobleman if she would like to dance. When she consented, another nobleman intervened and told him he had no business dancing with the young lady. The young draper stood his ground, however, 'saying that it was the holiday and he wanted to dance with this lady'. When the nobleman continued to complain, the draper threw him to the ground, and said 'that he [the draper] was as worthy a man as the nobleman to dance with her'. At this point, the fallen noble reached for his sword and likely would have killed the draper had not others intervened. A bourgeois named Fourneret scolded the draper, telling him 'he was a worthy man [*homme de bien*] in his own rank, but that the nobleman was of another quality altogether, as he was a gentleman and the issue of noble blood'. The angry draper then threw Fourneret to the ground too, as a general brawl erupted. When order was finally restored, and miraculously no one was killed or seriously injured, the rifts in the social fabric were still very visible. An attorney in the Parlement of Dijon demanded that the mayor, Jean Noel (who had just been re-elected two days earlier), do something about these 'rebels [*mutins*]'. The mayor thought the term 'rebel' was too strong, and declared that there had never been any rebels in Dijon. Clearly he did not want to escalate things further by widening a social rift into serious political division. This point was underlined by a group of wine-growers, who took serious offence at the way all the lower classes were being depicted as

---

12   For the fate of Protestantism in Dijon after 1561, see Holt, 'Wine, Community and Reformation'. Protestants were forbidden from standing for office or voting in the mayoral elections after 1561.

Election Festivals, Power and Society in Sixteenth-Century Burgundy   27

rebels. '[It was] the wine-growers who said that even when they had suffered [in the siege by the Swiss army in 1513] and had their homes in the suburbs burned to the ground, not one of them had resorted to mutiny, and still less was anyone inclined to do so at present. They were all good servants of the King, and there had never been any mutinous rebels in Dijon.' The mayor calmed the hotter heads of all social levels by promising 'to make good justice', though it appears no one was ever arrested or brought to trial for starting the mêlée.[13]

This episode is a perfect example, of course, of how easy it was for a *jour de fête* to become 'the world turned upside-down'. It was on such feast-days that a draper would be most likely to ask the fiancée of a nobleman to dance, knowing full well that such comportment would be entirely irregular on all other occasions. These were garden-variety social tensions in a hierarchical community, however, and ought not be associated with the political divisions that occasionally disrupted the elections in the 1520s.[14] What is most significant about this incident is that both the mayor and the wine-growers alike shared a common view of a loyal and devoted political community, and they both made pains to shore up the quotidian tensions in the body social by underscoring the harmony and community in the body politic. Thus, as in every other example of election festivals and rituals, the events themselves were full of potential for division and rifts in the community. At the same time, the rituals also allowed for the amelioration of those divisions and the restoration of the integrity of the whole community into the hierarchically structured social entity they all assumed God meant it to be.

To shift from a functionalist to a more historical perspective, the festivals and rituals associated with Dijon's mayoral elections in the sixteenth century were but one part of a culture that served to emphasize the communal ties between the élites and the popular classes. Thus, I disagree with those scholars who see the

---

13 Archives départementales de la Côte d'Or, B II 360/29, 25 26 June 1527.
14 One historian who has tried to do this, mistakenly in my view, is E. Nolin, 'Episodes de la lutte des classes à Dijon au XVIe siècle', *Annales de Bourgogne*, 36, 1964, pp. 270–75. Nolin argues that the election of 1527 itself was part of this class struggle, as all the lower classes (wine-growers above all) supported Noel against Pierre Sayve. This cannot be true, however, as in 1529 virtually all the wine-growers supported Pierre Sayve for re-election, as described above.

period between 1500 and 1800 as a constant battleground between élite culture and popular culture, with the former defeating and virtually eliminating the latter by 1800.[15] As I have tried to demonstrate through election rituals, there was a good deal of overlap and imbrication between élite and popular culture. Although the élites were always those who wielded power, they often relied on the lower classes to do so. The advent of the Reformation served as a catalyst to this cultural process, as Burgundians underscored the Catholic ties that bound together nobleman and wine-grower alike in the face of a Protestant threat that was equally dangerous to all. The result was that election turnouts were at their peak in the second half of the sixteenth century during the Wars of Religion, when all social classes felt most inclined to show their participation in the body politic. These communal ties not only enabled Dijon to withstand the threat of Protestantism, but they allowed the town to flex its political independence during the period of the Catholic League, as Dijon was one of a number of towns that refused to accept the authority as king of Henri IV, whom they perceived as a heretic. It was only after Henri abjured his Calvinist faith and became a Catholic in 1593 that any kind of rapprochement was possible.

Although Henri IV proved to be a good Catholic king to his Burgundian subjects, he was also well aware how much they used the ritual of the mayoral election to bolster their authority and independence from the crown in the civil wars. Thus, after making peace he began the process of dismantling the powers of election that the city had enjoyed for centuries. As early as 1599, Henri IV had requested that the city send him the names of the three candidates who received the most votes, so that he could personally select the mayor from among them.[16] The city fathers balked at this suggestion and complained to the Parlement for nearly a decade, when Henri finally issued an edict in June 1608 to that effect. His justification was that he wanted 'to prevent the disturbances and seditions that

---

15 For the most extreme of these views, see Jean Delumeau, *Le Catholicisme entre Luther et Voltaire*, Paris, 1971; Robert Muchembled, *Popular Culture and Elite Culture in France, 1400–1750*, trans. Lydia Cochrane, Baton Rouge, LA, 1985; and Peter Burke, *Popular Culture in Early Modern Europe*, London, 1978. Both Muchembled and Burke have somewhat moderated their original views in more recent publications.

16 AMD, B 236, fols.233ᵛ–93ʳ, June–October 1599.

Election Festivals, Power and Society in Sixteenth-Century Burgundy 29

take place during the elections in large towns throughout the kingdom, and notably in Dijon'. The King did promise, however, that having made his choice for mayor, 'the said [candidate] will be received and installed [in office] in the accustomed manner'. The whole point, of course, was that this form of the election itself was *not* in the accustomed manner. When nearly a year later, in May 1609, the city had still not agreed to the election reforms, Henri IV issued patent letters and a *lettre de jussion* requiring the city to send him the names of the three candidates with the most votes in the forthcoming election so that he could name the next mayor.[17] Although the King did select the candidate who received the most votes that year, the following year, in 1611, the regent for the young Louis XIII, Marie de' Medici, did not; and the election was in fact postponed while the city argued with the regency government over the proper format of the election.[18] The regent eventually consented to allow the old format to continue, but introduced a far more serious reform in the process. By patent letters of the King it was decreed in July 1611 that no one could vote in any election who had not paid at least four *livres tournois* in the *taille* (a personal income tax) for each of the preceding three years. This was explicitly designed to remove the wine-growers and artisans from the election altogether, because, as the patent letters stated clearly, 'the inhabitants who were the poorest and among the lowest condition of the people have been those who have almost always elected the mayor'.[19] Thus, in 1611 the majority of those who had voted in the mayoral elections for the previous century were excluded from taking part. Finally, in 1668 Louis XIV took the power to elect the mayor away from the rest of the population as well, as from that date forward it was the king alone who selected the mayor of Dijon. And while these changes in Dijon's elections festivals may have intruded into the body politic as uncomfortably as any of the actions by the absolutist state of Louis XIV, the rest of the festivals and rituals each St John the

---

17 AMD, B 12, cote 41 (carton), June 1608 and 31 May 1609; B 246, fols. 264^v–66^v, 18 June 1609.
18 AMD, B 248, fols. 1^r–25^v, 21 June 1610; fols. 42^r–44^v, 6–11. July 1610; fols. 257^r–59^r, 10 June 1611.
19 AMD, B 248, fols. 301^{r-v}, 27 August 1611.

Baptist's day continued as before, ensuring that at least the body social and the body of Christ would persevere in Dijon until the French Revolution.

TRIONFI OF THE HOLY DEAD: THE RELIC FESTIVALS OF BAROQUE BAVARIA

Trevor Johnson

On Sunday 31 May 1693, the small town of Kemnath in northern Bavaria hosted a very special festival. In preparation for the celebration, a route through its streets had been traced with fresh foliage, its houses has been adorned with brightly coloured cloths, flowers and paintings, and four triumphal arches, replete with symbolic embellishment, had been constructed in front of the parish church, the town hall and the two main gates. The city had become a stage on which townspeople and visitors, lining the streets and perching on rooftops, watched the colourful pageant unfold. From the suburbs, a lengthy procession slowly skirted the moat and walls, entered the town by the lower gate and wound its way through the streets and under the triumphal arches before ending up at the parish church, where a sermon was preached in the open to a crowd of over 6,000. Divided into forty-three groups, the procession was made up of mounted trumpeters and drummers, figures in Roman costumes, the town's craft guilds, groups of villagers from rural parishes, the Corpus Christi brotherhood, Franciscan friars, the junior and then senior secular clergy, magistrates, noblemen, mayors and councillors, noblewomen, male citizens, and at the rear the women of the town, in three groups of young girls, single women and matrons. Each section was headed by standard bearers and figures in Roman costume representing varied *genii*. Five floats incorporated *tableaux vivants*. At the heart of the procession, directly ahead of the abbot and escorted by a bodyguard of halberdiers, was borne the focus and cause of the celebration, the complete skeleton of the early Christian martyr, St Primianus, bedecked with jewels and encased within a glass reliquary. His holy bones had been recently excavated from the Roman catacombs of St Callistus and had been acquired by the little Bavarian town through the efforts of Kemnath's parish priest and the festival's organizer, Johann Arkhauer. An octave of special sermons and forty-one Masses added lustre to the solemnities.[1]

The Kemnath celebration was an unusual, unprecedented event for the town, but hardly a unique event for the Bavarian region during what might be termed the 'long' Counter-Reformation period of c. 1550–1750. It has been estimated that around a thousand relics of Roman martyrs, many of them complete skeletons, were translated from the Roman catacombs to Bavaria alone in the seventeenth and eighteenth centuries. Many of these translations were attended by festive celebrations of comparable splendour and similar form to those of St Primianus at Kemnath.[2] In addition, the period saw a series of celebrations occasioned by the exhumation and translation of holy relics which had lain long in the Bavarian earth. These various relic festivals formed a distinct sub-type of religious feast, during a period in which sacred celebration generally within the region was attaining new heights of elaboration and variety. In Counter-Reformation Bavaria, elite patronage and a vibrant popular religion allied to produce a particularly expressive festal culture, developing around both formal liturgical celebration and its associated quasi-liturgical practice. Bavarians, for example, bucked a trend elsewhere in Europe against popular religious theatricals by enthusiastically staging passion-plays, such as the regular performances at Oberammergau which began in fulfilment of a communal vow in the plague-year of 1634.[3] With equal enthusiasm

---

[1] Staatsarchiv Amberg (hereafter StAA), Geistliche Sachen 3395, 'Relation und ordentliche Beschreibung, wie Nemblichen Venerabiles Reliquiae Sti. Primiani Martyris, Nacher Statt Kimnath, in dem Fürstenthumb der Oberen Pfalz yberbracht [...] wordten'.

[2] Walter Pötzl, 'Volksfrömmigkeit' in Walter Brandmüller (ed.), Handbuch der bayerischen Kirchengeschichte, St Ottilien, 1993, II, pp. 871–961, especially pp. 918–29; Edgar Krausen, 'Die Verehrung römischer Katakombenheiliger in Altbayern im Zeitalter des Barock', Bayerisches Jahrbuch für Volkskunde, 1966–67, pp. 37–47.

[3] See Peter Burke, Popular Culture in Early Modern Europe, London, 1978, p. 235, on this instance of Bavarian exceptionalism, and, for Bavarian popular religious theatricals in

they mounted elaborate Corpus Christi and Holy Week processions, applauded Jesuit drama and *theatra sacra*, celebrated the *Kirchweih*, or dedicatory feast of their parochial churches, participated in rural missions, collaborated in confraternal and sodality festivals, attended jubilees, beatification, canonization and *te deum* celebrations and peregrinated to an astounding number of wonder-working shrines. On this last practice, the comment of Aventinus in his *Baierische Chronik* of 1533 ('generally speaking, the Bavarian people [...] enjoy going on pilgrimages and hold many pilgrimage-processions') still held good two centuries later.[4]

The focus in the following pages, though, will be on the relic festivals, which, in Bavaria as elsewhere, centred on rituals which had been formalized by the Council of Trent in a desire to ensure due authentication: firstly, the *inventio* of holy relics, that is to say their discovery (and subsequent 'recognition', approbation, 'elevation' and publicization), and secondly their *translatio*, or movement from one site to another. Such moments gave rise to a distinctive form of Baroque festival, characterized by carefully choreographed processions, triumphal entries and octaves of Masses and sermons. These otherwise ephemeral celebrations were often given an afterlife in print through detailed descriptions which typically provided a brief *vita* of the saint in question, details of the order of procession and a narrative of festival events and which sometimes reproduced the texts of specially composed festival hymns and sermons.[5] A measure of the impact and resonance of the festivals was the growth of lively cults of the saints whose relics had been greeted in this spectacular fashion, a devotion reflected in pilgrimages, donations to shrines and patterns of name-giving.

---

general, Leopold Schmidt, *Das Deutsche Volksschauspiel. Ein Handbuch*, Berlin, 1962, pp. 267–76.

4   Johannes Aventinus, *Baierische Chronik*, ed. Georg Leidinger, Jena, 1926, p. 10. There is an extensive literature on Bavarian local pilgrimage, largely arising from the German *Volkskunde* tradition. For references, see Rebekka Habermas, *Wallfahrt und Aufruhr. Zur Geschichte des Wunderglaubens in der frühen Neuzeit*, Frankfurt and New York, 1991, and Philip M. Soergel, *Wondrous in His Saints: Counter-Reformation Propaganda in Bavaria*, Berkeley and Los Angeles, CA and London, 1993. For an overview of Bavarian popular religion, including its specifically festival elements, see Pötzl, 'Volksfrömmigkeit'.

5   Ibid., p. 926.

34 *Trionfi* of the Holy Dead: the Relic Festivals of Baroque Bavaria

Unlike other Bavarian festivals, the relic pageants have so far received little scholarly attention, yet in association with their festal counterparts they illuminate something of the interaction between religious and political cultures and of the evolution of Baroque aesthetics in the age of confessionalization. Religious and quasi-religious festivals can be approached in a number of ways. Canonical feasts, like Corpus Christi, and popular celebrations, such as Carnival, can be analysed in a functionalist manner: how and to what extent does the festival contribute to (or work against) social cohesion? In the following pages, however, the concentration will be less on the functionality of these *trionfi* of the holy dead, something which cannot be assessed from the festival accounts alone, than on their symbolic hermeneutics, on the ways in which their form and iconography, as mediated by the festival literature, manifested a range of explicit and latent meanings. The focus will be on festivals as expressions of identity, or rather identities, since in this respect it would appear that they exhibited a typically Baroque polysemy.

Relics and the pietas bavarica

The period saw a tremendous displacement of relics, both into and within Germany. In the sixteenth century this included the flight of relics from Protestant into Catholic Germany, exemplified by the Bavarian acquisition of the remains of St Benno, the eleventh-century bishop of Meissen in Saxony, who had been canonized in 1523. Narrowly rescued from Protestant iconoclasm, the relics came into the hands of Duke Albrecht V of Bavaria in 1576 and four years later were placed in the Munich Frauenkirche for public veneration. As Philip Soergel has recently pointed out, the acquisition of Benno's bones was a major coup for the Bavarian dynasty at a time when the Wittelsbachs were anxious to present themselves as the foremost champions of Catholic orthodoxy within the Holy Roman Empire. Indeed, through the adjacent construction of a pantheon of ducal tombs, the elaborate monument to the saint became transformed into a grandiose expression of Wittelsbach identity and power.[6] The combination of political ambition and confessional polemic which was here the feature of a static memorial was also to find expression in the relic festivals associated with other cults within

---

6   Soergel, *Wondrous in his Saints*, pp. 181–91.

Trionfi of the Holy Dead: the Relic Festivals of Baroque Bavaria

Bavaria in the seventeenth and eighteenth centuries. A strong impetus continued to come from the dynasty, particularly during the long reign of Duke (after 1623 Elector) Maximilian I (1598–1651). Maximilian continued the policy of rescuing relics from the Protestant north: in 1648 the bones of SS Cosmas and Damian came to Munich from Bremen, whilst, in a deal with the Duke of Mecklenburg, more relics were acquired in exchange for a pack of hunting dogs.[7] However, Bavaria's first elector was also keen to associate indigenous Bavarian saints with an image of his duchy, people and dynasty as singularly destined to protect and promote the beleaguered Church. Hence his commission of the Jesuit, Matthäus Rader, to compose the *Bavaria Sancta* (1615–28), a compendium of the lives of the many sainted, beatified and venerable men and women who through the ages had been particularly associated with Bavaria. Alongside the Virgin, declared Patroness of Bavaria by Maximilian in 1616, this local pantheon was vital to the construction of a distinctive *pietas bavarica*, a devotional culture which harmonized Church, land and dynasty.[8] The frontispiece to the *Bavaria Sancta*, with its depiction of the Virgin and St Michael (the latter wearing the order of the Golden Fleece which had been bestowed on Maximilian in 1600) gazing admiringly while the Christ-child blesses a map of the duchy and Satan is trampled underfoot, represented this ideal clearly.[9]

---

7   Romuald Bauerreiss, *Kirchengeschichte Bayerns*, St Ottilien, 1977, VII, p. 312.

8   Gerhard P. Woeckel, *Pietas bavarica: Wallfahrt, Prozession und Ex-voto-Gabe im Haus Wittelsbach in Ettal, Wessobrunn, Altötting und der Landeshauptstadt München von der Gegenreformation bis zur Säkularisation und der 'renovatio ecclesiae'*, Weissenhorn, 1992.

9   Just in case it was not clear enough, though, Rader spelt it out: 'when you see *Bavaria Sancta* on the title-page', ran his Preface, 'with your considerable intelligence you will easily see how the title derives from the subject. For if you examine all the corners of Bavaria you will scarcely find one place where you do not stumble upon the glowing tracks of holiness and religion: cities, towns, villages, fields, forests, mountains and hills all breathe and exhibit the old, Catholic faith in Bavaria. Everywhere one finds holy houses, fine monasteries, new schools, illustrious relics [...]. The holy embraces so much of Bavarian soil that it would be tedious to go into detail. The whole land seems to be nothing but religion: one collective, popular shrine': cited in Peter Pfister, *Leben aus dem Glauben: das Bistum Freising*, vol. 3: *Reformation, Gegenreformation und Barockzeit*, Eckbolsheim, 1990, p. 36.

The *Bavaria Sancta* reflected (and doubtless helped to inspire) the seventeenth-century renewal of interest in the lipsanology, or relic-lore, of indigenous Bavarian saints. Although in part the revisitation of medieval hagiographical texts and holy grave sites was coloured by the 'new criticism' of the Bollandists and others, the devotional dimension was even more important. Cities, monasteries and, above all, the cathedral churches of Bavarian dioceses increasingly turned to their patron saints and sought to renew their patronage through festive translations of their corporeal remains. Musty bones were exhumed and placed in new, more prominent shrines. In 1612 the bishop of Regensburg, Wolfgang von Hausen, solemnly opened the shrine of his namesake, St Wolfgang, the chief patron of the diocese, and the following year translated the bones to a new altar.[10] At Freising, the remains of the holy Abbess Irmengard were similarly exposed in 1631, while at Neuhausen the relics of Blessed Winthir had been translated to a new and more prominent shrine in 1610.[11] In Augsburg, the bones of sainted figures from the early history of the diocese, the martyr Digna and the bishops Wikterp, Tozzo, Nidkar and Adalbero were translated to the new sacristy of the Benedictine abbey of SS Ulrich and Afra in 1619. In an effort to extend the cult a second solemn translation was celebrated in 1698. Five triumphal arches and a stage decorated with pictures and emblems were erected inside the church. A procession, featuring musicians in Roman costume, floats with figures of the five saints and five symbolic springs, carts with representations of the Church (Militant, Suffering and Triumphant) and a model of the refurbished sacristy, accompanied the relics of the

---

10   Georg Schwaiger, 'Der heilige Bischof Wolfgang von Regensburg (972–994). Geschichte, Legende und Verehrung', *Beiträge zur Geschichte des Bistums Regensburg*, 6, 1972, pp. 350–419 (p. 355).

11   Bauerreiss, *Kirchengeschichte Bayerns*, VII, p. 313. As the century progressed, numbers of the new shrines constructed for these old saints, including those of Blessed Berthold of Regensburg, St Rasso at Grafrath, the 'Three Poor Saints' of Griesstetten and Blessed Alruna at Niederaltaich, were of the large glass model typical of the reliquaries of the cartacomb saints. This trend towards the enhancement of display was supra-Bavarian: in 1699, in the Franconian prince-bishopric of Würzburg, the bones of the sainted medieval bishop, Bruno, were translated, in a festive procession, to a specially commissioned new altar, so constructed that it was possible to crawl through it to achieve more intimate contact with the relics: Pötzl, 'Volksfrömmigkeit', pp. 910–11.

'newly raised-up saints and patrons of the city and territory of Augsburg' from the cathedral to the abbey church. In addition to the usual Masses, sermons and the decree of a plenary indulgence, the week of solemnities included a 'festival academy' of public disputations. The celebrations were commemorated in two contemporary printed accounts.[12]

Such festivals were also a feature of the following century. In 1745, the bishopric of Eichstätt celebrated its millennial jubilee by processing the relics of its founder and leading patron, St Willibald. According to the published festival account, for 500 years the exact whereabouts of the saint's remains had been a mystery, but no sooner had the decision been made to celebrate the jubilee than the current bishop was 'divinely inspired' to discover the relics behind the cathedral's high altar. A week of celebrations was inaugurated by the procession on 5 September, which involved sixty-eight separate contingents and included *genii* with images of Willibald and Eichstätt's other saints and floats enacting scenes from their lives.[13] In Augsburg, meanwhile, relic festivals continued to play an important part in the reactivation of the cults of diocesan saints, most notably with the chief diocesan patrons, Ulrich and Afra, whose relics were solemnly exhumed and translated to new shrines in 1762 and 1804 respectively.[14] The latter celebrations were occasioned by the fifteen-hundredth anniversary of the saint's martyrdom. By this period, however, opinion on the appropriateness of such celebrations was divided. Many 'enlightened' Catholics were themselves sceptical of relic veneration, and many feared that ridicule might descend on the Church as a result of this blatant display. Sensitive to the cultural climate, the bishop insisted on a secret examination of the exhumed bones in order to ascertain their state of

---

12 Peter Rummel, 'Katholisches Leben in der Reichsstadt Augsburg (1650–1806)', *Jahrbuch des Vereins für Augsburger Bistumsgeschichte*, 18, 1984, pp. 9–161 (pp. 120–22).

13 Johannes Andreas de la Haye, *Die in seinem tausend-jährigen Alter feyerlichst erneuerte Herrlichkeit der Eichstättischen Kirch, bey ienem grossen Jübel- und Dank-Fest, welches wegen im abgewichenen 1745ten Jahr, durch die Gnad Gottes würcklich erreichten Tausend Jahren von Errichtung des Hoch-Stiffts, dann zu gleicher Zeit bechehenen glucklichisten Erfindung des Heiligen Wilibaldi ihres ersten glorwurdigisten Bischoffens mittels solemner Translation sothaner neu-erfundenen HH. Reliquien [...] celebrirt worden ist [...]*, Ingolstadt, 1746.

14 Rummel, 'Katholisches Leben', pp. 126–27.

survival (luckily they were intact, bar two missing toes) before the formal 'recognition' could be staged and the festival planned. The jubilee was celebrated in October 1804, with an estimated 100,000 participating, and the translation took place the following May.[15]

The Afra jubilee was the last great Bavarian relic celebration of the Old Reich and, despite its pomp, the defensiveness exhibited even by its promoters betrays the extensive encroachments of Enlightenment secularism. The earlier relic festivities of monastic and cathedral chapters, however, seem to have responded to other threats. In the first instance, one can interpret the festivals as a visible, devotional expression of the stubborn defence of privilege and tradition mounted by ancient ecclesiastical corporations against both the centripetal absolutism of the post-Tridentine papacy and political pressures from the Bavarian state. Diocesan relic festivals can be seen as expressions of localism, as, in Simon Ditchfield's words, 'vindicators of local diversity'.[16] Wolfgang, Willibald, Ulrich and the rest were potent emblems of the political and ecclesiastical autonomy of their dioceses, personifying, and thus mobilizing, individual and collective identification with a territory. Appropriate symbolism was of course not in itself a guarantee of effective propagandistic agency. Success indeed was held to depend on the ability of the saint to exercise real patronage, to intercede and to work miracles for the patronee. The contract implied in the relic festival, veneration in return for patronage, was an attempt to delineate, pin down and grasp the mysterious power of the sacred.[17] The same process was at work with the *Gnadenbilder*, or miraculous images of the saints, which proliferated in Bavaria in the same period. At the same time the resanctification of cathedrals and convents through veneration of their saintly patrons rebounded to the gain of the duchy of Bavaria,

---

15 Theodor Rolle, 'Die 1500-Jahrfeier des Martyriums der heiligen Afra im Jahre 1804/5', *Jahrbuch des Vereins für Augsburger Bistumsgeschichte*, 22, 1988, pp. 105–50.
16 Simon Ditchfield, 'Martyrs on the Move: Relics as Vindicators of Local Diversity in the Tridentine Church' in Diana Wood (ed.), *Martyrs and Martyrologies*, Oxford, 1993, pp. 283–94.
17 For discussion of the impact of such festivals on local religion in the Augbsurg diocese, see Hermann Hörger, 'Die "Ulrichsjubiläen" des 17. bis 19. Jahrhunderts und ihre Auswirkungen auf die Volksfrömmigkeit in Ulrichspfarreien', *Zeitschrift für bayerische Landesgeschichte*, 37, 1974, pp. 309–57.

Trionfi of the Holy Dead: the Relic Festivals of Baroque Bavaria 39

in so far as the areas of the spiritual jurisdiction of the bishops were under the political control of the Wittelsbach dynasty. Although secular and ecclesiastical authorities did not always appear to sing from the same hymn-sheet, their sponsorship of relic festivals united in promoting the *pietas bavarica*.

Secondly, such relic festivals contributed to a polemic and serviced a propaganda that was explicitly confessional. The festive translation of local relics, particularly those of diocesan founders, was a dramatic restatement of the continuity of Catholic identity, an identity expressed through a triumphalist assertion of the cult of the saints in general. Protestant rejection of the saints had itself to be rejected, through more intense, more passionate, more elaborate glorification of their deeds and veneration of their relics, as Rader had exhorted in the *Bavaria Sancta*. The revival of the cult of Wolfgang at Regensburg, for example, must be seen in the light of the difficult circumstances of the post-Reformation bishops, whose authority had been severely compromised by the defection of their city and of the Upper Palatinate, a major segment of their spiritual jurisdiction, to Protestantism. The Thirty Years War (1618–48), although physically devastating, brought about the windfall gain of the re-Catholicization of the latter territory, annexed by Maximilian of Bavaria in the 1620s. On the eve of the great conflict, the Wolfgang relic festivals were not only intended to reaffirm diocesan identity; they also symbolized episcopal aspirations that the saint's patrimony, the entire see of Regensburg, would be restored to the true faith.

What strikes one from the festival accounts is the durability of the confessional theme, from the stormy sectarian extremism of the Thirty Years War through to the supposedly more temperate confessional climate of the mid-eighteenth century. The published description of the Eichstätt jubilee relic festival of 1746 provides a late example of anti-Protestant polemic transmitted through the medium of festival. In a brief historical overview, its author treated the Reformation period in uncompromising terms:

> Practically no area of Germany escaped the manifold snares laid by Luther and his adherents. However, due to the careful precautions and Christian fortitude of its most zealous bishops then and since, the Eichstätt diocese has till now been miraculously preserved in its original zeal for the true faith,

even though (alas!) at the time some neighbouring principalities and lordships separated themselves from the mother-church of Eichstätt.[18]

Within the procession itself, the float dedicated to the eighth century of the history of the diocese portrayed the Eichstätt church, inspired by 'its courageous superior', in the act of excluding Lutheranism from its territory. It featured a scene of the foundation of the convent of Mariastein, dedicated to the Virgin, who was described as 'alone destroying all heresies'.[19] Finally, in his jubilee homily, Eichstätt's vicar-general returned to the theme. Addressing the saint, he identified Luther with the beast from Psalm 79 ('the boar out of the wood doth waste it and the wild beast of the field doth devour it'):

> The beast of Eisleben devoured the splendid vines of the greatest monasteries, numerous parishes and innumerable souls. Lest even greater damage occur again, redouble your pleas to God and maintain all the souls of your diocese in the exclusively salvific Catholic Christian faith, which you planted with your truly paternal and pious hand, until the end of the world![20]

Like those of the preceding century, the eighteenth-century relic translations and jubilees of diocesan patrons aimed to consolidate the confessional identity of their participants and spectators. They provided a salutary reminder of heretical dangers, whilst glorying past victories and demonstrating uninterrupted religious allegiance. Such celebrations of indigenous relics were, however, outnumbered by those of outsiders.

Holy Bodies

In the seventeenth century the ravages of the Thirty Years War and the recovery of previously reformed territories by Catholic states, as with the Bavarian annexation of the Upper Palatinate, necessitated the importation of new relics to replace their now lost pre-Reformation counterparts. Of such replacements Rome and its early-Christian catacombs proved to be by far the most prolific source. Rediscovered by chance in 1578, the subterranean cemeteries revealed the remains of thousands of Christian dead, all of whom, on the basis of selective interpretation of epigraphy

---

18 de la Haye, *Herrlichkeit der Eichstättischen Kirch*, p. 6.
19 Ibid., p. 14.
20 Ibid., p. 48.

Trionfi of the Holy Dead: the Relic Festivals of Baroque Bavaria   41

and such physical indicators as alleged 'phials of blood', were identified as early martyrs. Their bones, whenever possible assembled to form complete skeletons, were transferred to the Vatican, where the papal sacristan officially certified them as holy relics. Popularized through Antonio Bosio's *Roma sotteranea* (1632), the catacomb saints became the most sought-after relics in Catholic Europe.[21]

Austria and the Catholic regions of Switzerland and South Germany appear to have presented a particularly large market for relic exports from Rome. From the start, Bavaria was a key destination, translations of *Katakombenheiligen* beginning under Maximilian I with the arrival of the relics of St Modestus in Munich in 1610. Cordial relations between the papacy and the Wittelsbachs enabled the dynasty to act as facilitator in acquiring relics for Bavarian municipal and ecclesiastical corporations, between which immense competition developed to secure the bodies of the martyrs. The years of peace after 1648 saw a massive extension of the cult, reaching a peak around 1700.[22] At this time the festivals attending the translations were also at their most elaborate.

The basic structure of such festivals, at least of their mature, late seventeenth-century phase, has already been outlined through the example of the Kemnath celebrations of 1693. How, though, is the Bavarian enthusiasm for such festivals to be explained and their content interpreted? They shared with the celebrations of their indigenous Bavarian counterparts the motifs of dynasticism, localism and confessionalism but, in their varied component idioms, expressed these differently and introduced additional features. More flagrantly, perhaps because they were initially without any local associations, they supported a pure doctrinal didacticism, directed at the Catholic laity. Indeed one can find as a stated aim the reinforcement of orthodox post-Tridentine teaching on the cult of the saints. In June 1669 the skeleton of the catacomb saint, Crescentianus, was solemnly welcomed by the town of Amberg, the capital of Bavaria's Upper-Palatine province. The parish

---

21   For the most detailed study of the phenomenon, see Hansjakob Achermann, *Die Katakombenheiligen und ihre Translationen in der schweizerischen Quart des Bistums Konstanz*, Stans, 1979.

22   Pötzl, 'Volksfrömmigkeit', pp. 918–29; Krausen, 'Verehrung römischer Katakombenheiliger'; Trevor Johnson, 'Holy Fabrications: The Catacomb Saints and the Counter-Reformation in Bavaria', *Journal of Ecclesiastical History*, 47, 1996, pp. 274–97.

priest, Bernhard Neuhauser, had petitioned for such a relic, the better to indoctrinate his flock in this most basic of Catholic devotions:

> He argued [wrote one of his successors] that over the previous four years he had given the old converts of Amberg plenty of homilies on the cult of the saints. With this devotion, however, it was vital actually to place saintly relics before them and, so to speak, give them faith in [the saints'] intercession and helpfulness, in order for the cult of the saints which had been preached to them to remain all the more firmly in their hearts.[23]

Despite a last-minute attempt by the Amberg Jesuits to hijack it for their own college, Neuhauser succeeded in acquiring his relic: on 4 June 1669 the reliquary was processed through a series of triumphal arches from a suburban chapel to a newly restored altar in the parish church, accompanied on its journey by the suffragan bishop of Regensburg and 100 citizens bearing tapers and rosaries.[24]

Indoctrination is also manifest in the iconography of the triumphal arches erected for the translation of St Primianus to Kemnath, Amberg's Upper-Palatine neighbour. The largest displayed a pair of painted panels, the first of which depicted Primianus rising from a tomb accompanied by angels bearing bones and quotations from Psalms 33 and 138 ('the lord keepeth all his bones' and 'my bones are not hidden from thee'). The second panel showed Primianus again, now standing in the clouds and holding two thuribles, from which incense rose up towards the gleaming triangle of the Trinity and the motto 'Gott allein'. Below Primianus was an altar, from which another thurible vented incense which ascended to join the thuribles held by the saint. 'Bluet und gebein mein opfer sein' was the motto here. Johann Arkhauer, the festival organizer who had designed the scheme and later reported on the event, glossed the second image as a demonstration that 'the honour paid to the saints is paid to God Himself'.[25]

Nevertheless, the rich symbolism of the translations transcended a simple appeal to Tridentine orthodoxy, whilst the relics in question were more than striking props with which to enliven catechetical instruction. They were after all the remains of very special holy dead, the early Christian Roman martyrs, and the celebrations of their arrival in Bavaria could not fail to possess either a wider

---

23 StAA, Geistliche Sachen 713, 14 April 1701.
24 Ibid., 681.
25 Ibid., 3395, 'Relation'.

resonance or a polemical and confessional edge. At a time when Europe's wars of religion had fostered a cult of martyrdom on both sides of the sectarian divide, the reception of the catacomb saints offered a timely confirmation of congruity between contemporary Catholic stoicism and that of the early persecutions. The connection, in an age which prized continuity, was all the more effective given that the martyrs in question were representatives of an early Church which even Protestants had to concede was incontrovertibly pure. Meanwhile, their Roman provenance underscored the re-found universalism of the post-Tridentine Church and papacy. Bavaria had for long represented a confessional frontier, clinging to the old faith but exposed to influence from its Protestant neighbours, while its most recent territorial acquisition, the Upper Palatinate, had been subject to Calvinist rule and conversion prior to the Thirty Years War. Here at least the new cults of the *Katakombenheiligen*, along with those of the old diocesan patrons, were both symbols and agents of re-Catholicization. Neuhauser had hoped especially to impress the 'old converts' of his town. In 1693, Arkhauer, writing an account of the Primianus festival at Kemnath for his bishop and for the regional governor, described the week-long celebrations as 'especially' dedicated to 'the extirpation of heresy'.[26] Beyond a simple restatement of the faith, the relic festivals of the catacomb saints therefore enjoyed a second dimension as manifestations of confessional identity.

If the Roman provenance of the new relics was impressive, a further significant cluster of meanings was imparted to these festivals by the shameless corporeal integrity of the catacomb saints, a factor which distinguished them from most other relics of the holy dead. The complete skeletons, always described as 'whole bodies' rather than 'relics', seem to have been conceptualized rather differently from their fragmented confrères. Certainly their display, during the festivals and in their subsequent enshrinement, emphasized this feature. Generally relics were housed in *ostensoria* or display cases which obscured rather than revealed what were anyway semiotically neutral objects, totally dependent on adjacent inscriptions for identification (and through identification, power). By contrast, the large glass reliquaries of the intact catacomb saints were constructed for maximum visibility. Within them, armatures allowed the unmistakably human skeletons to be

---

26 Ibid.

posed in lifelike attitudes, standing, seated or, most often, reclining on cushions, their skulls turned towards the viewer. Often gems were positioned in the eye sockets, perhaps to impart an impression of vitality, and the bones (supplemented where necessary with wood or papier-mâché) were clothed in padded robes and bedecked with pearls, beads and the locally-fashioned tinsel decorative work known as *Klosterarbeit*. The Cistercian abbey of Waldsassen acquired ten catacomb saints in the eighteenth century, each displayed wearing a laurel crown and bearing emblems of his or her career and martyrdom (the skeleton of the soldier-saint, Theodosius, for example, sports a helmet and sword). From 1756 the abbey celebrated an annual 'Heilig-Leiber-Fest', a festival of the Holy Bodies.[27]

The corporeal integrity of the catacomb saints bespoke that of the Church itself, its catholicity and unity, as well as its holiness and apostolic descent, all the more intact for having jettisoned its heretics. It may also have fostered the localization of their cults. Indigenous Bavarian saints were easier candidates for symbols of civic, regional or territorial identity than the aliens from the catacombs. Typically, however, in the course of a festival a newly arrived martyr was declared patron of the host town, district or parish, and perhaps the whole bodies expressed more effectively than could abstract bone fragments the concept of an individual holy personality watching over and safeguarding a community. In Kantorowiczian terms, one might say, of the saint's two bodies, the mortal and the mystical, the devotees could claim exclusive and transparent possession of the first and, in consequence, guarantee the undivided attention of the second.[28] Through their form (the entry into and procession through a town) and through their iconography, the relic festivals eased this process of transition and adoption. At Kemnath, where Primianus was declared patron of the town during the festival, the

---

[27] Bärbel Hamacher, *Waldsassen*, Passau, 1992, p. 31; Manfred Knedlik, 'Karfreitagsprozessionen in Waldsassen im 18. Jahrhundert', *Oberpfälzer Heimat*, 38, 1994, pp. 112–22 (p. 114). On the form and decoration of the reliquaries, see Achermann, *Katakombenheiligen*, pp. 87–99; Pötzl, 'Volksfrömmigkeit', pp. 911, 919–20, 926–27. In his report on the Primianus festival at Kemnath in 1693, Father Arkauer described in detail the elaborate form of the reliquary, which even incorporated wheels for the easy manoeuvring of the relic: StAA, Geistliche Sachen 3395.

[28] Ernst Kantorowicz, *The King's Two Bodies: A Study in Medieval Political Theology*, Princeton, NJ, 1957.

triumphal arches featured the arms of the papacy, echoing the Roman provenance and universalizing tendencies implicit in the catacomb cult, but balanced them with the escutcheons of the local bishop, the electorate of Bavaria and the town itself. The festival was plainly a manifestation of civic pride and identity, embracing not only the citizenry but also villagers from the outlying rural parishes who processed into the town led by their priests. Kemnath's central place in the local sacred economy was further emphasized iconographically on one triumphal arch through emblematic references to the Armesburg, a nearby shrine which Johann Arkhauer had established in the 1670s with financial support from the Elector of Bavaria.

Association with an existing local pilgrimage was clearly a further useful means of promoting a new cult. In August 1698 the Cistercian abbey of Raitenhaslach celebrated its sexcentenary with a relic festival honouring a newly acquired family of catacomb saints: Ausanius, Concordia and their year-old daughter Fortunata. Here again the celebration took the form of a procession through a series of triumphal arches. A specially composed festival hymn asked rhetorically of the saints what it was that had made them flee from their Roman home to the 'lap' of Bavaria ('from the Tiber to the river Salzach') and confidently asserted:

> Ich glaub daß Maria gewesen
> Von Oetting der Magnet-Stein
> So gezogen unverwesen
> Eure heilige gebein.[29]

The reference, wrapped in the metaphor of magnetic attraction, was to the nearby town of Altötting and its ancient Marian shrine. A connection was thereby established between the trio of hitherto unknown saints and Bavaria's premier Marian pilgrimage, the focus of intense and widespread devotion, including that of the ruling Wittelsbach house. In an apparent reversal of precedence, one of the pageant's *tableaux* featured a personified Altötting kneeling before the arriving martyrs. Similarly the Benedictine convent of Geisenfeld festively received the relics of St Dionysius in July 1673; a miracle-book published shortly after by the nuns' confessor associated the miracles which the martyr had already begun to work with those of St Anna, whose *Gnadenbild* was already enshrined in the

---

29 Krausen, 'Verehrung römischer Katakombenheiliger', p. 43.

abbey. Here the two cults, old and new, seem to have become mutually reinforcing.[30]

The localization of the catacomb saints, their successful integration into the extant pantheon of local cults, can be gauged by devotional patterns established in the wake of the relic festivals. At Amberg, St Crescentianus appears to have been the focus of a small-scale pilgrimage for a number of years (if one can judge by donations received at his altar).[31] The same occurred with other catacomb saints in Bavaria, some of whom even acquired reputations for specialist miracles: St Felix protected his devotees at Gars against fire, St Donatus defended Freising against storms and, at Dillingen, St Faustus operated against cattle-disease. Patterns of name-giving, based on analyses of baptismal registers, also indicate an assimilation of the new cults into the Bavarian religious landscape.[32] It would seem that local religion was sufficiently plastic to accommodate the new saints without necessitating the displacement of existing cults. Imported relics from the catacombs rubbed shoulders (as it were) with ancient local bones or miraculous images, whose cults were reactivated at the same time. The necrology of the Lower-Bavarian Benedictine abbey of Niederaltaich records that when its church was restored in 1727, the abbot 'endowed and decorated it with the six holy bodies of SS Julia, Julius, Alruna, Magnus, Aurelia and Antonius, as well as with other holy relics, especially those of the sainted Bishop Pirmin, the first builder of the monastery of Niederaltaich'.[33]

Processions and trionfi

The Eichstätt procession of 1745 followed the same route as the city's Corpus Christi procession and, as for Corpus Christi, the streets were decorated with 'fresh green foliage', rugs, pictures, emblems and flowers. 'One might think', gushed the commemorative text, 'that Eichstätt had been transformed into a

---

30   Ibid., pp. 37–38.
31   Johnson, 'Holy Fabrications', pp. 294–96.
32   Krausen, 'Verehrung römischer Katakombenheliger'; Pötzl, 'Volksfrömmigkeit', pp. 926–28.
33   Georg Stadtmüller and Bonifaz Pfister OSB, *Geschichte der Abtei Niederaltaich, 741–1971*, Augsburg, 1971, pp. 235, 237, 243–44.

delightful pleasure garden'.[34] The Kemnath procession too wound its way through streets decorated with foliage and a prominent place was accorded the members of the town's recently established 'Corpus Christi' confraternity, splendid in their red habits and hoods. Many other relic pageants too shared the route and something of the style of the annual eucharistic festival: relics, like the host, enjoyed, for example, the privilege of being borne under splendid canopies. There was, of course, nothing unusual in the choice of the processional form *per se*, as this was a traditional method of exposing relics for veneration and, more importantly, for supplication, when recourse was had to their apotropaic qualities at moments of communal emergency. Moreover, from the inception of the feast of Corpus Christi relics accompanied the host in processions, appropriately enough when at least in Germany the wafer was viewed as an especially potent relic, and so again the association was a natural one. Furthermore, in a fusion of devotional and political idioms, Corpus Christi routes themselves often originated in those used for medieval royal entries.[35]

Yet, as Philip Soergel has recently emphasized, the Bavarian celebration of Corpus Christi had itself been significantly transformed since the mid-sixteenth century, through a combination of dynastic and ecclesiastical initiative. In contrast to Corpus Christi traditions in Western Europe, in Bavaria the involvement of guilds and confraternities, the costuming of participants and the employment of floats and *tableaux vivants* seem in the main to have appeared only after the Reformation and their introduction appears to have been confessionally inspired. Mimesis of biblical scenes had a 'propagandistic and polemical' function, designed to counter Protestant attacks on the eucharistic festival as an unscriptural and idolatrous innovation. As they increased their repertoire, Munich's Corpus Christi processions correspondingly grew in size (numbering 3,000 participants by 1582) while their political importance was enhanced by the attendance of the ruling Wittelsbachs and their court.[36] The style of the capital was copied elsewhere,

---

34 de la Haye, *Herrlichkeit der Eichstättischen Kirch*, p. 10.
35 Miri Rubin, *Corpus Christi: The Eucharist in Late Medieval Culture*, Cambridge, 1991, p. 243–71; Charles Zika, 'Hosts, Processions and Pilgrimages in Fifteenth-Century Germany', *Past and Present*, 118, 1988, pp. 25–64.
36 Soergel, *Wondrous in His Saints*, pp. 80–91.

although inevitably on a slightly more modest scale, throughout Bavaria. Sloppiness which detracted from the splendour and dignity of the performance was frowned upon: one unfortunate priest of the Regensburg diocese was censured by his consistorial court for using a beer glass to improvise repairs to the broken window of his monstrance during his village's Corpus Christi procession of 1648.[37] From the 1650's, ducal patronage and injunctions encouraged the revival of weekly eucharistic processions, held on Thursdays, permitting the message of the annual festival to resonate throughout the year.[38] Sermons and print defended and extolled the silent mystery of the Eucharist against its Protestant critics and defilers, while brotherhoods were established to popularize the cult. Corpus Christi then had become an important locus of Bavarian confessional propaganda. In sharing its new structure, as well as some of its details, the relic festivals partook too of its enhanced range of meanings: a manifestation of confessional identity and an association with the politico-religious ambitions of the ruling dynasty.

The relic processions also echoed another form of annual processional which spread throughout Bavaria in the seventeenth-century: the Holy Week procession. This had a penitential character, alien to the relic festivals, but the themes of sacrifice, martyrdom, and triumph over death linked them, as did the processional form, the use of floats and *tableaux vivants* and the iconographical motifs of palms and crosses.[39] The floats of the Primianus festival at Kemnath, for example, offered scenes of the saint in prison, strengthened for his martyrdom by the vision of an angel holding a cross and presented by the Virgin to the Trinity.[40] These would doubtless have reminded bystanders of the Sorrowful Mysteries of Christ's Passion as enacted during Holy Week processions. There are indications too in the records that props and costumes may have been re-used for various separate festal occasions.[41]

---

37 Bischöfliches Zentralarchiv Regensburg, Consistorial Protokolle, 3 February 1648.
38 StAA, Geistliche Sachen 860.
39 On Bavarian Holy Week processions, see Rummel, 'Katholisches Leben', pp. 68–95 (reproducing details of a splendid forty-seven-metre long watercolour of the 1747 procession); Knedlik, 'Karfreitagsprozessionen in Waldsassen'.
40 StAA, Geistliche Sachen 3395, 'Relation'.
41 For example, after the translation of the martyr Crescentianus to the parish church of St Martin in Amberg in 1669, the Jesuit college retained the costumes made for the

Trionfi of the Holy Dead: the Relic Festivals of Baroque Bavaria   49

In common with other Baroque processions, those which formed the centrepieces of the relic pageants offered a representation of the established order, ranking their participants according to their position within the ecclesiastical and lay hierarchy and rigidly emphasizing distinctions of social status, occupation, gender and age. Such representation, it must be remembered, was of an essentially fictive ideal of a harmonious and ordered community, the ideal of the élite who organized the festivals, and one must be wary of reading an ideological consensus, still less a social reality, into such expressions. Processions, though, offered more meanings in the seventeenth-century German Counter-Reformation context. There is a sense of assertiveness, perhaps of aggression, or even something quasi-militaristic, in the urge to get congregations on the move in ordered files. And, indeed, in bi-confessional German regions in the sixteenth and seventeenth centuries the Catholic marching-season did often threaten the precarious religious peace. In Regensburg in the 1620s the Protestant council repeatedly erected barricades to restrict the Catholic minority's Corpus Christi and Good Friday processions, while the Donauwörth crisis of 1607, which led directly to the formation of two opposing confessional alliances within the Empire, had as its primary cause a dispute over the control of processional space, sparked by the revival of rogations from the town's Benedictine abbey.[42] Although religious conflict *per se* had eased by the period of the heyday of the relic festivals, the salience of the processional form may have stirred memories, serving not merely to inspire the faithful but also to overawe waverers and intimidate confessional opponents.

If the relic festival echoed, and in a sense was parasitic upon regular religious festivals, such as Corpus Christi or Holy Week, it looked elsewhere too for borrowable ingredients. Indeed, in some ways the closest parallel to (and possible model for) the late seventeenth-century relic celebration, particularly that of the catacomb saint, was not the sacred feast of Corpus Christi but the secular pageant of the royal entry, the *trionfo*, or triumph, that 'toy' of princes, as Bacon

---

procession. The festival's organizing committee (the parish priest, mayor and electoral officials) described the costumes as 'useless' for the parish church, but valuable for the Jesuits' own 'endeavour', which presumably implied a utility for either Holy Week processions or the drama staged at the Amberg college: StAA, Geistliche Sachen 681.

42 Dollinger, p. 249–50; Ronald G. Asch, *The Thirty Years War: The Holy Roman Empire and Europe, 1618–1648*, Basingstoke and London, 1997, p. 27.

dismissively termed it.[43] The extramural departure point of the procession (with civic dignitaries leaving the city to welcome the entrant), the routine balancing of the mobile procession with static triumphal arches, the use of floats and carts with allegorical figures or *tableaux*, the classical (especially imperial Roman) costuming and the self-referential motif of the host city, its local topography emblematized in the festal iconography, were all key specific features of the Renaissance and Baroque royal *trionfo* as much as they seem to have been of the relic festival. In general both shared the same infrequency and the same *Gesamtkunstwerk*-quality, the sense of iconographic and scenographic overload, which leads Roger Chartier to describe the entry as 'a festival of festivals'.[44] In Bavaria the heyday of the relic celebration coincided with an extension of the festal culture of the electoral court under Electors Ferdinand Maria and Maximilian II Emanuel. Along with operas, ballets, tournaments, *naumachiae*, banquets, comedies, hunts, illuminations, parades and winter sleigh-rides, triumphal entries, such as those staged by Maximilian Emanuel in Munich after the lifting of the siege of Vienna in 1683, or on the occasion of his marriage in 1685, were a key component of this festal repertoire.[45]

Like the *trionfi* of the secular ruler, although clearly in different ways, the relic festivals stressed the themes of triumphant heroism and sovereign majesty. The triumphal theme comes through strongly in the catacomb-saint festivals. The holy skeletons habitually sported the laurels of conquering heroes. As martyrs for Christ, their deaths were regarded as almost gladiatorial victories: the martyrs were the spiritual conquerors of their heathen and demonic persecutors. At the Raitenhaslach festival of 1698, for example, a celebration of the martyrs Ausanius, Concordia and Fortunata, the decor of the triumphal arches featured an angel

---

43 Francis Bacon, *The Essayes or Counsels Civill and Morall of Francis Bacon Lord Verulam*, London, 1906 edn, pp. 115–16.
44 Roger Chartier, 'Phantasie und Disziplin. Das Fest in Frankreich vom 15. bis 18. Jahrhundert' in Richard van Dülmen and Norbert Schindler (eds), *Volkskultur. Zur Wiederentdeckung des vergessenen Alltags (16.–20. Jahrhundert)*, Frankfurt am Main, 1984, pp. 153–76 (p. 163).
45 Eberhard Straub, *Repraesentatio Maiestatis oder churbayerische Freudenfeste. Die höfischen Feste in der Münchener Residenz vom 16. bis zum Ende des 18. Jahrhunderts*, Munich, 1969, pp. 174–318.

Trionfi of the Holy Dead: the Relic Festivals of Baroque Bavaria   51

bearing the motto 'ex caede triumphus' ('triumph from slaughter') and allegorical figures of courage and fortitude. In dying they won eternal glory: the city of Amberg received in a solemn procession what was described as the 'glorious body' of the martyr, Fortunatus, in 1692. At Kemnath the hymn *Victori* was sung in honour of the martyr Primianus.[46]

The festivals also celebrated the 'sovereign' power of the saints. Their majesty could be pictured as deriving from their position in the hierarchy of the divine heavenly court, which in the Baroque imagination was conceived as a speculum of the absolutist royal court. At the same time, as either ancient or new patrons, they were in a sense the spiritual sovereigns of their host towns, their gilded reliquaries a species of throne.[47] The corporeal integrity of the relics and the glittering *Klosterarbeit* may have helped to reinforce this idea. Through form, as much as content, the religious festival both received dignity and legitimacy from the secular sphere, but simultaneously reflected it back, sacralizing the authority of the prince, whose escutcheons decorated the triumphal arches and whose officials marched in the train of the saints and martyrs, in a typically Baroque transference between sacred and profane.[48]

Macabre Curiosities

Time and again, when studying the festival descriptions and their accompanying illustrations, or viewing the occasional surviving reliquary *in situ*, one's attention is

---

46   Krausen, 'Verehrung römischer Katakombenheliger', p. 42; StAA, Geistliche Sachen 713 and 3395, 'Relation'.

47   In a doubtless hyperbolic confusion of categories, Johann Arkhauer referred to the newly nominated civic patron, St Primianus, as Kemnath's 'guardian angel': StAA, Geistliche Sachen 3395, 'Relation'.

48   This fusion of elements was of course as much medieval as early modern practice. One must recall too that, in an inversion of the festivals described here, relics were typically brought out on the occasion of royal entries, as emblems of local identity and means of sacralizing the oaths of mutual loyalty sworn on such occasions between ruler and subjects. For early modern examples from the Duchy of Lorraine, see Kate Currey, 'The Political and Social Significance of Court Festivals in Lorraine, 1563–1624', unpublished DPhil dissertation, University of Sussex, 1996, p. 123.

arrested by the most bare and stripped of images, the shocking intimacy of the revealed human skeleton and its grinning death's head. The impact of the relic-festivals, and the popularity, especially, of the 'whole bodies' of the catacomb saints, was surely connected with the *frisson* of this macabre encounter, something clearly felt by early modern Bavarians, but in ways which are now impossible to recapture fully.

The Baroque was of course no stranger to macabre and skeletal images in a religious setting. Indeed it abounded in them, and representations of the dissected human body could be said to have achieved a new level of detail following the publication of the *De humanae corporis fabrica* of Vesalius in 1543. The skull as *memento mori* was a stock feature of contemporary *vanitas* art and of funeral sculpture, as well as a melancholic stage prop for tragic drama.[49] Real human skulls were also used as props to dramatize the penitential messages of the rural missions undertaken by the Jesuits in Bavaria from the early eighteenth century.[50] The *Totentanz* also seems to have had a recrudescence in Counter-Reformation Bavaria: seventeenth- and eighteenth-century examples of the Dance of Death can be found throughout the electorate, from its northern border at Wondreb and Roding in the Upper Palatinate to its southern extremity at Füssen in the Bavarian Alps.[51] Human bones were displayed in ossuary chapels, the visible expression of the cult of the dead and the charity towards the Holy Souls suffering the torments of Purgatory promoted by the Counter-Reformation Church. Many ossuaries were

---

49 For discussion of the latter theme in the context of English drama, see Andrew Sofer, 'The Skull on the Renaissance Stage: Imagination and the Erotic Life of Props', *English Literary Renaissance*, 28, 1998, pp. 47–74.

50 Trevor Johnson, 'Blood, Tears and Xavier-Water: Jesuit Missionaries and Popular Religion in the Eighteenth-Century Upper Palatinate' in Bob Scribner and Trevor Johnson (eds), *Popular Religion in Germany and Central Europe, 1400–1800*, Basingstoke and London, 1996, pp. 183–202 (p. 193).

51 Rolf Jacob, 'Der Totentanz in Wondreb', *Oberpfälzer Heimat*, 35, 1991, pp. 202–16; Reinhold Böhm, *Der Füssener Totentanz und das Fortwirken der Totentanzidee im Ostallgäuer und Außerferner Raum*, 3rd edn, Füssen, 1990.

Trionfi of the Holy Dead: the Relic Festivals of Baroque Bavaria   53

restored after the Thirty Years War and their presence in churchyards was often mandated in diocesan constitutions.[52]

The Spanish historian José Antonio Maravall has linked the Baroque fascination with representations of death to a familiarization with violence occasioned by post-Reformation Europe's wars of religion, but also to an accompanying cultural ambition to lay bare the cruel realities of the human condition in order to contain and dominate it. Accordingly, the macabre, in particular the iconographic use of the human skeleton, was presented as a public spectacle:

> And such a spectacle could tell one many things. Its carefully realized representation of how one ends up after death could contain a severe warning about what lies beyond, or also a reminder about what happens when one has not known how to defend oneself from enemies, or perhaps a mere anatomy lesson, or the barbarous confirmation of what the force of those in power can do to one if one dares to confront them. The representation of the skeleton, then, had multiple functions in the baroque, and if we cannot deny that the principal function corresponded to an ascetic-religious meaning, resonances alluding to the danger of the social and political world were never lacking [...] an entire series of concepts — time, change, decay, etc. — that were fundamentally interwined in baroque mentality were connected with this event of the transition of death [...].[53]

Although they dealt with actual bones rather than painted or sculptural renderings of them (or, more accurately, in addition to such renderings), the relic festivals of Bavaria and other Catholic regions in the long Counter-Reformation were part of this Baroque culture of the macabre. Yet in place of horror or terror, the expected response was awe, veneration and, not least, affection: in this particular death's-head had to be seen the visage of a saint, a holy patron, protector and helper. Perhaps the clothing and decoration of the skeletons (including often the placement of jewels in the eye sockets, giving the sense of a gaze returned), which seem so much a feature of their presentation, were not incidental but actually vital to the softening of an otherwise grotesque spectacle.

---

52 On ossuaries and other aspects of the cult of the dead in the Upper Palatinate, see Walter Hartinger, *...denen Gott genad! Totenbrauchtum und Armen-Seelen-Glaube in der Oberpfalz*, Regensburg, 1979.

53 José Antonio Maravall, *Culture of the Baroque: Analysis of a Historical Structure*, trans. Terry Cochran, Manchester, 1986, p. 165.

Above all, though, it was the very elevation of a canonical ritual into a festival which is most striking.

The popular response to this was, however, ambiguous. On the one hand, the proliferation of pilgrimages, name-giving and other devotions around the relics suggests a successful reception of the cults, what the organizers of the relic festivals would have regarded as a correct 'reading' or 'viewing' of them. In 1701, the parish priest of Amberg reported how several years previously a party of officials from Bamberg had visited the town and asked permission to view the shrine of the catacomb saint, Crescentianus.

> A few years later, one of them, named Otto, found himself suffering from a protracted and painful disease of the arms and legs. Since the many remedies he tried brought no improvement, he made a vow to this saint, *towards whom he had felt a great affection right from when he first saw him in his tomb*, and offered him four silver [ex-votos in the shape of] arms and legs. Upon making the vow he was immediately cured.[54]

Here, according to the pilgrim himself, the sight of the relic had triggered an emotional response, one of 'affection', which was entirely appropriate. In 1669, however, within two weeks of the enshrinement of the saint, an incident involving the relic which reveals a rather different way of seeing had been brought to the attention of the local magistrates. An Amberg innkeeper, Hans Wegele, was charged with forcing open the reliquary in an act of 'sacrilegious vandalism' in order to reveal its contents to satisfy the curiosity of some men from Nuremberg to whom he was giving a tour of the town. Despite the testimony of eyewitnesses, Wegele protested his innocence, stating that when he examined it the reliquary was already unlocked and claiming that the verger's daughter was reputed to be willing to open up the reliquary for a tip to anyone who was curious to see inside it. The innkeeper was fined and the incident quickly blew over.[55] It offers a tantalizing glimpse of a response very different from that intended by the organizers of the relic festivals, a different species of fascination but one which was perhaps an inevitable product of them. The festivals, indeed, can be seen as the dramatizations

---

54 StAA, Geistliche Sachen 713; emphasis added.
55 Ibid., 681.

Trionfi of the Holy Dead: the Relic Festivals of Baroque Bavaria   55

of macabre curiosities which in their grotesque freakishness were as equally typical of the Baroque as the religious emotions evoked by sacred immanence.[56]

Conclusion

The Afra festivities in Augsburg in 1804–05 can be taken as marking the end of the particular festival type we have been examining, even though relics themselves continued to be significant objects of devotion. The Holy Roman Empire itself limped on only for another year. The mass migration of bodies from the catacombs also stopped in the nineteenth century. In Bavaria the demise of the relic festival coincided with the massive secularization of church property of 1803 and a decline of pilgrimages and traditional religious festival under the pressures of enlightenment statism.[57] Today the saints in question attract minimal devotion, but inspire some curiosity, when their surviving reliquaries are not discreetly veiled.

How then can we sum up this festival type? Structurally, it borrowed freely from other festivals. Its organizers, almost always clerics, were festal magpies, pinching elements from other celebrations, both sacred and profane. These were then creatively reassembled, just as the skeletons of their subjects were themselves ambitiously reconstituted. The products of this *bricolage* were not great pieces of dramatic, scenographic or architectonic art. Stripped of classical allusions, their design and execution lacked the refinement and complexity of the court culture which seems partly at least to have inspired them, whilst at the same time they lacked the verve of more direct popular cultural products. These hybrid festivals were, however, splendid shows and, although clerically led, were founded upon popular participation, channelled especially through the contribution of confraternities.

Above all, the relic festivals exhibited a programme, recoverable from the glosses of their organizers and commentators, from their iconography and from

---

56 On the monstrous and the freakish in the Baroque, see Timothy Hampton, 'Introduction: Baroques' in Hampton (ed.), *Baroque Topographies: Literature/History/Philosophy* (Yale French Studies, no. 80), New Haven, CT, 1991, pp. 1–9.

57 On these developments, and particularly the attacks on traditional local pilgrimages, see Habermas, *Wallfahrt und Aufruhr*, pp. 105–89.

their form. Over the long process of confessionalization, they joined with other Bavarian festivals in promoting an identification with Church and state. Isidoro Moreno Navarro, a student of the rituals surrounding sacred images in modern Spain, has described communal festivals as representing 'rituals of division' when regarded from within the community in which they are celebrated, but as also constituting important 'signs of identification' for the community as a whole.[58] The Bavarian relic festivals might have fostered competition between different confraternities and religious corporations (the contest in Amberg between the Jesuit college and the parish church for the body of St Crescentianus is an example of the latter), but they simultaneously nurtured both a local identity and, more significantly, a confessional one.

Catholic identity in this period was, it appears, predicated upon veneration of the saints and an attitude of expectancy toward the miraculous intervention of the sacred realm in the mundane. Defence of this became a key ingredient of the religious polemic and propaganda to which the relic festivals were a contribution. The salience of the festivals over the long century after the Peace of Westphalia is a reminder too that, like other subjectivities, confessional identity required constant construction and reinforcement: hence the didactic imperatives behind the festivals and the salience of didactic elements within them and within their attendant rhetorical infrastructure of sermons, homilies and printed accounts. The relic festivals furthermore are evidence that confessionalization entailed positive reinforcement of a value system as well as the negative technologies of control and discipline which have recently preoccupied historians.[59] Surrounded by all the devices that Baroque festival culture could muster, and evoking mixed emotions, the relics of the Bavarian saints, old and new, were uniquely powerful if ambiguous signs.

---

58 Isidoro Moreno Navarro, 'Niveles de significación de los iconos religiosos y rituales de reproducción de identidad en Andalucía' in Pierre Cordoba and Jean-Pierre Étienvre (eds), *La Fiesta, la ceremonia, el rito*, Granada, 1990, pp. 91–103 (p. 95).

59 Space prohibits further discussion of the confessionalization debate here. See Heinz Schilling, 'Die Konfessionalisierung von Kirche, Staat und Gesellschaft — Profil, Leistung, Defizite und Perspektiven eines geschichtswissenschaftlichen Paradigmas' in Wolfgang Reinhard and Heinz Schilling (eds), *Die Katholische Konfessionalisierung*, Münster, 1995, pp. 1–47, for a restatement of the thesis applied to a Catholic context.

PEACE FESTIVALS AND THE CULTURE OF MEMORY IN EARLY MODERN SOUTH GERMAN CITIES

Claire Gantet

As the Thirty Years War had begun with a feast-day,[1] it ended also with feast-day celebrations, the peace festivals (*Friedensfeste*). If historiography has analysed the identity and subversive nature of the feast-day gatherings which provoked the revolts,[2] the neutralizing and euphemizing qualities of their collective violence continue to remain open to examination. Given the norm that all wars are likely to end in a climate of euphoria and festivity, the diffusion and length of celebrations in the case of the treaties of Westphalia have drawn few historical investigations. I can account for more than 200 different peace festivals celebrated in the course of the peace treaties which lasted from 1648 to 1660 and ultimately brought an end to

---

1 In 1606 at Donauwörth, one of the eight Imperial cities where Catholics and Protestants enjoyed the same political and juridical rights. During the procession of Saint Mark, reliquaries and banners were seized and ridiculed by Protestants who repeated their violations the following year; Maximilian of Bavaria occupied the town in December 1608 and forbade Protestant worship. The drama destroyed all accord between Catholics and Protestants, blocked the Reichstag and created the Union and the League.

2 See the works of Emmanuel Le Roy Ladurie, Yves-Marie Bercé, Roger Chartier in France; the books of Natalie Z. Davis, Richard C. Trexler, Edward Muir in the English-speaking countries; and the studies of Norbert Schindler in Germany.

the overall conflict. These peace festivals commemorated the peace as a historical event. But they were such an integral part of life in the towns and were so inherent to local civic culture that they sometimes became institutionalized and took place every year. Even today, two peace festivals continue to be celebrated: the festival of Coburg in Ernestine Saxony, reinstated in 1971 to be held once every decade, and particularly the Augsburg festival in Swabia, where the event has been celebrated every year, and has been recognized since 1950 as a public holiday. It is the only public holiday specific to one city in the whole of Germany.

Peace festivals have been treated from two points of view: as the collective memory of the treaties they commemorated, or as an empty memory of the events of the Thirty Years War that they evoked. One needs both to construct the memory of the war and to forget the troubles of the war.

I would like to show in this study of peace festivals the originally religious dimension of the perception of the peace of Westphalia and then the way in which references to the Thirty Years War have contributed to forming a national — even nationalist — culture. I will analyse when and where the festivals took place, and then examine their institutionalization.

Four Waves of Celebratory Activity

The peace at the end of the Thirty Years War was welcomed with festivities located above all in the centres of political negotiation and in the areas most affected by the war. The signatures of the different peace treaties ending the overall conflict punctuate the four waves of festivity between May 1648 and August 1660.

The first festivals were celebrated at Münster, Osnabrück and in the Netherlands, making official the peace signed on 15 May 1648 between Spain and the United Provinces. After eighty years of war, the Peace of Münster officially conferred independence on the United Provinces, and was commemorated as the establishment and guarantee of liberty and independence of the new Republic. But if the restoration of peace was celebrated in the northern trading cities like Amsterdam, it was also celebrated in the southern Catholic cities, such as Antwerp, which had been politically and economically disadvantaged in both war and peace. These essentially civic manifestations were focused around the town hall.³ The fragile new Republic was divided by the conflicting interests of pacifist merchants on the one hand and Calvinist preachers and the Orange party on the other. The euphoric need to forget, moreover, went hand in hand with that of remembering, in order to pass on the souvenir of suffering; if peace has its apologists it also has its Cassandras.⁴

The second and third festival periods occurred within the boundaries of the Holy Roman Empire, with the signature of the treaties of Westphalia at the end of 1648 and in 1649, and then their ratification in Nuremberg in 1650. The focus of these celebrations was also the political unity of the empire, the end of the war of religion.

The years 1648–50 represented a period between the signature of the peace and the real departure of the troops.⁵ As long as the troops were quartered in the country, and usually unpaid, people feared that the peace would not last long. Hence only in 1650, the year marking the real break with war, did festivals flourish: ninety-two festivals are attested for 1650, or almost half of the total number I have found for the whole period under research. The principal event of 1650 was the conclusion of the Recess of Nuremberg (*Nürnberger Exekutionstag*), ratifying the treaties of Westphalia and ordering the details relating to the departure of the occupying troops. Nuremberg, resuming the ancient tradition of an imperial town, became the centre of celebrations in 1650: I have counted eighteen successive festivals from 1648 to 1650, including two exceptionally lavish festivals,⁶ that of 4–5 June organized by the Swedish general Wrangel, and

---

3   See Matthäus Merian, *Theatri Europæi. Sechster und letzter Theil...*, Frankfurt am Main (hereafter *Theatri Europæi*), 1663, pp. 474–76.

4   'Il n'est pas de la Pais entre les Etats, comme des réconciliations particulières: celles ci ne peuvent subsister avec le moindre ombrage de soupçon, en matière d'Etat, toute confiance doit être assaisonnée de beaucoup de prudance, ennemie de négligence... c'est la maîtresse piece & la clef de l'observation des traités... Et comment, je vous prie, entretenir cette jalouzie si nécessaire, sans une mémoire prézante des offances passées, qui conserve l'impression d'une juste crainte?': *Devs Harangves panégyriqves, L'vne de la paix, l'avtre de la concorde. A Nosseignevrs Des provinces libres & unies des pays-bas...*, Amsterdam, 1648, f. A 5ʳ⁻ᵛ.

5   See Antje Oschmann, *Der Nürnberger Exekutionstag 1649–1650. Das Ende des Dreißigjährigen Krieges in Deutschland*, Münster, 1991.

6   Merian, *Theatri Europæi*, pp. 937–1084.

particularly that of 25–26 June commanded by the imperial general Piccolomini: these examples assume the proportions of princely festivals (*Hoffeste*), with balls, a banquet sumptuous not only gastronomically (six courses in succession) but also allegorically (the menu including the 'dove of peace' and temples of concord as table decorations), with immense firework displays to finish the show. The whole design of these celebrations was orchestrated to enhance their allegorical significance. Underlying the programmes, composed by poets and playwrights of the *Fruchtbringende Gesellschaft* and the *Pegnisischer Blumenorden*, was the notion of peace beyond all political and social consideration, while at the same time symbol and allegory were to render even war aesthetic.

The influence of the Nuremberg festivals was immediate. At least fifty festivals were celebrated in the Holy Roman Empire between 26 June 1650, the date of the official ratification of the Recess of Nuremberg, and the end of that year. I have found poems by Sigmund von Birken, Johann Klaj and Georg Philipp Harsdörffer recopied by a village official in the Coburg territories. These three poets gained imitators organizing sumptuous festivities from Weimar (with Johann Thomas) to Coburg (with Michael Franck). But it was more than the appeal of their allegorical context which provoked such manifestations — their real significance lay in the departure of the occupying troops, marking a real and tangible peace. For example, it was decided that a peace festival would be celebrated in Coburg as in the rest of Ernestine Saxony on 19 August because this was the date set by the Recess of Nuremberg for the departure of the occupation force. The peace festival of Frankenthal was delayed until 1652, because agreement on the departure of unpaid Swedish troops was only reached in that year.

In the Holy Roman Empire, peace festivals were organized by local authorities on dates with local significance. This differs considerably from the centralized commemorations organized during the French Revolution. In the political capitals of the Empire, peace celebrations were limited to the tradition of the Te Deum compositions and fireworks. The richest of these manifestations was in Prague, the capital of the rebellious kingdom where war had begun, and where it ended on Sunday 24 of July 1650: peace was celebrated with carillon chimes, a Te Deum in every church, 108 volley-firings, trumpets accompanied by such popular displays as window illuminations, maypoles planted on every corner and bonfires.

The fourth group of festivals took place in 1660, commemorating the Treaty of the Pyrenees, cementing the alliance between France and Spain. In a Paris besieged and starving under the Fronde at the end of 1648, where any event was a pretext for the production of mazarinades (pamphlets or songs against Cardinal Mazarin), news of the Peace of Westphalia was mixed with news of the peace between the King and the Parlement. Rumours of a total European peace initially circulated, then pamphlets prevailed justifying the 'delay of the peace agreement' due to Spain's perfidious behaviour or due to the revival of the Fronde in the Parlement of Paris. The King's return to the capital, on the symbolic date of Saint Louis's Day, was celebrated as a festival of peace, but a ritual peace. In contrast, the Peace of the Pyrenees was conducted in great pomp and circumstance in Paris at the beginning of February and again in August 1660. More than peace, the celebration marked the victory against the Habsburgs, the end of 'Spanish predominance', sealed with the marriage of Louis XIV and the Infanta Maria-Theresia. As a result, the festival of the Parisian peace assumed the form of a ceremonial king's *entrée*[7] — the most extravagant of the *Ancien Régime*. While earlier processions passed from the gates of the city to the Cathedral of Notre-Dame and involved the actual handing over of the keys to the king in exchange for his confirmation of privileges, this festival became a demonstration of royal power and extended from the Faubourg Saint-Antoine to the centre of the city. The 1660 festivities contrast with those of 1649: the procession crossed the rue Saint-Antoine where Condé had beaten the royal army with the support of the people of Paris; it pursued its course towards the Pont Notre-Dame on which the barricades had been built during the uprising against Mazarin. The 1660 festival in this sense was an exorcism of the Fronde. The Peace of the Pyrenees, which put an end to all hostilities, was also celebrated in Germany, at Memmingen and at Augsburg for example, by extraordinary peace festivals on 4 July and 8 August 1660.

Despite the diversity of the political contexts in which they appeared, these festivities shared common features. In the first place they combined three elements: a lavish meal implied the re-establishment of a gargantuan tradition, the restoration of the body, martyred by the war; a world of light and decoration suggested that it

---

7   See Karl Möseneder, *Zeremoniell und monumentale Poesie: die «Entrée solennelle» Ludwigs XIV. 1660 in Paris*, Habil.-Schrift Regensburg 1980, Berlin, 1983.

was again possible to dismiss the night of war with illuminations and fireworks; and finally the festivals' necessarily urban character. I have even encountered country festivals in urban territories, taking purely religious forms (*Buß- und Bettag*). All festivals accord a role to children. The anecdote told at Nuremberg concerning the gathering of children on wooden horses in the quartering party of Piccolomini who, having laughed about it, decided to mint a commemoration double ducat, finds its parallel in Paris in 1649. When at the age of eleven Louis XIV received some children fighting each other with wooden swords, he laughed and invited their leader to a feast on St John the Baptist's day. In all peace festivals, children are at the forefront of the celebration: it is through children that memory lives on. These festivities all have a dual nature, public and official, as an application of authority in the symbolic space of the town (fountains of wine from the town hall, from Nuremberg to Amsterdam), and carnivalesque: the symbols of war are reversed by 'recycling', as the same trumpets and the same drums handled by the armies in manoeuvre now announce peace; the canons henceforward resound with military salutes, and tears of joy take the place of the tears of blood, retaining all the rituals of exorcism.

What Did the Peace Mean? Confessional and City Festivals

At least 217 different peace festivals can be counted between 1648 and 1660 in Europe, including 195 in the Holy Roman Empire, which is hardly surprising given the importance of the Empire in early modern Europe and during the Thirty Years War. Within the Empire, nearly half of the total of festivals occurred in Franconia, Württemberg and Swabia. Maps of festival diffusion and concentration cross two types of geography: that of the Protestant sites (for example, festivals in Saxony), and that of the urban network (for many of the festivals in Franconia and Swabia). These festivals were both confessional and urban.

One is immediately struck by the rarity of peace festivals in Catholic territories: the 1648 peace was celebrated neither in Munich nor in Altötting, the two

Bavarian centres. At the frontier town of Freiburg im Breisgau,[8] on the border of Habsburg territories and not far from the free town (*Reichsstadt*) of Strasburg, peace was announced on 13 December 1648 and a Te Deum was sung on 15 December. In addition, a pilgrimage to Einsiedeln was organized in gratitude for the peace.

Catholic memory of the Thirty Years War was more focused on the Battle of the White Mountain (1620) than on the peace. This battle was perceived as the signal for the re-Catholicization of the Empire. In celebration of the victory, precise replicas of the Loretto sanctuary were built between 1626 and 1633 in Prague, at the imperial castle (*Hradschin*), in Vienna, in Silesia, in Moravia and in southern Germany. The wife of J. B. Martinitz, one of the defenestrated victims, brought an offering with an *ex-voto* to the sanctuary of Altötting which depicted two great Catholic families (the Slawata and the Lobkowicz) and the Jesuits, who had been driven out of Bohemia before 1620. Thus Altötting, which had inherited the body of Tilly, became the great sanctuary under the protection of the Bavarian dukes.

The peace festivals of the years 1648–60 were not only confessional in character but also urban. They were especially numerous in the free towns of the Empire where there was every need to affirm loyalty to the Emperor and the Empire which had been so badly treated in the war, particularly during the Swedish period. This need also justified the intensity of festival activity in Saxony, the guardian of the Imperial Constitution.

Institutionalization of the peace festivals was a southern characteristic which could assume three forms: as a reinterpretation of previous children's festivals (such as the *Maientag* at Göppingen), as the establishment of a religious festival (at Oettingen, Pfadelbach and to a certain extent Coburg) and finally as an annual event like the peace festivals in Lindau and Augsburg. In this latter case, confessional parity[9] (a system of municipal government by which all civic posts

---

8   See Heiko Haumann and Hans Schadek (eds), *Geschichte der Stadt Freiburg im Breisgau*, 3 vols, Stuttgart, 1992–96, II (1994), *Vom Bauernkrieg bis zum Ende der habsburger Herrschaft*.

9   See Étienne François, *Protestants et catholiques en Allemagne. Identités et pluralisme, Augsbourg, 1648–1806*, Paris, 1993.

were shared equally — or alternately if the number was uneven — between Protestants and Catholics independently of their respective demographical size) was the main motive of institutionalization. The Peace of Westphalia, which officially recognized the same juridical rights for Catholics, Protestants and the Reformed Church, codified the parity system and was naturally celebrated in particular by the Protestants of towns with equal representation who in 1648 felt they had been saved from annihilation. The need to guarantee the Peace of Westphalia, as a civic and a religious peace, was realized through the institutionalized nature of festivals whose annual recurrence already guaranteed the longevity of the peace, particularly since the coexistence of Catholics and Protestants engendered an excessive ritualization of gestures in daily life and the emphatic celebration of the festivals. The festival both exhibited confessional tensions and sublimated them through its diversionary character.

Two Cases: Augsburg and Coburg

The two richest examples are the festivities of Augsburg and Coburg. Admittedly these two towns possessed very different features. Coburg, located geographically in southern Germany but politically in Ernestine Saxony, was a small entirely Protestant stronghold, the 'residence' of the Duke of Saxe-Coburg, but in many respects it remained a large rural market town protected by the forest of Franconia. Augsburg was a major cultural centre, an imperial free city whose urban government was based on confessional parity. It had no territory, which reinforced the civic conscience of the inhabitants. Both these towns shared a symbolic role in the history of the Reformation. It was to the Coburg fortress (*Veste Coburg*) that Luther had escaped under the impact of the imperial ban. Augsburg was the town where the Protestant Confession was presented to Charles V in 1530 and where the peace of 1555 was signed. In these two towns, festivals reinforced an exemplary and demonstrative form of Protestantism.

The Augsburg peace festival was conceived from the outset as an annual celebration. It was planned in advance but was delayed by the lengthy establishment of the peace stipulations. News of the conclusion of the Nuremberg Recess reached Augsburg on 28 June, the military troops were evacuated on 30

Peace Festivals in Early Modern South German Cities   65

July,[10] and the festival was announced on 3 August, to take place on 8 August. It was spread over two days: the 'main peace festival' (*hohes Friedensfest*) and a 'children's peace festival' (*Kinderfriedensfest*) the following Wednesday. The best indication of this urge to create a festival tradition resides in the distribution of engravings to children from 1651 on (until 1789).[11] From the outset it was decided that each year the engraving would illustrate, like the illustrated Bible, a passage from the Bible in the order of the biblical books (apart from a few scenes of a more allegorical or historical nature). In a sense a whole book was conceived, as each year the children turned to a new page.

The first peace festival was a euphoric celebration; the churches were filled with maypoles, flowers, sand, and allegorical or historical inscriptions mixing Augsburg history with that of the Reformation:

Den 8. dito Montags ist durch Gottes sonderlich gnad / wie gemeldt / von den Euangel[ischen]: ein sehr herrliches Danckfrid[ens]: u[nd] frewdenfest inn allen 6. Pfarren mit musicieren / singen beten Dancken u[nd] communiciren gehalten / von den Papisten aber wie an an andern gemeine wercktagen gearbeitet / auch so gar holtz gen marckh geführt worden / Dann die thor vormittag geöffnet gewesen u[nd] den gantzen tag offen verbliben. [...]: Daran inn S. Anna Kirchen die obere oder der Juncker u[nd] der undere boorkirchen auch beide Chor / das Fuggerische u[nd] hindere Chor mit schönen langen - herrlichen Tapazereÿen hinder her an gmäur behengt gewesen / so umb die dann allerleÿ schöne figuren u[nd] Historien / oder aber blumenwerck / u[nd] an denen hoher oder boorkirchen gehangen / gemeiner Statt insignia mitten under dem blum werck / weil selbige dem Magistrat Zugehörig / gestanden [...] Barfüsser Kürch ist gleicher gestalt mit Maÿen schön gezieret gewesen / von statt der Tapezereÿen mit schönen tafeln / so an den Kirchensäulen u[nd] an der hohen boorkirchen auffgehenget worden / alß Herrn M. Weberi Senioris / Herrn M. Gabelij Senioris / Herrn M. Pauli Denischij / Herrn D. Lutheri / Königß inn Schweden / Hertzog Bernhardi von Weinmaÿr der Königl[ichen]: Princessin inn Schweden Christinæ etc. bildnussen / u[nd] kleinen gemalten täfelen / so inn der Kirch auff dem golstemß der manns stuhle gestanden / ihr schöne geschribne früch u[nd] Reimen von gipffer Fractur schrifftig über den Kirchenthüren aussen u[nd] innen. Alß: Durch frid kann freud / ô freud / ô frid [...] Dises Tags ist der Gottesdienst inn allen Kirchen vor 5. uhren inn

---

10 See Chronik von Clemens Jäger, f. 103ʳ.
11 See Horst Jesse, *Friedensgemälde 1650–1789. Zum Hohen Friedensfest am 8. August in Augsburg*, Pfaffenhofen/Ilm, 1981.

sehr volckreicher versamlung mit der Music von Orgel schlagen u[nd] singen angefangen worden [...].[12]

It was a festival controlled by the Protestant authorities, but it was also a total festival, over-saturated with signs submerging the spectator in luxuriant vegetation with objects, colours and scents engaging all his senses. The festival as representation was taken to the heights of extravagance.

In 1650, the festival attracted many of the faithful: 981 communicants passed through the single church of the *Barfüsser*, and over 200 children gathered at the children's peace festival. In comparison, at the jubilee of the peace of Augsburg on 25 September 1655, only 697 communicants were counted in the same church. But the feast generated violence that led to accidents. Although organized by civic and Protestant authorities, the festival was potentially subversive, because the represented, symbolic, order often enough clashed with the actual order. By limiting the Augsburg peace festival to the churches, the ceremonies neutralized the space that Protestants shared with Catholics in everyday life. The festival was reduced to a single procession formed exclusively by children. During the Coburg peace festival, in contrast, the procession headed by children was swelled by members of the council, women and the corporations, who, while singing psalms, crossed the town from the ramparts to the churches, the castle and to the *Veste Coburg*, before returning to the marketplace along the streets lined with patrician houses.

In terms of rites, anthropologically speaking, the festival was a system of inclusions and exclusions. It was celebrated only by Protestants. Catholics later responded by re-establishing the carnival — a traditional target of Protestant criticism — and by the emphatic celebration of Corpus Christi (officially considered in Augsburg from 1806 as the counterpart of the peace festival). On the days of the peace festival, a public holiday for Protestants, Catholics responded symbolically by redoubling their zeal, particularly in activities that were normally shared with Protestants. If the festival excluded some groups (the Catholics), certain members of the community in turn turned away from the festival: beggars,

---

12 Staats- und Stadtbibliothek Augsburg: 4 Cod. Aug. 238, Barthol: Bavari Aug: Anonymi Diarium (Bartholomäus Beyer) ff. 135^v–137^r–^{v}.

Peace Festivals in Early Modern South German Cities 67

the hungry and the poor. A pastor from the Coburg region, Martin Bötzinger, reports in 1650:

Kurze Zeit danach hieß es abermals, daß im Lande Friede sei, der Friede von Osnabrück und Münster, sagte mein Schulmeister — aber ich habe es nicht eher geglaubt, als bis ich in Coburg das große Friedensfest mitgefeiert habe, das für den Sebaldustag des Jahres 1650 angesagt war [...]. Viele sind gewesen, die sind sich in die Arme gefallen und haben geweint, daß einem dabei das Herz brechen konnte, wieder andere schrien auf und wollten sich von niemand trösten lassen, während etliche, die mit Gütern geschoben und mit Nahrungsmitteln gewuchert hatten, einsam standen und der allgemeinen Verachtung preisgegeben waren, ja einem ist sogar ins Angesicht gespien worden.[13]

What was there in fact to celebrate in the still war-stricken years of 1648–50? The Augsburg peace festival took place every year on 8 August, in commemoration of 8 August 1629, the date of the enforcement of the Restitution Edict: then all pastors under threat of expulsion had been forced to convert to Catholicism, Protestant churches and schools in the town had been closed and worship, both in the forms of collective and individual prayer, forbidden, and gallows had been built on the town hall square. The peace festival was different from a mere public commemoration of the 'miracle of the Peace of Westphalia', which saved Protestants from expulsion; it was also a celebration of the traumatism of war.

The Formation of a Culture of Memory: Festival and Jubilee

How did these memorial festivals fashion a memory of the Thirty Years War ? How did references to the Thirty Years War contribute in their turn to the formation of a national culture ?

The memory of the Thirty Years War lasted throughout the period so that the Peace of Nymegen was celebrated in Augsburg by a big peace festival on 8 August 1679. At the beginning of the eighteenth century, the Spanish war of succession, which was the first war to affect the region again, reinforced at the same time the

---

13 *Leben und Leiden des Pfarrers Martin Bötzinger während des dreißigjährigen Krieges*, Dem Deutsch der Gegenwart angenähert von Oskar Wünscher, Eisenach, 1925 (Thüringer Heimatbücher, 2), pp. 42–43.

memory of the Thirty Years War. It then became manifest that the period of Augsburg's glory was over and the peace could only function as a mirror, a nostalgic projection of a golden age of gilded peace.

But the peace festival found a new dynamic in the jubilees of the Reformation, whose institutionalization has been compared with that of the peace festivals. This correlation between jubilees and peace festivals shows up most clearly at Augsburg: Protestants celebrated jubilees as peace festivals to make up for the jubilees they previously had to miss.[14] From 1655 on, the peace festivals and particularly the children's peace festivals inspired the programme of the jubilees of the Reformation. This resulted in greater elaboration of the peace festival and its integration not only with Augsburg history but also with Reformation history, culminating in 1730 with the two-hundredth anniversary of the Confession of Augsburg. The jubilee of the Reformation was modelled on the peace festival; the latter then adorned churches with the same decor as used for the Reformation jubilee, the same sermons were delivered, the same cantata composed and the same engraved prints distributed to the children. Celebrating the Confession of Augsburg also meant celebrating the Peace of Westphalia. The identification of the Reformation jubilees with the peace festival tradition was so strongly felt in Augsburg that in 1748, for the one-hundredth anniversary of the Westphalia treaties, the Protestant authorities deliberated over which aspect they should celebrate: a Reformation jubilee, an extraordinary peace festival or simple commemoration ? Taking into consideration the earlier date of the peace festival, the commemoration of the Westphalia treaties was celebrated not on 24 October, the date of the treaties' signature, but on 8 August, as a sumptuous peace festival.[15]

---

14 The first Reformation jubilee at Augsburg was that of the peace of Augsburg in 1655: the 1617 jubilee was only celebrated in a low-key fashion (all censored sermons remained only in manuscript form), reflecting the mounting tension prior to the Thirty Years War; the Confession of Augsburg jubilee in 1630 was celebrated in silence because Augsburg was then occupied by the imperial camp and officially returned to the Catholic fold.

15 Stadtarchiv Augsburg: Evangelisches Wesensarchiv, Acta 534.

Towards a National Children's Festival

The weakening of the polemical content of the festival is reflected in the dissociation of its confessional and civic elements (in other words its attachment to jubilees). At the end of the eighteenth century, the expense and the polemical nature of peace festivals came under greater criticism. From 3 August 1796, the Protestant section of the Augsburg council took restrictive measures to celebrate the peace festival in silence as a normal Sunday office.[16] In 1806, following the incorporation of the free imperial cities into the Kingdom of Bavaria (*Mediatisierung*), the great festival of the Peace of Augsburg assumed the name of *Toleranz- und Friedensfest* (the festival of tolerance and peace) without, however, losing any of its Protestant character. It was confined to a religious feast-day while the children's version became a celebration for Protestant schools. Protestants were to respect Sunday as a day of rest, and Catholics were not to work on the day of the peace festival. In Coburg a major debate emerged as to whether one could continue to celebrate this imperial festival since the Empire no longer existed.[17] Parallel to this retreat on local interests, the direct memory of the Thirty Years War at the beginning of the nineteenth century was eclipsed by that of the liberation wars and suffered from demographical, economic and social changes as well as from the effect of the incorporation into the state of the imperial free cities. All these changes modified the festival's civic spirit.

Three tendencies characterize the evolution of peace festivals in the nineteenth century: their nationalization (paralleling the nationalization of the memory of the Thirty Years War), their militarization and their child-orientation.

The evolution of the Dinkelsbühl school festival, the *Kinderzeche*,[18] provides the clearest example of these transitions. It was originally celebrated by Catholics and Protestants alike. After 1648, it was celebrated with particular sumptuousness as a festival of confessional parity. After 1806, children in front of the town hall, armed with wooden guns, recited poems and sang songs dedicated to the King of

---

16 Ibid., Acta 830.
17 Staatsarchiv Coburg: Kons. (Acta Consistorialia), 171.
18 Stadtarchiv Dinkelsbühl Kinderzeche alte Akten: 479, 1, 1, Verschiedene Gegenstände 1831–1920; 479, 1, 2, Einzelakten 1836–1912/13; 479, 1, 3, Akten zur Säkularfeier 1848–1854; 479, 1, 3, Rechnungsbücher.

Bavaria. Although the festival remained Protestant, participation was open to the entire city: decorations, initially limited to school precincts, appeared in the hospital church, at the city-gates, on the marketplace and in the town hall, while the procession involved an increasing number of children following an increasingly extensive itinerary through the city. In 1848, the commemoration of the treaties of Westphalia coincided with the commemoration of the *Kinderzeche*, and the pastor Johann-Conrad Unold-Zangmeister, inspired by a chronicle reference, linked the *Kinderzeche* directly to the Thirty Years War. Henceforward the child-leader (*Oberst*) recited a poem of thanksgiving to Gustavus Adolphus, who had threatened the city but allowed himself to be placated by the intercession of children and had thus saved it from war and destruction. According to this now lost chronicle, two school festivals originally existed — one Protestant and the other Catholic; however, the Protestant version evolved much more sumptuously after the signature of the treaties of Westphalia and commemorated the entry of Gustavus Adolphus into the town. During the entry of the Swedish King and his commander Sperreuth, Protestant children had danced in their schools. From 1848 on, the children in the procession dressed in what they imagined to be the costumes of the Swedish army during the Thirty Years War, and in 1868 they assembled in a *Knabenkapelle* and lead the procession accompanied by 'Swedish' music. The diversionary appeal increased; its success was a product of romantic nostalgia and the hero-cult which developed around the figure of Gustavus Adolphus as a national Protestant king after the 1830s.

In 1832 the commemoration of the Battle of Lützen and the death of the Swedish King were celebrated with extravagance: a Gothicizing cenotaph was built at Lützen from drawings by Karl Friedrich Schinkel[19] and inaugurated with much ceremony. In the same vein, the first authentically dated monuments to the Thirty Years War were erected (near Nuremberg, for example), including a living monument known at its creation as the *Gustav-Adolph-Werk*. The latter was meant to preserve the memory of the dead King, as during the foundation of the new empire in 1871 in the flourishing of local 'comedies'. Productions such as the

---

19   See *Schinkel-Ehrung in der DDR. Karl Friedrich Schinkel 1781–1841*, ed. Staatliche Musee zu Berlin/DDR, Ausstellungskatalog 1830–1980 im Alten Museum Berlin, Berlin, 1980, 426 pp.

Meistertrunk at Rothenburg ob der Tauber, or the play *Anno 1634* at Nördlingen, are prime examples. A play by Georg Wolfgang Stahl was performed at Dinkelsbühl in 1897 and has since remained the basis of the child- and folklore-oriented *Kinderzeche*. The memory of the Thirty Years War had turned into folklore, having lost its confessional and civic identity.

Conclusion

It may be asked in conclusion what influence the confessional cultures enjoyed in the formation of the memory of the Thirty Years War. Was there any real difference between the offerings made at sanctuaries by those who made vows to the Virgin during the war, grateful for their survival, and those who had vowed to celebrate peace festivals and made vows to thank the Lord for escaping the war? On both accounts there was a return to the past to overcome the rupture which the Thirty Years War represented. Catholic and Protestant memories were less opposed in inner depth than in the outward forms of piety they practised. With regard to the reception of the Council of Trent, Catholics continued to venerate the Virgin and her miracles; in contrast, Protestants attached their own celebratory traditions to significant dates. But both Catholics and Protestants sought to overcome despair by joy — either through commemorative irony, or through carnivalesque laughter to forget.

THE POLITICIZATION OF TRADITIONAL FESTIVALS IN GERMANY, 1815–48

James M. Brophy

In 1820 Hessian police arrested balladeers and hurdy-gurdy men at fair grounds in the Hanau region for singing songs that heroicized Karl Ludwig Sand, a newly minted martyr for the liberal-national cause, whose execution provided ideal material for street entertainment.[1] In fact, poems, etchings, stories, pantomime and street ballads about Sand circulated widely throughout Germany and even produced alarm among French censors.[2] The monitoring of 'seditious' popular amusements at fairs and markets might initially appear as little more than colourful marginalia to the larger narrative of repressive politics of Vormärz

---

1   My thanks to the German Academic Exchange Service and the National Endowment for the Humanities for their support with this ongoing research project.

2   For the poems, songs and illustrations of 'Sands Tod', as well as the documentation of the arrest and eviction of entertainers using this material at fairs in Hesse, see Hessisches Staatsarchiv Marburg (HStAM), Rep. 24a, nr. 85; and Rep. 180, nr. 29; for versions of Karl Sand songs from 1833, 1840 and 1847, see John Meier, *Volksliedstudien*, Strassburg, 1917, pp. 177–213; for an example of Sand pamphlet literature, see *Ausfuehrliche Darstellung von Karl Ludwig Sands letzten Tagen und Augenblicken*, Stuttgart, 1820, versions of which also included a lithographic portrait and appended song. For French censorship of Sand literature, see Rudolf Schenda, *Volk ohne Buch: Studien zur Sozialgeschichte der populären Lesestoffe 1770–1910*, Munich, 1977, p. 237; for the problems of Sand representations in Prussia, especially the pantomine 'Kotzbues Todt', see GStA Berlin, Rep. 77, tit. 1000, nr. 8, Bd. 1, pp. 14, 16, 19–20, 23–26.

Germany (1815–48), but the subject deserves greater scrutiny. Although Sand's murder of August Kotzebue endures in modern memory as the official justification for the Carlsbad Decrees (1819), these popular representations, more than the laws themselves, exposed many non-élite and illiterate groups to the existence of an oppositional political culture. These popular media not only evince the degree to which political ideas were beginning to saturate German life but also suggest the manner in which political publics broadened beyond associational life. With justification, state authorities and police viewed popular entertainment and their public spaces as a potential threat. Such public gatherings as fairs, markets, festivals and carnivals, the space and atmosphere of which provided the necessary sites for popular politics, thus become an important element for understanding the expansion of political life in the modern era.

In the last fifteen years a spate of studies have re-evaluated the significance of festive culture and its spaces in German history.[3] This body of literature has

---

3   Ernst Walter Zeeden, 'Feste und Politik in Deutschland', *Bericht über die 35. Versammlung deutscher Historiker in Berlin: 3. bis 7. Oktober 1984*, Stuttgart, 1985; Michael Maurer, 'Feste und Feiern als historischer Forschungsgegenstand', *Historische Zeitschrift*, 253, 1991, pp. 101–31; George L. Mosse, *The Nationalization of the Masses: Political Symbolism and Mass Movements in Germany from the Napoleonic Wars through the Third Reich*, New York, 1975; Jonathan Sperber, 'Festivals of National Unity in the German Revolution of 1848–49', *Past and Present*, 1992, 136, pp. 114–38; K. Möckl (ed.), *Hof und Hofgesellschaft in den deutschen Staaten im 19. und beginnende 20. Jahrhundert*, Boppard am Rhein, 1990; David E. Barclay, 'Ritual, Ceremonial, and the "Invention" of a Monarchical Tradition in Nineteenth-Century Prussia' in Heinz Duchhardt et al. (eds), *European Monarchy: Its Evolution and Practice from Roman Antiquity to Modern Time*, Stuttgart, 1992; Werner K. Blessing, *Staat und Kirche in der Gesellschaft. Institutionelle Autorität und mentaler Wandel in Bayern während des 19. Jahrhundert*, Göttingen, 1982; Klaus Tenfelde, 'Mining Festivals in the Nineteenth Century', *Journal of Contemporary History*, 12, 1978, pp. 377–412. The historiographical trend is hardly isolated to German history: see Lynn Hunt, *Politics, Culture, and Class in the French Revolution*, Berkeley, CA, 1984; Eric Hobsbawm, 'Mass-Producing Traditions: Europe, 1870–1914' in Eric Hobsbawm and Terence Ranger (eds), *The Invention of Tradition*, Cambridge, 1983; Susan G. Davis, *Parades and Power: Street Theater in Nineteenth-Century Philadelphia*, Philadelphia, PA, 1986; Sean Wilentz, 'Artisan Republican Festivals and the Rise of Class Conflict' in Michael H. Frisch and Daniel J. Walkowitz (eds), *Working-Class America: Essays on Labor, Community and American Society*, Urbana, IL, 1983, pp. 37–77; Pierre Nora, *Les Lieux de mémoire*, 3 vols, Paris,

The Politicization of Traditional Festivals in Germany, 1815–48   75

drawn new attention to the festivals' idioms, symbols and rituals which articulated new forms of citizenship ideals. The newer research has shown particular interest for those bourgeois festivals created for explicit political or cultural purposes.[4] Used in a sequential narrative, such gatherings as the Wartburg Festival (1817), the Nürnberger Feier of Dürer (1828), the Hambach Fest (1832), the Gutenberg Festivals (1837/40), the Kölner Dombaufest (1842), the various revolutionary festivals of 1848–49 and the Schiller Festivals (1859) mark the evolving forms of representative publicity for nineteenth-century bourgeois political culture, especially when situated alongside the other jubilees, monument-building movements and bourgeois cultural associations which constituted the social formations of Germany's liberal-national movement.[5] Certainly this new avenue of research could be extended to explain how festive rituals, public representations of power and oppositional political discourse affected popular culture and shaped the political agency of common social groups.[6]

1984–92; Mona Ozouf, *Festivals and the French Revolution*, trans. Alan Sheridan, Cambridge, MA, 1988.

[4] Dieter Düding, *Organisierter gesellschaftlicher Nationalismus in Deutschland (1808–1847). Bedeutung der Turner und Sängervereine für die deutsche Nationalbewegung*, Munich, 1984; Manfred Hettling and Paul Nolte (eds), *Bürgerliche Feste: Symbolische Formen politischen Handelns im 19. Jahrhundert*, Göttingen, 1993; Charlotte Tacke, *Denkmal im sozialen Raum: Nationale Symbole in Deutschland und Frankreich im 19. Jahrhundert*, Göttingen, 1995; Ute Schneider, *Politischer Festkultur im 19. Jahrhundert. Die Rheinprovinz von der französischen Zeit bis zum Ende des ersten Weltkrieges 1806–1918*, Essen, 1995; idem, 'Die Revolution — ein Fest?' in Ottfried Dascher and Everhard Kleinertz (eds), *Petitionen und Barrikaden. Rheinische Revolutionen 1848/49*, Münster, 1998, pp. 234–37; Stefanie Pröbsting, 'Die Schillerfeiern von 1859. Instrument oder Ersatz der Nation?', Staatsexamensarbeit, University of Münster, 1992.

[5] A good example of building a narrative through festivals can be seen in Dieter Düding, Peter Friedmann and Paul Münch (eds), *Öffentliche Festkultur: Politische Feste in Deutschland von der Aufklärung bis zum Ersten Weltkrieg*, Reinbek, 1988. See also Peter Stein, 'Sozialgeschichtliche Signatur 1815–1848' in *Zwischen Revolution und Restauration 1815–1848*, vol. 5, *Hansers Sozialgeschichte der deutschen Literatur vom 16. Jahrhundert bis zur Gegenwart*, ed. Gert Sauermeister and Ulrich Schmid, Munich, 1998, p. 608, n. 23.

[6] For a promising start to this important research agenda, see Wolfgang Kaschuba, 'Ritual und Fest. Das Volk auf der Straße. Figurationen und Funktionen populärer Öffentlichkeit zwischen Frühneuzeit und Moderne' in Richard van Dülmen (ed.), *Dynamik der Tradition:*

Central to this literature's innovative dimension is its attention to the sociopolitical construction of public space. The social control of public space and its cultural representations and discourses about that space defines an important aspect of political power and sovereignty.[7] Following the rise of rights-bearing doctrines of individualism and the French Revolution's practice of popular sovereignty, the uses of public space became more complex, contested, variegated. In Germany the politics of the Napoleonic era undercut absolutism's claim that the body politic (and the social field that it occupied) was an extension of the king's sovereignty.[8] Major social reforms (abolition of serfdom and guilds, freedom of movement and occupation) and the political mobilization of social groups, which transformed state subjects into political citizens, forever changed social identities and public life.[9] During the revolutionary era, public space

---

Studien zur Kulturforschung IV, Frankfurt am Main, 1992; Richard van Dülmen and Carola Lipp, 'Wasser und Brot. Politische Kultur im Alltag der Vormärz- und Revolutionsjahre', *Geschichte und Gesellschaft*, 10, 1984, pp. 320–51; Hans Medick, 'Plebejische Kultur, plebejische Öffentlichkeit, plebejische Ökonomie. Über Erfahrungen und Verhaltensweisen Besitzarmer und Besitzloser in der Übergangsphase zum Kapitalismus' in Robert Berdahl (ed.), *Klassen und Kultur. Sozialanthropologische Perspektiven in der Geschichtsschreibung*, Frankfurt, 1982; Josef Mooser, 'Unterschichten in Deutschland 1770–1820' in Helmut Berding et al. (eds), *Deutschland und Frankreich im Zeitalter der Französischen Revolution*, Frankfurt am Main, 1989; Jonathan Sperber, 'Echoes of the French Revolution in the Rhineland, 1830–1849', *Central European History*, 22, 1989, pp. 200–17; idem, *Rhineland Radicals: The Democratic Movement and the Revolution of 1848–49*, Princeton, NJ, 1991; Hans-Gerhard Husung, *Protest und Repression im Vormärz. Norddeutschland zwischen Restauration und Revolution*, Göttingen, 1983; Charlotte Tacke, 'Feste der Revolution in Deutschland und Italien' in Dieter Dowe, Heinz-Gerhard Haupt and Dieter Langewiesche (eds), *Europa 1848. Revolution und Reform*, Bonn, 1998, pp. 1045–88.

7   For an insightful discussion on the cultural implications on the organization of space, see Mary Poovey, *Making a Social Body: British Cultural Formation, 1830–1864*, Chicago, IL, 1995, pp. 25–53.

8   German forms of absolutism never attained the fuller claims of control that French absolutism did, but the ability of cities, corporations and guilds to challenge absolutist sovereignty weakened over the course of the early modern period.

9   Otto Dann, *Nation und Nationalismus in Deutschland 1770–1990*, Munich, 1993, pp. 56ff; Karen Hagemann, 'Of "Manly Valor" and "German Honor": Nation, War, and Masculinity in the Age of the Prussian Uprising against Napoleon', *Central European History*, 30, 1997, pp. 187–220.

became a crowded marketplace of varying representations of the body politic, in which old-regime absolutists, French occupational authorities, German Jacobins, pious Catholics, 'awakened' religious commentators, German citizen-patriots and others vied for dominance of public opinion and, ultimately, the new cultural idioms and symbols that would reconstitute post-revolutionary citizenship and sovereignty. Perhaps herein lies the critical difference between the political worlds and social spaces of the eighteenth and nineteenth centuries. Although eighteenth-century artisans, farmers and burghers certainly used public space (strikes, processions, riots) to stake claims to privileges eroded and honours lost, the trajectory of political change was limited to estate society and its framework of political rights.[10] By contrast, the precedent of the French Revolution's constitutionalism and popular sovereignty moved nineteenth-century politics beyond traditional conceptions of liberty. Situated in a broader problem of post-revolutionary popular politics, the perception and practice of traditional festivity manifested itself in a new register.

Issues of politicization in post-Napoleonic Germany are not new to German historiography, but it is none the less fair to characterize existing research as resting primarily on public-sphere models and functionalist socio-economic arguments. With the former, voluntary associations and print culture are assigned major roles in transforming nineteenth-century society.[11] To be sure, locating and

---

10 Arno Herzig, *Unterschichtenprotest in Deutschland 1790–1870*, Göttingen, 1988; Andreas Grießinger, *Das symbolische Kapital der Ehre. Streikbewegungen und kollektives Bewußtsein deutscher Handwerksgesellen im 18. Jahrhundert*, Frankfurt am Main, 1981; Robert A. Schneider, *The Ceremonial City: Toulouse Observed, 1738–1780*, Princeton, NJ, 1995.

11 Fritz Valjavec, *Die Entstehung der politischen Strömungen in Deutschland 1770–1815*, Munich, 1951; Reinhart Koselleck, *Kritik und Krise. Ein Beitrag zur Pathogenese der bürgerlichen Welt*, Freiburg, 1959; Jürgen Habermas, *Strukturwandel der Öffentlichkeit. Untersuchungen zu einer Kategorie der bürgerlichen Gesellschaft*, Neuwied, 1962; Otto Dann, 'Die Anfänge politischer Vereinsbildung in Deutschland' in Ulrich Engelhardt et al. (eds), *Soziale Bewegung und politische Verfassung: Beiträge zur Geschichte der modernen Welt*, Stuttgart, 1976, pp. 197–232; Otto Dann (ed.), *Vereinswesen und bürgerliche Gesellschaft*, Cologne, 1984; idem (ed.), *Lesegesellschaften und bürgerliche Emanzipation: Ein europäischer Vergleich*, Munich, 1981; Ulrich Hermann, 'Die Lesegesellschaften des 18. Jahrhundert und der gesellschaftliche Aufbruch des deutschen Bürgertums' in Hermann

explaining the importance of these new spaces where people could assemble as free-thinking individuals, engage in debate, and thus form a 'public' opinion independent of Church and state remains foundational. But casting voluntary associations as the leading player in the rise of modern politics is only half the story. Alongside the new mental interiority of sensibility and critical-rational musing brought about by novels, newspapers, criticism and the milieu of reading circles, historians have not satisfactorily shown why modern political culture took hold so rapidly in the decades after 1815. The social formation of reading clubs cannot account for the widespread political mobilization that made the Revolution of 1848–49, and the years leading up to it, the dramatic social process that it was.

The link between socio-economic crises and political action also takes on first-order importance, but studies on economic modernization and political protest do a poor job in accounting for the cultural codes, mental habits and social environment that vernacularized political choices.[12] How economic forces and

---

(ed.), *'Die Bildung des Bürgers'. Die Formierung der bürgerlichen Gesellschaft und die Gebildeten im 18. Jahrhundert*, Weinheim, 1989; idem, 'Geheime Organisierung und politisches Engagement im deutschen Bürgertum des frühen 19. Jahrhunderts. Der Tugendbund Streit in Preußen' in Peter Christian Ludz (ed.), *Geheime Gesellschaften*, Heidelberg, 1979; Dieter Dowe, *Aktion und Organization. Arbeiterbewegung, sozialistische und kommunistische Bewegung in der preußischen Rheinprovinz 1820–1852*, Hannover, 1970; Thomas Nipperdey, 'Verein als soziale Struktur in Deutschland im späten 18. und frühen 19. Jahrhundert' in H. Bockmann et al. (eds), *Geschichtswissenschaft und Vereinswesen im 19. Jahrhundert*, Göttingen, 1972; Wolfgang Hardtwig, *Vereinswesen in Deutschland 1620–1870. Sozialgeschichte der Idee freier Vereinigung anhand der Begriffe Gesellschaft, Geheimgesellschaft, Verein, Assoziation, Genossenschaft, Gewerkschaft*, Stuttgart, 1987; idem, 'Strukturmerkmale und Entwicklungstendenzen des Vereinswesens in Deutschland' in Dann (ed.), *Vereinswesen*; Dieter Düding, *Organisierter gesellschaftlicher Nationalismus in Deutschland (1808–1847): Bedeutung der Turner und Sängerverein für die deutsche Nationalbewegung*, Munich, 1984; Franklin Köpitzsch (ed.), *Aufklärung, Absolutismus und Bürgertum in Deutschland*, Munich, 1976; idem, *Gründzüge einer Sozialgeschichte der Aufklärung in Hamburg und Altona*, 2 vols., Hamburg, 1982. For a larger argument that traces the development of European public opinion, see Franco Venturi, *The End of the Old Regime in Europe, 1776–1789*, 2 vols, Princeton, NJ, 1991, *Volume 1: The Great States of the West*, trans. R. Burr Litchfield.

12 The outstanding structural analysis of society and economy for this period remains Hans-Ulrich Wehler's *Deutsche Gesellschaftsgeschichte, Bd. 2, Von der Reformära bis zur*

public-sphere discourses interpenetrated with public space and popular culture has yet to be examined with satisfactory specificity. Widespread political mobilization in western Germany can only be explained by understanding how political discourses penetrated and were assimilated into popular cultural forms. This period's fusion of politics and popular culture arose out of specific historical circumstances. Bracketed between the incipient public-sphere institutions of absolutism (associations, salons, journals) and the formal public-sphere structures of post-1848 European politics (parliaments, uncensored press, political parties) lies the period 1815–48, a post-old-regime society forced to adapt forms of popular culture for political life because governments blocked the development of formal channels for political expression in a developed public sphere. Consequently, Germany's first modern political public encountered ideas and moulded opinions through festive life and market culture.

After 1815 the political encoding of public and private space became more of a problem than ever before. The laws that enabled the government to erect a new apparatus of surveillance and control over public space in the period 1815–48 is perhaps the most telling evidence of this tension. The Carlsbad Decrees of 1819 underscored the attempt of state authorities to clamp down on press, universities, political assemblies and the display of politically subversive insignia. The German Confederation's Six Articles of October 1832, which followed a series of tumultuous German responses to the July Revolution and the mass demonstration of the Hambach Fest in May 1832, tightened governmental control over print culture and public space, for these contentious areas of civil society no longer served state power. Not surprisingly, such spheres of popular culture as colportage and street entertainment also fell under new rigours of surveillance and licensing.[13]

---

industriellen und politischen 'Deutschen Doppelrevolution 1815–1848/49, Munich, 1987, see too the excellent study of bread riots and street politics in Manfred Gailius, *Strasse und Brot. Sozialer Protest in den deutschen Staaten unter besonderer Berücksichtigung Preußens, 1847–1849*, Göttingen, 1990; and idem and H. Volkmann (eds), *Der Kampf um das tägliche Brot. Nahrungsmangel, Versorgungspolitik und Protest 1770–1799*, Opladen, 1994.

13   Petzoldt, *Bänkelsang*, p. 21ff.; Schenda, *Volk ohne Buch*, p. 233. For a sample of the new vigilance over colporteurs, see the 15 January 1811 circular from the Prussian Minister of the

Yet official attempts to deny oppositional political culture its share of public space was a dismal failure. The reasons are numerous, but one large reason was the role played by traditional festivals and fairs (*Jahrmärkte* and *Messen*). In this period the festive cycle of urban and rural traditional life underwent degrees of politicization that contributed to the process of forming political publics. In view of the highly restrictive measures against public assembly in the German Confederation after 1819, such festivities as carnivals, parish festivals, annual markets and fairs often became the only public gatherings that connected regional cultures with the oppositional ideas of the political public sphere. These sites of sociability constituted 'contradictory space':[14] on the one hand, they served cultural and economic needs vital for Church, economy and local communities; on the other, oppositional political cultures, denied their own festive outlets, resurfaced at these sites, thus politicizing economic exchange and 'traditional' rites. The 'abuses' of traditional festivals were not lost on government officials, who sought to limit the duration and existence of traditional customs. To use the Prussian state as an example, it sought to put temporal and spatial limits on pilgrimages and religious processions in 1825, on parish festivals in 1832 and on carnival between 1827 and 1834.[15] Within this decade, the Prussian state made a

---

Interior that introduced the need to have all materials from colporteurs stamped: GStA Berlin, Rep. 77, Tit. II Censur Sachen, Gen. Nr. 7, Bd. 1, p. 1; see also Hessian police reports from 1824, in HStAM, Rep. 17g, Gef. 74, nr. 9.

14   Henri Le Febvre, *The Production of Space*, trans. Donald Nicholson-Smith, Oxford, 1991, pp. 264–68, 280–82, 320–21.

15   For the discussion on restricting carnival, see Landeshauptarchiv Koblenz, Best. 403, nrs. 2616, 7061, 2159 and Best. 441, nr. 23984; for pilgrimages and processions, see Hauptstaatsarchiv Düsseldorf (hereafter HstAD), Oberpräsident Ingersleben, Coblenz, to Regierung Aachen, 9 Sept 1825, HStAD, nr. 4880, unpag.; for *Kirmes*, see HStAD, Reg. Aachen, Nr. 4882, unpag., which makes numerous references and reactions to the 2 October 1832 ordinance that limited *Kirmes* to two days and which documents the continuous government discussion, beginning in 1816, which advocated a law to limit *Kirmes* festivities; for further material, see HStAD, Regierung Köln, nr. 59, *passim*. The Catholic Church, it should be noted, fully approved of the state's plans. Since the eighteenth century the Church had issued decrees to rein in the excesses associated with pilgrimages, and issued another circular in 1826. For the Church position on this matter, see the Historisches Archiv des Erzbistum Kölns (AEK), Gen I 4.4,1, unpag., esp. the decree from Archbishop Spiegel from 26 May 1826.

concerted effort to place new restrictions on a range of traditional festive practices. Although economic efficiency and morality are the commonly cited reasons, the problems of maintaining control of public crowds and nurturing respect for state authority lurk as additional motivations.

The politicization of traditional festivity in the Vormärz period is, furthermore, not isolated. Pilgrimages, processions, the winter festival of carnival, May rites of spring, summer solstice festivals and the parish festivals of summer and autumn blurred their traditional symbolism with contemporary politicized messages. Cyclical festive time intersected with modern linear political time, which reinscribed festive culture with new meanings.[16] In a similar fashion, the carnivalesque dimension of markets and fairs (jugglers, organ-grinders, singers, colporteurs, fortune tellers, excessive consumers of food and alcohol) also enabled politicized forms of laughter and entertainment to affect festive space of rural and urban market-grounds. And because the spaces of traditional festivals and fairgrounds form a significant component of local communicative networks, the politicization of this public space merits the historian's attention. These transformed milieux can be profitably interpreted, following Pierre Bourdieu, as 'a structuring structure, which organizes practices and the perception of practices'.[17] Whether conscious or unconscious, festive practices affected the

---

16 Peter Sahlins has demonstrated this point with nineteenth-century French political culture: see his *Forest Rites: The War of the Demoiselles in Nineteenth-Century France*, Cambridge, MA, 1994, pp. 61–96; see also Douglas A. Reid, 'Interpreting the Festive Calendar: Wakes and Fairs as Carnivals' in Robert D. Storch (ed.), *Popular Culture and Custom in Nineteenth-Century England*, London, 1982.

17 Pierre Bourdieu's *Distinction: A Social Critique of the Judgement of Taste*, trans. Richard Nice, Cambridge, MA, 1984, p. 170. Bourdieu has been used extensively to understand the cultivation of taste and the cultural markers of class distinction, but his notions of how space, consumption and taste affect and reflect mental habits and social behaviour can be equally applied to the political *habitus* of nineteenth-century social groups. Dieter Groh, for example, suggests reading E. P. Thompson through Bourdieu in his Introduction to Thompson's German edition of *Plebeische Kultur und moralische Ökonomie. Aufsätze zur englischen Sozialgeschichte des 18. und 19. Jahrhunderts*, Frankfurt am Main, 1980. See, more recently, Ingrid Gilcher-Holthey, 'Kulturelle und symbolische Praktiken: das Unternehmen Pierre Bourdieu' in Wolfgang Hardtwig and Hans-Ulrich Wehler (eds), *Kulturgeschichte Heute*, Göttingen, 1996, pp. 111–30. Wolfgang Kaschuba has also

values, perceptions and behaviour of individuals. In the Vormärz era festivals produced sites in which social differences, class distinctions and regional political grievances came to the fore. By assimilating the emblems and symbolic practices of political difference, festive culture affected in turn the sociocultural identities of individuals. In this fashion, I argue that politicized festivity altered the *habitus* of common social groups, for it offered a recurring vehicle through which people in rural and urban areas encountered, if not also acquired, political choices in post-Napoleonic Germany.

This chapter examines popular festivity in two ways. First, it analyses the reform of public carnival in the Rhineland as a prominent example of how a 'traditional' festival became explicitly instrumentalized by different bourgeois political interests to articulate views not otherwise permissible. Secondly, the chapter turns to the ways in which traditional festive space politicized German society in the first half of the nineteenth century. Customary gatherings, this chapter argues, became important sites for the distribution and visual projection of new political discourses circulating in the public sphere. By recognizing how customary forms of sociability and exchange became transformed into communicative instruments for partisan politics, one can begin to appreciate the dynamic of rapid politicization in the period 1815–48.

Rhenish Carnival Between Restoration and Revolution

Carnival season in the Rhineland stretches over a long part of the winter festive cycle. After the reformation of the festival in Cologne in 1823, it began in November, opened its public meetings after New Year's Day, and organized the

---

incorporated Bourdieu's theses into his important wide-ranging survey, *Lebenswelt und Kultur der Unterbürgerlichen Schichten im 19. und 20. Jahrhundert*, Munich, 1990. With different theoretical emphases, Thomas Lindenberger's *Strassenpolitik. Zur Sozialgeschichte der öffentlichen Ordnung in Berlin 1900 bis 1914*, Berlin, 1991, and Lynn Abrams's *Workers' Culture in Imperial Germany: Leisure and Recreation in the Rhineland and Westphalia*, New York, 1992, underscore the importance of street life for interpreting working-class politics and culture. See, also Dagmar Kift (ed.), *Kirmes-Kneipe-Kino. Arbeiterkultur im Ruhrgebiet zwischen Kommerz und Kontrolle (1850–1914)*, Paderborn, 1992.

The Politicization of Traditional Festivals in Germany, 1815–48   83

parade, ball, banquets and many other public celebrations during the festival's climax during the week before Ash Wednesday.[18] Although carnival life is deeply embedded in Rhenish culture (conservative estimates date it from the high medieval period), it underwent drastic change after the French occupied the Rhineland. The French revolutionary government not only prohibited public carnival festivities, but it also abolished guilds, the apprentices and journeymen of which were the driving organizational forces of traditional carnival. Public carnival was reduced to dispersed, spontaneous revelry, while balls and parties continued on a private level. Upon inheriting the middle and lower sections of the Rhineland in 1815, the Prussians found a tradition in disarray but none the less alive. Moreover, the festival's tradition of misrule resurfaced. When carnival followed the machine-breaking riots in Eupen in 1821, the Landrat asked his superiors for extra police and gendarmerie personnel, because 'the carnival days offer the opportunity for the ill-tempered types to gather and, after excessive consumption of spirits [...] are provoked to carrying out malicious acts'.[19]

When carnival was formally revived in 1823 in the Rhenish metropole of Cologne, the public festivities took on a wholly different form and function, enabling bourgeoisie groups to articulate both cultural and political criticism.[20] The restructuring of carnival in Cologne merits attention, for it became the model for all major cities in the Rhineland. Of all the *Fasching-Fastnacht-Karneval*

---

18   The following section on carnival largely draws on material from my earlier essay, 'Carnival and Citizenship: The Politics of Carnival Culture in the Prussian Rhineland, 1823–1848', *Journal of Social History*, 30, 1997, pp. 873–904.

19   Landrat v. Schiebler zu Eupen, to Regierung Aachen, Innenministerium, 15 Feb 1822, HStAD, Reg. Aachen, nr. 231, p. 89.

20   Anton Fahne, *Der Carneval mit Rücksicht auf verwandte Erscheinungen: Ein Beitrag zur Kirchen- und Sitten-Geschichte*, Cologne, 1854, reprint 1972, pp. 155ff.; Wilhelm Walter, *Der Karneval in Köln von den ältesten Zeiten bis zum Jahre 1815*, Cologne, 1815, pp. 9ff.; Joseph Klersch, *Volkstum und Volksleben in Köln: Ein Beitrag zur historischen Soziologie der Stadt*, Cologne, 1965, pp. 93ff.; Peter Fuchs and Max L. Schwering, *Kölner Karneval: Zur Kulturgeschichte der Fastnacht*, vol. 1, Cologne, 1972, pp. 25–43. For the most recent scholarly treatment of carnival in Cologne, Aachen and Düsseldorf, see Christina Frohn, *'Löblich wird ein tolles Streben, Wenn es kurz ist und mit Sinn, Karneval in Köln, Düsseldorf und Aachen 1823–1914*, Doctorarbeit, Rheinische Friedrich-Wilhelms-Universität, Bonn, 1998.

activities in Germany, only the Rhineland employed the principle of voluntary association (*Verein*), a leading tenet of enlightened civil society that enabled people (mostly men) to gather in clubs as free-thinking equals, outside the purview of Church and state. In view of the official restoration of rank and corporatist society in 1815, and the Prussian state's stubborn adherence to it throughout the Vormärz, the use of the associational principle by carnivalists betokened muted political criticism. This innovation began in 1823 with Cologne's *Grosse Karneval Gesellschaft*, a bourgeois society that constituted its executive council and its general assembly in liberal-parliamentary terms.[21] All members of the general assembly elected members to the executive council, and members possessed the right to speak as equals in the long weekly sessions which met from New Year's Day to the end of the carnival season. As an 1826 carnival flier claimed, 'The difference between estates is lifted, pleasure walks free.'[22] After 1827 the society members wore a fool's cap in sittings, lionizing the wisdom of the fool — a trope for common man and equality. In their literature and speeches carnivalists further named the society's speaker 'president', the small council his 'state ministry' and the general assembly a 'Reichstag'.[23] Although the early carnivalists' notions of *egalité* and *fraternité* were quite limited, the structure and levelling symbolisms of the weekly sessions none the less endorsed the bourgeois political credo of individualism. The appeal of associational carnival spread throughout the Rhineland. Carnivalists in Aachen, Bonn, Coblenz, Düsseldorf, Karlsruhe, Mainz, Mannheim and Trier adopted the format of the bourgeois voluntary association, thus infusing the rule of fools with principles of open discussion and liberal governance.[24] Although not always

---

21 For a contextualization of Cologne's carnival life with the city's broader — and vibrant — bourgeois associational networks, see Gisela Mettela, *Bürgertum in Köln 1775–1870. Gemeinsinn und freie Association*, Munich, 1998, pp. 157–270.

22 Kölnisches Stadtmusuem (hereafter KSM), Graphische Sammlung (GS), Wurf Zettel 1806–1827, 1826, 1a-m, nr. 1. Significantly this flier is written in the Kölsch dialect: 'Däh Ungerschaid des Standes däh is gehovven, De Freud spazehret frei'.

23 Fahne, *Carneval*, pp. 172–75.

24 For overview of politicized carnival in the Prussian Rhineland, see C. Frohn, *Löblich wird ein tolles Streben*, passim; Michael Müller, 'Karneval als Politikum. Zum Verhältnis zwischen Preussen und dem Rheinland im 19. Jahrhundert' in Kurt Düwell and Wolfgang

The Politicization of Traditional Festivals in Germany, 1815–48   85

intentionally, these carnival clubs had created a social space in which to build political opinion and acted as outlets to disseminate views on politics and ideals of citizenship not otherwise permissible.[25]

The principal vehicle for political satire was the *Sitzung*, the official meetings of carnival associations, whose verse, songs and speeches often contested the bounds of censorship. Although the larger associations erected stages for their satiric oratory, smaller sittings used wooden washtubs as podiums. The washtub was a traditional carnival symbol of honesty, in which all ideas and issues — society's 'dirty linen' — were scrubbed clean to emerge as the 'naked truth'.[26] The politically coloured persiflage and verse of washtub speeches (*Büttenrede*) became a hallmark of the restored Rhenish carnival. Through lampooning, jesting and mocking, speakers transgressed norms of social and political criticism. Hence this specific carnival rite promoted freer forms of expression, which, in turn, furthered critical reflection on social relations. And its oral form enabled ideas circulating in bourgeois print culture to spill into artisan and labouring circles, which had less access to printed political commentary.

There are few extant *Büttenreden* from the Vormärz era, but the pamphlets, fliers and printed lyrics during carnival document the overall political subversion

---

Köllmann (eds), *Von der Entstehung der Provinzen bis zur Reichsgründung, Bd. I*, Wuppertal, 1982; for Mainz, see Anton Maria Keim, *11mal politischer Karneval — Weltgeschichte aus der Bütt. Geschichte der demokratischen Narrentradition vom Rhein*, Mainz, 1966; and Bianka Stahl, 'Formen und Funktionen des Fastnachtfeierns in Geschichte und Gegenwart, dargestellt an den wichtigsten Aktivitäten der Mainzer Fastnachtsvereine und Garden', dissertation, Bielefeld, 1981; for Karlsruhe, Peter Pretsch, *'Geöffnetes Narren-Turney'. Geschichte der Karlruher Fastnacht im Spiegel gesellschaftlicher und politischer Entwicklungen*, Karlsruhe, 1995.

25   Hence, alongside the more traditional reading circles, table societies and educational associations, carnival clubs also played a role in promoting the 'rational-critical' discourse that developed public opinion, which is for Jürgen Habermas the critical institution for the rise of bourgeois civil society. See his *Strukturwandel der Öffentlichkeit: Untersuchungen zu einer Kategorie der bürgerlichen Gesellschaft*, Frankfurt am Main, revised edn, 1990. For a fuller argument on this point, and the need to modify the Habermasian model of the public sphere for nineteenth-century bourgeois political culture, see Brophy, 'Carnival and Citizenship'.

26   Dietz-Rüdiger Moser, *Fasching-Fastnacht-Karneval. Das Fest der verkehrten Welt*, Graz, 1986, pp. 285–86.

of carnival. In the 1830s, mock public notices, which proscribed carnival-season behaviour in pretentious official language, ridiculed Prussian authorities, whose genuine ordinances on masking and comportment stood everywhere.[27] Mock advertisements also scoffed at the Prussian government with puns that called attention to censorship and political subordination, while Cologne's carnival theatre posters lampooned Prussian officers and aristocrats.[28] In the first decade of restored carnival, Cobbles and Cologne also printed daily carnival newspapers whose free-thinking attitude and references to censor-free print led to recurring problems with the state and the eventual suspension of their operation in 1828 and 1830.[29] In 1828 Carnival's potential for political satire moved the Prussian King to deny Bonn a public carnival altogether: 'From a policing perspective this objectionable, anomalous popular festivity can never be allowed in a university town.'[30]

To be sure, the original reformers of carnival in the 1820s were neither democrats nor radical liberals wishing to overturn political order for a new vision of society. Rather, the patricians and urban élites instrumentalized carnival in Cologne to convey a politics of cultural identity over which Prussia had no control. Threatened with the centralizing political hegemony of Berlin, city élites used carnival to project their identity as municipal and cultural leaders of a city that had undergone a series of blows to its status. The university had moved to Bonn; French occupation and secularization had stripped the city of cultural treasures; and, most importantly, city governance, once the exclusive preserve of

---

27   See, for example, 'Publikandum', KSM, GS, Wurf Zettel 1806–27, 1825/3.
28   'Producten-Fabrik in Köln', KSM, GS, Wurf Zettel 1831–35, 1832/6,7,9; 'Das Pantoffel-Regiment', Wurf Zettel 1836–37, 1836/6,7,8; see also the poster from 10 February 1847, KSM, GS, Karneval Theater 1835–70, 1847/2.
29   Fahne, *Carneval*, pp. 199–201, offers samplings of journalism that ran into trouble with the censors; for the censoring and dissolution of newspapers, see Oberbürgermeister zu Coblenz to Regierung in Coblenz, 22 August 1828, Landeshauptarchiv Koblenz (LHK), Rep. 441, nr. 23984, unpag.; Ingersleben to Coblenzer Carnival Committee, 19 Dez. 1828, LHK, Rep. 2616, 67. See 73, 75 for further problems in 1829 in Coblenz; Polizei-Inspector Struensee report to Ingersleben, 21 November 1829, LHK, Rep. 403, nr. 2616, 87-89; Müller, 'Karneval als Politikum', p. 210
30   Friedrich Wilhelm III to Interior Minister Schuckmann, 20 March 1828, LHK, Rep. 403, nr. 2616, p. 45; GStA Berlin, Rep. 77, Tit. 499, nr. 6, Bd. 1, p. 29.

patricians, was replaced by French and Prussian forms of state-appointed mayors and regional governors. Through the celebration of local dialect (*Kölsch*), customs and folkloric characters, bourgeois patricians, merchants and cultural leaders transformed public space during carnival, rendering invisible the political sovereignty of Prussia. They sought to create a distinctly Rhenish festival, the symbolic universe of which evoked a unified city embracing the leadership status of its propertied and educated local élites. The Romantic celebration of Rhenish folkloric traditions might initially appear to have little in common with political concerns, but this festival, by resuscitating urban and regional identities, had an explicit political function. The festive practices (parades, balls, sittings) demarcated the limits of Prussian governance, visually articulating local bourgeois leadership. The festival articulated the desire for Cologne and Rhenish élites to be assimilated into the Prussian establishment as co-equals and not as annexed subordinates.

How carnivalists criticized Prussian politics and militarism varied greatly, but one can recognize increasingly sharpened tones through the 1830s and explicitly radical manifestations in the 1840s. This trend is explained not only by the increasing gap between state and society in Vormärz but also by the spread of organized carnival to students, artisans and intellectuals, who employed carnival for more democratic purposes. In the 1840s, such groups replaced the subtle criticism of the 1820s and 1830s with explicit scorn. Bonn students used the carnival washtub to excoriate Prussian politics of paternalism; Trier's carnival society printed advertisements for 'Communist cigars with an excellent democratic taste' and decorated parade floats with slogans of equality and freedom; and Vallendar's public parade was cancelled because of its explicit democratic sympathies.[31] In 1844 Düsseldorf's government officials informed their superiors that the city's newly formed 'Haupt-Carnival-Verein', whose members were 'so-called liberals, mostly young jurists [...] [who] articulated political opinions under the cloak of carnival 'amusement' and exposed their

---

31 Regierungspräsident Gerlach to Innenminister von Arnim, 22 February 1844, LHK, Rep. 403, nr. 7061, pp. 115–22; Müller, 'Karneval als Politikum', p. 215; Wilhelm Capitain, *Geschichte der Karnevals-Gesellschaft 'Die Bemoosten' und des Vallendarer Karnevals*, Cologne, 1930, pp. 11–15.

illegal viewpoints to their audiences'.[32] The same Verein also issued honorary memberships to well-known radicals (for example, George Sand, Ferdinand Freiligrath, Hoffmann von Fallersleben, Charles Dickens) but was dissolved after mocking a minor Prussian official.[33] In spite of this ban, 'this malicious party' nevertheless met at a tavern and immediately ran foul of the authorities by booing and hissing the Prussian royal anthem played by the inn's orchestra.[34]

These Carnival clubs became bolder in the years leading up to the Revolution. In Cologne, a new carnival society, headed by the democratic cigar-dealer Franz Raveaux, openly mocked Prussian officials as 'dumb and wretched [...] cowardly and unjust' and staged skits 'intended to arouse hate and contempt against the government'.[35] Following songs of lament and woe, reported officials, carnivalists wishfully called for the imminent occupation of the Rhineland by the French. An 1844 toast by a Düsseldorf carnivalist made the connection between carnival misrule and a freer civil society: 'We too belong to an order; it is indeed not the Order of the Swan [a Royal Prussian order], but rather the larger Order of Freedom, whose task it is to enlighten people of their true interests and proper rights and to defend them.'[36] Similarly, an 1846 circular of the society characterized its club as fools in the 'service of humanity' who 'possessed the right to shout in despot's faces: that is dumb!' 'Indeed it is only a guerrilla war', stated the circular, 'but the victory will not be denied us'.[37]

Clearly the fool's cap had become a thin disguise for serious political discourse; carnival societies had become vehicles to articulate suppressed political opinion. In 1844, upon learning about police surveillance of society meetings, a

---

32 Regierungs-Präsident Spiegel to Oberpräsident, 24 February 1844, LHK, Rep. 403, nr. 7061, pp. 126–27; Landrat Frentz to Spiegel, 2 Feb. 1844, LHK, Rep. 7061, p. 31.
33 For a list of honorary members see LHK, Rep. 403, nr. 7061, p. 349; Sperber, *Rhineland Radicals*, p. 100.
34 Regierungspräsident von Spiegel an Innenminister Graf v. Arnim, 8 February 1844, LHK, Rep. 403, nr. 7061, pp. 49–53; Müller, 'Karneval als Politikum', p. 213.
35 Innenminister Bodelschwingh to Oberpräsident Eichmann, 18 January 1847, LHK, nr. 7061, p. 299; and an intercepted letter describing a sitting of Raveaux's club in January 1847, pp. 301–02.
36 Report of Police Inspector Brendamour, 11 February 1844, LHK, Rep. 403, nr. 7061, p. 67.
37 Circular of 1 January 1846, LHK, Rep. 403, nr. 7061, pp. 266–67.

Düsseldorf carnivalist took off his cap and shouted: 'I speak to you not as a fool, but as a serious man who will not tolerate such treatment!'[38] The Florresei-Gesellschaft in Aachen also sought to speak as serious men. The club proposed that carnival 'form a parliamentary school' and 'make public discussion of all matters accessible to citizens'.[39] Because of this political tendency, carnival clubs attracted prominent democratic and liberal leaders in the 1840s, who emerged as leaders in 1848–49. David Hansemann, Franz Raveaux, Gottfried Kinkel, Georg Weerth and Carl D'Ester all participated in carnival activities in the 1840s. Hermann Heinrich Becker, Gottfried Boecker, Carl Cramer, Wilhelm Hospelt and Carl Wilhelm Wülfing were other active democrats in 1848 previously involved with carnival organizations.[40]

Carnival, though unique in its symbolic practices, should however be understood as a variant of bourgeois associational life particularly successful in reaching larger publics because of its ability to graft itself onto traditional festive space. Choir and gymnast societies also strove to transform their public functions, and the processions and public rituals of religious brotherhoods and sharpshooter societies also blurred the line between associational and public space. Yet none of these could compare with the traditional popularity of carnival's revelry and rites. Consequently, carnivalists were far better poised to reach larger audiences and publicize their messages in a more appealing manner. Not surprisingly, Prussian authorities sought in 1828 to limit public carnival only to those regions that could prove historic continuity with the pre-French period. Their success in limiting the influence of carnival's misrule in Rhenish villages is questionable, but they did contain the menace to the Rhineland. Upon learning of carnival clubs forming in

---

38 Landrat Frentz (Düsseldorf) to Regierungs-Präsident Spiegel, 2 February 1844, LHK, Rep. 403, nr. 7061, p. 30; also quoted in Sperber, *Rhineland Radicals*, p. 101.
39 Müller, 'Karneval als Politikum', p. 214.
40 See Marcel Seyppel, *Die demokratische Gesellschaft in Köln 1848/49: Städtische Gesellschaft und Parteientstehung während der bürgerlichen Revolution*, Cologne, 1991; for Hansemann's carnival activity in 1847, see Müller, 'Karneval als Politikum', p. 214; for Weerth's participation in the Cologne carnival in 1841–42, see Uwe Zemke, *Georg Weerth. Ein Leben zwischen Literatur, Politik und Handel*, Düsseldorf, 1989, p. 22.

Königsberg and Berlin in the 1840s, the government moved swiftly to dissolve the new associations.[41]

Political Accents of Traditional Festivals

While governments could prohibit the explicit festive culture of liberalism with a fair degree of success, they could not effectively control the politicization of festive spaces which had no direct relationship to oppositional politics. State governments were, of course, not above trying to prohibit festivals that threatened security. In the summer of 1819, for example, Hessian officials cancelled several parish festivals in the Niederaula region when the circulation of a proclamation exhorting rebellion posed, they believed, the threat of tumult.[42] But such attempts were rare and short-lived, thus making the contestatory codes and symbolic practices that linked local festive traditions with larger political discourses and networks a significant topic for nineteenth-century social historians.

Many traditional folk customs underwent blatant politicization. Following the July Revolution of 1830, for example, villagers in Baden, the Bavarian Palatinate and the Prussian Rhineland politicized the spring rite of May trees by renaming them liberty trees.[43] The spring rite of renewal, fertility and courtship was recast

---

41 For Königsberg, see Decree of Friedrich Wilhlem IV, 6 January 1845, GStA Berlin, Rep. 77, Tit. 499, nr. 20, p. 2; for Berlin, see circular from Ministry of Interior, 14 Feb. 1845, GStA Berlin, Rep. 77, Tit. 499, nr. 19, p. 4.

42 HSAM, Rep. 24a, nr. 85, 31 Aug. and 15 Sept. 1819, unpaginated.

43 Wolfgang Schieder, 'Der rheinpfälzische Liberalismus von 1832 als politische Protestbewegung' in H. Berding et al. (eds), *Vom Staat des Ancien Regime zum modernen Parteienstaat. Festschrift für Theodor Schieder*, Munich, 1978, p. 195; Sperber, 'Echoes of the French Revolution' (see note 6 above), pp. 201, 203; Karl H. Wegert, *German Radicals Confront the Common People: Revolutionary Politics and Popular Politics, 1789–1849*, Mainz, 1992, pp. 159, 163. Wegert's central thesis that historians distort the political character of popular gatherings in the Vormärz by confusing 'the rugged, superstitious, alcohol-suffused world of artisan and peasant with the world of Biedermier respectability' is not persuasive (p. 159). Wegert disregards a large body of evidence that shows the role of popular groups in expanding political publics after the July Revolution of 1830. For a balanced assessment of this issue, see Wolfram Siemann, *Vom Staatenbund zum Nationalstaat. Deutschland 1806–1871*, Munich, 1995, pp. 343–49.

as a Jacobin symbol of protest against political suppression.[44] Ceremonial plantings of liberty trees, writes Jonathan Sperber, 'occurred in at least fifty different localities in the spring of 1832, complete with a parade of the civic guard, speeches, music and drinking, following closely the forms adopted by the Rhenish Jacobins in the 1790s'.[45] Summer solstice festivals, widely celebrated on the feast day of St John (24 June), also succumbed to politicization after bourgeois associations used the day to honour Johannes Gutenberg. These 'secular' celebrations extolled the importance of Gutenberg and the printing press for the Reformation and for enlightened civilization, but in doing so the festivals paid implicit homage to the freedoms of press and thought.[46]

Folk customs practised during carnival and parish festivals also took on political accents. The most prominent of these is the *Katzenmusik*, a charivari or rough music, the symbolic ritual censuring of individuals who transgressed community morals. Jonathan Sperber's research on the popular forces driving the Revolution of 1848 in the Rhineland has shown how these collective actions undermined various forms of authority in the Vormärz period. Traditionally used to ostracize individuals for adultery or remarriage, *Katzenmusiken* were now directed against officials whose taxes were perceived to be immorally high, against rationalist priests undermining traditional Catholicism, and against ecclesiastical authorities who supported the side of Prussia during the 'Cologne Troubles' (*Kölner Wirren*, 1837) In the 1840s the villagers of Adenau (Eifel), demanding lower taxes, drove their Landrat out of town with a violent *Katzenmusik*; similarly, the tax collector of Trittenheim (Mosel) was menaced in 1848 with a charivari as part of a larger tax boycott in the Trier province. Cologne democrats in 1848 also organized charivaris against government officials who took measures against democrats and against officers of the Bürgerwehr who

---

44   For a broader history of the liberty tree's evolving symbolisms, see David J. Harden, 'Liberty Caps and Liberty Trees', *Past and Present*, 146, 1995, pp. 66–102.

45   Sperber, 'Echoes of the French Revolution', p. 203.

46   For a good overview of these festivals, see Jürgen Steen, 'Vormärzliche Gutenbergfeste, 1837 and 1840' in Dieter Düding et al. (eds), *Öffentliche Festkultur: Politische Feste in Deutschland von der Aufklärung bis zum Ersten Weltkrieg*, Reinbek, 1988, pp. 147–65. Steen, however, does not mention the important fact that these 'secular' festivals were appropriating the feast-day of St John (24 June).

deployed their men more for preservation of order than for the interests of the revolution. Even moderate bourgeois liberals could find themselves the victims of a *Katzenmusik*. A charivari by democrats against August von der Heydt, the moderate Elberfelder liberal banker who had championed constitutionalism, ended up in a street brawl between Prussian loyalists and German constitutionalists. Likewise a radicalized Cologne crowd in June 1848 pelted Ludolf Camphausen's house with stones while singing hateful songs, before being dispersed by the Bürgerwehr.[47] Equally important, though, were other village customs that accompanied weddings, births, wakes and funerals — rituals which traditionally affirmed the community's assent — that took on increasing tones of class hostility and political antagonism. As early as 1819, Prussian officials in the Rhineland requested that several traditions be banned.[48]

But traditional festive spaces of Vormärz Germany mostly became implicated in politics indirectly, by providing social spaces that accommodated competing political discourses which challenged ruling political authority on a number of levels. These sites enabled groups to circulate ideas and images of oppositional politics among heterogeneous crowds. In doing so, such festive spaces as parish festivals, commercial fairs and annual markets blurred the distinction between political, cultural and economic spheres. The remainder of this chapter seeks to foreground the ways in which various social groups politicized traditional festivals and fairs with clothing, crowd protest, music, popular entertainment, literature and material culture.

Symbolic forms of protest with personal attire nettled officials throughout the restoration and Vormärz periods. Democratic *Gesellen* and members of student fraternities wore their *Burschenschaft* colours as well as black, red and gold in various combinations to project their political sympathies; although outlawed in 1819, the fashion only continued, either with 'clever' subtlety or with

---

47 All above examples come from Jonathan Sperber, who incisively shows how *Katzenmusiken* became integrated into the popular politics of 1848: *Rhineland Radicals*, pp. 86–88, 180, 243, 285, 316, 335.
48 Hauptstaatsarchiv Düsseldorf (HStAD), Reg. Köln, nr. 59, pp. 4–8; HStAD, Reg. Aachen, Nr. 4790, 'Verbot der sogenannten Charivaris bey Hochzeiten', unpaginated.

'incomprehensible boldness and publicity'.[49] In 1822, a Breslau university spy complained that young people not connected with the university had also started to wear politically encoded watch bands.[50] Certain hair styles and beard shapes marked one's alliance to the constitutional cause, just as *Altdeutsch* clothing served a similar function. The latter fashion of loose blouses, large cloaks, long hair and the display of oak leaves and daggers, a prominent form of dress at the Wartburg festival of 1817, acted as political markers of protest against restored princely particularism.[51] In 1822, the lord mayor of Cologne, in recommending tight restrictions on parish festivals' time limit and public behaviour, expressed the desirability of banning the wearing of regional costume (*Gottestrachten*). The time-honoured tradition of wearing ceremonial costume on religious festivals, the lord mayor suggested, was tainted by the sartorial affinities it held with the 'old German' costumes of the recent national festivals.[52] Although the lord mayor admitted the impossibility of banning traditional costume, the comment highlighted the recent politicization of 'tradition'.

Following the unsuccessful Polish insurrection of 1831 and the Hambach Fest of 1832, 'Polish jackets' and 'Hambacher hats' replaced old German costume as the preferred signifiers of liberal political sympathies for men, while women wore aprons and kerchiefs bearing Hambach iconography. At a parish festival in Deutz in 1832, the wearing of Hambacher hats by a group of young men provoked argument and rioting. Those wearing Hambacher hats were thrown in the Rhine, beaten with sticks and driven from the festival's dance-halls.[53] Inter-village youth violence and brawling related to courting had long been problems at these local

---

49 See the complaint of Außerordentlicher Regierungs Bevollmächtiger, 27 June 1822, regarding the habit of Breslau students of wearing black cravats and gold breast-pins to display their colours, which he recommended be outlawed: GStA Berlin, Rep. 77, Tit. 13, nr. 17, Bd. 1, p. 59ᵛ; for comments on students' boldness, 9 May 1822, see ibid., p. 9.
50 Universität Breslau to Regierungsrat Neumann, 22 January 1822, ibid., p. 65.
51 The iconographical references are found in the pamphlet *Ausfuehrliche Darstellung von Karl Ludwig Sands letzten Tagen und Augenblicken*, Stuttgart, 1820.
52 Minutes of meeting of Oberbürgermeister, 1 February 1822, Historisches Archiv der Stadt Köln (hereafter HAStK), Best. 400, nr. V, 13A, 7, unpaginated.
53 Deutzer Landrat to Kgl. Reg., Abteilung des Innenministeriums, 16 October 1832, HStAD, Reg. Köln, nr. 59, p. 27v.

festivals, but political issues began to affect social relations at local fairs in the 1830s. In October 1832, in the immediate aftermath of the Hambach Fest and its public revival of constitutional liberalism, Prussian officials passed an ordinance that limited parish celebrations to two days and further prohibited public activities after eleven o'clock in the evening.[54]

The defiance of crowds toward public authority also constituted forms of protest. In the 1830s Prussian authorities expressed increasing alarm when crowds greeted the order of policemen to disperse with laughter and derision.[55] For this reason, crowds at parish festivals (*Kirmes*, *Kirchmessen* or *Kirchweihfeste*) became a perennial worry for public authorities because of the frequent problem of youths taunting soldiers. Belgian–Dutch border disputes between 1830 and 1839 led Prussia to increase its military presence on its Belgian and Dutch borders, which in turn created numerous problems between civilians and military. In the 1830s spectacular brawls between soldiers and young civilian men took place throughout the western areas of the province. These fights mostly flared up at *Kirmes* and post-*Kirmes* drinking at taverns and effectively replaced timeless inter-village youth rivalries with a state–society dichotomy bearing a new look.[56] City festivals, too, became sites of anti-government behaviour. The St Ursula parish festival in 1838 occasioned a riot and a window-breaking charivari against state officials in response to the arrest of Archbishop Clemens August Droste zu Vischering.[57] The newly instated archbishop refused to abide by his predecessor's policy and acquiesce in the Prussian law of children following the faith of the

---

54 Letter of Bonn Landrat to Köln Regierung, 19 November 1832, HStAD, Regierung Köln, nr. 59, p. 44ᵛ. Not surprisingly, this ordinance was repeatedly broken, just as the Silesian province's ordinances of 1815, 1816, 1820 and 1842 that *Kirmes* only be held in November were routinely ignored. For the Silesian problem see 'Vorstellung des [...] Caspar Meusel in Betracht der Kirmesfeier zur ungesetzlichen Zeit', 27 Juni 1845, GStA Berlin, Rep. 77, tit. 499, nr. 21, unpaginated.

55 See, for example, the specific incident in Aachen on 2 April 1833, in which the police failed to disperse a crowd of 100–150 people, HStAD, Reg. Aachen, nr. 22, p. 14ᵛ.

56 For the dozens of brawls in the administrative districts of Erkelenz, Eupen, Aachen, Düren, Heinsberg, Geilenkirchen, Jülich and Malmedy, see HStAD, Reg. Aachen, nrs. 225, 227, 229, 232, 234, 237, 240, 242.

57 Friedrich Keinemann, *Das Kölner Ereignis, sein Widerhall in der Rheinprovinz und in Westfalen*. vol. 1, *Darstellung*, Münster, 1974, pp. 155–60.

father, which conflicted with canonical law. Not only did the arrest of the archbishop unleash a fury of legal and illegal publications — thus dramatically reconfiguring Prussia's public sphere — but also changed the sociocultural milieu of common Rhenish Catholics and their perceptions of Prussian governance. Feeling marginalized and disadvantaged in a predominantly Protestant state, Catholics embraced their festivals and customs with demonstrative enthusiasm. In spite of church and state bans on overnight pilgrimages and certain processions, such forms of popular piety grew in popularity over the course of the Vormärz period. Historians have paid much attention to the church-orchestrated Trier Pilgrimage of 1844, which organized over 500,000 Catholics to view the holy robe,[58] but of equal interest are the smaller, unauthorized pilgrimages and processions that mushroomed in the Rhineland in the 1830s and 1840s. Whereas the Trier spectacle was an officially organized demonstration of Catholic solidarity, the earlier pilgrimages manifested a reinvigoration of popular piety and an expansion of lay brotherhoods, which mostly organized the events.[59]

Displays of piety should not be directly equated with politicization, but the practice of Catholicism none the less took on embattled dimensions, for the Prussian state appeared to flout its role as guarantor of religious freedom. Dozens of priests, Catholic publicists and Catholic associations evoked the image of a Church under siege and ascribed martyr-like qualities to those who put canonical law before Prussian ordinances. Consequently, the religious life of the liturgical cyclical year became entwined with the secular life of state politics. 'Controversy sermons', homilies designed to stir up antagonism and anti-government sentiments, are the most telling evidence of this process; state officials monitored dozens of priests because of their inflammatory comments in the pulpits, resulting in warnings and arrests.[60] Such sermons further assumed religious significance when delivered as Advent reflections, Lenten homilies and Easter messages. The

---

58 The best analysis of the Trier pilgrimage remains Wolfgang Schieder, 'Kirche und Revolution. Sozialgeschichtliche Aspekte der Treirer Wallfahrt von 1844', *Archiv für Sozialgeschichte*, 14, 1974, pp. 419–54.

59 HStAD, Reg. Aachen, nr. 4880, passim. For a balanced discussion on pilgrimages and brotherhoods, see Jürgen Herres, *Städtische Gesellschaft und katholische Vereine im Rheinland 1840–1870*, Essen, 1996, pp. 193–233.

60 AEK Gen I 4.16, unpaginated.

arrest of Father Beckers in Cologne and Father Binterim in Düsseldorf (Bilk) produced public outcry and spontaneous demonstrations which the government perceived as anti-government activity. Cologne Catholics used the opportunity of St Clemens' feast-day (23 January) to pelt soldiers on watch with stones.[61] Similarly, the many processions between Easter and Corpus Christi assumed a provocative accent. Both priests and government officials were quick to note the antagonistic ill-will between confessions when Catholics displayed statues and venerated paintings in Protestant areas.[62] The call of one anti-government pamphlet to found a festival and processions for St Joseph to celebrate all-Catholic marriages pointed up the political instrumentalization of festive culture.[63] In sum, the heightened differentiation between Catholicism and Protestantism brought about a critical awareness among common social groups toward Prussian citizenship. Political historians speak blithely of the *Beilegung* (reconciliation) of the Cologne Troubles in 1842, when Friedrich Wilhelm IV made amends, but bracketing the crisis to four years overlooks the long-term perceptual frameworks of ordinary Catholics whose political *habitus* remained forever changed.

This tumultuous period in the Rhineland provides the proper background to view the climax of state violence against civilians at traditional festivals: the St Martin Parish Festival of 1846. After the Cologne troubles, tensions simmered in the city. In June 1840 a Cologne throng insulted soldiers and pelted them with rocks, necessitating increased patrols of the gendarmerie.[64] Throughout the 1840s crowds at the parish fairs of the Großer Sankt Martin parish in Cologne exhibited little respect for Prussian authority, which by prohibiting the use of fireworks had challenged a time-honoured tradition of the city's old market square. In 1844 and 1845, crowds had grown accustomed to intervening in the attempts of police and

---

61 Kienemann, *Kölner Ereignis*, pp. 159–60
62 AEK Gen I 4.12, unpaginated.
63 See Police Director Ludemann (Aachen) to Regierungs Präsidium Aachen, 4 April 1838, HStAD, Reg Aachen Präsidialbüro, nr. 2235, for a copy of the pamphlet 'Der Catholische Bruder- und Schwesternbund. Ein Ostergeschenk für katholische Jünglinge und Mädchen', pp. 143ff., which proposed 23 January as a festival to celebrate all-Catholic marriages.
64 Cologne Police Director to Regierung in Cologne, 25 June 1840, HStAD, Regierung Köln, nr. 62, p. 43.

soldiers to apprehend youths setting off fireworks, behaviour that certainly offended the military-style 'citadel practice' of Prussian police.[65] On 3–4 August 1846, the ostentatious show of troops stationed in the parish neighbourhood put an end to the fireworks, but the stone-throwing and taunts by the crowd unleashed a rampage of soldiers on the Cologne citizenry. The pent-up aggression produced a rare level of violence against unarmed citizens that left dozens injured and a cooper's journeyman bayoneted to death. The incident provoked a crowd of thousands to congregate the next day outside the Rathaus, leading to negotiations that removed the troops from within city walls and created an unarmed Bürgerwehr. Similarly, thousands attended the burial of the apprentice Heinrich Statz, an act through which the crowd's mourning and anger became a dramaturgical expression of political opposition. Carl D'Ester, the radical democrat, used the burial service to excoriate the Berlin government. The event sharpened the embittered resentment of the Cologne citizenry toward Prussian rule.[66] Combined with two other events of that year, the highly politicized Choir Festival and the campaign and election for the newly restructured municipal government, the St Martin debacle marked 1846 as a watershed year in Cologne's political development.[67] With hindsight, historians have viewed the event as a dress rehearsal for 1848.

Music, too, politicized festival, fairs and markets. In 1832, Prussian officials confiscated from fair vendors French music boxes that played 'Chlopicky's waltz', because of its well-known association with the Polish uprising,[68] but were

---

65 For the political import of the symbolic and physical force of the Prussian police's 'citadel practice', see Alf Lüdtke, *Police and State in Prussia, 1815–1850*, trans. Pete Burgess, Cambridge, 1989.
66 For the St Martin's parish fair riot in 1846, see HAStK, Best. 400, 14E, 21½; GStA Berlin, Rep. 77, Tit. 505, nr. 2, Bd. 3, pp. 14–109. See the solid analyses by Marcel Seypel, *Die Demokratische Gesellschaft in Köln 1848/49. Städtische Gesellschaft und Parteientstehung während der bürgerlichen Revolution*, Cologne, 1991, pp. 43–47; and Sperber, *Rhineland Radicals*, pp. 129–31. For earlier problems with Cologne parish festivals, see HAStK, Best. 400, nr. V, 13A (1820s), p. 7; ibid, Best. 400, 14E, 21½ (1840s); HStAD, Reg. Köln, nr. 62, pp. 4–13ᵛ (1836), 43 (1840), 48ff. (1843) and 71ff. (1844); GStA Berlin, Rep. 77, tit. 499, nr. 21 (1840s).
67 Mettela, *Bürgertum in Köln*, p. 6.
68 GStA Berlin, Rep. 77, tit. 500, nr. 8, p. 28.

powerless in prohibiting the sale of sheet music of Hambacher and Polish waltzes, the titles of which gave tribute to liberal constitutional politics.[69] The following year Cologne revellers changed the title and lyrics of a well-known carnival song ('Karneval ist noch nicht verloren') to 'Poland is not yet lost', in an obvious gesture of support.[70] The political lyrics of balladeers transformed the annual fairs and markets into unruly public space.[71] Street entertainers sang the patriotic lyrics of Ernst Moritz Arndt, Max v. Schenkendorf and Theodore Körner from the Wars of Liberation, recycled endless versions of Karl Sand's tale throughout the 1820s and delivered songs about Poland and Greece in the 1830s.[72] In the 1840s they composed songs about Heinrich Ludwig Tschech, the unsuccessful assassin of Friedrich Wilhelm IV, and Friedrich Hecker, the much-celebrated democrat.[73] Famine in the 1840s and the weavers' uprisings of the 1840s provided a new cycle of songs, the topicality and drama of which packed a punch. To be sure, the majority of these market songs rested on the traditional genres of dreadful crimes and shocking deeds to draw crowds and sell fliers, but even these formulaic standards sometimes did not get through the censor. Singing of a world out of joint and of widespread disaster suggested the absence of law and order, if not

69 P. Ditmar, C. Foerster and J. Kermann (eds), *Hambacher Fest. Freiheit und Einheit, Deutschland und Europa* [Katalog zur Dauerausstellung des Landes Rheinland Pfalz zur Geschichte des Hambacher Festes], Mainz, 1990, 5th edn, pp. 161, 163, 166.
70 Police Report of 8 March 1833, GStA Berlin, Rep. 77, Tit. 499, nr. 6, Bd. 1, p. 73.
71 The role of song as a carrier of political ideas, for example, has not been well integrated into political narratives; the politicization of *Volkslieder* and *Bänkelsang* and their social spaces (taverns and markets) have yet to receive proper historical scrutiny. For literary and folkoric treatments of *Bänkelsang*, see Leander Petzoldt, *Bänkelsang. Vom historischen Bänkelsang zum literarischen Chanson*, Stuttgart, 1974; K. V. Riedel, *Der Bänkelsang. Wesen und Funktion einer volkstümlichen Kunst*, Hamburg, 1963; Fritz Brüggemann, *Bänkelgesang vor Goethe*, Leipzig, 1937. For a good example of integrating song into political history, see Laura Mason, *Singing the French Revolution: Popular Culture and Politics, 1787–1799*, Ithaca, NY, 1996. Regina Schulte also shows how poaching songs can be integrated into analyses of popular politics: *Village in Court: Arson, Infanticide, and Poaching in the Court Records of Upper Bavaria, 1848–1910*, New York, 1994.
72 Fritz Peters, *Freimarkt in Bremen: Geschichte eines Jahrmarkts*, Bremen, 1962, p. 141; Rudolf Schenda, *Volk ohne Buch*, p. 237; Wolfgang Braungart (ed.), *Bänkelsang — Bilder — Kommentare*, Stuttgart, 1985, pp. 152–57.
73 Petzoldt, *Bänkelsang*, pp. 104–08.

also the pressing need to change society.[74] While the degree of political charge of *Bänkelsang* and *Jahrmarktlieder* is up for debate, certainly it is time for social and political historians to recognize the key role that fairgrounds and such ballads played in vernacularizing political news for common consumption. Certainly it affected bourgeois cultural production, showing that communication does not always 'trickle down'. The omnipresence of bench-singing and its quotidian simplicity moved Heinrich Heine and Hoffmann von Fallersleben to mimic its meter and melodramatic tone in their political verse of the 1840s, just as Goethe drew on the tradition in his novellas.[75] The bench-singers' parodies and ballads further found their way into mass print culture after 1844 with *Fliegende Blätter*, the satirical newspaper.[76] Frank Wedekind later stylized the genre into a high-cultural form, which Brecht subsequently refashioned for his politically didactic plays.

Peep-show men further added a political edge to fairgrounds. Because they provided extemporized narrative to the series of pictures that adults and children paid money to see, the opportunity for piquant satire was always present. Adolph Glaßbrenner, the Berlin humorist, included in his multi-volume sketches of popular humour and everyday life *Berlin wie es ist und — trinkt,* a dialogue of a Berlin peep-show man:

> [picture of a new addition to Berlin's Tiergarten park]. Third boy: 'Say why are there so many blue sign posts by the paths?' Peep-show man: 'The roads are marked only so that even out in God's free nature you remember that you're ruled by a just authority. Rrrr! another picture! [picture of Philadelphia] Those figures you see in the foreground are German

---

74 Braungart (ed.), *Bänkelsang*, pp. 418–19.
75 Petzoldt, *Bänkelsang*, pp. 104–08; Tom Cheesman, *The Shocking Ballad Picture Show: German Popular Literature and Cultural History*, Providence, RI, 1994, pp. 161–88. For the larger sociocultural argument that uses popular entertainment to mark the impact of secular individualism on family and community after the *Volksaufklärung* of the late eighteenth century, see chapters 3 and 4. Cheesman's discussion, however, does not focus on the particular political accents of bench-singing that arose in the Vormärz period.
76 Karl Riha, 'Schießt ja auf keinen König nicht. Parodistische Bänkellieder und politische Spottgedichte im Umkreis der Revolution von 1848/49' in Riha, *Moritat, Bänkelsang, Protestballade. Zur Geschichte des engagierten Liedes in Deutschland*, Frankfurt am Main, 1975, p. 43.

emigrants, who left their native homeland because they could no longer feed themselves and were oppressed'. Second boy: 'But my father always reads to us from the newspapers that things are so bad in America!' Peep-show man: 'Is that right. The newspapers tell us lies about that so that people won't emigrate, but things are better in America (he looks around), they've got freedom there. Rrrr! another picture!'[77]

Glassbrenner's verisimilitude is borne out by a number of printed peep-show songs from the 1840s with explicitly political themes, but given the strengthened state censorship after the July Revolution, the best material clearly never saw the printed page.[78] 'Das Guckkastenlied vom großen Hecker' (The Peep-box Song of the Great Hecker), the popular parody of 1848, indirectly paid tribute to the peep-box tradition of political commentary. But even peep-show men themselves often acted as political markers. In the 1815–48 period, crippled war veterans of the Wars of Liberation were granted hurdy-gurdy and peep-box licenses by the Prussian government to ensure them a livelihood. Similarly to the function of war cripples in printed caricatures of the day, they were a 'graphic reminder of the people's sacrifices during the 1813–14 Wars of Liberation and a symbol of the earlier king's promise of a constitution in 1815'.[79]

Festive space also became politicized with the circulation of literature. As we have seen, carnival associations in Cologne, Coblenz, Mainz, Karlsruhe and other cities produced their own newspapers and accompanying broadsheets, fliers, mock-proclamations and witty verse, which ranged from the edifying to the excoriating. But crowds at festivals and markets also attracted colporteurs and second-hand dealers, who sought to sell all types of printed material: chapbooks, calendars, almanacs, devotional literature, song-sheets, penny dreadfuls, but also journals, newspapers and commentaries. The colporteur traded in information of every kind, from superstitious remedies, irrational prophecies, salacious fiction and medical quackery to pious sermons and inspirational literature. But the colporteur was also the carrier of other ideas; not only did he deliver political

---

[77] Mary Lee Townsend, quoting (and translating) Glaßbrenner in *Forbidden Laughter: Popular Humor and the Limits of Repression in Nineteenth-Century Prussia*, Ann Arbor, MI, 1992, pp. 48–49.

[78] Petzold, *Bänkelsang*, pp. 106–07.

[79] Townsend, *Forbidden Laughter*, p. 168.

news from other regions but also sold provocative literature that excited and agitated: Protestant tracts in Catholic regions, republican essays from Switzerland and 'offensive' censored songs, caricatures and fliers.[80] In view of the extraordinarily high circulation figures of broadsheets during the Napoleonic era — those of Arndt's song-sheets approached 100,000 — and given the custom of extensively recycling literature and newspapers, there is little doubt of a supply of politicized popular literature for colporteurs to hawk in the 1820s.[81]

The sale and display of images — caricatures, political allegories and visual lampoons — at bookshops and public markets especially worried officials. Advances in printing and lithography in the 1820s brought about the potential for cheap, mass distribution of pictures, enabling printers to meet the growing demand for politically charged images. The dozens of censored images by Prussian officials in the 1830s and 1840s suggested a lively market for oppositional representations.[82] Whether illiterate audiences could apprehend political criticism from iconographic cues is a controversial issue,[83] but the Prussian government certainly believed that images constituted a more accessible form of subversive communication than printed text. In 1842 the provincial governor of the Rhine province prohibited the practice of Rhenish booksellers to display political *Zerrbilder*, which enabled the 'common man' to build critical political opinions.[84] In 1843 the Prussian government, responding to the growing numbers of lithographic caricatures (which included extremely unflattering sketches of Friedrich Wilhelm IV) promulgated new censorship laws to include images and caricatures.[85] Such illegal material circulated mostly through

---

80   Schenda, *Volk ohne Buch*, p. 268; HSAM, Rep. 17g, Gef. 74, nr. 9.
81   For publication figures, see Siemann, *Vom Staatenbund zum Nationalstaat* (see note 43 above), p. 306.
82   GStA Berlin, Rep. 77, tit. 2, Gen. nr. 7, Bd. I and II, see also Townsend, *Forbidden Laughter*.
83   For a discussion of the problem of 'reading' images, see Lawrence G. Duggan, 'Was Art really the "Book of the Illiterate"?', *Word and Image*, 5, 1989, pp. 227–51.
84   Oberpräs. Schaper an kgl. Reg. In Coblenz, 2 Dec. 1842, GStA Berlin, Rep. 77, tit. 2, Gen. nr. 7, Bd. II, 'Die Censur und Unterdrückung anstoessiger Kupferstiche und Gemaelde, 1832–43, p. 195.
85   *Gesetz-Sammlung* 1843, p. 25, nr. 2324 (AKO 4 February 1843).

bookshops, but colporteurs, tavern keepers and vendors at the Leipzig and Frankfurt fairs also played a large role in distributing such material. In 1833, for example, Prussian officials cited the Frankfurt fair as an outlet for political contraband in a report on 'speculating Jewish smugglers' selling censored lithographs of the Polish insurrection.[86]

The presence of political contraband at fairs and markets and the willingness of certain vendors to engage in illegal trade highlights the politicization of market culture and, conversely, the commercialization of politics. The links between material culture, commercial gain and political identity (whether subversive or loyal to the state) and the degree to which the market shaped political culture has not been properly assessed. German states strove early — from the end of the Napoleonic era — to forbid the commodification of political allegiance, regardless of political stripe. The Prussian government in 1814–15 initially censored the attempt of a medal business to strike a woman's medallion that replicated the Prussian coat of arms. The government distrusted the manufacturer's aim to provide women with a political marker, which was revealed in a newspaper advertisement for the medal: 'Just as men wear the national cockade, so is it proper and correct to wish that the female sex would also be offered an outward sign to show their patriotic spirit'.[87] In 1822, the political police apparatus of the German Confederation relentlessly pursued the businessmen who manufactured and distributed thousands of daggers to university towns, the motto of which — 'Honour, Fatherland, Freedom' — was deemed seditious.[88] In this period smoking became something of an oppositional act and a politicized commercial venture. In 1827 Prussian police arrested two wood turners for manufacturing pipes, the heads of which depicted a naked woman with the inscription, 'Freedom of Press, Public Opinion, Reduction of Armies and Freedom of the Seas'.[89] Apprentices in Düsseldorf also smoked from pipes, the

---

86 Königsberger Police President to Interior Minister Brenn, 13 March 1833, GStA Berlin, Rep. 77, tit. 500, nr. 8, p. 7–8.
87 GStA Berlin, Rep. 77, tit. II, Censur-Sachen Gen., nr. 13, pp. 1–2. The advertisement appeared in the *Spener'sche Zeitung* in July 1814.
88 Oberpolizei Direktor zu Kassel an Polizeidirektor zu Marburg, 11 February 1822, HSAM, Rep. 24a, nr. 80, unpaginated.
89 GStA Berlin, Rep. 77, II Censur Sachen Gen., nr. 7, Bd. 1, p. 92.

heads of which depicted the oil canvas of Carl Friedrich Lessing's 'Hussitenpredigt' (1834), a painting widely interpreted as an oppositional allegory to the religious and censorship politics of the Prussian state.[90] Students and other democratic elements flouted regulations forbidding smoking outdoors, causing observers to associate public smoking as a politically oppositional gesture.[91]

Following the Hambach Fest of 1832, images of such leaders as Philipp Jacob Siebenpfeiffer and Johann Georg Wirth appeared on a host of goods. Markets sold lithographic portraits, tobacco pipes, china plates, beer mugs, cotton handkerchiefs, aprons, bonnets and a host of other inexpensive politicized trinkets.[92] The suppression of the Polish Uprising in 1831 occasioned the sale of tin Polish soldiers, so-called Freedom Fighters, which Prussian officials promptly confiscated.[93] In 1832–33, alongside a spate of lithographic portraits of the Polish patriots, an assortment of goods (handkerchiefs, snuffboxes, plates, mugs) inscribed with Polish nationalist support appeared in German markets.[94] Women's associations also held public lotteries in 1831 and 1833 to raise money for exiled Polish revolutionaries and arrested Hambach participants, thus politicizing women's public activities, charitable games of chance and the social space within which the lotteries were held.[95] In Baden, women connected with the Vaterlandsverein, the association which advocated freedom of press and had helped organize the Hambach Fest, visited numerous parish festivals in 1832 to

---

90 Hanna Gagel, 'Düsseldorfer Malerschule in der politischen Situation des Vormärz und 1848' in *Düsseldorfer Malerschule* [catalogue to exhibition], Düsseldorf, 1979, p. 69.
91 Wolfgang Schivelbusch, *Das Paradies, der Geschmack und die Vernunft. Eine Geschichte der Genußmittel*, Frankfurt am Main, 1990, p. 141; Townsend, *Forbidden Laughter*, pp. 113–15. Townsend offers an insightful discussion of the 1843 print by O. Gennerich, 'Deutsche Opposition' (displayed on p. 114), which portrays a young man smoking in public directly in front of a no-smoking sign, while three observers view the act in shock. Townsend fails to note, however, that Gennerich unambiguously linked his smoker to democratic politics by evidence of his 'democratic' hat and cockade.
92 Ditmar et al. (eds), *Hambacher Fest* (see note 69 above), pp. 116, 117, 138, 141, 162, 164 and 166 presents illustrations of some these items.
93 GStA Berlin, Rep. 77, tit. 500, nr. 8, pp. 28–37.
94 Ibid., p. 18^v.
95 Ditmar et al. (eds), *Hambacher Fest*, pp. 58–59, 189.

collect money to defray the legal costs of arrested Hambach leaders.[96] (These public charitable actions were undertaken again for the Silesian weavers in the 1840s.) Similarly, carnival bon-bons wrapped in black, red and gold wrappers politicized the simple act of eating candy in festive space.[97]

Such examples underscore the growing commodification of politics. The political public sphere had extended into material culture and consumption, showing the flexibility and ingenuity of oppositional political culture to exploit the 'free trade' of market goods in an era when speech and press were severely restricted.[98] Politically inscribed goods reshaped public life; they politicized consumption and provided a new form of communication. The shared language of politicized goods provided people with the means to project subversive ideas and allegiances in an era of pronounced political reaction and censorship.[99] These goods, by moving beyond the printed word, strove to create a new social space of communicative freedom.[100] Of course, the function of politicized goods greatly depended on the user and the situation. In some instances, such as in carnival sittings or at May-tree celebrations, drinking from Hambach glasses or taking snuff from 'Polish Freedom' boxes affirmed among friends solidarity to a political community. Yet in the socially diverse marketplace or the heterogeneous crowds of a parish festival, political insignia might serve as a provocative, antagonistic advertisement. Yet again, the same forms of projection might be used only privately as domestic reminders of one's political convictions. In any case, although the meaning of the political markers changed with the context, these material forms of political culture were none the less visible carriers of ideas and

---

96 Ibid., p. 194.
97 Ibid., pp. 178, 187; a politically bitter couplet also appeared on the wrapper: 'Und du mein Volk läßt das Geschehen/ Läßt deine Manneskraft im Kerker untergehen'.
98 For a discussion of market culture and its relationship to politics, see Paul Nolte, "Der Markt und seine Kultur — ein neues Paradigma der amerikanischen Geschichte?', *Historische Zeitschrift*, 264, 1997, pp. 329–60.
99 These insights are largely indebted to T. H. Breen's on the political ramifications of colonial consumption in his '"Baubles of Britain": The American and Consumer Revolutions of the Eighteenth Century', *Past and Present*, 119, 1988, pp. 73–104.
100 Siemann, *Vom Staatenbund zum Nationalstaat*, p. 220.

theories otherwise only accessible through élite, clandestine political literature.[101] Although superficial and multivalent in their meaning, such symbols played a large role in publicizing the existence of political opposition.

Conclusion

This chapter posits that any persuasive explanation of how popular politics and partisan political culture emerged in the early nineteenth century must focus on the historical development of social space and its relationships to political power. Such an explanation moves well beyond this chapter's restricted subject of festive space. The politicization of taverns, public reading practices, religious spaces and commercial practices are just some of the many spheres of public space that would need to be researched when addressing the development of modern political cultures. None the less, the politicization of traditional festivals and fairs constitute an important chapter in explaining how common people developed an awareness of difference and opposition, which thus provided the potential for a modern partisan sensibility to emerge in both urban and rural regions. In the period 1815–48 these festive spaces not only acted as influential sites to acculturate insulated communities to new political forces but also to vernacularize such political forces to local conditions and temperaments. Hence, alongside arguments that characterize the period of 1815–48 as one of ceaseless crisis that necessarily produced political change, we should also seek to understand how social environments and mental habits evolved to assimilate the notion of political action and make possible the phenomenon of mass political movements. By circulating and externalizing the symbols and ideas of liberal, constitutional and democratic political reform, this form of 'street politics' acted as an important, resonant communicative force that extended and strengthened the public impact of the invented festivals and print culture of oppositional political culture. In sum,

---

101 Moreover, for women to have worn Hambach skirts and for students to possess politically inscribed daggers, there were entrepreneurs supplying the demand. Because the motivation for profit was presumably as important as the political content of the goods, the economic dynamics of market culture must be considered along with political dimensions when discussing the rise of popular politics.

the politicization (and secularization) of festive space is part of the long-term structural changes in German rural, village and urban life that reconstituted the social body by exposing new social groups to the political life of Germany. This political public emerged with greater visibility in 1848-49, even if bourgeois leaders were unprepared, and sometimes unwilling, to work with this common public sphere.

WINE FESTIVALS IN CONTEMPORARY FRANCE: RESHAPING POWER THROUGH TIME IN BURGUNDY

Marion Demossier

Since the 1930s, Europe has witnessed a development of rural tourism which has been accompanied by a renaissance of local festivals. These events have frequently been ignored by historians and social anthropologists who have dismissed them as mere folklore. In recent years, however, a number of important studies[1] have shown that they can provide a rich source for the understanding of the social and symbolic relationships within a given community. By their very nature, festivals occur for brief, sometimes intense, periods of time, highlighting the social structures, conflicts and tensions of a particular society. Drawing on my research into the wine festivals of Burgundy, I will concentrate upon the annual Saint-Vincent-Tournante, which is the largest in the region, and in particular on that held in 1991 in the village of Puligny Montrachet.[2] Through the organization of the

---

1   See L. Dumont, *La Tarasque: Essai de description d'un fait local du point de vue ethnographique*, Paris, 1987; D. Fabre, *La Fête en Languedoc*, Toulouse, 1977; A. Corbin, N. Gérôme and D. Tartakowsky, *Les Usages politiques des fêtes au XIXè siècle*, Paris, 1994.

2   The last Saint-Vincent-Tournante took place in the village in 1961. There is a hierarchy of villages holding the festival: the more famous villages are allowed to hold it every twenty to thirty years.

celebration, it is possible to examine the social and political relations of the participants and their position within the community. The Saint-Vincent-Tournante offers a further advantage for investigation because it is a cyclical festival, returning to the same village approximately once in every generation and allowing both the local people and the anthropologist[3] to analyse the effects of social, economic and political changes.

When examining the power relationship between the State and local communities, anthropologists have traditionally assumed that conflict was inevitable. As for their definition of power and authority within a particular society,[4] they have almost without exception emphasized the importance of tradition in conferring status within non-industrial societies which is contrasted with that derived from personal and material achievement in the Western world. In criticizing this approach, T. H. Eriksen has argued that in our modern societies, 'achievement does not count for everything' and that 'social background and family networks' may be no less important.[5] The example of the Saint-Vincent-Tournante confirms that the simple dichotomies of State versus local community, or of non-industrial as opposed to capitalist societies, are insufficiently nuanced for any attempt to explain the structure and conduct of social and political behaviour in contemporary rural society. This chapter will, therefore, analyse the power relationship in a given community by following the organization and management of the festival and by assessing the changes in the political and social sphere of the village.

---

[3] Anthropological research was conducted in order to prepare a documentary on the festival.

[4] According to Max Weber, authority is taken for granted by opposition with power that is continuously challenged and must be defended. Steven Lukes (*Essays in Social Theory*, London, 1977) has suggested that power could be studied on three levels: in the process of decision-making, in looking at non-decision and in including muted or powerless groups. I have tried in this chapter to look at the festival as a whole without privileging any particular one of these approaches.

[5] T. H. Eriksen, *Small Places, Large Issues, an Introduction to Social and Cultural Anthropology*, London, 1995, p. 147.

I

In Burgundy, and especially the Côte d'Or, each village of winegrowers has a *confrérie*, many of them dating back to the nineteenth century, which is charged with organizing a celebration every 22 January in honour of their patron saint, St Vincent. Since 1947, there has grown up alongside these village festivities a regional event, the Saint-Vincent-Tournante, which has become one of the most important in Burgundy, attracting an international audience. The Saint-Vincent-Tournante is now a vast commercial operation, with a budget in 1991 of some 3.5 million francs, welcoming more than 100,000 visitors in just two days, who between them consumed at least 30,000 bottles of wine. In the course of the festival, glasses were sold at twenty-five francs each, permitting the customer to taste as much of the local wine as he or she wished. With forty visitors treated for 'alcoholic coma', it is easy to visualize the consequences, and to understand why the festival offers a rich field of investigation for the anthropologist.

The origins of the Saint-Vincent-Tournante are to be found in the context of the great economic depression of the 1930s which hit Burgundy particularly hard. In 1934, the international Confrérie des Chevaliers du taste-vin was created in Burgundy by two local notables, Camille Rodier, chairman of the Tourist Office of Nuits-Saint-Georges, and Camille Faiveley, wine-merchant. Their aim in establishing this Bacchic society was twofold. Firstly, they intended to build an attractive Rabelaisian festival in order to promote the wines from the region. Their second aim was to play the role of a medium between two connected but hostile worlds, the wine-growers and the landowners or wine-merchants. The crisis of the 1930s produced serious tensions between these two social groups. It was the wine-merchants who bought the grapes from the wine-growers, produced and marketed the wine. When they stopped buying, this soon meant hardship for the wine-growers. The wine-merchants themselves were also in difficulties because they were left with large unsold and expensive stocks. The threat of social conflict was very real, and Rodier and Faiveley undoubtedly hoped to defuse tension whilst giving a much-needed boost to local commerce. It was a great success and the Confrérie des Chevaliers du taste-vin has subsequently served as a model throughout France and elsewhere in Europe, and similar *confréries* now promote the wines of regions such as Champlitte, Saumur and Alsace. Today, the role of the Confrérie is to choose the village which will hold the Saint-Vincent-Tournante and to oversee the organization of the festival. In practice, the festival rotates amongst the wine-growing communities of the Côte d'Or and returns every twenty or thirty years to its point of departure.

The Saint-Vincent-Tournante is a two-day festival which follows the pattern of traditional village celebrations. A procession culminating in a Mass at the local church provides the original core of the event, but a whole series of more modern elements have been grafted onto this. After a hearty *casse-croûte*, the representatives chosen by the seventy-two *confréries* and *sociétés viticoles* of Burgundy march off behind floats carrying the statues of St Vincent and the banners and standards of their confraternities. They make a tour of the village and its principal vineyards before arriving at the church for a special mass and sermon which is transmitted to the teeming crowds outside on a giant screen. While the faithful are gathered together, the profane simultaneously begin the first wine-tastings offered to those who have bought a glass bearing the arms of the village. Once the mass is completed, the *chevaliers du taste-vin* conduct a ceremony of induction into their *confrérie* for some of the oldest and most respected of the local *vignerons*. The main participants in the festival and their guests then divide into three groups for the banquets of honour. One of the local catholic notables hosts a reception for the local clergy, while the *chevaliers du taste-vin* gather in their fief, the Château du Clos-de-Vougeot, with their guests — many of whom are figures of international repute in the arts, politics or the business world — plus two *vignerons* from each of the participating villages. Finally the wine-growers from the host village and their guests, drawn mainly from the professional and commercial world of wine, hold their own banquet. With the three orders thus 'à table', the festival is thrown open to the public, with the crowds swarming through the host village, wine-tasting, and often drunkenness following close behind. The sacred has given way to the profane, the Church to the pagan rites of Bacchus and to the popular atmosphere of an inebriated fairground which leaves the uninformed observer in total confusion.

The organization of such a festival requires more than a year of intensive preparation, and it is important to remember that it involves tremendous financial risk. The host village depends upon the sale of glasses to balance its budget and as the Saint-Vincent-Tournante is held in January a sudden blizzard could spell

Wine Festivals in Contemporary France

disaster. The responsibilities and dangers involved impose great strain upon the village solidarity which is so dear to the self-image of wine-growing communities. By observing the preparation and conduct of the festival from its inception, the anthropologist can therefore learn much about local society. To manage the event, the village of Puligny-Montrachet, host to the Saint-Vincent-Tournante of 1991, established ten committees overseeing, for example, the decoration of the village, publicity, the banquets and so on, thus allowing different individuals and social groups to participate in the festival. The *chevaliers du taste-vin* supervise these preparations and endeavour to preserve the traditional ethos of the festival by trying, usually unsuccessfully, to ensure that the wine cellars remain closed during the celebration of mass. They also consult local notables in order to choose from amongst the senior *vignerons* of the organizing village, those who will be inducted into their *confrérie*. According to one observer: 'It is above all their years of work in the vineyard which matters, these are people who started their professional lives when they were thirteen or fourteen and never stopped until their retirement'.[6] As the Chevaliers du taste-vin is composed of the region's notables, leading wine merchants, politicians and a collection of international personalities, to be 'inducted' is a great honour.

By acting as mediators between local society and the wider world, the notables ensure that the festival functions harmoniously in their village. They define the rules of behaviour and give the tone to the ceremonial. The notables themselves can be defined as those who have accumulated a social, cultural and professional capital to complement their economic position. More often than not, they possess some of the largest domains in the village and are engaged in the commercialization of their production rather than the cultivation of the vine. As we shall see, the distinction between notable and *vigneron* is still a valid one. The village of Puligny-Montrachet was composed in 1991 of two wine-merchants and one landlord, seen as 'notables', and ten wine growers, some small *vignerons* (twenty-two have between one and five hectares) and finally some part-time

---

[6] 'Ce sont surtout leur ancienneté dans le travail de la vigne qui compte, ce sont des gens qui ont commencé à travailler dans les vignes à treize ou quatorze ans et qui n'ont jamais quitté leur métier jusqu'à la retraite.' All quotations here and below are taken from personal communications with the author.

workers. It is the landlord and the group of wealthy owners who are primarily responsible for organizing the event. Although the social structure has been largely static since 1930, with a small number of notables and a large majority of wine-growers, there is nevertheless an ongoing process of renewal. In their daily discourse, the *vignerons* define themselves as 'workers in the vineyard' and describe the landlords as 'those who don't work in the vineyard'. This simple dichotomy is given greater force by the undoubted distinction in terms of clothes, gestures, lifestyle and language — all of which point to the existence of two separate social worlds. Amongst the *vignerons* of the Côte d'Or, the notables are, however, a minority compared with the individual wine-grower families, who are now dominant on a professional and political level. Many of the families of *vignerons* who are today so ubiquitous in the Burgundian villages are the descendants of day-labourers, share-croppers and wealthy proprietors of the nineteenth century who benefited from the break-up of the large estates following the phylloxera crisis of 1880 and the economic depression of the 1930s. While many of these families can trace their roots back to the seventeenth century, there are also newcomers anxious to integrate themselves into the professional and social world of the vines. To complete this overview of the social composition of Puligny-Montrachet, it is necessary to consider the relatively large number of retired people, the employees of the wine trade and various salaried workers who commute to the neighbouring towns of Beaune, Châlon-sur-Saône or Dijon. Many of these people participated in the preparation of the festival, and especially in the decoration of the village. They were, however, rarely present in the organizing committees and their involvement was not essential. Ultimately the Saint-Vincent-Tournante is a celebration of the values and lives of the *vignerons* and it provides an opening into the structure of their politics and society.

II

In the Burgundian wine communities, power and authority are defined not only in terms of family pedigree and kinship ties, but also by individual relations to the professional world of the vine. What is peculiar to societies of *vignerons* both in France and elsewhere in Europe is their intermediate position between the rural and the urban, the peasantry and the commercial sector and the economy of 'auto-

Wine Festivals in Contemporary France 113

subsistance' and that of capitalism. Within the villages themselves, several types of authority are in competition both in the economic and political fields, and the Saint-Vincent-Tournante provides an opportunity for conflict as well as self-evaluation.

The Saint-Vincent-Tournante of 1991 was particularly revealing in terms of the redefinition of power at the local level. The municipal elections of 1977 had seen the electoral triumph of Jean-René Chartron (right-wing), from an old family of the wine merchants from Puligny, whose father and grand-father had already held the office of *maire*. In 1990, however, Jean-René was called upon to resign by the municipal council for the alleged abuse of his political position to obtain the *appellation* of *grand cru* for one of his vineyards.[7] At the next elections he was defeated by an outsider of left-wing sympathies, who was employed in Châlon-sur-Saône, and represented those in the village unconnected to the production of wine. Throughout the preparation of the festival, there was friction between the new municipal authorities and the *vignerons*, whose political allegiance was more conservative. One classic example of their disputes concerned the role of the Church in the forthcoming festival. Despite the decline of the influence of the *curé* in village life (on average there is one *curé* for between five and ten villages), religion continues to serve as a point of reference in political terms. In the collective memory, the old divisions between clerical and anti-clerical are still present and affect the alignment of the principal families. Religion also determined attitudes towards the Saint-Vincent-Tournante, as one informer exclaimed: 'Him, he was a red, he never went to Mass, he refused to have anything to do with the festival.' As for the priests themselves, they do not adopt a leading role in the event, occupying themselves only with the sermon and Mass. Their attempt to emphasize the religious character of the cult of St Vincent amidst the material and more pagan aspects is something of a losing battle. Popular reaction can be summed up by the declaration of one *vigneron*: 'The priest, he said that we are

---

7 There are four different appellations: regional (occupying 38 per cent of the Burgundian planting area), villages (37 per cent), *premiers crus* (20 per cent), *grands crus* (20 per cent). Pinot noir is grown on three-quarters of the available planting area.

rich, but it is an exaggeration'.[8] If the clergy has been pushed to the sidelines, it is others from within the community who have come to the fore.

The Saint-Vincent-Tournante also makes it possible to identify the strategies employed by the different individuals, families and social groups to reinforce, protect or advance their power and spheres of influence. In 1991, one of the key figures in this process was the leading notable, Monsieur Vincent Leflaive. He was president of honour of the Saint-Vincent-Tournante, a *chevalier du Mérite Agricole*[9] and owner of one of the most prestigious estates in the region. Leflaive represents the classic example of a medium between local society and the world beyond, and his participation in the Saint-Vincent-Tournante was essential. He oversaw the administration of the festival, organized the necessary village assemblies and committees, chose those who would be inducted into the Confrérie des Chevaliers du taste-vin and presided over the banquet of the *vignerons*. It is not an exaggeration to state that he defined the place of each member of the village in the ceremony as a whole. How can the authority of Leflaive be explained? Perhaps the most important feature to note is the profound *ancrage* (or deep roots) of the family Leflaive, in both the village and its vineyards. Following the local saying: 'To be part of the village, you need three graves in the cemetery or fifty years of being part of the community.'[10] On this score the Leflaives have nothing to fear. In the publicity material for their domain, the arms of the family are clearly underlined with the dates 1735–1985, and a genealogical tree conveniently provides proof both of their long presence in the Puligny-Montrachet and of their 'letters of nobility'. This social authority is complemented by economic power. The estate owned by Vincent Leflaive is one of the most distinguished in the region and is notable for its successful commercialization, with nearly all of its production sold overseas (mainly in the United States) or directly to restaurants. The estate itself consists of more than twenty hectares (compared to an average of five hectares only) including the most prestigious vineyards which in themselves add further lustre to his image. Social and economic influence is

---

8   'Le curé, il dit qu'on est des nantis, faut pas exagérer.'
9   High distinction in the rural and political sphere. The award is one of national recognition.
10 'Tant qu'on a pas trois tombes au cimetière ou cinquante ans d'existence au village, on est pas du village, ça n'ira pas.'

reinforced by the weight of professional office. Leflaive held the post of president of the Syndicat Viticole, a crucial position for mediating between local and national affairs. As the award of the Mérite Agricole demonstrates, his reputation extends well beyond the village, although it can give rise to expressions of jealousy. As one *vigneronne* explained: 'but my husband, he was dreaming of having this award [...] because he has done a lot for the village but Mr Leflaive got it and my husband thought he deserved to have it more, he has been devoted to Puligny'.[11] It is, however, interesting to note that although the notion of *ancrage* is so crucial to the definition of the notable, Leflaive has only resided permanently in the village since 1977. Until that point, it was his brother who ran the domain, while Vincent had, since 1950, worked for international enterprises in Indochina and the United States. It was the name of the family which facilitated his personal *ancrage*.

Amongst the principal collaborators of Vincent Leflaive in 1991 was the president of the Saint-Vincent-Tournante, Louis Carillon or, as he was more commonly known, 'Loulou Carillon'. Although he also possessed a profound *ancrage* in the village, his roots are solidly entrenched amidst the *vignerons* rather than the notability. In addition to being president of the Saint-Vincent-Tournante, Carillon is a leader of the political right, which after 1990 was in opposition to the municipal council. Throughout the festival, he was to be seen at the head of the community of *vignerons*, notably during the procession and at the banquet, where he sat alongside Leflaive. He was also the central figure around whom the Chevaliers du taste-vin and the other representatives of the region coalesced during the festival itself. The family Carillon has been present at Puligny-Montrachet since at least 1632 and numerous ties of kinship unite it with the neighbouring villages. Louis's father was a *vigneron* of repute, and his wife the daughter of the steward of the Leflaive domain, who was responsible, in part, for establishing its great reputation. Such strong and significant ties ensure both authority and influence in the community of *vignerons*. Despite his position as a leader of the right, Carillon was able to act as a mediator with his political

---

11 'M'enfin, mon mari, il aurait trop voulu avoir le poireau [...] une médaille, une reconnaissance envers quelqu'un parce que vous avez fait du bien [...]. Monsieur Leflaive l'a eu justement ces derniers temps....et mon mari dit, je me suis dévoué et je l'ai pas eu.'

opponents, for example, in finding a compromise on the vexed question of whether the wine cellars should remain open during Mass, as well as placing individuals on the various organizing committees according to their personal beliefs and political sympathies. He was also active in conciliating the often conflicting interests of the *vignerons* and the rest of the village by being present at all committees and by supervising closely their actions. Finally, Carillon personally directed the monthly plenary meetings of the commissioners. By personality and his *métier* of *vigneron*, Carillon was clearly of those 'who work in the vines' and not a notable in the same sense as Leflaive, and his house, comportment and lifestyle confirm that observation. He was nevertheless vital to the success of the festival, as one local noted: 'There is one chairman who is recognized by the majority and everybody has decided that he is the right person.'[12]

A third group which distinguished itself by its willingness to participate in the preparation of the Saint-Vincent-Tournante were the newcomers, or perhaps more precisely, those who lacked an *ancrage* or pedigree enabling them to be fully recognized by the village. As one *vigneron* observed: 'us, we did that in order to be recognized', that is to say that the festival provided a means of integration. Several families could be included in this category, but it is interesting to examine some particularly pertinent examples of those individuals who have already achieved recognition on a professional and economic level. Two cases are especially striking, those of Gérard Boudot, manager of the *domaine* Sauzet, and the family Maroslovac, for both of whom the Saint-Vincent-Tournante marked a milestone on the path to social integration. As Mr Maroslavac said, 'We get known and we get loved.'[13]

Gérard Boudot and Stephen Maroslovac had in common the fact that they both actively participated in the preparations for the festival, while their wives chaired a committee. Mme Boudot organized the banquet of the *vignerons*, and Mme Maroslovac the commission responsible for the decoration of the village. It is noteworthy that both women identified the desire for integration as a principal motive for their actions and they believed that their involvement would advance that end. A second shared point of reference was the relatively large scale of their

---

12 'Il y a un président du comité, tout le monde a décidé que c'était lui et personne d'autre.'
13 'On se fait connaître, on se fait aimer.'

respective domains, Boudot managing some twelve hectares, while that of the Maroslovac consists of more than twenty hectares. Moreover both families assume direct responsibility for the commercialization of their product. These are economically powerful clans and it would not be unfair to claim that as *vignerons* they enjoy an international reputation. Yet within the geographically confined space of Puligny-Montrachet, where it is necessary to have 'three graves in the cemetery' to belong, they lack true recognition. The Saint-Vincent-Tournante provided a vehicle by which to overcome the remaining obstacles to integration. Gérard Boudot, for example, was a newcomer to the village. Formerly a professional rugby player, he married a granddaughter of the *domaine* Sauzet. When, on the death of the grandfather, the inheritance was divided, some twelve hectares passed to the young couple. In recent years, thanks to the efforts of Gérard, the domain has acquired the reputation of being the best in Puligny-Montrachet.

As for the Maroslovacs, they offer a clear case of rapid social and economic ascension which was not initially accompanied by social acceptance. After leaving his native Yugoslavia in 1930, Maroslovac senior came as a labourer to Burgundy. Two years later, he installed himself at Puligny, working as an agricultural labourer in the vineyards. Little by little, he accumulated the capital necessary to buy his own vines and by 1991 he possessed over twenty hectares, making his domain one of the largest in the village. His sons and grandsons have followed in his footsteps, acquiring vines of their own, and they will inherit the domain in their turn. It was, however, his son, Stephen, who participated in the Saint-Vincent-Tournante. He remarked: 'It is very difficult to integrate ourselves, we have always been seen as foreigners.' The festival marked a turning-point and brought belated recognition for Maroslovac senior, who was one of those chosen for induction into the Confrérie des Chevaliers du taste-vin. As his son noted: 'He was very proud because he was inducted with the older wine-growers of Puligny. At the end of your life, it is something.'[14] It was his fifty years spent working in the vineyards which, in principle, was the basis of his recognition, but this recognition only came at the end of his labours.

---

14 'Il a retiré une gloire personnelle parce qu'il était intronisé avec les plus vieux vignerons du village. A la fin de sa vie, c'était vraiment quelque chose.'

III

Through these examples of social ascension, the process of integration is fundamental because it determines the extent of social recognition, confirming with it the status and power which are attached thereto. In this respect, the next Saint-Vincent-Tournante, due in twenty or twenty-five years time, will be a crucial moment for our two case-studies. Moreover, all of our examples reveal the mechanisms defining notability, authority and legitimacy in the context of village society. In examining them, I have attempted to illustrate the different forms of social representation and to see how the festival redefines or restores the equilibrium amongst competing social groups. In 1991, it was clear that one of the principal points of dispute was between the wine community, deeply concerned from a professional and commercial standpoint about the wider image conveyed, and the village which controlled the festival. A number of key mediators held the positions of leadership and managed the problems and disputes involved in the organization of the event. The categories of notable and *vigneron* were fundamental to the power structure and in the distribution of roles within the village. The new *maire*, for example, was almost completely absent from the scene and neither he nor the other members of the village unconnected to the wine trade could do anything more than yield to the direction proposed by the *vignerons*. As Laffond observed: 'In this Saint-Vincent people from very different backgrounds were brought together and that posed a very tricky problem, you have the Saint-Vincent of the organizers, you have the influential people within the village itself and it is them who are the most advantaged from a financial point of view.'[15] With different groups seeking to advance their own agendas the ability to find mediators such as Carillon and Leflaive capable of resolving conflict is essential. Certainly the next Saint-Vincent-Tournante risks to produce more serious tension between the minority, the economically powerful wine community and the rest of the village.

To conclude, economic strength seems to determine the division of power within the village, notably between those involved in the wine trade and those

---

15 'Dans cette Saint Vincent sont réunis des gens de conditions différentes, alors ça pose un problème et c'est de plus en plus difficile, vous avez à la Saint Vincent des organisateurs, vous avez des gens influents dans un village, ce sont ceux qui sont le plus favorisés financièrement.'

outside of it. Yet within the wine community itself, another factor is predominant: the *ancrage* and family pedigree of the individual within that society. The organization of the festival clearly reproduced these long-established social hierarchies, although the picture was less static than it might at first appear. By its cyclical nature, the Saint-Vincent-Tournante places the social structure of the village under fresh scrutiny every thirty years and it has served both as a mechanism for facilitating and legitimizing social change. In the collective memory, the ideal of notability has remained tied to the role of the large proprietors as an essential medium between the village and the world outside. As one *vigneron* noted: 'Chartron, he was elected twice, he was a wine-merchant and landlord. At the time, we appreciated having a mayor with an important social situation. He shielded us with his authority.'[16]

If such a perception of authority is shared by the *vignerons*, however, it holds no relevance to the newcomers to the village and particularly those unconnected to the wine trade, as the elections of 1990 demonstrated. It is easy to predict that in the future conflict may occur as a result. However, the Saint-Vincent-Tournante of 1991 still allowed the participants to indulge in an image of a mythical golden age of the vine, that of harmonious dualities of proprietors and *vignerons*, cultivators and merchants, 'vigne et du vin'. Today two of the principal actors in the Saint-Vincent-Tournante of 1991 are dead, but the community will have to wait for at least another twenty years to prepare a new balance of its social relations. This new balance would have to take into account a fundamental change since 1930s: the greater commercialization of the *vignerons*.

---

16 'Chartron, il a dû faire un mandat de maire, il était négociant en vins, propriétaire et à l'époque, on aimait avoir un maire avec une position sociale importante, il servait de bouclier. C'est ce qu je dis à Leflaive qui est toujours président du syndicat. Vous êtes notre bouclier.'

PART II

MONARCHIC, DYNASTIC AND COURT FESTIVALS

HABSBURG FESTIVALS IN THE EARLY MODERN PERIOD

Karl Vocelka

As in many other countries, festivities in Austria have constituted one of the main topics of early descriptive and narrative historiography of the nineteenth century. Historians from this time have most often concentrated their interest on courtly and aristocratic events, but in some cases — when good documentation existed — also on festivities of the inhabitants of major cities. Although the studies of the nineteenth century were based on contemporary descriptions, they nevertheless often simply translated the contemporary texts into modern language.[1]

A different, critical and interpretative new approach to the topic of festivities has developed in the last few decades, mainly since the 1970s.[2] Studies published

---

[1] As one example among many, see E. Otto, 'Zur Geschichte des deutschen Fürstenlebens, namentlich der Hoffestlichkeiten im 16. und 17. Jahrhundert', *Zeitschrift für Kulturgeschichte*, 8, 1901, pp. 335–53.

[2] R. Alewyn and K. Sälzle, *Das große Welttheater. Die Epoche der höfischen Feste in Dokument und Deutung*, Hamburg, 1959, now in a second edition as *Neuauflage als* in Beck'sche Reihe, 389, Munich, 1989; E. Straub, *Repraesentatio Maiestatis oder churbayerische Freudenfeste. Die höfischen Feste in der Münchener Residenz vom 16. bis zum 18. Jahrhundert*, Munich, 1969 (= *Miscellanea Bavarica Monacensia*, 14); H. Tintelnot, 'Die Bedeutung der "festa theatrale" für das dynastische und künstlerische Leben im Barock', *Archiv für Kulturgeschichte*, 37, 1955, pp. 336–51; J. Jaquot, *Les Fêtes de la renaissance*, 3 vols, Paris, 1956–72; H. Commenda, 'Adelige Lustbarkeiten in Linz vom

since then constitute part of a general methodological revolution in historiography, with an orientation towards social and cultural paradigms. None the less, old-fashioned themes such as diplomatic and political history still prevail within a great deal of German-speaking historiography. As an example, I would like to mention a description which I published several years ago with four of my former students of the coronation ceremonies of Maximilian II in Bohemia, the Empire and Hungary in the years 1562–63.[3] As a source we utilized the eyewitness accounts of Hans Habersack, which are full of cultural, ceremonial and detailed prosopographic information. The critique of one mainstream historian was directed, however, not at details of our study, but rather at the fact that the text contained no information about political history; he therefore questioned if it was worth publishing at all.[4]

But in spite of the narrow orientation of many Austrian and German historians towards political, biographical and local history, new trends of European historiography have also greatly influenced the approach to history. The importance of the history of everyday life (*Alltagsgeschichte*), the emphasis on social history, including that of élites — based on the research of Norbert Elias — and a new approach to popular culture have all strengthened and enhanced interest in festivities. Festivals form a central topic within both the traditional

---

16.bis zum 18.Jahrhundert', *Historisches Jahrbuch der Stadt Linz*, 1958, pp. 141–80; K. Vocelka, 'Manier — Groteske — Fest — Triumph. Zur Geistesgeschichte der frühen Neuzeit', *Österreich in Geschichte und Literatur*, 21, 1977, pp. 137–50; idem, 'Die Wiener Feste der frühen Neuzeit in waffenkundlicher Sicht', *Studien zur Wiener Geschichte. Festschrift aus Anlaß des hundertfünfundzwanzigjährigen Bestehens des Vereines für Geschichte der Stadt Wien* (= *Jahrbuch des Vereins für Geschichte der Stadt Wien*, 34, 1978), pp. 133–48; *Europäische Hofkultur im 16. und 17. Jahrhundert*, 2 vols, Hamburg, 1981 (= *Wolfenbütteler Arbeiten zur Barockforschung*, 9); J. J. Berns, *Höfische Festkultur in Braunschweig-Wolfenbüttel 1590–1666*, Amsterdam, 1981 (= *Daphnis*, 10); U. Kardoff, *Vom Glanz rauschender Feste*, Zürich, 1989; U. Schultz (ed.): *Das Fest. Eine Kulturgeschichte von der Antike bis zur Gegenwart*, Munich, 1988; W. Haug and R. Warning (eds), *Das Fest*, Munich, 1989 (= *Poetik und Hermeneutik*, 14).

3   F. Edelmayer, L. Kammerhofer, M. C. Mandlmayr, W. Prenner and K. G. Vocelka, *Die Krönungen Maximilians II. zum König von Böhmen, Römischen König und König von Ungarn (1562/63) nach der Beschreibung des Hans Habersack, ediert nach cvp 7890*, Vienna, 1990 (= *Fontes rerum Austriacarum Erste Abteilung Scriptores*, 13).

4   Review signed Schz., *Archiv für Reformationsgeschichte*, 20, 1991, pp. 144–45

Geistesgeschichte as well as the new philological methods of text-interpretation which stress the textual and symbolic character of such events.[5]

Roger Chartier states that the intensification of research on festivities compensates for the defects of our modern cultural system in which festivities have little importance, as opposed to the traditional pre-modern one in which festivities played a great role. This observation, which is unquestionably correct, shows that the spirit of the age — the *Zeitgeist* — favours research on festivities.[6] As we have lost what Jan Huizinga called the 'tension between holiday and everyday', we look back — sometimes nostalgically — to the early modern period in which this tension was still present.[7]

Of course, many different kinds of festivities have been discussed as topics of historical, art-historical, theatre-historical, musicological, ethnological and philological research. In accordance with international trends, special interest in popular festivals, especially carnival, has been pursued also in Austria.[8] None the less, most studies still centre on the upper classes of society. This is of course also a question of the existence of sources; it is clear that the court festivals of the Habsburgs have left more traces in archives than, for instance, a village festival in the countryside.

---

5   See, for example, J. Kuczynski, *Geschichte des Alltags des deutschen Volkes 1600–1945*, 6 vols, Cologne, 1980–85, for the early modern period see vols I and II.

6   R. Chartier, 'Phantasie und Disziplin. Das Fest in Frankreich vom 15. bis zum 18. Jahrhundert' in R. van Dülmen and N. Schindler (eds), *Volkskultur. Zur Wiederentdeckung des vergessenen Alltags (16.–20. Jahrhundert)*, Frankfurt am Main, 1987 (= *Fischer Taschenbuch*, 3460), p. 153.

7   J. Huizinga, *Herbst des Mittelalters. Studien über Lebens- und Geistesformen des 14. und 15. Jahrhunderts in Frankreich und in den Niederlanden*, 11th edn, Stuttgart, 1975, pp. 1ff.

8   There are many books and articles on this topic. See, for example, M. M. Bachtin, *Literatur und Karneval. Zur Romantheorie und Lachkultur*, Frankfurt am Main, 1990 (= *Fischer Taschenbücher*, 7434); *Fasnacht*, Tübingen, 1964; H. Moser, 'Kritisches zu neuen Hypothesen der Fastnachtsforschung', *Jahrbuch für Volkskunde*, 5, 1982, pp. 9–50; N. Schindler, 'Karneval, Kirche und die verkehrte Welt. Zur Funktion der Lachkultur im 16. Jahrhundert', *Jahrbuch für Volkskunde*, 7, 1984, pp. 9–57, B. Scribner, 'Reformation, Karneval und die "verkehrte Welt"' in van Dülmen and Schindler (eds), *Volkskultur*, pp. 117–52; and C. Müller, *Sozialdisziplinierung während Fastnacht und Fastenzeit in Tirol zwischen 1530 und 1650*, Vienna, 1995.

The social determination of the quantity and quality of sources means that only the ruling classes, who reported on their life themselves, also give evidence of their festive culture, whereas the majority of sources contain only indirect evidence about groups other than the court, the aristocrats and the Church. Most members of the lower strata of society were — as we all know — simply not able to write. The festivities of peasants and lower classes must therefore be reconstructed mainly from hidden hints and remarks in the documentation of ecclesiastic institutions or manorial lords, which constituted the ruling group (*Obrigkeit*) for them.

As opposed to the limited material available for the lower classes, numerous different kinds of sources of high quality exist for all élite festivals: printed or handwritten descriptions of heralds and professional festival organizers (*Herold- und Pritschenmeisterdichtung*), as well as descriptions and interpretations of humanists and artists who arranged festivities or were responsible for the artistic milieu in connection with them, for example, well-known painters such as Giuseppe Arcimboldo. The economic and organizational context of such festivities is well documented in archive documents, including ceremonial and logistic plans such as how to house and feed the festival participants. Financial records such as accounting reports contain important information on the artists, artisans and merchants who contributed to specific festivals. Handwritten sources, for example, in the manuscript sections of libraries, contain poems, orations and musical *intermezzi* connected to those festivals. Pictures exist for many festivities, and in some cases illustrations of the written descriptions of events, contemporary independent paintings or illustrations which document different phases of such events. In many cases we can also find objects connected with festivities in museums, for example, wedding presents, or armour and weapons manufactured for the tournaments which took place on such occasions.[9]

---

9   A. Stöckelle, 'Geburten und Taufen am barocken Kaiserhof', *Österreich in Geschichte und Literatur*, 18, 1974, pp. 129–41; A. Stöckelle, 'Taufzeremoniell und politische Patenschaften am Kaiserhof', *Mitteilungen des Instituts für Österreichische Geschichtsforschung*, 90, 1982, pp. 271–337; K. Vocelka, *Habsburgische Hochzeiten 1550–1600. Kulturgeschichtliche Studien zum manieristischen Repräsentationsfest*, Vienna, Graz and Cologne, 1976 (= *Veröffentlichungen der Kommission für Neuere Geschichte Österreichs*, 65), or B. Grohs, 'Italienische Hochzeiten. Die Vermählung der

Habsburg Festivals in the Early Modern Period 127

The interpretative framework of this focus on court festivities has been constructed by theories concerning the formation of a specific court society in the Baroque period, the *höfische Gesellschaft*, as Norbert Elias calls it,[10] and the interest in representation of the courts and dynasties, which also allow comparisons to other court centres. There has been an unconscious acceptance of traditional historiographic interest in the political and military competition in Europe in the early modern period which took place mainly between France and the Habsburgs in Vienna and Spain. This competition, however, was fought not only on the battlefields but also in the theatres, firework displays, operas and tournaments of the courts.

This chapter concentrates on the court festivities of the Habsburg family in the sixteenth and seventeenth centuries, which have been popular subjects in books and articles over the last decades. After a closer look at this literature we soon realize that a great part of the research so far has focused on festivities which might best be described with a term coined by Arnold van Genep: 'rites of passage' (*rites de passage*).[11] Birth and baptismal ceremonies, weddings, coronations and funerals are the main topics of this new interest in festivities. In the terminology of the German tradition of European ethnology (*Volkskunde*), a differentiation has developed between festivities of the year-cycle (*Feste des Jahreslaufes*) and festivities of the life-cycle (*Feste des Lebenslaufes*). Whereas most festivities of the life-cycle have been researched as case-studies during the

---

Erzherzoginnen Barbara und Johanna von Habsburg im Jahre 1565', *Mitteilungen des Instituts für Österreichische Geschichtsforschung*, 96, 1988, pp. 331–82; E. Scheicher, 'Ein Fest am Hofe Erzherzogs Ferdinands II.', *Jahrbuch der kunsthistorischen Sammlungen in Wien*, 77, 1981, pp. 119–53; M. Hawlik-van de Water, *'Der schöne Tod'. Zeremonialstrukturen des Wiener Hofes bei Tod und Begräbnis zwischen 1640 und 1740*, Vienna, 1989.

10 N. Elias, *Die höfische Gesellschaft. Untersuchungen zur Soziologie des Königtums und der höfischen Aristokratie, mit einer Einleitung Soziologie und Geschichtswissenschaft*, Neuwied and Berlin, 1969 (= *Soziologische Texte*, 54); N. Elias., *Über den Prozeß der Zivilisation. Soziogenetische und psychogenetische Untersuchungen*, 2 vols, Berne and Munich, 1969. See also M. Reisenleitner, 'Die Bedeutung der Werke und Theorien Norberrt Elias für die Erforschung der Frühen Neuzeit', *Frühneuzeit-Info*, 1, 1990, pp. 47–57.

11 A. van Genep, *Übergangsriten (rites de passage)*, Frankfurt and New York, 1981.

last several years, research concerning the year-cycle is still a subject waiting to be tapped. More detailed research of the court festivities of the year would help us to strengthen the contact to the well-elaborated and studied field of Habsburg piety which constitutes a central point of interest for the mentality of the Habsburg family.[12] Within the framework of a family for whom Catholic piety played such an important role, ecclesiastic holidays were always events to be celebrated, but in the Middle Ages the piety of the Habsburgs was relatively unobtrusive compared to other families or social groups. Church festivities have always been determined by the ecclesiastic calendar, with the major stations of the life of Christ such as Christmas and Easter dominating, but in the Middle Ages the calendar of the saints, including all local saints, and that of the Virgin Mary were of growing importance.

Let us first concentrate the festivities of the life-cycle. Most of these festivities — and certainly those most important culturally — were festivals planned by the ruler. The concept and programme of these festivals mirrored clearly the rulers' own concept of power and the importance of the dynastic family. The ideology of the ruling system of the Middle Ages and the early modern period cannot be understood without a thorough study of the ideology behind it, which consists of a mixture of ancient and Christian elements. These elements were comprehensible at the time for most of the élites who participated in the festivities, though there are some cases which show that not everyone could really follow the elaborate mythological festive programmes. Other festivities, however, were arranged by the aristocrats *for* the ruler and not *by* the ruler himself. Until now the analysis of festivities has not paid enough attention to the differentiation between the organizers — working on the presumption that there was no difference because of the common cultural background of élite social groups. More attention to this point may be useful in future research.

Following the Middle Ages the different festivities of the life-cycle lasted for several days each, framed by tournaments, hunting expeditions, banquets, dance and church ceremonies, which changed in taste and fashion during the course of

---

12 K. Vocelka and L. Heller, *Die Lebenswelten der Habsburger. Kultur- und Mentalitätsgeschichte einer Familie*, Graz, Vienna and Cologne, 1997, pp. 13–38, and A. Coreth, *Pietas Austriaca. Österreichische Frömmigkeit im Barock*, Vienna, 1982.

Habsburg Festivals in the Early Modern Period 129

the centuries but stayed the same in their respective symbolic meaning. The circle of participants of such courtly events was strictly limited to the absolute élite of aristocrats and high-ranking clergymen. Another demonstration of this were the rules for the tournaments, whose participants had to prove that they belonged to certain aristocratic families who were allowed to joust according to specific aristocratic rules. This was called *turnierfähig* in German and formed a special differentiation within the aristocratic class. Many Habsburgs loved tournaments and spent enormous sums of money on armour, some of which today forms the core of what is undoubtedly the world's most important collection of arms, in Vienna.[13]

With the beginning of the early modern period, festivities in the Habsburg monarchy began to change. This was a time in which the Habsburgs became one of the most important dynasties in Europe — ruling, on the one hand, Spain and its colonies, Burgundy and great parts of Italy, and, on the other, the Holy Roman Empire, including Austria and Bohemia and at least a part of Hungary. The influence of Humanism and the Renaissance, the model of Italian festival culture and the rich Burgundian heritage challenged the imperial court in Vienna — festivals became complex structures which included different arts and made use of mythological and allegorical knowledge. In the sixteenth century, festivities in the Habsburg court were a kind of *Gesamtkunstwerk* which involved all the artists and scholars of the court.[14] They built triumphal arches, painted allegorical and mythological paintings and sketched costumes for the cavalcades, processions and entrance ceremonies, composed music and performed theatre. Humanists wrote mythological programmes for the tournaments and later on for the operas which celebrated the Habsburg virtues in government and the specific role of the family in Europe. From the reign of Maximilian I, this consciousness of the mission of the House of Habsburg developed to become a central topic of festivals as well as of panegyric writings.[15]

The Renaissance enforced the tradition of imperial representation and combined it with the notion of this mission of the Habsburg family, who attempted to create,

---

13   See *Katalog der Leibrüstkammer*, 2 vols, Vienna, 1976 and 1990.
14   Vocelka, *Habsburgische Hochzeiten*, p. 26.
15   Vocelka and Heller, *Die Lebenswelten der Habsburger*, pp. 117ff.

in fictive genealogies, lines of descent from Caesar, Aeneas or at least ancient Roman clans, such as the Colonna or the Pierleoni families.[16] Elements of ancient Roman representation were used in Habsburg festivals, especially the motif of triumph, which was rooted in the Italian Renaissance and its revival of the idea of *trionfo*.[17] Triumphal arches were one expression of this, and the same motif is visible in other examples of fine art, such as in 'Ehrenpforte', Maximilian I's famous series of illustrations. Arches were employed much more extensively in temporary festival architecture — a field of experimentation for real architecture. These ephemeral constructions of wood and linen, decorated with stucco and paint, were used in all major festivities of this time. They used elements of form from antiquity, such as obelisks, pyramids and porticoes, and were decorated with sophisticated mythological and allegorical scenes. The most famous examples of these triumphal arches were imitated and copied, their fame spread through sketchbooks and etchings, often called *apparato delle feste*.[18]

Apart from these static elements of festive culture, there was also great interest in mechanical motion. Triumphal carriages with festal decorations — in the tradition of the Italian *carro* — were used already in sixteenth-century events and created a long tradition of similar objects still used today in festive processions such as modern carnival or wine festivals. The surprising element of these carriages was the fact that no persons or animals were visible, so spectators had the impression they moved of their own accord; in one recent study in this field they were called 'forerunners of automobiles'. This fascination with technology is also evident in the use of fireworks, which were supervised by specialists, and in the illumination of houses in cities, and must be seen in the context of a city which was usually completely dark at night.[19]

---

16 On Habsburg genealogical thinking, see, for example, A. Lhotsky, *Aufsätze und Vorträge*, 5 vols, Vienna, 1970–76, and M. Tanner, *The Last Descendant of Aeneas: The Hapsburgs and the Mythic Image of the Emperor*, New Haven, CT and London, 1993.

17 W. Weisbach, *Trionfi*, Berlin, 1919; H. S. Versnel, *Triumphus: An Inquiry into the Origin, Development and Meaning of the Roman Triumph*, Leiden, 1970.

18 H. Blaha, 'Österreichische Triumph- und Ehrenpforten der Renaissance und des Barock', unpublished PhD dissertation, University of Vienna, 1950.

19 A. Lotz, *Das Feuerwerk. Seine Geschichte und Bibliographie*, Leipzig, 1941; G. Sievernich and H. Budde, *Das Buch der Feuerwerkskunst. Farbenfeuer am Himmel Asiens und*

Habsburg Festivals in the Early Modern Period 131

Naturally a strong propagandistic element existed in all these festivities, although the term is relative and must be viewed differently for a period which had no propaganda comparable to that of the present. It was only necessary to influence the élites who participated in the festivals themselves or read the illustrated descriptions or the texts of theatre libretti. Copies of such descriptions and libretti — sometimes accompanied by a handwritten imperial letter — were sent to different European courts as part of the political competition in symbolic values, mentioned above.

Manneristic festivities in the sixteenth century were seen mainly in the courts of Ferdinand I and his sons Maximilian II, Ferdinand of Tyrol and Karl, who ruled Inner-Austria, but also during the early years of the rule of Rudolf II at his court in Vienna and later in Prague. Rudolf reduced the number and size of the public festivities at his court, a fact which may be explained by his mental illness.[20] Yet the representational festivals of the sixteenth century were still no more than the overture to a climax of festival culture to come. Many elements in tournaments and other spectacles already point towards the development of a magnificent Baroque heyday of culture at the imperial court in Vienna. The core of this festive culture of the seventeenth century consisted of the performance of operas which developed under Italian influence.[21] Habsburg rulers showed a strong personal interest in music. All emperors from Ferdinand III to Charles VI composed music themselves and spent enormous sums of money every year on cultural activities. Despite the importance of personal factors — the Habsburgs' education included musical instruction, and many marriages took place between Habsburg rulers and Italian princesses — this theatrical climax cannot be separated from social and economic developments.[22] As Norbert Elias has shown, the development of absolutism as a ruling system made it necessary to domesticate the aristocracy. Aristocrats were attracted by a court that had a monopoly on

---

Europas, Nördlingen, 1987; G. Kohler (ed.), *Die schöne Kunst der Verschwendung. Fest und Feuerwerk in der europäischen Geschichte*, Zürich, 1990.

20 K. Vocelka, *Die politische Propaganda Kaiser Rudolfs II. (1576–1612)*, Vienna, 1981 (= *Veröffentlichungen der Kommission für die Geschichte Österreichs*, 9).

21 H. Seifert, *Der Sig-prangende Hochzeit-Gott. Hochzeitsfeste am Wiener Hof der Habsburger und ihre Allegorik 1622–1699*, Vienna, 1988 (= *Dramma per musica*, 2).

22 Vocelka and Heller, *Die Lebenswelten der Habsburger*, pp. 263–87.

social prospects; they thus lost local importance and influence, and with that the possibility of resistance, and had to be kept busy at the court. Festivities must be seen in this context. Another symptom of these changes is the growing household of the emperor — from several hundred aristocrats at the beginning of the sixteenth century to more than 2,000 at the beginning of the eighteenth.[23]

The audience of aristocrats, at whom most of the festivities were addressed, also influenced the content of festivals. Their language was élitist, both in a literal sense — Latin, Spanish, Italian or French were used — but also in a metaphorical sense, as the language was not comprehensible to all. It was full of allusions to the classical course of studies for the élite, and one could not understand a festival without the study of classical Latin literature and without acquaintance with the language of symbols and personifications. The wealth of knowledge required makes deciphering such a programme also an adventure today: it often ends with disappointment as we cannot understand the symbolic text of the period in its entirety.

It is interesting that only a few of the festivities of the life-cycle stressed religious elements and ideas, though they were connected with religious ceremonies such as baptism, weddings and funerals. The symbolic language of these events was pagan and mythological, influenced by Renaissance and Humanistic ideas. Their main goal was representation, to demonstrate Habsburg power and virtues, and in this context only one of them, the virtue of piety (*pietas*), was regularly included in the programmes.

With the Counter-Reformation victorious in the Habsburg Empire after 1620, when the Battle of the White Mountain (Bilá Hora) near Prague laid the foundation for a radical and brutal re-Catholization of all the Habsburg-ruled countries, except Hungary, religious topics became more important than ever. The representative character of festivities was now paralleled by an explicitly Catholic character. These two elements occur together in many festivities, but can also be separated in different festive occasions. Again, social considerations might provide some explanation. Court festivities were originally, and increasingly became,

---

23 See Elias, *Die höfische Gesellschaft*, and H. C. Ehalt, *Ausdrucksformen absolutistischer Herrschaft. Der Wiener Hof im 17. und 18. Jahrhundert*, Vienna, 1980 (= *Sozial- und wirtschaftswissenschaftliche Studien*, 14).

exclusive occasions for élites to meet, but these élites had already been converted to Catholicism early on. Only a few of the court aristocrats were still Protestants; in most of the Habsburg-ruled countries no religion but Catholicism was now tolerated. Conversion had become the entrance-ticket to Habsburg court society. These court aristocrats had been educated in Jesuit schools, or at least sent their children to such institutions, and required no such propaganda. Therefore the necessity of Catholic indoctrination arose more obviously in the cities and in the countryside, in the sphere of influence of the local manorial lords. Schools and sermons, and indeed the whole system of enforcement of social discipline, were the natural tools for the Counter-Reformation, but festivities also played an important role, as they reached the crowds who required indoctrination.[24]

Many occasions could be analysed in this context: Jesuit theatre, the worship of saints and their relics by the Habsburgs, as well as pilgrimages which the court undertook to Altötting in Bavaria and later especially to Mariazell, the *Magna mater Austriae*. I shall discuss just one of these ecclesiastical events in greater detail here: the Corpus Christi procession. The question of transubstantiation was without doubt the central theological issue of the Reformation period. Here not only Catholics and the Reformation movements differed, but the Reformers could not agree amongst themselves. Lutheran, Zwinglian and Calvinist movements were unable to co-operate to the extent they would have liked, as they could not reach a compromise on this vexed issue.[25]

---

24 K. Vocelka, 'Public Opinion and the Phenomenon of Sozialdisziplinierung in the Habsburg Monarchy' in C. W. Ingrao (ed.), *State and Society in Early Modern Austria*, West Lafayettte, 1994, pp. 119–38. R. J. W. Evans (ed.), *Crown, Church and Estates. Central European Politics in the Sixteenth and Seventeenth Centuries*, Basingstoke, 1991; F. M. Dolinar (ed.), *Katholische Reformation und Gegenreformation in Innerösterreich 1564–1628* (title also in Slovene and Italian), Klagenfurt, 1994; W. Reinhard, 'Gegenreformation als Modernisierung. Prolegomena zu einer Theorie des konfessionellen Zeitalters' *Archiv für Reformationsgeschichte*, 68, 1977, pp. 226–52.

25 M Schmaus and A. Grillmeier (eds), *Handbuch der Dogmengeschichte. IV. Sakramente, Eschatologie*, Fasz. 4a, 'Eucharistie in der Schrift und Patristik' (by J. Beck), Freiburg, 1979, and Fasz. 4b, 'Eucharistie in Mittelalter und Neuzeit' (by B. Neunheuser), Freiburg, 1963; M. Rubin, *Corpus Christi: The Eucharist in Late Medieval Culture*, Cambridge, 1961.

The position of the Catholics was clear: Christ was physically present in the bread and wine (which could be drunk only by the priest) used in the church service, and this position was openly demonstrated in the veneration of the Eucharist. One dominating aspect of Habsburg piety (*pietas Austriaca*), in addition to the veneration of the Cross and Mary the Virgin, was the veneration of the Eucharist, rooted in a legend about the first Habsburg ruler in the empire, Rudolf I, who was elected in 1273. Rudolf was said to have given his hunting horse to a priest who wanted to cross a river with the Eucharist to administer the Sacrament to a dying person. On the next day Rudolf refused to take the horse back, as it had carried the body of Christ.[26]

This specific veneration of the Eucharist found many expressions in Habsburg tradition, but the most visible was the Corpus Christi festival. Many Habsburg rulers since Charles V, who participated in a Corpus Christi procession as early as 1530, openly demonstrated their veneration of the Eucharist by taking part in this solemn ritual. It was not so much in the sixteenth century, when many of the subjects of the Austrian Habsburg-ruled countries were Protestants, but later in the baroque period that it became a duty for a Habsburg ruler to participate in the procession, walking in the immediate vicinity of the monstrance. The tradition of the ruler walking directly behind the Eucharist was carried on not only until 1918, but is still continued today, as all Austrian presidents — with the exception of the socialist atheist ones — have imitated the role of the God-like ruler and participated (and continue to participate) in the Corpus Christi procession.[27]

There is no specific decorative element in this festivity — no fancy dress, no artistic decoration, no triumphal arches (though there is a series of Gobelin tapestries in Madrid, 'The Triumph of the Eucharist', based on Rubens's paintings); on the contrary, the ruler displayed his modesty by walking with an *armselig Kranz von Rosen*, a pitiful crown of roses on his head like any other person, demonstrating his humility in the face of God. Symbols like these were

---

26 Coreth, *Pietas Austriaca*, pp. 18ff.
27 U. Kammerhofer-Aggermann, 'Quellenvergleich zu den Fronleichnamsprozessionen in den Städten Graz und Salzburg vor und nach der Reformationszeit. Die Rolle der Corporis-Christi Bruderschaften in der Fronleichnamsprozession', *Volksfrömmigkeit, Referate der österreichischen Volkskundetagung*, Graz, 1989 (= *Buchreihe der österreichischen Zeitschrift für Volkskunde*, Neue Folge, 8, Vienna, 1990), pp. 267–83.

intended to influence the entire population — not only the élites — in the process of the Counter-Reformation which emphasized the sacraments, the interpretation of which was finally settled by the Catholic Church in the Council of Trent in the 1560s.

For future research on festivities in the context of the Habsburg Empire more attention needs to be paid to religious festivities. The ambiguity of the God-like Habsburg ruler, on the one hand, and the religious humble Habsburg, on the other, cannot be understood by studying court festivals alone. Tensions within Baroque culture are an intrinsic element of this culture itself, and without a closer examination of this bi-polarity our understanding of the festivals of the early modern period will remain a very limited one.

'FOUR WEDDINGS AND A FUNERAL': FESTIVAL FORMS AND DYNASTIC CONSOLIDATION IN DUCAL LORRAINE 1563–1624

Kate Currey

Court historians, and especially historians of court festival, have long been aware of the function of court spectacle in promulgating the power of rule.[1] Festival has come to be seen no longer as mere diversion, but as an active component of government. Many recent studies have concentrated chiefly upon festival symbolism in order to interpret the underlying message of control.[2] Others adopt a 'total' approach, where every possible aspect of the festal event is recreated, often through the production of facsimile editions of festival texts and even, in one case, televisation.[3]

---

[1] A representative expression of this attitude comes from Jean Marie Apostolidès, 'le spectacle est une nécessité intrinsèquement liée à l'exercice de pouvoir': *Le Roi-machine. Spectacle et politique au temps de Louis XIV*, Paris, 1981, p. 8.

[2] For an excellent example of this type of study, see Steven N. Orso, *Art and Death at the Spanish Habsburg Court: The Royal Exequies for Philip IV*, Columbia, MO, 1989.

[3] See, for example, V. E. Graham and W. McAllister Johnson, *The Paris Entries of Charles IX and Elisabeth of Austria*, Toronto, 1978. The 1589 wedding *intermezzi* for Christina of Lorraine and Ferdinando de Medici were televised in December 1990: see *Una Stravaganza dei Medici. The Florentine Intermedi of 1589*, Channel 4 Television, London, 1990.

However, festival forms are as, if not more, important than festival symbolism in conveying the ruler's intentions. As with festival symbolism, much research has been undertaken as to how festival forms were deployed in this way. Forms associated with royal ceremonial such as entries and funerals have attracted particular attention, as there the relationship between the form and its function has been assumed to be self-evident.[4] Valuable work has also been undertaken on the vogue for certain types of courtly entertainment such as ballets or chivalric spectacle.[5]

Even more recently, Peter Burke has demonstrated that Louis XIV's court propagandists self-consciously deployed a range of media forms to transmit an integrated message of political power.[6] I will undertake something similar here in relation to festival forms deployed by the dukes of Lorraine between 1563 and 1624. It would seem that Charles III of Lorraine (1559–1608) fostered those festival forms which supported his aspirations towards his duchy's royal status. It can be argued that royal France (which had already monopolized those forms conventionally associated with the representation of power) was Charles III's chief template. Indeed, he had direct experience of French court life, having spent his adolescence there during the troubled period of Lorraine's regency in the 1550s 'dans un climat favorable à l'absolutisme'.[7]

---

[4] French royal ceremonial has been subject to close attention. On French royal entries, in addition to *The Paris Entries* cited in note 3, see L. M. Bryant, *The King and the City in the Parisian Royal Entry Ceremony: Politics, Ritual and Art in the Renaissance*, Geneva, 1986. On funerals, see R. E. Giesey, *The Royal Funeral Ceremony in Renaissance France*, Geneva, 1960.

[5] On ballet, see Margaret McGowan, *L'Art du ballet de cour en France*, Paris, 1963. On chivalric spectacle, see Helen Watanabe O'Kelly, *Triumphall Shews: Tournaments at the German-speaking Courts in their European Context, 1560–1730*, Berlin, 1992.

[6] Peter Burke, *The Fabrication of Louis XIV*, New Haven, CT and London, 1992.

[7] After the death of Duc François, a quarrel developed between his widow, Christine de Denmark, and her brother-in-law, Nicolas, Comte de Vaudémont, who feared that Christine would involve the Empire in the dispute. The simplest solution was to remove the young Charles III: see Paulette Choné, *Emblèmes et pensée symbolique en Lorraine (1525–1633)*, Paris, 1991, p. 132, n. 12.

Festival Forms and Dynastic Consolidation in Ducal Lorraine 1563–1624

I am not the only scholar who believes that Charles III wished to emulate royal France through his fostering of festival forms.[8] Charles III was married to Claude de France, daughter of Catherine de' Medici and King Henri II in 1559. This appears to have been a policy designed to bring Lorraine closer within the orbit of French control. Its longer-term outcome would seem to have had the opposite effect. Instead, Charles III, aware of the fissures developing in the Valois dynasty, nurtured the ambition of acquiring the French throne for his eldest son and heir, Henri, Marquis du Pont, who was born in 1563.[9]

In the remainder of this chapter, I will analyse a range of festival forms in vogue at the court of Nancy during the reigns of Charles III (1563–1608) and Henri II (1608–24). These include forms associated with ceremonial moments in the life of the dynasty, such as pastoral, entries and funerals. They also include forms of court entertainment such as theatre, ballets and chivalric spectacle. In each case, the choice of form conveyed a message of political intent which was just as important of the symbolic content of these festivals. Forms can be valuable referents. This is because the festival culture of Europe's early modern courts centred not just upon the transmission of symbolism, but also of form. It was the exchange of form which led to fundamental changes in Lorraine's festival traditions. Therefore, what also emerges from this chapter is a sense of changing taste in festivals at the court of Lorraine during the successive reigns of Charles III and Henri II.

Let me begin this survey of festival forms by looking more closely at pastorals. This form often conveyed a subtext of governance and control, where the figure of the ruler symbolized the Good Shepherd.[10] Baptismal ceremonies marking births in

---

8 Choné, Giesey and Rothrock feel that it is possible to infer a French influence upon Charles III. Indeed, the latter comments that 'we must assume the interchange of ideas' occurred between the two: see O. R. Rothrock, 'Jacques Callot and Court Theatre (1608–1619): Studies in Court Theatre and its Printed Propaganda in the Background of Callot's Artistic Individuality', unpublished PhD dissertation, Princeton University, 1987, p. 28.

9 For an account of Charles III's designs upon the French throne, see L. Davillé, *Les Prétentions de Charles III à la couronne de France*, Paris, 1909.

10 On the political function of pastoral, see Luigi Monga, *Le Genre pastoral au XVIe siècle: Sannazar et Belleau*, Paris, 1974.

the house of Lorraine occurred with relative frequency between 1563 and 1624.[11] Although pastorals were popular at courts with which Lorraine had contact, there it was deployed just twice across the period; once in 1564 for the birth of Charles III's heir, Henri, Duc de Bar in 1564 and again in 1602 for that Henri, Marquis d'Hattonchatel. The latter was heir to Charles III's younger son, François, Comte de Vaudémont. This could suggest that the pastoral genre had been deliberately chosen to celebrate the birth of ducal heirs. The existence of published accounts referring to each occasion also seems to confirm their importance.[12]

The christening celebrations at Bar-le-Duc in May 1564 are remarkable for the presence and close involvement of the French court. Superficially, this was simply a family celebration, but Catherine de' Medici was using the event as a staging post on her strategic tour of France with the future Charles IX.[13] Speculation has also taken place as to whether the French presence in Lorraine marked an attempt at territorial expansion similar to King Henri II's German expedition of 1552 which resulted in the occupation of the bishoprics of Metz, Toul and Verdun.[14] Relations between Lorraine and France gradually disintegrated in the latter half of the sixteenth century. The strongly French presence at the 1564 christening was intended to remind Charles III that his duchy was a French satellite, as Bar-le-Duc was partly under royal control.[15]

Something of this political undercurrent may be inferred from the treatment of the 1564 christening in Belleau's *Bergerie*. Belleau was a French court poet and member of the *Pléiade*, which also included Ronsard. In a normal festival account,

---

11 As recorded by C. Chapellier, 'Dates des naissances, morts et mariages de plusieurs princes et princesses de Lorraine', *Journal de la Société d'Archéologie de Lorraine*, 1876, pp. 108–18.

12 These are Rémy Belleau, *La Bergerie* (Paris, 1565), reprint, ed. Doris Delacourcelle, Geneva, 1954, and Nicolas Romain, *La Salmée: Pastorelle comique ou fable bocagère*, Pont-à-Mousson, 1602.

13 For an account of this expedition, see J. Boutier, A. Dewerpe and D. Nordman, *Un tour de France royal: Le Voyage de Charles IX (1564–66)*, Paris, 1984.

14 Ibid., pp. 74–75.

15 On the right bank of the river Meuse, Bar was subject to the dukes of Lorraine (the *Barrois non-mouvant*). On the left bank, it was subject to France (the *Barrois mouvant*).

the event of central importance is the subject of the text.[16] This is not the case with the *Bergerie*. Instead, the celebrations at Bar are subsumed within a narrative structure which relocates them to the Guise family seat at Joinville. The occasion has been uprooted from its native soil and transplanted to the French court. The intention here is quite clear. Through its treatment in the *Bergerie*, the birth of an heir to Charles III is played down and absorbed as an event of marginal importance to the French court.

The essential difference between Romain's *Salmée* and the *Bergerie* is that the former has an exclusive connection with the court of Lorraine. In a verse prelude to the piece, Romain acknowledges his cultural debt to the poets of the *Pléiade*.[17] However, he is at pains to point out that he is a Lorrainer and a very different product from his French counterparts. Romain is celebrating an event which he regards as of central importance to the duchy of Lorraine, not a mere dynastic sideshow at the Valois court. Yet was the birth of an heir to Charles III's younger son, François, Comte de Vaudémont, an event of such dynastic significance that it warranted evocation through a pastoral? Perhaps not, but the event alluded to another of greater potential danger to Lorraine, the fact that the marriage of Charles III's heir, Henri, Marquis du Pont, to Catherine de Bourbon, sister of King Henri IV of France, was childless. It could be argued that both the *Bergerie* and *Salmée* are imbued with dynastic rivalry. Whilst the former attempts to contain a potentially disloyal satellite, the latter plays up the rivalry which could undermine Lorraine's entire ducal dynasty. It shows that a festival form, such as that of the pastoral, can be used to draw deliberate parallels between political occurrences. Here, the birth of an heir to François de Vaudémont far surpasses that of Henri, marquis du Pont.

Of all festival forms, perhaps entries articulate the message of the ruler's supremacy with the greatest force. This is certainly the case with entries staged in Nancy, Remiremont and Metz during the late sixteenth and early seventeenth

---

16 For a useful survey of the festival literature genre, see Helen Watanabe O'Kelly, 'Festival Books in Europe from the Renaissance to the Rococo', *The Seventeenth Century*, 3, 1988, pp. 181–201.

17 Romain, *La Salmée*, p. 15

centuries.[18] Ducal investitures provided a pretext for entries to Nancy, but the form was not imbued with any particular political symbolism in the period prior to the reign of Charles III.[19] However, Charles III's investitural entry was a radical departure from the norm. It was postponed until 1562 because Charles refused to accept the limitations which the wording of the oath imposed upon his powers.[20]

The issue of Charles III's exposure to royal propaganda at the French court has already been raised. It is tempting to see his reluctance to accede to the demands of ceremonial form as evidence of this. The Nanceian entry of 1562 is not the only case of Charles III tampering with the entry form for his own ends. This also occurred over Charles's 1579 entry to the abbey town of Remiremont in the Vôsges, which was the scene of a sovereignty dispute between Lorraine and the Empire.[21] Charles asserted his rather than the Empire's authority over the town by altering the wording of the oath. He proclaimed himself its *souverain* rather than its *gardien*.[22] Surely these changes to accepted ceremonial form show Charles III's determination to make the entry suit his aims as a proto-absolutist ruler.[23]

Other entries staged in Lorraine during this period fit the typology of the civic triumph examined in a recent study by Gordon Kipling.[24] One such occasion was the entry staged by the Nanceian municipality in 1606 to celebrate the marriage of Margherita Gonzaga to Henri, duc de Bar. Several factors make this entry a

---

18 On ducal entries in the later seventeenth century, see Chantal Humbert, 'Décorations éphémères et thème dynastique à la cour de Lorraine (1650–1736)', *Le Pays Lorrain*, 1980, pp. 125–58.

19 This took the form of a religious ceremony and an oath solemnizing the bond between the Duke and his subjects.

20 See Choné, *Emblèmes*, p. 132, n. 12.

21 For more on ducal entries to Remiremont, see Bernard Puton, *Entrées et serments des ducs de Lorraine à Remiremont*, extract from the *Bulletin de la Société Philomathique Vosgienne*, Saint-Dié, 1888–89.

22 Ibid., p. 51

23 No doubt he was comparing his situation with the duchies of Burgundy or Brittany, whose 'power at times equalled that of the king': see J. H. Burns, 'The Idea of Absolutism' in John Miller (ed.) *Absolutism in Seventeenth Century Europe*, Basingstoke and London, 1990, pp. 1–20, p. 3.

24 Gordon Kipling, *Theatre, Liturgy and Ritual in the Medieval Civic Triumph*, Oxford, 1998, p. 4.

politically important event. One was that its focus was the duchess, not the duke. Another was that the traditional form of the investitural entry had an elaborate symbolic programme grafted onto it.[25] The entry's political message was the hoped-for continuation of the ducal dynasty through the birth of heirs, especially given the death of the groom's infertile first wife, Catherine de Bourbon in 1604.

Nanceian entries continued to evolve throughout the reign of Henri II. Although his investitural entry to Nancy in April 1610 retained its traditional form, that staged by the city authorities to celebrate his survival of an assassination attempt that May was significantly different. This difference was mainly expressed in the added accretion of symbolic detail to convey ducal authority. Despite this, the form of the entry was largely unaltered.[26]

A reference has been made to civic entries in the context of ducal Lorraine. They were also a consistent presence in French-ruled Metz, staged in 1587, 1603 and 1624 respectively. Perhaps the most important of these occasions was the 1603 entry held for the visit of Henri IV of France and Marie de' Medici.[27] In my view, the consistent deployment of a form expressive of royal authority on contested Lorraine territory would have made Charles III all the more determined to bolster his own ducal authority. Whilst Messin entries concerned that city's loyalty to France, those of Lorraine reinforced the duchy's political independence, symbolized by its adoption of quasi-royal ceremonial form.

Funerals gave dynasties another opportunity to celebrate their continuity. The artificial decor of funeral trappings, whether family trees, *chapelles ardentes* or effigies, attempted to forge permanence from a mortal ruler's achievements.[28] Much of their symbolism is focused upon the genealogical origins and continuity of

---

25 For more on the symbolism of this occasion, see Choné, *Emblèmes*, pp. 161–69.
26 Ibid., p. 161.
27 A primary account of this event exists: see Abraham Fabert, *Voyage du Roy à Metz*, Metz, 1610.
28 For example, poems were written which mimicked 'tombs': see Madeleine Maurel, 'Fastes mortuaires et déploration: Essai sur la signification du baroque funèbre dans la poésie française', *XVIIe Siècle*, 82, 1969, pp. 36–64.

Europe's ruling houses.[29] Charles III's elaborate 1608 obsequies epitomize this type of dynastic emulation. As Giesey convincingly argues, the funerals of royal France were their likely model.[30] In the case of funeral, this process had begun as early as the late fifteenth century. It can be regarded as the longest standing evidence of the quasi-royal aspirations of the rulers of Lorraine.

Nanceian court funerals demonstrate how a festival form with an established pedigree was introduced and adapted to fit the requirements of a ducal rather than royal dynasty. The essential difference was seen in the adaptation of ritual and the symbolic echo of French royal funeral at the event's climax. Here the *héraut d'armes* made the triple pronouncement: 'Le Duc est mort, son Corps est icy inhumé, et ses cerimonies [...] sont accomplies'.[31] The final phase in the ritual was the ceremonial disbanding of Charles III's household, symbolized by the breaking of its *Grand Maistre*'s baton of office.[32]

If one is to follow Kantorowicz's 'two bodies' model, royal power was continuous and undying.[33] That of ducal rulers died with them and had to be reactivated in the person of the ruler's heir. It was customary for ducal heirs to attend their predecessor's funeral as a substitute for a later coronation ritual. At royal funerals, heirs were not present and celebrated their accession at their coronation. Ironically, all of Charles III's deployment of devices imitative of French ritual (such as his effigy) could not alter this essential point of difference between royal and ducal power.

It cannot be denied that Charles III's death ended a period of political stability for his duchy. None the less, his funeral stressed the continuation of effective government even after his death. Perhaps Charles III's funeral overemphasized his

---

29 On the genealogical preoccupations of early modern rulers, see Marie Tanner, *The Last Descendant of Aeneas: The Hapsburgs and the Mythic Image of the Emperor*, New Haven, CT and London, 1993.

30 See Giesey, *Royal Funeral*, and also his *Cérémonial et puissance souveraine*, Paris, 1987, where the relationship between ducal and royal funeral ceremony is discussed in more detail.

31 Claude de La Ruelle, *Discours des cérémonies*, Nancy, 1609, p. 198.

32 Ibid., pp. 204–05.

33 For more on this, see E. H. Kantorowicz, *The King's Two Bodies: A Study in Medieval Political Theology*, Princeton, NJ, 1957.

Festival Forms and Dynastic Consolidation in Ducal Lorraine 1563–1624

indispensability for Lorraine. Its projection of an idealized image of ducal power along, as it were, royal lines, was one with which Charles III's heir was unable to compete. Charles III's obsequies had a dual perspective. First, they allowed Charles III to convey a political message to contemporary courts; that his emulation of royal France was a metaphor for his duchy's powers. Secondly, they were the creation of court functionaries who owed their existence to the court, and who were the architects of their ruler's image.[34]

Courtly entertainment could also be exploited for its message of dynastic consolidation. In the remainder of this chapter I will assess the part played by theatre, ballet and chivalric spectacle in projecting this message. Theatre is distinct from these other forms in that it was not explicitly generated within the court context. Its presence was externalized, represented by the presence of itinerant theatre groups at the court and the dramatic repertoire at the Jesuit university of Pont-à-Mousson. Primary evidence suggests that theatre in sixteenth-century Lorraine developed in tandem with that of France.[35] Classical tragedy was taking the place of mystery plays as the more popular dramatic form. Regular references also occur to an awareness in the duchy of the current French theatrical repertoire, including works by Gringoire, Garnier and Jodelle.[36]

It is Lorraine's Jesuit theatre which is seen to have supplied the intermediate developmental phase between late medieval religious drama and classical theatre proper.[37] Whilst Jesuit theatre shared the didactic message of mystery plays, it also possessed many of the characteristics of the newly emerging French tragic form; rhetorical dialogue, minimal staging and the deployment of a chorus.[38] Scholars have argued that the duchy's native classical tragedy evolved from a fusion of the separate theatre traditions of the Nanceian court and the Jesuit University. It was

---

34 See Burke, *Fabrication*, ch. 4, 'The Construction of the System', pp. 49–59.
35 Archives départementales de Meurthe-et-Moselle, B1175, B1206 etc., cited in Kate Currey, 'The Political and Social Significance of Court Festivals in Lorraine 1563–1624', DPhil dissertation, University of Sussex, 1996, p. 246, n. 110.
36 Alain Cullière, 'La Vie culturelle en Lorraine dans la seconde moitié du XVIe siècle', PhD dissertation, Université de Nancy II, 1978, p. 332.
37 Ibid., p. 333.
38 Ibid.

ducal patronage of the university which provided the contextual link between the two settings.[39]

The bridging of these separate spheres is exemplified in the career of Nanceian court officer and author Nicolas Romain. Romain (the aforementioned author of the pastoral *Salmée*) was educated at the university and thence pursued a career as court functionary in the household of Charles III's younger son, François, comte de Vaudémont.[40] Romain's literary output shows explicit connections to the dramatic genres current both at the university and in Europe. His play *Maurice* (1606) borrows the themes and subject-matter of a typical Jesuit drama.[41] In deference to his ducal patron, Romain adopts a less didactic style, more likely to appeal to a courtly audience reared on popular French tragedy. As has already been discussed, Romain's *Salmée* showed his ability to adapt a current genre to suit local circumstances.

Court ballet came late to Nancy. It is not recorded there until 1594. This seems at odds with the fact that ballet was already well established at two courts with which Nancy had regular contact: Florence and France.[42] Music and informal dance, the 'raw ingredients' of ballet, if you like, were already in vogue at Nancy, so how can we explain ballet's late appearance? One reason could be the early death (in 1574) of Charles III's wife, Claude de France. This could well have inhibited the further development of ballet, which she might otherwise have influenced through her participation.

Another theory is that the adoption of ballet at the court of Lorraine reflected Charles III's cultural competition with Europe's other courts.[43] One of the main elements of Charles III's policy were the marriages he brokered for his many children. These in turn influenced the cultural life of the Nanceian court. For example, the marriages of his heir Henri to Catherine de Bourbon (1599) and Margherita Gonzaga (1606) brought to Nancy their experience of court ballet. Both were to play an active part in developing ballet at Nancy.

---

39 Ibid., p. 332.
40 For more on Romain's career, see Currey, 'The Political and Social Significance', p. 317.
41 On Jesuit drama, see W. H. McCabe, *An Introduction to Jesuit Theater*, Missouri, MO, 1983.
42 Choné, *Emblèmes*, p. 181.
43 Ibid.

Festival Forms and Dynastic Consolidation in Ducal Lorraine 1563–1624 147

Ballet none the less declined in popularity after 1616.[44] This could be due to the fact that it was a late addition to the court's festival repertoire. Several other factors have been offered to explain this fact. One is that the death of court artist Jacques de Bellange deprived Lorraine's ballet of one of its greatest exponents.[45] Another view is that ballet was too expensive.[46] Expensive chivalric entertainments, however, were still staged throughout this period. It is more likely that the decline of ballet relates to the fact that the popularity of music was also waning at this time.[47]

The cultural climate of the court altered during the reign of Henri II. It favoured chivalric spectacle rather than ballet.[48] This could have been dictated by the social composition of the court, dominated as it was by a group of court favourites led by Louis de Guise, Baron d'Ancerville. Whilst this group had participated in court ballets during their youth, their mature taste appears to have leaned more towards military festivals than dance.[49]

This brings me on to chivalric festival which, at the court of Nancy, was popular throughout the sixteenth and mid-seventeenth centuries. Different forms abounded, including jousts, tilts, running at the ring, horse combats, foot combats and carousels.[50] This taste for chivalric spectacle was on a par with the rest of Europe — with the possible exception of jousts, restricted in France after Henri II died after taking part in such a contest in 1559.[51] Tilts declined in popularity after 1618, although an engraving by Jacques Callot depicts an example held between 1628–29.[52] References to foot combats occur in the Nanceian archives after 1585 and to

---

44 Ibid., p. 192.
45 See Currey, 'The Political and Social Significance', p. 289, n. 68.
46 Choné, *Emblèmes*, p. 192.
47 See René Depoutot, 'La Musique à la cour de Lorraine au temps de Jacques Callot' in *L'Art en Lorraine au temps de Jacques Callot* (ed. Musée des Beaux-Arts, Nancy), Paris, 1992, pp. 119–29 (p. 119).
48 Choné, *Emblèmes*, p. 193.
49 Archives départementales de Meurthe-et-Moselle, B 1388.
50 Currey, 'The Political and Social Significance', p. 291, n. 83.
51 A. Young, *Tudor and Jacobean Tournaments*, London, 1987, pp. 16–17.
52 O'Kelly, *Triumphall Shews*, p. 18.

running at the ring after 1591.[53] Funeral orations written for Charles III in 1608 mention his youthful participation in one form, the 'courir à bague'.[54] That carousels at the court of Nancy reflected European trends is reflected by archival references to competing teams and thematic structures in 'tournois' and 'caroselles' of 1564, 1595, 1614 and 1616.[55] The 1627 *Combat à la Barrière* was a large-scale carousel with an elaborate symbolic programme. This indicates that Nancy's chivalric forms were as flourishing as any others in Europe.

As I hope to have demonstrated here, festival forms at Nancy can be examined as an index to gauge the political intentions of Charles III and Henri II. Lorraine was not a cultural backwater; rather its cultural traditions developed in active response to European trends. Some of its festival forms were the mainstays of courtly celebration, such as ballet and chivalric spectacle. Others, such as theatre, existed outside the court context, but were in regular contact with it. Even entertainment could articulate a message of supremacy. For example, ballets echoed Valois tradition; chivalry represented the duchy's competitive Catholic militancy; and theatre underscored the close ties between the court and the Jesuits of Pont-à-Mousson.

Other forms punctuated the lives and reigns of Lorraine's rulers: pastoral, entries and funeral. Indeed, the rarity of the pastoral form at the court highlighted the political impact of the births of its heirs as fêted in Belleau's *Bergerie* and Romain's *Salmée*. The most striking changes occurred to entries and funeral, those forms associated with the continuity of rule. Under Charles III and his publicists, both forms became vehicles for a wider public and international message: that of the duchy's political supremacy. This policy originated with Charles III's experience of French royal festivals and his own dissatisfaction with the ritual limitations of ducal investitures. Charles III fostered festival form's role as the bearer of his political intention, a function which was hitherto monopolized by symbolism, an artificial emphasis, which I hope this chapter has helped (in some part) to redress.

---

53 See note 50 above.
54 Léonard Périn, *Oraisons funèbres*, Pont-à-Mousson, 1608, p. 26.
55 Young, *Tudor and Jacobean Tournaments*, p. 22.

THE PETRINE YEAR: ANNIVERSARIES AND FESTIVALS IN THE REIGN OF PETER I (1682–1725)

Lindsey Hughes

The reign of Peter the Great of Russia forms a watershed in Russian history which is associated with a number of transitions, both real and constructed: from isolated 'Eastern' tsardom to major 'Western' power, from religious to secular, from Moscow to St Petersburg. Peter's contemporaries often employed metaphors which suggested that Russia was 'created' in Peter's reign: in a speech at the celebrations for the peace of Nystadt between Russia and Sweden in 1721, for example, the chancellor Gavrila Golovkin declared that Peter had brought Russia from 'nothingness into being [*iz nebytiia v bytie*]', while Archbishop Feofan Prokopovich's oration at Peter's funeral in 1725 included the image of Peter 'giving birth' to Russia.[1] In the process of creating the new Russia (like Pygmalion carving out Galatea), Peter changed concepts of time, transferring his country to the same time-scale as much of the rest of Europe and propagating ideas of

---

1   Golovkin's speech in *Polnoe Sobranie Zakonov Rossiiskoi Imperii*, first series, 45 vols, St Petersburg, 1830–43 (hereafter *PSZ*), VI, no. 3840, p. 445. Oration (1725) in Feofan Prokopovich, *Sochineniia*, ed. I. P. Eremin, Moscow and Leningrad, 1961, pp. 126–29. There is a translation in Marc Raeff (ed.), *Peter the Great Changes Russia*, Lexington, MA, 1972, pp. 39–43. This work, which likens Peter to Samson (strong defender of the fatherland), Japhet (creator of the fleet), Moses (law-giver), Solomon (bringer of reason and wisdom) and David and Constantine (reformer of the Church) appears to draw on the model of Lutheran funeral orations.

'catching up' and making 'progress' which would have been both unfamiliar and uncongenial to his Muscovite predecessors. Everything he did was infused with a sense of urgency. 'Thank you for your letter', he wrote to the newly formed Senate in 1711, 'and for the improvements you have made; in the future you need to work to have everything prepared well ahead of time, because wasted time, like death, cannot be reversed.'[2] It is not surprising, given this sense of haste and purpose, that the calendar did not escape Peter's attention. From the way their years were numbered to the anniversaries they were supposed to celebrate, Russians were to be reminded constantly of the Tsar-Reformer.

This chapter examines the feasts and anniversaries which were considered worthy of official celebration at court in the last years of Peter's reign. (Even Peter could not hope radically to reform the festive timetable of the mass of the population, a topic to which we shall return towards the end.) How did Peter's ritual year differ from that of his seventeenth-century predecessors? What do the differences tell us about the nature of Peter's reforms, especially with reference to the ongoing debate about the 'secularization' of Russian culture during his reign? I shall be concerned with the court's year-cycle rather than with the life-cycle of rulers. Rites of passage such as baptisms, funerals and weddings are only touched upon, as is the manner of celebration of extended festival periods such as Yuletide and Shrovetide and the wholesale adoption of classical imagery.[3]

The Muscovite court calendar, which took shape during the sixteenth century, revolved around the Orthodox liturgical year, the anniversaries of living and dead members of the royal family, selected saints' days and special anniversaries of national events, which were usually linked with the feasts of miracle-working icons

---

[2] *Pis'ma i bumagi Imperatora Petra Velikogo*, vol. XI, part 1, Moscow, 1962, p. 281 (8 June 1711).

[3] On weddings, funeral and coronations, see Richard Wortman, *Scenarios of Power: Myth and Ceremony in the Russian Monarchy, Vol. 1: From Peter the Great to the Death of Nicholas I*, Princeton, NJ, 1995, and my book *Russia in the Age of Peter the Great*, New Haven, CT and London, 1998, Chapter 8, 'The Petrine Court', pp. 248–97. Also, my articles 'Peter the Great's Two Weddings: Changing Images of Women in a Transitional Age' in R. Marsh (ed.), *Women in Russia and Ukraine*, Cambridge, 1996, pp. 31–44, and 'The Courts of Moscow and St Petersburg' in John Adamson (ed.), *The Courts of Europe During the Ancien Régime (1500–1750)* (forthcoming).

of the Mother of God (see Table 1). Different reigns saw different emphases. For example, certain saints' festivals were celebrated as name-days when royal personages were alive and were the occasion for requiem masses after their death. Tsar Aleksei (reigned 1645–76) and his son Fedor (1676–82) frequently made pilgrimages to churches and monasteries in the Moscow region and celebrated local festivals. In the regency of Sophia (1682–89), festivals associated with the Novodevichii and Donskoi convents and the name-days of royal women were prominent,[4] while in the period immediately after Sophia's overthrow Patriarch Ioakhim and his successor Adrian revived the feasts of prominent Moscow prelates.[5] As the century drew to a close, Peter's elder brother and co-tsar Ivan (1682–96), whose disabilities restricted him to a purely ceremonial role, maintained a busy timetable of public devotions,[6] but Peter was absent from the Kremlin for long periods, drilling troops, sailing and building ships and, from 1695, actively campaigning against the Turks. More and more frequently it was recorded that he 'did not deign to attend' ceremonies.[7] Prince Boris Kurakin, the future ambassador to the Dutch Republic, recorded:

> First the ceremonial processions to the cathedral were abandoned and Tsar Ivan Alekseevich started to go alone; also the royal robes were abandoned and Peter wore simple dress. Public audiences were mostly curtailed (such as were given to visiting prelates and envoys from the hetman, for which there were public processions). Now there were simple receptions.[8]

When Ivan died in January 1696, the old court calendar was already doomed, although major Kremlin services and processions were held even during Peter's

---

4   See Lindsey Hughes, 'Sophia, "Autocrat of All the Russias": Titles, Ritual and Eulogy in the Regency of Sophia Alekseevna (1682–89)', *Canadian Slavonic Papers*, 28, 1986, pp. 266–86.
5   See, for example, the palace records *Dvortsovye razriady* (*DR*), 4 vols, St Petersburg, 1852–55, IV, pp. 522–23 (Feast of Metropolitan Filipp of Moscow, 9 January 1690).
6   See ibid., pp. 839–910 (records for 1694).
7   See, ibid, p. 548: 'But the great sovereign tsar and great prince Peter Alekseevich did not go to vespers or to the liturgy in the Cathedral [*vykhodu ne bylo*]'.
8   B. A. Kurakin, 'Gistoriia o tsare Petre Alekseeviche' (written in the 1720s) in N. I. Pavlenko (comp.), *Rossiiu podnial na dyby*, 2 vols, Moscow, 1987, I, pp. 381–82.

absence abroad in 1697–98.[9] The old cycle of rituals was more or less killed off when Patriarch Adrian breathed his last in October 1700 and Peter failed to appoint a successor. The Byzantine-inspired 'symphony' of Church and tsardom expired with Adrian and with it the basic ideological underpinnings of the Muscovite court year which relied upon this ancient partnership.

For all Peter's reputation for being a 'great contemner of all pomp and ostentation about his own person',[10] thereafter it was a case of new ceremonial rather than no ceremonial. Some thirty special anniversaries were added to the court calendar during Peter's reign, although not all were celebrated with the same pomp or regularity (see Table 2).[11] At the same time, the number of church festivals celebrated *publicly* was reduced to about twenty. Lesser religious feasts, including most Russian and Byzantine saints' days, disappeared from the public calendar, although they continued to be honoured, as appropriate, in churches and monasteries. Those demoted included all the feasts of Russian prelate saints such as the metropolitans of Moscow Filipp, Petr and Aleksei and the first patriarch, Iov, all of whom provided unwelcome reminders (to Peter) of the Church's once powerful political role.[12] Certain largely devotional (although politically and

---

9   *DR*, IV, pp. 1048–53 (1697), a list of secular personnel designated to attend ceremonies during Peter's absence, provides a good indication of the festivals which were given prominence at this late date: 1 September, 1 October, 22 October, 6 January, Easter week and the week following, *prepolovenie*, 21 May, 23 June, 8 July, 11 July, 20 July, 28 July, 1 August, 15 August and week preceding.

10 J.-G. Korb, *Diary of an Austrian Secretary of Legation at the Court of Czar Peter the Great*, trans. and ed. Count MacDonnell, 2 vols, 1863, reprint, London, 1968, II, p. 155.

11 See *Kalendar' ili mesiatsoslov khristianskii po staromu shtiliu ili izchisleniiu, na leto ot voploshcheniia Boga Slova 1725* (Moscow, 1724), reprinted in P. Pekarskii, *Nauka i literatura pri Petre I*, 2 vols, St Petersburg, 1862, II, pp. 625–26; also 'Reestr torzhestvennym i viktorial'nym dniam, kakie byli prazdnuemy v Sankt-Peterburge v 1723 g. s molebstviem ili bez onogo', in *Opisanie dokumentov i del, khraniashikhsia v arkhive Sviateishego Pravitel'stvuiushego Sinoda*, III, no. 394, prilozh. XLI, pp. cxix–cci; *Pokhodnye zhurnaly Petra I 1695–1726*, St Petersburg, 1853–55. For palace records in the period to 1700, see *DR*.

12 See *DR*, IV, pp. 849, 866–67 (1694), when Tsar Ivan attended liturgies for Metropolitans Filipp (8 January) and Aleksei (12 February). In the 1710s Peter instructed the secretary Ivan Iur'ev, who was compiling a *Book of Orders*, to omit episodes in which early Russian princes deferred to clergymen, consulted with church hierarchs or gave generous gifts to

Anniversaries and Festivals in the Reign of Peter I (1682–1725)   153

ideologically coloured) court rituals, which had once occupied a substantial part of the royal timetable, disappeared completely, notably the royal family's 'secret outings' (*tainye vykhody*) to visit the inmates of almshouses and prisons, formal royal processions (*shestviia*) (when several churches in the vicinity of the Kremlin might be visited) and lengthy excursions (*pokhody*) to monasteries (for example, for the feast of St Sergii on 25 September).[13] Likewise, regular services of remembrance (*panikhidy*) on the anniversaries of the deaths and name-days of deceased Romanovs, including Tsars Mikhail, Aleksei and Fedor, lapsed. Peter had long since begun to neglect such observances. In 1689, for example, he was severely criticized for missing services in memory of his brother Tsar Fedor on 27 April (requiem mass on the anniversary of his death) and 8 June (the feast of his patron, St Theodore Stratilates).[14]

The first clear break with the Muscovite calendar came in 1700, when Peter replaced the old Orthodox manner of numbering years from the creation of the world or the birth of Adam (calculated as 5509 BC) with dates from the birth of Christ. He adopted the Julian or Old Style calendar (which was still in use in a number of Protestant countries, including England), decreeing that the year would begin on 1 January rather than 1 September. Muscovite New Year was a strictly religious occasion, when tsar and patriarch walked in a procession of crosses and icons in the Kremlin and pious speeches were delivered.[15] Along with a number of other traditions, these rituals had begun to fall into disuse in the later 1690s, especially during Peter's absence on his Grand Embassy to the West in 1697–98. In the words of the Imperial Secretary Johannes Korb, after the Tsar's return the

---

churches and monasteries: see D. Serov, *Stepennaia kniga redaktsiia Ivan Iur'eva (1716–1718 gg.)*, dissertation abstract, Leningrad, 1991, pp. 15–16.

13 See O. G. Ageeva, *Obshchestvennaia i kul'turnaia zhizn' Peterburga I chetverti XVIII v.*, dissertation abstract, AN SSSR Institut istorii, Moscow, 1991, pp. 16–17. On the political underpinnings of royal outings, see Nancy S. Kollmann, 'Pilgrimage, Procession and Symbolic Space in Sixteenth-Century Russia' in Michael S. Flier and Daniel Rowland (eds), *Medieval Russian Culture, Vol. 2* (California Slavic Studies, 19), Berkeley, Los Angeles, CA and London, 1994, pp. 163–81.

14 *DR*, IV, p. 433.

15 See, for example, the description of the New Year ritual (*deistvo novogo leta*) in September 1693 in *DR*, IV, pp. 821–23. Only Ivan attended, dressed in red velvet robes.

anniversary was 'left unrevived as things worn out and obsolete. It was considered that the worship of by-gone generations was needlessly superstitious in allowing majesty to be wrapped up with so many sacred rites'.[16]

Decrees issued on 19 and 20 December 1699 (in the year 7208, according to the old reckoning) declared that not only many European Christian nations but also Orthodox Slavic people started their year on 1 January.[17] Peter's new prescription for celebrating this 'goodly undertaking and the new century' introduced markedly secular elements alongside the usual church services.[18] In this characteristic example of 'enjoyment by decree', details were specified: festive greenery of a prescribed type was to be displayed; a public firework display on Red Square was to be complemented by better-off citizens firing celebratory salvoes from guns and muskets and letting off rockets, while poorer residents were instructed to pool their resources to provide a few flares and beacons. Protests from traditionalists that the Almighty must have created the world in autumn when there was an abundance of produce and clement weather for the first man and woman were brushed aside. Oddly, palace records include an entry for the celebration of a mass for the new year on 1 September 1700, to which Peter sent secular officials, who thus marked the new year for a second time,[19] but this duplication does not seem to have been repeated after Patriarch Adrian's death (on 15 October 1700). Die-hards continued to gather in secret to celebrate on 1 September, however; pro-government churchmen, on the other hand, often used 1 January to issue patriotic New Year's resolutions.[20]

---

16 Korb, *Diary*, I, p. 159. Korb was in Moscow for 1 September 1698.
17 *PSZ*, III, no. 1735, pp. 680–81; ibid., no. 1736, pp. 681–82; I. A. Zheliabuzhskii, 'Zapiski' in A. B. Bogdanov (ed.), *Rossiia pri tsarevne Sof'e i Petre*, Moscow, 1990, pp. 281–83. A foretaste of these edicts appears in a personal order (*ukaz*) of 17 November 1699 which includes the instruction: 'The year is to be written from the birth of Christ in all business matters' (*PSZ*, III, nos. 1735, 1718, p. 671).
18 On the latter, see *DR*, IV, p. 1111.
19 Ibid., p. 1155.
20 H.-F. de Bassewitz, 'Zapiski grafa Bassevicha, sluzhashchie k poiasneniia nekotorykh sobytii iz vremeni tsarstvovaniia Petra Velikogo (1713–1725)', *Russkii arkhiv*, 3, 1865, p. 237. See Archbishop Feofilakt Lopatinskii's sermon in the Dormition Cathedral in 1722, on the theme of the peace with Sweden, in V. P. Grebeniuk (ed.), *Panegiricheskaia literatura petrovskogo vremeni*, Moscow, 1979, pp. 255–64.

The next important date in the Petrine calendar — Epiphany on 6 January — shows that some traditions proved remarkably resilient, albeit with a modern update. On this date sixteenth- and seventeenth-century tsars customarily attended the blessing of the waters by the patriarch on the banks of the Moskva river below the Kremlin, at a spot designated as the 'Jordan'. In Peter's time the tone of the proceedings began to change from religious to military. In 1699, for example, men of the Preobrazhenskii and Semenovskii guards turned out and fired a salute.[21] The Dutch painter Cornelius de Bruyn witnessed the event in 1702, when a huge procession of clergy performed the ritual. He remarked that previously the festival had been celebrated 'with much more pomp and solemnity than at present, it having been customary for their Majesties and the Grandees of state to be present thereat'.[22] Even so, the ceremony survived to be transferred to the river Neva in St Petersburg. A German traveller witnessed it in 1711, when several thousand people attended, the minister from Hanover, F. C. Weber, in 1715 and Friedrich von Bergholz in 1722, when Peter attended as colonel of his regiment.[23] Court records for 6 January 1724 describe a late example: after matins in St Isaac's cathedral (dedicated to St Isaac of Dalmatia, whose feast falls on 30 May, Peter's birthday), the guards were drawn up and marched to the Trinity Quay near the Winter Palace, where Tsaritsa Catherine watched from a window. Peter marched at the head of the Preobrazhenskii guards in his colonel's uniform. The Tsar, Tsaritsa and their daughters attended mass in the Trinity Cathedral, 'and after mass there was a procession of the Cross to the Jordan. When the divine service at the

---

21 Zheliabuzhskii, 'Zapiski', p. 267. Another blessing of the 'Jordan' (*iordan* or *erdan*) ceremony (Procession of the Life-Giving Cross, 1 August, also associated with the baptism of Rus' in 988) received a modern update. See, for example, record for 1690 when, in addition to the Kremlin parade, Peter held his own ceremonies at Preobrazhenskoe when cannons in a mock fortress were lined up and fired, with drums and salutes: *DR*, IV, pp. 571–72.

22 Cornelius de Bruyn, *Travels into Muscovy, Persia, and Part of the East Indies; containing an Accurate Description of what is most remarkable in those Countries*, 2 vols, London, 1737, II, pp. 22–24.

23 *Exacter Relation von der ... neu erbauten Festung und Stadt St. Petersburg ... von H.G.*, Leipzig, 1713, pp. 78–79; F. C. Weber, *The Present State of Russia*, 2 vols, London, 1723, I, p. 85; F. W. von Bergholz, *Dnevnik kammer-iunkera Berkhgol'tsa, vedennye im v Rossii v tsarstvovanie Petra Velikogo s 1721–1725 g.*, part 2 (1722), Moscow, 1858, pp. 22–25,

Jordan was over, the standards of all the battalions were taken to the Jordan and sprinkled with [holy] water and there was a gun salute from the fortress, then the soldiers fired a round of rifle shots.'[24] The same ceremony was enacted a year later, just a few weeks before Peter fell ill and died.[25] It survived into the reign of Nicholas II.

Another Muscovite ritual, the Palm Sunday procession, in which the tsar on foot led a donkey bearing the patriarch across Red Square (a ceremony said to have been instituted by Emperor Constantine the Great), had already fallen into disuse when the patriarchate fell vacant in 1700.[26] Even the symbolic subservience of the secular power to the sacred was unacceptable to Peter, but echoes of Palm Sunday may be detected in Hosanna-type greetings ('Blessed is he that cometh in the name of the Lord') offered to Peter by eminent churchmen on various occasions later in his reign. The honour previously given to the patriarch was thus usurped by the tsar, while the demoted patriarch was indirectly ridiculed in mock ceremonies involving the Prince-Pope (head of Peter's All-Drunken Assembly), with pigs, bears or goats substituted for the Biblical ass.[27] Easter Week as a whole, the high point of the Muscovite liturgical calendar, was duly celebrated

---

24 *Pokhodnyi zhurnal za 1724*, pp. 30–31.

25 *Pokhodnyi zhurnal za 1725*, p. 1. See also *Sbornik vypisok iz arkhivnykh bumag o Petre Velikom*, 2 vols, Moscow, 1872, II, p. 119 (1691).

26 Entries in *DR* for 5 April 1691 (IV, pp. 398–401), 20 March 1692 (pp. 659–63), 9 April 1693 (pp. 775–79). Peter attended the last one: see Michael Flier, 'Breaking the Code: The Image of the Tsar in the Muscovite Palm Sunday Ritual' in Flier and Rowland (eds), *Medieval Russian Culture*, pp. 213–42; L. Hughes, 'Did Peter I Abolish the Palm Sunday Ceremony?', *Newsletter of the Study Group on 18th-Century Russia*, 24, 1996, pp. 62–65; Ju. M. Lotman and B. A. Uspenskij, 'Echoes of the Notion "Moscow as the Third Rome" in Peter the Great's Ideology' in Lotman and Uspenskij, *The Semiotics of Russian Culture*, Ann Arbor, MI, 1984, p. 60. Ivan Golikov records that Peter led a horse on which the prince-pope Nikita Zotov was seated: Golikov, *Deianiia Petra Velikogo*, 12 vols, Moscow, 1838, VI, p. 277.

27 See V. M. Zhivov and B. A. Uspenskii, 'Tsar' i Bog: Semioticheskie aspekty sakralizatsii monarkha v Rossii' in B. A. Uspenskii (ed.), *Iazyky kul'tury i problemy perevodimosti*, Moscow, 1987, pp. 112–15; F. W. von Bergholz, *Dnevnik kammer-iunkera Berkhgol'tsa*, 3rd edn, vol. 1 (Moscow, 1902), pp. 118–19. On the All-Drunken Assembly or Synod, see James Cracraft, *The Church Reform of Peter the Great*, London, 1971, pp. 10–19.

Anniversaries and Festivals in the Reign of Peter I (1682–1725)

throughout Peter's reign, but on a plainer and more private scale. The religious intensity which had kept his predecessors occupied day and night in devotions and elaborate processions was alien to Peter. He attended more church services than usual during Easter Week and took communion, but as far as I can ascertain he no longer participated in foot-washing ceremonies, consecrations of holy water, parades of the relics of saints or processions of crosses behind the shroud, as had his predecessors.[28]

The celebration of the first royal name-day (*imeniny* or *angel*) of the reformed year on 3 February — that of Peter's eldest daughter Anna (born 1708) — continued a Muscovite tradition.[29] In the seventeenth century the emphasis had been on religious devotions, which often occupied the whole court in two days of church services, on the eve and on the day itself. Even the more secular feasting was accompanied by the distribution of alms to the poor and receptions for clergy. In Peter's reign the devotional aspect was not lost completely, but the emphasis changed. In 1721, for example, the feast of SS Simeon and Anna was marked by a celebration of mass, a dinner, the launch of a ship and a party at the Post Office, 'where there were fireworks and a lot of rockets'.[30] Whereas at the Muscovite court, with its regimen of female seclusion, special name-day gifts of food and drink were distributed to courtiers and priests on behalf of the women, who remained in their separate apartments, in Peter's reign the royal women, dressed in the latest Western fashion, could preside over their own parties in mixed company. In the Petrine calendar the name-days of Peter, Catherine and their children were designated for public celebration (Peter's feast of SS Peter and Paul on 29 June was marked with special festivities), but not, it should be noted, the name-day of his son by his first marriage, Tsarevich Alexis (condemned to death for treason in 1718) or Alexis's children. The feast of Alexis Man of God on 17 March (also the name-day of Peter's father) was not marked once the Tsarevich fell into

---

28 See, for example, the court calendars for Easter 1720, *Pokhodnyi zhurnal za 1720*, pp. 14–15; *Pokhodnyi zhurnal za 1721*, pp. 31–32.

29 On the manner of celebration in Moscow, see G. Kotoshikhin, *O Rossii v tsarstvovanie Alekseiia Mikhailovicha*, St Petersburg, 1906, p. 18.

30 *Pokhodnyi zhurnal za 1720*, pp. 19–21.

disfavour.[31] The name-days of favoured newcomers, on the other hand, were given special prominence, as for example when Peter ordered the composition of new verses to hymns to St Catherine for his wife's name-day in 1723.[32] Peter's favourite, Alexander Menshikov, shared in the celebrations of the feast of the newly prominent St Alexander Nevskii (see below).

Birthday celebrations were a more recent phenomenon. These and other royal anniversaries (*vysokotorzhestvennye tsarskie dni*) had been marked in the seventeenth century as private family occasions, but under Peter they appeared on the official calendar along with other royal dates.[33] (His own birthday on 30 May was always an occasion for drinking and banquets.) The printed calendar for 1725 included not only the coronation of Tsars Ivan and Peter (25 June) but also Catherine's coronation in 1724 as consort (24 May) and the royal couple's wedding anniversary (19 February). In 1723 the latter celebration featured firework devices with monograms, hearts and a Cupid which flew into a temple when Peter lit the touch-paper.[34] In other words, members of the royal family were fêted as secular personalities in their own right rather than indirectly through the images and virtues of their patron saints, as had been the case during the Muscovite period.[35]

Peter clearly enjoyed the drinking, dancing and fireworks which accompanied family occasions (his harsh treatment of his eldest son notwithstanding, he was devoted to his wife and daughters), but the anniversaries closest to his heart were victory days (*viktorial'nye dni*). The nearest Muscovite equivalents were festivals for miracle-working icons, notably the annual procession of crosses and icons from the Kremlin cathedral of the Dormition to the Donskoi Convent on 19 August (marking Moscow's victory over the Tatar khan Murat Girei in 1591); that to the Cathedral of the Icon of the Kazan' Mother of God on Red Square on 22 October (the liberation of Moscow from the Poles in 1612); and the feasts of the icons of

---

31 Earlier examples of its use in *DR*, IV, p. 1125 (17 March 1700).
32 Arkhiv Leningradskogo Otdeleniia Instituta Istorii, fond 270, d. 104, 1. 123, 19 October 1723, to the Synod.
33 Ageeva, *Obshchestvennaia i kul'turnaia zhizn'*, p. 13.
34 V. I. Vasil'ev, *Starinnye feierverki v Rossii (XVII–perv. ch. XVIII v.)*, Leningrad, 1960, p. 51.
35 See discussion in Wortman, *Scenarios of Power*, pp. 62–63.

the Mothers of God of Vladimir on 23 June (Ivan III's stand-off against the Tatars in 1480) and Smolensk on 28 July (the capture of Smolensk from the Poles in 1514, commemorated by the founding of the Novodevichii Convent, the procession's destination). Despite their association with victories, the processions had a primarily religious emphasis, celebrating divine intervention in the military fortunes of the Muscovite state. Accounts make no special mention of military insignia or historical battles.[36] Under Peter, notable victories won during the Great Northern War without the intervention of miraculous images (although icons continued to be carried on campaigns) were added to the calendar (see Table 2). An edict of 18 October 1723 addressed the problem of 'when and where to fire guns for victories': 'For past victories a general salute is to be fired everywhere only for the battle of Poltava; for Lewenhaupt [Lesnaia] only in the place where the court is situated. The two naval victories [Hangö and Grenham], on the same day 27 July, are to be celebrated in Kronstadt, and all the others only in those towns which were taken on those particular dates.'[37] (In 1716 Menshikov wrote to Admiral Fedor Apraksin: 'The day after tomorrow we shall celebrate the anniversary of the naval battle at Hangut, with which I congratulate Your Excellency. May God grant you a new victory, which I wish with all my heart.')[38]

Petrine victory day anniversaries had both religious and secular elements: *ordin dukhovny* and *ordin politicheskii*. Orthodox services (which in St Petersburg were usually held in the Holy Trinity cathedral opposite the Peter-Paul fortress) were followed by a variety of parades and gun salutes, assemblies, balls and firework displays.[39] In June 1710, for example, the first anniversary of the victory at Poltava was celebrated in St Petersburg with a church service, gun salutes from the fortress and ships, a mini-regatta and fireworks followed by a feast.[40] The parades were embellished with the stock classical components of the Renaissance

---

36 See, for example, an account of the 22 October procession in 1693: *DR*, IV, pp. 829-33. Ivan presided alone: ibid. p. 895 (23 June 1694). See E. B. Mozgovaia. 'Sintez iskusstv v triumfakh pervoi chetverti XVIII veka', *Problemy sinteza iskusstv i arkhitektury*, 21, Leningrad, 1985, p. 67.

37 *PSZ*, VII, no. 4327, p. 134.

38 V. N. Berkh, *Zhizneopisanie general-admirala F. M. Apraksina*, St Petersburg, 1825, p. 89.

39 Ageeva, *Obshchestvennaia i kul'turnaia zhizn'*, p. 11.

40 Iust Iul', 'Iz zapisok datskogo poslannika Iusta Iulia', *Russkii arkhiv*, 1892, p. 9 (8 July).

advent, first seen at the triumphal procession following Peter's victory at Azov in 1696, and initially they had to be explained to a public unfamiliar with such Western-inspired spectacle. A 1704 description of triumphal gates outside the Moscow Academy stated:

> I think, Orthodox reader, you will marvel at these triumphal gates (as in past years) which are based not on divine scripture but on secular stories, not upon holy images but on secular historians or the work of versifiers [...]. You should know that this is not a temple or a church created in the name of one of the saints but has a political [*politichnaia*] meaning; this is civic praise by those who toil with their labour for the security of the fatherland.[41]

Military anniversaries were often marked by specially composed sermons and panegyrics, sometimes issued in printed pamphlets. For example, *The Key to the House of David*, a sermon composed in 1719 by Gavril Buzhinskii on the seventeenth anniversary of the capture of Schlüsselburg, explained that the latter was 'the key [*kliuch*] that opened the way to the foundation of the ruling city of St Petersburg — the key to the East Sea and North Sea'. Buzhinskii further explained that the key to the house of David was actually the word of God, thereby combining a religious message with patriotic sentiments.[42] Archbishop Feofan Prokopovich was a master of the art of rhetoric, as exemplified by his sermons on Poltava (1717) and Hangut and Grengham (1720), both of which attribute Russia's victory to the grace of God but also make 'political' points about Peter's wisdom and his solicitude for Russia's welfare.[43] New motifs combined with older Orthodox ones: on 27 July 1721, the anniversary of Hangö and the Feast of St Panteleimon, a ship named the St Panteleimon was launched.[44] (Prokopovich countered conservative protests that fleets were 'ungodly' by pointing out that

---

41 Vasil'ev, *Starinnye feierverki*, p. 25: 'siia ne sut' khram ili tserkov' v imia nekoego ot sviatykh sozdannaia, no politichnaia, si est' grazhdanskaia pokhvala truzhdaiushchimsia o tselosti otechetstva i trudy svoimi'. Variation of text in Grebeniuk, *Panegiricheskaia literatura*, p. 154. The author was Joseph Turoboiskii, rector of the Moscow Academy.
42 *Kliuch domu Davidova* (published in 1722) in ibid., pp. 91–92.
43 See Prokopovich, *Sochineniia*, pp. 48–59, 103–12.
44 *Pokhodnyi zhurnal za 1721*, p. 53.

God had created seas as a means of communication between countries and that to denounce Peter's navy was to show ingratitude to God.)[45]

The Treaty of Nystadt, which ended the Great Northern War, signed on 30 August 1721, fell into a category of its own. 'For such divine mercy we must give threefold thanks', wrote Peter, 'the first as soon as this news is received, the second on 22 October, the third on 28 January, the latter two to be carried out simultaneously all over the realm.' All three occasions were to be marked with three rounds of cannon fire.[46] Subsequently, the anniversary was fixed at 30 August and combined with the Feast of St Alexander Nevskii, the thirteenth-century prince of Novgorod who had beaten both the Swedes and the Teutonic Knights in the vicinity of St Petersburg. It is significant that in 1724 the Synod ruled that the iconographic depiction of St Alexander as a monk was to be discontinued; only the warrior-prince model was to be used, thus downgrading the monastic vows he took late in life.[47] Peter was not averse to introducing new saints' days into his calendar as long as they served his purposes. Alexander's relics were duly transferred to St Petersburg to the newly founded monastery dedicated to him.

One of the last anniversaries to be instituted was the festival of Peter's first sailing boat, the 'grandfather of the Russian navy', which was brought from Moscow to St Petersburg in 1723. In 1724 Peter ordered that the boat was to be brought out each year on 30 August, and to be kept in the Alexander Nevskii Monastery.[48] Thus victory over the Swedes, a medieval warrior-prince with Baltic

---

45 'Slovo pokhvalnoe o flote rossiiskom' (1720) in Grebeniuk, *Panegiricheskaia literatura*, p. 236; Prokopovich, *Sochineniia*, pp. 103–12.
46 'Reskripty i ukazy' in *Osmnadtsatyi vek. Istoricheskii sbornik izdannyi P. Bartenevym*, 6 vols, 1869, IV, p. 68 (Letter to Governor of Riga, 9 September 1721). On first celebrations, see *Pokhodnyi zhurnal za 1721*, p. 59. The date 22 October, it will be recalled, was the feast of the icon of the Mother of God of Kazan', traditionally associated with the liberation of Moscow in 1612 but also, earlier, with Ivan IV's conquest of Kazan'.
47 Grebeniuk, *Panegiricheskaia literatura*, p. 87. See also Wortman, *Scenarios of Power*, p. 62.
48 *PSZ*, VII, no. 4562, p. 345 (2 September 1724). On the boat, see Minna Sarantola-Weiss, 'Peter the Great's First Boat, "Grandfather of the Russian Navy"' in Maria di Salvo and Lindsey Hughes (eds), *A Window on Russia: Papers from the V International Conference of the Study Group on Eighteenth-Century Russia, Gargnano, 1994*, Rome, 1996, pp. 37–41.

connections and the foundation of the Russian navy were all linked. Shortly after Peter's death, his successor Catherine (at Menshikov's instigation) instituted the Order of Alexander Nevskii, to be issued to all the holders of the Order of St Andrew from the rank of major-general and above and worn only on St Alexander's Day, 30 August.[49]

St Andrew's Day on 30 November was given new prominence from 1699 as the feast of the knights of that order, the first to be instituted in Russia. Despite St Andrew's association with Russia through the legend of his visit to the land of Rus', his feast had not been particularly prominent in the Muscovite calendar. For Peter, however, Andrew had personal associations. In addition to being a fisherman (that is, a sailor), he was also the brother of St Peter and hence regarded as one of the Tsar's patrons, and he was no doubt also recommended to Peter by his Scottish friends Patrick Gordon and James Bruce.[50] From 1700 St Andrew's diagonal cross appeared (in blue on a white background) on regimental and naval flags, replacing the iconic symbols which decorated Muscovite military standards.

Thus Peter the Great set his personal imprint upon the shape of the Russian year as firmly as he did on the way Russians dressed. As in the case of Western fashion and shaving, which were imposed on the urban population in the period 1698–1705, the changes introduced by Peter were not merely practical or even aesthetic but also political and ideological. They reflected Peter's brand of rulership. In the words of Feofan Prokopovich:

> A sovereign monarch can lawfully command of the people not only whatever is necessary for the obvious good of his country, but indeed whatever he pleases, provided that it is not harmful to the people and not contrary to the will of God. The foundation of his power, as stated above, is the fact that the people has renounced in his favour its right to decide the common weal, and has conferred on him all power over itself: this includes civil and

---

49 Bergholz, *Dnevnik kammer-iunkera Berkhgol'tsa*, 1725, p. 87.
50 See G. Vilinbakhov, 'Otrazhenie idei absoliutizma v simvolike Petrovskikh znamen' in Vilinbakhov, *Kul'tura i iskusstvo Rossii XVIII veka*, Leningrad, 1981, pp. 15–17; idem., 'K istorii uchrezhdeniia ordena Andreia Pervozvannogo' in Vilinbakhov, *Kul'tura i iskusstvo petrovskogo vremeni*, Leningrad, 1977, pp. 144–48. Vilinbakhov argues that Andrew had the advantage over St Peter of not being directly associated with the Vatican.

ecclesiastical ordinances of every kind, changes in customs and dress, house-building, procedures and ceremonies at feasts, weddings, funerals [...].[51]

But the exercise of the sovereign will in matters of custom and tradition evoked violent protest, not least against the destruction of the traditional calendar. The following denunciation, recorded in Peter's secret chancellery, the Preobrazhenskii Prikaz, is characteristic: 'Now the counting of years in Moscow has been changed and the great sovereign has ordered Hungarian dress to be worn, and the Great Fast [Lent] in Moscow has been shortened, and after Easter Sunday it is said that they will begin to eat meat on Wednesdays and Fridays.'[52] A prevalent idea was that Peter had 'stolen' time from God. According to the old Orthodox calendar, a new century, 7200, had already begun (on 1 September 1692); thus by announcing another new century in 1700 the Tsar had 'stolen' (or perhaps lost) eight years.[53]

Some churchmen refused to celebrate new-fangled feasts. The monk Aleksei of the Alexander Monastery at Svir, for example, refused to mark Catherine's name-day on the grounds that her marriage to the Tsar was illegal. Peter, he claimed, was spiritually related (*imel dukhovnoe srodstvo*) to the Tsaritsa since her godmother at her baptism had been his sister Natal'ia Alekseevna. Hence Catherine was Peter's niece. He accused Peter and his assistants of failing to keep the fasts (a habit allegedly acquired from the 'fallen Western church of Rome'). Aleksei was defrocked, tortured and broken on the wheel in 1720.[54] The manner of celebration was also denounced by traditionalists: Peter's ungodly innovations were said to include the shaving of beards, German dress, the wearing of ribbons and loops (orders) around the neck, smoking and chewing tobacco, comedies, masquerades, feasts and balls.[55]

Despite some evidence of protest, the great mass of the population remained indifferent to or even unaware of the details of the court timetable in St Petersburg

---

51 'Justice of the Monarch's Right', in *Peter the Great: His Law on the Imperial Succession. The Official Commentary*, trans. and ed. Antony Lentin, Oxford, 1996, pp. 56–57; *PSZ*, VII, no. 4870, p. 628.
52 N. B. Golikova, *Politicheskie protsessy pri Petre I*, Moscow, 1957, p. 133.
53 E. Shmurlo, *Petr Velikii v otsenke sovremennikov i potomstva*, St Petersburg, 1912, 'Primechaniia', p. 2.
54 G. V. Esipov, *Raskol'nich'i dela XVIII stoletiia*, 2 vols, St Petersburg, 1861, II, pp. 134–55.
55 Examples taken from Shmurlo, *Petr Velikii v otsenke sovremennikov i potomstva*.

and Moscow. Both these urban centres were a giant step away from the everyday cycle of rural concerns. Just as Russian peasants went on wearing their beards and bark sandals, so they continued to observe traditional feasts and saints' days, especially feasts associated with the agricultural year (George, Nicholas, Elijah), with livestock (Koz'ma and Dem'ian), healing and fertility (Paraskeva, Anastasiia) and other areas of immediate interest to peasants.[56] Nor can it be argued that Peter *secularized* the calendar. Rather, he changed its priorities and balance, designating a more limited public sphere than previously for the Church, which now celebrated most of its festivals without the participation of the Tsar and other dignitaries and was obliged to put in an appearance with incense and choirs at such newly devised Petrine occasions as ship-launches and triumphal parades. Thus, although one can agree broadly with the idea that Petrine propaganda had 'two basic aims: to confirm new cultural values and discredit old ones', in the area of anniversaries, as elsewhere, Peter often revised and adapted old values rather than destroying them completely.[57] As a recent study of St Petersburg cultural life admits, for ideological reasons Soviet scholars all too often focused on the *new* and underplayed or excluded the *old*, especially religious aspects.[58] Ultimately, the Petrine calendar may be read as a statement of Petrine priorities and ideals: opting for a January start to the year in order to be in line with the practice of the 'many European Christian nations' with which Russia now had regular contacts; public celebration of royal anniversaries, including birthdays, to shift the emphasis from patron saints to secular individuals; 'victory days' to underline national achievements; the elevation of a new selection of saints — Andrew, Alexander, Peter and Paul — and demotion of the holy band of Muscovite prelates, especially the ones who had asserted their independent authority over monarchs. A new capital (the city of St Peter) provided a new setting and churches gained new dedications. (It is interesting how few of Peter's newly built churches were

---

56 Nobles, too, especially women outside St Petersburg, celebrated such festivals.
57 See, for example, arguments in V. M. Zhivov, 'Azbuchnaia reforma Petra I kak semioticheskoe preobrazovanie', *Uchenye zapiski Tartuskogo gos. universiteta*, vol. 720, 1986, pp. 55–66.
58 Ageeva, *Obshchestvennaia i kul'turnaia zhizn'*, p. 2: 'The study of the festive life of St Petersburg allows us to demonstrate the dualistic, contradictory character of the changes taking place there, the dualism of state policy.'

dedicated to the feasts of the Mother of God, protector of Moscow.) The reduction in the number of religious ceremonies which required the full-time royal presence reflected not so much Peter's 'impiety' as his timetable — waging wars, building ships, attending Senate, drafting legislation, travelling abroad — which was aimed more towards the service of the state (the common good) than to the worship of God, although Peter probably did not make a clear distinction between the two. Likewise his 'courtiers' spent more prolonged periods on active military service than had their predecessors, much less time performing ceremonial duties and standing or parading around in church than the boyars of old. The Tsar had cast off the heavy brocade robes which had restricted the movement of his predecessors to a dignified processional pace in favour of practical tunic and breeches, supplemented by the trappings of a Roman emperor for official images. Thus unencumbered, he led — and churchmen, who had once determined the shape and pace of the court's year, had no choice but to follow.

Table 1: The Muscovite Year

Major festivals and anniversaries celebrated at the Muscovite court in the period 1676–1700[59]

1 September	New Year's Day
8	Nativity of the Mother of God
14	Exultation of the Cross
17	St Sophia
25	St. Sergii of Radonezh (Vision of the Mother of God)
1 October	Protecting Veil of the Mother of God
22	Icon of the Kazan' Mother of God
21 November	Presentation of the Mother of God
27	Icon of the Sign of the Mother of God
6 December	St Nicholas

---

[59] Based on records in *DR*, IV. Different reigns saw different emphases: not all the above dates were celebrated every year. Requiem masses on the anniversaries of royal deaths were not always held on precisely the same dates every year. Only the name-days of ruling monarchs and consorts have been included.

21	Metropolitan Peter of Moscow
25	Christmas
6 January	Epiphany. Blessing of waters
9	Metropolitan Philip of Moscow
16/17	Requiem for Tsarevich Aleksei Alekseevich (d. 1671)
28/29	Requiem for Tsar Aleksei (d. 1676)
2 February	Presentation of Our Lord in the Temple (Candlemas)
12	Metropolitan Alexis of Moscow
15	Requiem for Tsaritsa Evdokia Luk'ianovna (d. 1645)
23	Requiem for Tsaritsa Maria Miloslavskaia (d. 1669)
February–June	Moveable feasts or fasts of Shrovetide (*miasopustnaia* or *syrnaia nedelia*), Lent (*Velikii post*), Palm Sunday (*Verbnoe Voskresenie, Vaii*); Easter week (*Strastnaia velikaia nedelia*): Maundy Thursday (*Velikii Chetvertok*, washing of feet); Good Friday (*Velikii piatkok*, parade of relics); Holy Saturday (*Velikaia Subbota*, parade of shroud); Easter Sunday (*Svetloe Khristovo Voskresenie*)
	[Week after Easter = daily processions from Dormition Cathedral to other Kremlin cathedrals and churches]
	Wednesday of the fourth week after Easter (*prepolovenie piatidesiatnitsy*); Ascension (*Voznesenie* — Thursday of sixth week after Easter); Trinity Sunday (*Troitsa, piatidesiatnitsa* — 49th day after Easter)
9–10 March	Icon of Fedorovskaia Mother of God
17	Alexis Man of God (requiem for Tsar Aleksei)
25	Annunciation
5 April	Patriarch Job of Moscow
27	Requiem for Tsar Fedor (d. 1682)
20 May	Transfer of the relics of Metropolitan Aleksei of Moscow
21	Icon of the Vladimir Mother of God (Sretenie)
	SS Constantine and Helena
8 June	St Theodore Stratilates (Fedor's nameday)
15	Metropolitan Iona of Moscow
23	Icon of the Vladimir Mother of God (procession)

24	Birth of John the Baptist
29	SS Peter and Paul (Peter's name-day)
2 July	Deposition of the Robe of the Mother of God
5	St Sergii of Radonezh
8	Icon of the Kazan' Mother of God (procession)
10	Deposition of the Robe of The Saviour in Moscow (from 1625)
11	Icon of Rzevsk Mother of God
12/13	Requiem for Tsar Mikhail (d. 1645)
20	Prophet Elijah
28	Icon of Smolensk Mother of God (procession to Novodevichii Convent)
1 August	Procession of the Life-Giving Cross (blessing of water, associated with baptism of Rus'). First day of Dormition fast
6	Transfiguration
	[Week before Dormition = daily processions of Cross]
15	Dormition of the Mother of God
16	Icon of Saviour Not Made by Hands
17/18	Requiem for Tsaritsa Evdokia Luk'ianovna
19	Icon of Don Mother of God (procession to Donskoi Monastery)
26	Martyrs Adrian and Natalia: name-day of Tsaritsa Natalia Kirillovna, Tsarevna Natalia Alekseevna
29	Beheading of John the Baptist

Table 2: The Petrine Year

Major festivals and anniversaries celebrated at the Russian court after the end of the Great Northern War (1721)

1 January	*New Year's Day (from 1700)
6	Epiphany
February/March/April	Shrovetide/Easter
3 February	*SS Simeon & Anna: name-day of Anna Petrovna
19	*Marriage of Peter and Catherine (1712)
5 April	*Catherine's birthday
7 May	*Catherine's coronation (1724)

168   Anniversaries and Festivals in the Reign of Peter I (1682–1725)

30	*Peter's birthday (St Isaac of Dalmatia)
25 June	*Coronation of Ivan and Peter (1682)
27	*Battle of Poltava (1709) (St Samson)
29	*SS Peter and Paul: name-day of Peter and his grandson
27 July	*Battles of Hangö (1714) and Grengham (1720) (St Panteleimon)
9 August	*Narva (1704) (St Matthew)
26	*St Natalia: name-day of Natalia Alekseevna (Peter's sister, d. 1716), Natalia Alekseevna (Peter's granddaughter, b. 1714), Natalia Petrovna (Peter's daughter, born 1718)
30	*St Alexander Nevskii (changed from 23 November); official anniversary of Peace of Nystadt (1721); 'Grandfather of the Russian Navy' (1723)
5 September	*St Elizabeth: name-day of Elizaveta Petrovna
28	*Battle of Lesnaia (1708) ('The Mother of Poltava')
11 October	*Battle of Nöteborg (1702)
18	Battle of Kalisz (1706)
24 November	*St Catherine: name-day of Empress Catherine; institution of Order of St Catherine (1714)
30	*St Andrew (Day of Knights of Order of St Andrew from 1699)
18 December	Birthday of Elizaveta Petrovna
25	Christmas/Yuletide

* = Included in lists of 'ceremonial, festive and victory days, which are celebrated annually' in *Kalendar' ili mesiatsoslov khristianskii po staromu shtiliu ili izchisleniiu, na leto ot voploshcheniia Boga Slova 1725* (Moscow, 1724).

THE TRANSFORMATION OF CEREMONIAL: DUCAL WEDDINGS IN BRUNSWICK, c. 1760–1800

Thomas Biskup

I

In early November 1790, Brunswick made preparations for the festivities to take place at the ceremonial entry of Prince Carl Georg August, the eldest son of Duke Carl Wilhelm Ferdinand and hereditary Prince of Brunswick, and his young wife Friederike Louise Wilhelmine of Orange. The couple returned to Brunswick from The Hague, where the wedding ceremony had taken place on 16 October, under the eyes of Friederike's father, the Dutch stadtholder William V. The marriage was, of course, a politically arranged enterprise: in 1787, Duke Carl Wilhelm Ferdinand had, in his function as a Prussian general, suppressed the revolution of the 'Dutch patriots' and saved the stadtholder's regime, which also had family links to the Duke through the wife of Prince William, a Prussian princess and cousin of Carl Wilhelm Ferdinand. The new connection between the houses of Brunswick and Orange thus renewed older family bonds. More importantly, it was the visible expression of the new pro-Prussian course steered by the stadtholder and the new coalition formed by Britain, Prussia and the Netherlands, which

---

This chapter is based on a paper given at the 1998 conference of the Society for Court Studies, London. I would like to thank Thomas Ahnert, Professor Derek Beales and Dr Joachim Whaley (all of the University of Cambridge) for their help with earlier versions of this paper.

supplanted the Dutch alliance with France that had been forged in the American War of Independence.[1]

The newly wed couple were welcomed with elaborate celebrations,[2] and the occasion spawned a vast array of pamphlets: dozens of poems and songs, sermons and books were published and all sorts of souvenirs were sold, ranging from engravings and medals to coffee cups bearing the images of the princely couple. The celebrations started on 10 November with the entry of the couple and ended after four days with a grand court *masquerade* in the opera. Sermons in the city's churches focused on the happy event and there were special meetings of associations and clubs like the Freemasons or the German Society, a meeting place for professors and students of nearby Helmstedt University.[3] The events surrounding 10 November were certainly one of the most wide-ranging public festivals that had taken place in Brunswick until then. A thousand-strong militia of burghers was specially set up to welcome the ducal couple outside the city and escort them to the palace. A number of smaller welcoming ceremonies were organized along their way, including veritable theatre scenes. The highlight was the illumination of the entire city on the evening of 13 November, which saw hundreds of houses decorated with candles, mottoes or small triumphal arches.[4]

---

[1] For the Dutch context, see J. Israel, *The Dutch Republic: Its Rise, Greatness and Fall, 1477–1806*, Oxford, 1995, pp. 1113–19; the best general history of eighteenth-century Brunswick is P. Albrecht, *Die Förderung des Landesausbaues im Herzogtum Braunschweig-Wolfenbüttel im Spiegel der Verwaltungsakten des 18. Jahrhunderts (1671–1806)*, Brunswick, 1980.

[2] Collections of all the pamphlets published on this occasion can be found in the Niedersächsisches Staatsarchiv Wolfenbüttel (NdStaWF), M 3067–3097, and Stadtarchiv Braunschweig (StaBS), H VIII B I, 131.

[3] Part of such a sermon is published in the *Braunschweigisches Magazin*, 45, 1790, pp. 665–68. The German Society held a meeting on 17 November and the Freemasons on 24 November 1790. See the printed invitation by the chairman of the German Society, F. A. Wiedenot, *Zur Feier der frohen Zurückkunft des ... Herrn Karl Georg August ... mit ... Friederike Louise Wilhelmine wird in einer öffentlichen Versammlung der Herzoglichen Deutschen Gesellschaft zu Helmstädt am 17ten November 1790 ...*, Helmstedt, 1790. For the Freemasons, see Wäterling, *Maurerische Feyer der festlichen Ankunft des Durchlauchtigsten Erbprinzen Carl Georg August und Seiner Frau Gemahlin*, Brunswick, 1790.

[4] The decorations are described in J. H. Campe, *Denkmal der Liebe eines guten Volks zu seinen guten Fürsten, oder Beschreibung des allgemeinen Volksfestes welches die Ankunft*

All these spectacles were attended by large crowds: according to one reporter, there were more than 20,000 spectators, while another even speaks of 25,000.[5] These numbers may be exaggerated, but there is abundant evidence that indeed thousands lined the streets and, moreover, took active part in one or other of the celebrations.

Nineteenth-century monarchist historians were not astonished by this response to a monarchical event. They considered them as natural expressions of the age-old attachment of the population to the ruling dynasty.[6] Modern historians, however, have tended to dismiss these and similar celebrations as 'mere propaganda' and 'false over-sentimentality'.[7] Such criticisms are not new: for example, the radical *Vormärz* poet Georg Büchner satirized royal appearances in his comedy *Leonce und Lena*, where the local authorities command the inhabitants of a backward village to welcome a royal couple. The local teacher accurately practises the difficult 'Vivat' ('One has to consider that it is Latin!'), while the bailiff admonishes the docile peasants to show the proper emotions — otherwise they would suffer the consequences.[8]

However, although much scholarly attention has been heaped on Renaissance and Baroque court festivals, on the one hand, and the bourgeois festivals of the

---

des Herrn Erbprinzen und der Frau Erbprinzessin Hochf. Durchl. zu Braunschweig veranlaßte, Brunswick, 1790, pp. 43–152; the palace was also decorated with eight spherical lamps, see NdStaWF, 2 Alt 4120, 'Vergütung für das Anzünden und Reinigen von 8 Kugellaternen auf der Schloßbalustrade in Braunschweig sowie unter den Bogen und dem dortigen Corps de Logis'.

5 Campe, *Denkma der Liebel*, p. xxxv; J. C. D. Curio, *Braunschweigs Jubel am 10ten November 1790. Bey der feyerlichen Einholung des Durchlauchtigsten Erbprinzen Carl Georg August und Seiner Frau Gemahlin der Durchlauchtigsten Prinzeßin von Nassau-Oranien Friederike Wilhelmine Louise. Als ein Andenken der treuesten Liebe dieser Stadt gegen Ihre Fürsten. Diesem sind die sämmtlichen an diesem frohen Tage erschienenen Gedichte beygefügt*, Brunswick, 1790, p. 75.

6 See, for example, O. v. Heinemann, 'Karl Wilhelm Ferdinand und die Französische Revolution' in his *Aus der Vergangenheit des Welfischen Hauses*, Wolfenbüttel, 1881.

7 R. Oberschelp, *Die Französische Revolution in Niedersachsen 1789–1803*, Hildesheim, 1989, pp. 5, 319.

8 Georg Büchner, 'Leonce und Lena', Act III, Scene 2; B. Dedner (ed.), *Leonce und Lena. Kritische Studienausgabe*, Frankfurt am Main. 1987, pp. 72–73.

nineteenth century, on the other, we know little about monarchical ceremonial in later eighteenth-century Germany and the response of the people to it.[9] Most studies dealing with the representation of the German monarchies concentrate on the so-called rise of absolutism and its heyday in the seventeenth and early eighteenth centuries. The decades after the Seven Years War are seen as a period when an exhausted *ancien régime* indulged in empty displays which had nothing to do with social reality. In this view, princely festivals lost their significance as representing the worldly hierarchy and thus became politically meaningless, though aesthetically still refined, parties.[10] One recent example of this approach is a study by Carmen Ziwes, who examined another bridal journey, the journey of Marie Antoinette from Vienna to Paris in 1770. The ceremonial which greeted the imperial princess in the city of Freiburg was, in Ziwes's words, 'without any message' and demonstrates how 'the festival culture, which was used by the absolutist state as a manifest expression of its ideology, had already faded and was further on the decline'.[11] In this view, the decline of ceremonial in the age of Enlightenment documents the erosion of absolutism, and the crisis of representation was in truth a crisis of legitimacy.

Certainly, enlightened writers did regard the pomp and circumstances of ceremonial and princely displays as superficial masquerades and a waste of resources. In Germany's 'Moral weeklies' (*Moralische Wochenschriften*) it became a commonplace to juxtapose the uprightness of a merchant burgher with the falsity of the aristocratic courtier. A new canon of values, including hard work and merit, family happiness and sociability, was propagated in the countless

---

9   For a survey of recent literature on festivals see the review article by M. Maurer, 'Feste und Feiern als historischer Gegenstand', *Historische Zeitschrift*, 252, 1991, pp. 101–30.

10 E. Straub, *Repraesentatio Maiestatis oder churbayerische Freudenfeste. Die höfischen Feste in der Münchner Residenz vom 16. bis zum Ende des 18. Jahrhunderts*, Munich, 1969, pp. 319–36.

11 C. Ziwes, 'Die Brautfahrt der Marie Antoinette 1770: Festlichkeiten, Zeremoniell und ständische Rahmenbedingungen am Beispiel der Station Freiburg' in K. Gerteis (ed.), *Zum Wandel von Zeremoniell und Gesellschaftsritualen in der Zeit der Aufklärung*, Hamburg, 1992, p. 67. Straub even links the decline of symbolic representation to the rise of an abstract notion of the state; see his *Repraesentatio Maiestatis*, p. 336.

Ducal Weddings in Brunswick, c. 1760–1800 173

periodicals and almanacs of the emerging 'public sphere'.[12] However, instead of speaking of a decline of 'representational culture' representing a crisis of the legitimation of monarchy, I should rather like to speak of a change of royal representation in the last decades of the eighteenth century.

In Brunswick, two phases in the development of ducal festivals can be distinguished: the decades before the 1770s were a period when exclusive court festivals were staged as part of a ceremonial designed to overawe the subjects and, more importantly, to gain prestige on the European stage, whereas during the 1790s court festivals were, in deed and in word, transformed into inclusive public festivals both to document and create internal stability and harmony.

II

Weddings had always played an important role as occasions for grand festivals at the Brunswick court. This was partly due to the ambitious marriage policy pursued by the dukes, and partly to the fact that for a smaller, and poorer, Protestant country which did not often see the entries of foreign rulers or ambassadors and which did not know state occasions such as coronations, weddings were a rare opportunity for the representation of ducal grandeur. In the course of the eighteenth century, Brunswick princesses became Roman empresses, queens of Prussia and England, and duchesses of Württemberg and Weimar, where Anna Amalia presided over the rise of German classicism. To mention just two particularly glamorous occasions: in 1733, Carl I, then hereditary prince, married Philippine Charlotte, daughter of Friedrich Wilhelm I of Prussia, and her brother Friedrich, the Prussian crown prince and future Friedrich II, married Carl's sister Elisabeth Christine; and in 1764, the then hereditary Prince Carl Wilhelm Ferdinand returned from his wedding in England to the British Princess Augusta. Most of these festivals took place in the summer palace of Salzdahlum that had been erected by Duke Anton Ulrich in the seventeenth century and represented

---

12 The concept of a 'public sphere' which was independent from courts goes back to Habermas, *The Structural Transformation of the Public Sphere*, Cambridge, 1989. The standard work for the 'new values' is still W. Martens, *Die Botschaft der Tugend. Die Aufklärung im Spiegel der deutschen moralischen Wochenschriften*, Munich, 1968.

one of the first German examples of a monarchical residence in the style of Versailles, well outside the ducal residence in Wolfenbüttel and the capital city of Brunswick. Consequently, the festivals were limited to the court and usually consisted of a series of church services, operas, balls and hunting parties, which were documented in representative *folio* volumes that were sent to other courts.

The entry of Carl Wilhelm Ferdinand and his wife in February 1764 — a situation almost identical with the one in 1790 — took place in the city of Brunswick, but was none the less an exclusive affair: only a small number of loyal addresses had been printed, most of which derived from ducal dependants like the Italian court poet Grattinara or the engraver Anton August Beck, who hoped to gain the title of Ducal Engraver.[13] An article in the local paper described the entry of Carl Wilhelm Ferdinand and Augusta meticulously.[14] Characteristically, the *Gazette de Brunswic* was a French paper, which reflects the dominance of French in court life and the dominance of the court in the 'public life' of 1760s Brunswick. As usual, the whole party was welcomed in tents outside the city, before entering Brunswick in a grand procession that displayed the full pomp of which a minor German prince was capable. The ducal family was distributed over eight six-in-hand carriages which were escorted by hundreds of Gardes du Corps and hussars with gold-embroidered uniforms, local nobles and court officials, ranging from the *Grand Maître de la Cour* to the more exotic *Grand Forêtier*. The crowd of locals and foreigners watching the procession was ignored almost altogether: apart from their being kept in order, they are only mentioned in one

---

13 A. A. Beck, *Braunschweigs Freude über die hohe und glückliche Vermählung Des Durchlauchtigsten Fürsten und Herrn, Herrn Carl Wilhelm Ferdinand ...*, Brunswick, 1764; D. Grattinara, *Amore Amante Serenata per le felicissime nozze di ... Carlo Giulielmo Ferdinando ...*, Brunswick, 1764. For Grattinara, see L. Ritter-Santini (ed.), *Eine Reise der Aufklärung. Lessing in Italien 1775*, Berlin, 1993, pp. 494–95. The other poems and addresses were A. S. von Goue, *Ode auf die hohe Vermählung des ... Herrn Carl Wilhelm Ferdinand ...*, Brunswick, 1764; H. C. Laue, *Als der Durchlauchtigste Fürst und Herr, Herr Carl Wilhelm Ferdinand ... mit ... Frau Augusta ... ihr Hochfürstliches Beylager vollzogen ...*, Helmstedt, 1764; C. LeBeau, *A Son Altesse Serenissime Monseigneur Charles-Guillaume-Ferdinand, Prince Hereditaire ...*, Helmstedt, 1764.

14 'Relation des Solemnités observées a Brunswic, le 21 Fevrier, & les jours suivans pour l'arrivée de S.A.R. Madame la Princesses Hereditaire', *Gazette de Brunswic*, 1764, 17, pp. 66–68.

sentence in the articles reporting on the event, as being duly 'impressed' by the entry of the new hereditary princess, which highlights the exclusive character of the 1764 celebration and reflects the baroque theory of ceremonial:[15] the court staged its ceremonial, whereas the inhabitants of Brunswick appear as passive observers, being closely observed by soldiers lest too much public joy might make a mess of the accurately arranged procession. For the court correspondents, the celebrations were successful because their stage (for example, the decorations in the palace or the opera) and their staging were 'ingénieuses & admirables': the criterion was *inventio*, the capability of 'inventing' and combining allegorical motifs in a novel way, which had been the focus of the Baroque 'art of ceremonial' and of course derives from ancient rhetoric.[16] The *peuple*, that is everything which did not belong to the court sphere, simply did not matter.

Festivals like the 1764 wedding were an essential part of the policy of dynastic ambition, which the Brunswick dukes had pursued since the seventeenth century. Duke Anton Ulrich (1671–1714) had both built up a standing army with the help of French subsidies and made his court one of the largest in Germany.[17] Like many Protestant courts in the eighteenth century, the Brunswick court laid its emphasis more on the patronage of music, literature and sciences than the fine arts. Which did not make it much cheaper: in 1693, the court consumed around 120,000 thalers per annum, a large part of which was spent on an opera house that held an audience of 2,500 (more than 1 per cent of the population). However, the

---

15 The article speaks of a 'concours extraordinaire des Citoyens & des Etrangers empressés de voir S.A.R. Me la Princesse Hereditaire ...': ibid., p. 67.

16 A classic of the 'art of ceremonial' is J. B. von Rohr, *Einleitung zur Ceremonielwissenschaft der grossen Herren*, Berlin, 1733, reprint ed. M. Schlechte, Weinheim, 1990. The importance of the *Inventio* concept is stressed by Schlechte in her Epilogue, pp. 38–39. See also Ziwes, 'Brautfahrt', p. 68.

17 O. v. Heinemann, *Geschichte von Braunschweig und Hannover*, 3 vols., Hannover, 1857, iii, pp. 162–267; G. Gerkens, *Das fürstliche Lustschloß Salzdahlum und sein Erbauer Herzog Anton Ulrich von Braunschweig-Wolfenbüttel*, Brunswick, 1974, pp. 32–37; C. E. Vehse, *Geschichte der Höfe des Hauses Braunschweig in Deutschland und England. Die Hofhaltungen zu Hannover, London und Braunschweig*, Hamburg, 1853; for data on court and country, see also the useful survey of V. Bauer, *Die höfische Gesellschaft in Deutschland von der Mitte des 17. bis zum Ausgang des 18. Jahrhunderts. Versuch einer Typologie*, Tübingen, 1993, pp. 73–75, 93–96.

dukes' various attempts to surpass their main rivals to become north-west Germany's dominant power failed, as the resources of the territory were not sufficient to support such an ambitious policy. The duchy of Brunswick-Wolfenbüttel covered only *c.* 3,700 square miles; the population numbered around 160,000 in the early eighteenth century and just over 200,000 by 1800. It was the Guelph cousins in neighbouring Hanover who finally prevailed over the older line. None the less, Anton Ulrich and his successors continued to maintain one of the most lavish courts in Germany and an army the principality could not afford. This was by no means unusual in eighteenth-century Germany. Rivalry within the 'court society of the Empire'[18] — that is, the various German princes as a whole — demanded that a ruler tried to increase his prestige and the 'honour' of his dynasty. Thus most German princes — even if they had no chance whatsoever of playing an international role — tried to increase their status and to enlarge their territories, and the image of a splendid court was almost as essential as the actual policy and military resources standing behind it.[19] Carl I (1735–1780), the father of Carl Wilhelm Ferdinand, was the last Brunswick duke to display the whole range of absolutist means of representation, following the tradition of his predecessors. Having moved the residence from provincial Wolfenbüttel to the much larger city of Brunswick in 1753, he tried to maintain simultaneously a disproportionately large army and a grand court, which he expanded to more than 400 persons, and which included an Italian opera, a French ballet and a German court theatre, which alone received an annual subsidy of 70,000 thalers (5 per cent of the principality's revenues). He also added large numbers of paintings to the already famous family collections, which included the library of Duke Augustus (1636–66) and the picture gallery of Duke Anton Ulrich.

It was above all the cost of this policy of dynastic aspiration which finally brought Brunswick to the verge of bankruptcy, as the high spending caused even

---

18 A. Winterling, *Der Hof der Kurfürsten von Köln, 1688–1794: Eine Fallstudie zur Bedeutung 'absolutistischer' Hofhaltung*, Bonn, 1986, p. 156.

19 An excellent analysis of the dynastic policies in general is provided by P. Wilson, *War, State and Society in Württemberg, 1677–1793*, Cambridge, 1995, ch. 1 and 2.

more debts.[20] By the 1750s, court expenditure had risen to more than 16 per cent of the principality's revenues. By 1763, more than eleven million thalers of debt had accumulated (compared to annual revenues of 1.5 million thalers), and the principality was in serious danger of losing part of its territory, which had been given as a security for a loan.

Only the radical measures taken by the hereditary prince Carl Wilhelm Ferdinand saved the principality. Like Joseph II or Margrave Carl Friedrich of Baden, he belonged to a new generation of princes who had already been deeply influenced by the Enlightenment in their youth, and who were characterized by a comparatively simple life-style, modesty, hard work and a distinctive sense of duty. He had become co-regent in 1770 and continued his new policy when he succeeded his father in 1780. Carl Wilhelm Ferdinand was the first Brunswick ruler to realize that the principality's resources were far too limited for any efforts to keep pace with larger territories. This did not mean that Carl Wilhelm Ferdinand was without personal ambitions. However, he did not pursue his career as the ruler of tiny Brunswick but as a Prussian general and, after the death of Friedrich the Great, as *éminence grise* at the Berlin court.[21] His personal ambitions were, so to speak, sublimated in his role in Prussia and thus separated from the interest of his principality. The priority of the 'new course' was to establish tight controls over government spending. Staff costs in the bureaucracy were limited as far as possible. Court expenditure was cut to 110,000 thalers, just half the amount spent by Carl I, the court was much reduced, and grand festivals ceased for the time being. This policy of fiscal austerity was effective and helped reduce the budget deficit as well as reduce the debt burden step by step.[22] After 1778, the upward trend in revenues eased the situation, and after 1785 Brunswick was virtually running a surplus economy. The new course culminated in an edict issued in 1794 that gave the estates a large measure of control over the finances of

---

20 Heinemann, *Geschichte von Braunschweig*, III, p. 266; W. Deeters, 'Das erste Jahrzehnt des braunschweigischen Finanzkollegiums von 1773–1785', *Braunschweigisches Jahrbuch*, 56, 1975, p. 107.

21 S. Stern, *Karl Wilhelm Ferdinand Herzog zu Braunschweig und Lüneburg*, Hildesheim, 1921, pp. 134–211, 282–351.

22 The financial policy is painstakingly reconstructed in Deeters, 'Das erste Jahrzehnt', pp. 101–20.

the principality, which represented an unprecedented self-restriction of an hitherto 'absolute' monarch.[23]

For the educated élite in Brunswick, the new course was proof of the ability of enlightened monarchy to solve essential problems like 'public' credit, which had brought down the French monarchy, without jeopardizing law and order. Of course, it is difficult to assess the impact the Duke's new course actually had on the prosperity and well-being of his subjects. What is important, however, is that it was seen as crucial by contemporaries. As Johann Joachim Eschenburg, professor at the Collegium Carolinum and one of the leading *Aufklärer*, remarked on his private copy of the debt edict, 'O our prince, in vain your fatherly love believes that your edict preserves your grateful country from future debts. On the contrary, this edict makes it deeply indebted to you.'[24]

III

Until the 1760s, the court had been *the* centre of political decision-making, economic initiatives and cultural life in the principality. There the enlightened élite had been attracted by projects like the Collegium Carolinum, which soon became a leading educational institution with an appeal to students from all over Germany and even from England. But the court lost its virtual monopoly on culture after the Seven Years War, both due to the reduction of the court and a wider process of change, in particular the rise of the public sphere and the increasing commercialization of culture which went along with it.

In the second half of the eighteenth century, Brunswick became a north German centre of commerce, publishing and Enlightenment culture second only to

---

23 There is no study on this important edict or its context. It was published in the *Braunschweigische Anzeigen* in May 1794 and the *Berlinische Monatsschrift* in June 1794. It was also printed separately.

24 StaBS, H VIII A, Eschenburg papers, nr. 1070, Bl. 33a: 'Umsonst, o unser Fürst, glaubt deine Vaterhuld, / durch dies Edict, durch später Enkel Spahren, / dein dankerfülltes Land für Schulden zu bewahren; / du bringst es auch dadurch in untilgbare Schuld. / Eschenburg.' The best biography of Eschenburg is F. Meyen, *Johann Joachim Eschenburg, 1743–1820. Professor am Collegium Carolinum*, Brunswick, 1957. Still useful is F. Spehr, 'Eschenburg', *Allgemeine Deutsche Biographie*, vol. 6, reprint, Berlin, 1968, pp. 346–47.

Hamburg. Part of this process was the rise of reading societies and all sorts of clubs and associations. In Brunswick, the first small reading society had been established in 1765; by the 1790s, Brunswick boasted five lending libraries, two 'reading cabinets', five reading societies and more than a dozen (mostly commercial) reading circles specializing in journals. Moreover, most inns and coffee houses, clubs and Freemasons' lodges also offered small libraries, as did several smaller clubs and associations which did not have rooms of their own but met in inns.[25] In these places, local papers such as the popular *Braunschweigische Zeitung* and the official state paper *Braunschweigische Anzeigen*, as well as national journals, some of which were also published in Brunswick, were freely available throughout the 1790s. The most important of these associations was the Großer Club, the Great Club, which had been established in 1780 and provided a meeting place for the nobility, higher state officials and local notables such as the Gravenhorst brothers, who were among the most prominent organizers of the 1790 celebrations.[26] Another aspect of this wider process of change was the increasing commercialization of culture. Of course, this process was not very far advanced — in particular if compared to contemporary Britain — but writers like Johann Carl Daniel Curio represented a new type of publicist who tried to make money by reporting on — and in a way thus creating — spectacular events like the balloon ascent of the French adventurer Blanchard in 1788. This had been a skilfully prepared commercial enterprise, where journalists, inn-keepers, producers of various souvenir articles, the local theatre-company, Blanchard himself and the ducal government — which hoped to attract money-spending

---

25 M. Graf, *Buch- und Lesekultur in der Residenzstadt Braunschweig zur Zeit der Spätaufklärung unter Herzog Karl Wilhelm Ferdinand (1770–1806)*, Frankfurt am Main, 1994; for the decreasing attraction of the court, see also G. Frühsorge, 'J. F. W. Jerusalem: Der Gelehrte als Hof-Mann' in K. Pollmann (ed.), *Abt Johann Friedrich Wilhelm Jerusalem (1709–1789). Beiträge zu einem Colloquium anläßlich seines 200. Todestages*, Brunswick, 1991, pp. 43–44.

26 L. Hänselmann, *Das erste Jahrhundert des Großen Clubs in Braunschweig*, Brunswick, 1880.

foreigners — co-operated to create a new kind of mass spectacle, which did not fit into the traditional categories of monarchical celebration or civic festival.[27]

The events of November 1790 combined these developments with the celebration of monarchy in a novel way. Most associations used the entry of the hereditary prince to arrange special meetings and stimulated their members to participate in public festivities such as the illumination. As never before on the occasion of a ducal event, the press reported lengthily on the 1790 celebrations, starting with detailed reports on the wedding ceremony in The Hague and the progress of the couple on their way to Brunswick.[28] One souvenir book edited by the mercurial journalist Curio was sold as early as 13 November,[29] while Curio's rival Joachim Heinrich Campe needed four days longer to publish his contribution.[30] Both were available in luxury editions for the rich as well as in cheaper editions for the poor: the price of Campe's 370-page book, for instance, started at one groschen, while the most expensive edition was printed on 'fine Swiss paper' and cost not less than eighteen groschen, more than the average servant earned per day.[31] The descriptions of the triumphal entry in turn spawned festivals in other places, which did not want to be left behind the capital: the town of Holzminden, for example, arranged a public festival celebrating the ducal family, after its burghers had learned about the Brunswick celebrations through newspaper articles.[32] The celebrations in Brunswick, on the other hand, had been boosted by the articles published in local and national papers, which described and commented on the coronation of Emperor Leopold II in Frankfurt the month before.[33]

---

27 G. Biegel, 'Der Ballonaufstieg von François Blanchard in Braunschweig am 10. August 1788'; *Braunschweig-Archiv*, 1993.
28 *Gnädigst privilegirte Braunschweigische Zeitung für Städte, Flecken und Dörfer*, 1790, 84.
29 *Braunschweigische Anzeigen*, 1790, 89, p. 1593.
30 *Braunschweigische Anzeigen*, 1790, 90, pp. 1610–11.
31 *Braunschweigische Anzeigen*, 1790, 93, p. 1659.
32 A report of the Holzminden celebrations is in *Braunschweigische Zeitung für Städte*, 1790, p. 95.
33 Ibid., 1790, pp. 84 and 85; Leopold's coronation is reassessed in R. Haaser, 'Das Zeremoniell der beiden letzten deutsch-römischen Kaiserkrönungen in Frankfurt am Main und seine Rezeption zwischen Spätaufklärung und Frühromantik' in J. J. Berns and T. Rahn

The educationalist Campe gave the festival a wider significance, which is reflected by the rather cumbersome title of his book, *Monument to the love of a good people to his good prince or description of the general popular festival that took place in Brunswick on occasion of the arrival of the hereditary prince and the hereditary princess of Brunswick*. The key word is *Volksfest* — popular festival — which points to the concept of the public festival, which was so dear to many enlightened writers.

Since the mid-century festivals had been a central problem for the *Aufklärer*, who had consistently criticized the existing practices of festival culture, both popular and monarchical, which were seen as both economically damaging and morally corrupting. However, German intellectuals also recognized the popular appeal of festivals and the potential they thus provided for spreading the gospel of Enlightenment among larger sections of the population. Taking up Rousseau's idea of patriotic festivals (in his *Lettre à d'Alembert* of 1758), they thus developed a new concept of 'popular festivals' fostering state patriotism, morality, economy and order. Campe, whose *Braunschweigisches Journal* had taken an active part in this debate, and other commentators took up this concept in their interpretation of the ducal entry.[34] Campe offers an interpretative framework for the entry celebrations by comparing them to the situation in other German states and in France, where the Festival of the Federation had been celebrated a few months before. What is important for him is not the dynastic marriage itself but the response of the people to it as an indicator of the popularity of the ruler:

> Watch this, you rulers of the world! See and hear why it is that the leaders of peoples tremble and are frightened by their subjects. [...] This is not the fault of the subjects, as all men are a good-natured and benign species, grateful to those who lead them to happiness, and most of all grateful to

---

(eds), *Zeremoniell als höfische Ästhetik in Spätmittelalter und Früher Neuzeit*, Tübingen, 1995, pp. 600–31.

34 Anon., 'Etwas von Nationalfesten und Volksfreuden, zur Beherzigung für die, welche über das Volk zu gebieten haben', *Braunschweigisches Journal*, 1789. 2; 'v. d. R.', 'Ueber den Aufsatz von National-Festen und Volksfreuden im 8ten Stück des Br. Journals 1789', ibid., 1790, 2.

their princes, if only they do more or less what they undertook to do as their most holy obligation.[35]

The message is clear: by attributing the popularity of the Duke and the stability of the political landscape of Brunswick to the 'benevolent' reign of Carl Wilhelm Ferdinand, who did everything for the well-being of his subjects, Campe's book also represents a warning to those rulers who ignore the just wishes of the population. Thus Campe's celebration of monarchy in 1790 follows the same argument as his celebration of the Revolution in France in his 'Letters from Paris' in 1789.[36] Countering claims that unrestricted Enlightenment leads to unrest and revolution — a common line of attack after 1789 — Campe takes Brunswick as the proof that no fear of Enlightenment was justified, as Brunswick, one of the most generous territories as far as freedom of the press and other core demands of the *Aufklärer* were concerned, was also one of the calmest. Arguing that enlightened government does not produce revolution but, on the contrary, increasing attachment to the existing order, Campe makes the entry celebrations a demonstration of loyalty. As the success of a show of loyalty is measured by the number of attendants and the depth of the emotions displayed, he has to prove, first, that the celebrations were, indeed, an expression of attachment to the ruler and, secondly, that they included all sections of the population.

Thus Campe is at pains to distinguish between staged festivals any despot could order and expressions of genuine loyalty to a true 'father of the people'. For him, the ultimate proof of this is precisely the lack of 'ceremonial magnificence'.[37] Contrasting the joy of the Brunswick population with the elaborate welcome festivals which were part of previous absolutist representation, Campe makes the simplicity of the festivities a major criterion for the loyalty of the population. 'True love' can do — indeed, has to do — without merely external pomp.

Most commentators stressed both the sincerity of the joy and its extent: it was general approval that counted, not only the approval of the small stratum making

---

35 Campe, *Denkmal der Liebe*, III, p. ix.
36 The 'Letters' were published in book form as *Briefe aus Paris zur Zeit der Revolution geschrieben*, Brunswick, 1790.
37 Ibid., p. iv.

up the public sphere. As the Helmstedt professor Remer wrote, the 'public sphere' of more or less élitist periodicals and clubs was not representative of the entire population.[38] There was no other way to represent what he called 'general opinion' than to make clear that the celebrations were a truly public festival that included all sections of the population. The much-praised stability of Brunswick could best be demonstrated by making the celebrations as inclusive as possible. Thus even die-hard conservatives like the preacher Johann Wilhelm Georg Wolff took large crowds as positive signs of attachment to the Duke and the present order.[39] Consequently, no report on the celebrations forgets to emphasize that *all* orders took part *voluntarily*, including the fringes of society. Hence, the poor figured prominently in the celebrations and their descriptions. Also, Jews were included and praised as true 'patriots'. This indicates under which word all the various orders and groups of society were summarized: 'patriots' were all those who worked for the fatherland in the place where God had set them. Thus, even the peasant could be a patriot — as long as he remained content to be a peasant.

The sheer number of burghers engaged in the celebrations was impressive indeed. Curio alone lists 918 persons by name, most of whom were members of the militia corps, which numbered around 1400 men in all.[40] These corps were almost exclusively drawn from the 'middle classes', people belonging to the group of 'tradesmen' in the wider sense, a definition including wholesalers as well as artisans, who were the strongest single group of the Brunswick population. The burghers' corps had organized itself on a meeting at the rifle club in early October, whose members elected the innkeeper and wine-merchant Johann Hermann Angot

---

38 J. A. Remer, *Die charakteristischen Züge des Bildes eines vorzüglichen Regenten der mittlern deutschen Staaten. Eine Rede bei Sr. Durchlauchten des Herrn Erbprinzen von Braunschweig und Lüneburg ... frohen Zurückkunft ...*, Helmstedt, 1790.

39 J. W. G. Wolff, *Ueber den Mangel der Achtung für die nöthige Ordnung im bürgerlichen Leben, als einen herrschenden Fehler unsrer Zeiten ...*, Brunswick, 1790.

40 Curio, *Braunschweigs Jubel*; Curio only mentions the names of the socially higher-ranking corps. Papen, the mayor, speaks of 1,700 who had subscribed to one of the corps but it is more likely that the number was smaller, as the members of the four socially lower-standing corps of merchants' servants, the two butchers' guilds and the tailors, numbered about 450–500, which would have to be added to the 848 members listed by Curio.

(1721–1800) as their 'general'.[41] He was the manager of two inns, one of which he had leased through direct intervention of the Duke himself only two years earlier. After his apprenticeship in Brunswick, Angot had travelled all over Germany. The highlight of these travels was his stay in Frankfurt in 1745, where he watched the coronation ceremony of Franz I, 'the splendour of which I have never forgotten', as he noted in his handwritten autobiography almost sixty years later.[42] With imperial pomp in mind, Angot tried hard to match the model in 1790. Unfortunately, the illumination of the city in celebration of the ducal wedding ended in disaster for the inn-keeper, whose militia escorted the carriages driving the court around the illuminated city. Once the procession had reached the Castle square, Angot tried to turn his horse to greet the Duke, who watched the procession from a window. However, the horse stepped into a hole in the street, the saddle belt came undone and Angot fell off his horse backwards, which temporarily ended his role as militia general. This accident was of course not mentioned in any of the reports describing the illumination, which was supposed to be a highlight of the public part of the festival. Indeed, the scene of the accident was the very focus of the attention, as the *Burgplatz* was surrounded by a ring of torches lighting the lion monument in its centre, which had been erected by Henry the Lion in 1166 and become the symbol of dynasty and country.

IV

The core elements of the Brunswick celebrations were part of a thousand-year-old tradition, the *adventus* of secular and ecclesiastical princes: the welcome outside the town; the decoration (and illumination) of the town itself; the solemn procession of the entering person and his suite; the town-dwellers lining the route.[43] Even the prominent role of children and white-clad maids of honour had

---

41 A lively report of the 1790 celebrations is given in the memoirs Angot himself had written for his family: 'Denkschrift für die Meinigen', StaBS, Angot papers, H VIII A: 78.
42 Ibid, p. 10.
43 K. Tenfelde, 'Adventus: Die fürstliche Einholung als städtisches Fest' in P. Hugger (ed.), *Stadt und Fest. Zu Geschichte und Gegenwart europäischer Festkultur*, Stuttgart, 1987, pp. 45–60. For Germany in general, see W. Dotzauer, 'Die Ankunft des Herrschers: Der

been a constituent element of entry ceremonial for centuries.[44] In 1790s Brunswick, all these elements were given a new meaning in the context of a changing world. Under Carl I, festivals had still been the articulation of ducal power (or a power the dukes would have liked to possess); the 1790 entry, however, was supposed to be a demonstration of political stability and social harmony.

In an age of turmoil and seemingly uncontrollable change, most *Aufklärer*, the clergy and also wider sections of the Brunswick population came to regard the Duke as the symbol and guarantee of stability as well as the continuation of enlightened reforms. Certainly, the ducal government and local notables co-operated closely in organizing the celebrations, but there can be no doubt that they enjoyed the support of many humbler men. The organization of the 1790 festival was aided by the network of associations and newspapers that had developed in the second half of the century. Indeed, it appears that a public celebration of monarchy on the scale of the 1790 festival would not have been possible had there not been an established and working public sphere. Combining a traditional monarchical ritual with the features of new mass spectacles, the educated and the propertied classes transformed, in writing even more than in reality, a formerly exclusive court affair into a public festival, both to assure themselves of this stability and to call upon the lower classes to respect the existing order.

The equation of state and family, which shines through all publications, with the ruler as omnipotent father of the country and his subjects as dependent children, had long been used by advocates of absolute monarchy. In the eighteenth century, however, the image of the ideal father changed significantly. The emphasis shifted, from the unlimited and even arbitrary power a distant *pater familias* wielded to the care and responsibility a kind and affectionate father showed his wife and children. Similarly, the image of princes changed from that of the unapproachable despot to the loving, patriarchal *Landesvater*. The mutual love and trust of father and family, as it is depicted in sentimental literature as well as in the educational tracts of Campe, corresponded to the mutual love

---

fürstliche "Einzug" in die Stadt (bis zum Ende des Alten Reichs)', *Archiv für Kulturgeschichte*, 55, 1973, pp. 245-88.
44   Tenfelde, 'Adventus', p. 47.

between ruler and subjects which also figures so prominently in the publications of November 1790.[45]

Affection for the ruler took the place of fear, and similarly the ceremonial of distinction and distancing was changed into a ceremonial of intimacy. The monarch, who had been placed far away from his subjects by 'Baroque' ceremonial, was now being perceived as an ordinary human being and had to legitimize his elevated rank through performance and hard work for the well-being of his subjects. Once he had earned it, the people of course had to fulfil their side of the contract and be obedient and loving subjects; authors like Remer and Wolff were quick to remind the people of this duty.

The court, which had been central to earlier festivals, was now being marginalized; the immediate and intimate relationship between ruler and people was celebrated, bypassing the court. By the end of the century, the 'benevolent' brand of 'enlightened' monarchy in Brunswick had gained a fresh, if in the long run problematic, public legitimation, which is mirrored in the change (to avoid the word 'decline') of ceremonial. The court, however, became increasingly dangerous as the symbolic representation of monarchy, in a time when the traditional academic critique of court life combined with the new set of 'enlightened', 'bourgeois' values and found access to wide sections of the population.

Ceremonial was not necessarily condemned to a slow death, although it had become something of a 'dirty word' by the late eighteenth century. Perhaps paradoxically, those writers condemning 'Baroque' ceremonial argued for a new form of ceremonial, the 'patriotic festival'. What Campe and others disliked was not, as they said, ceremonial as such, but the specific forms and contents of traditional princely ceremonial. If 'improved' and elevated to the rank of 'patriotic festival', the same occasion (even with almost the same choreography) could come back with a vengeance.

---

45 J. H. Campe, *Theophron oder der erfahrne Rathgeber für die unerfahrne Jugend. Ein Vermächtniß für seine gewesenen Pflegesöhne und für alle erwachsnere junge Leute, welche Gebracuh davon machen wollen*, Hamburg, 1783; for sentimental patriarchalism in general, see B. A. Sörensen, *Herrschaft und Zärtlichkeit. Der Patriarchalismus und das Drama im 18. Jahrhundert*, Munich, 1984.

Peter I and Catherine sailing in St Petersburg: from an engraving by A. Zubov, 1716.

The 1896 Hungarian Millennial Procession passes in front of the Supreme Court building: 'the imposing building forms a gigantic background [...] the group depicted on this photograph is reminiscent of a wonderful dream which the world has never seen before' (from *Das Huldigungs-Banderium vom 8ten Juni 1896 verewigt in Wort und Bild unter der Redaktion Stanislaus Tumárisz*, ed. Julius Laurencic, Budapest, 1896).

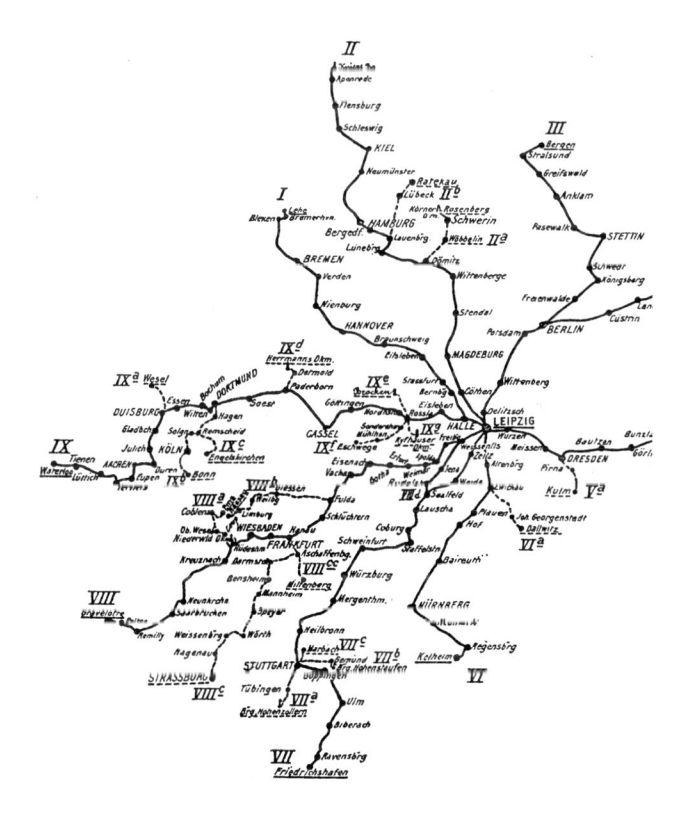

Survey map of the routes taken by the messengers of the German Gymnasts' Movement on 16–18 October 1913 (from *Deutsche Turn-Zeitung*, Leipzig, 1913, p. 742).

Konsum (German state department store) advertisement: 'Konsum prepares for Christmas'; the caption below reads 'Our rich array of goods is the result of our workers' hard work for the victory of socialism!' (Leipzig: VEB Graphische Werkstätten, 1958, reproduced from *Deutsches Historisches Museum Magazin*, 5, 1995, 14, p. 35).

Woman and children gazing at a Christmas tree and what we are to understand to be a portrait of their fallen husband and father (from *Deutsche Kriegsweihnacht*, 1944, p. 123). This Nazi publication appeared annually during the war years.

THE 1896 MILLENNIAL FESTIVITIES IN HUNGARY: AN EXERCISE IN PATRIOTIC AND DYNASTIC PROPAGANDA

Thomas Barcsay

At precisely midnight on 31 December 1895, the church bells of Hungary pealed in unison to signal the arrival of the long-awaited millennial year: 1896 was to be a year of joyous celebration, of festivals, processions, impressive acts of state and the inauguration of monumental public works projects. The grandest festivities would naturally take place in Budapest, the country's booming capital, but even remote and obscure hamlets were urged to do their bit and participate, however humbly, in the national festivities. What exactly was being commemorated during this year of national euphoria? Officially, it was the one-thousandth anniversary of the arrival of Árpád and his Magyar warriors in the Carpathian basin. In Hungarian, it was the *Honfoglalás* or the 'conquest of the homeland'. Although there was to be much talk about this being also 'the one-thousandth anniversary of the Hungarian state', such a claim was not strictly accurate, since an organized Hungarian kingdom on the Western model was not established until some 100 years after Árpád crossed the Carpathians at the Pass of Verecke.

The notion of celebrating great and significant events from the past was far from unusual in the nineteenth century — an age which revelled in the pleasures of historical commemoration. Wittenberg, for example, had marked the three-hundredth anniversary of the Reformation by commissioning a huge bronze statue of Luther to adorn the square where the great reformer had publicly burned the papal bull excommunicating him. Some seventy years later, in 1889, France commemorated the one-hundredth anniversary of the Revolution by staging a great international exhibition in Paris, whose symbol — the Eiffel Tower — was to represent all that was new and progressive in the Third Republic. The Hungarian millennial year thus fitted into a general European pattern; what was unusual, however, was the length, scale and expense of the celebrations.

The idea of marking the one-thousandth anniversary of the Magyar conquest was first raised during the hopeless days of neo-absolutism which followed the defeat of the Hungarian War of Independence in 1849. But the first concrete proposal was not to be made until 1868, when the Pest city council passed a resolution to this effect.[1] By this time much had changed since the 1850s. Hungary was now an equal partner in the Austro-Hungarian Empire and on the threshold of a half-century of remarkable economic progress. Although the idea was taken up with enthusiasm by the novelist Mór Jókai and by other prominent intellectuals, nothing much was done at an official level until 1882.

In that year, the government asked the Hungarian Academy of Sciences to set an official date for the arrival of the Magyars in the Carpathian Basin. After much scholarly wrangling, it was finally decided that successive waves of Magyars probably arrived some time between 888 and 900.[2] Eventually, the government chose 1895 for the commemoration; the Minister of Commerce used this date when presenting a formal proposal on the millennial year to parliament in 1891. It soon became clear, however, that the date would have to be changed. The great public works projects the government wanted completed for the anniversary could not possibly be ready in time. Accordingly, the millennial celebrations had to be put off, by one year, to 1896.[3]

A special Millennial Commission was set up in 1892 to co-ordinate various public and private projects; at the same time, financial support for a national

---

1 Katalin Sinkó, 'A valóság története avagy a történelem valósága' in *Lélek és forma, magyar művészet 1896–1914* [exhibition catalogue], Budapest, 1986, p. 13.
2 Ibid, p. 14.
3 Mór Gelléri (ed.), *Führer durch die Millenium Landes-Ausstellung auf Grund Officieller Daten*, Budapest, 1896, pp. 44–45.

exhibition — destined to be the focal point of the celebrations — was guaranteed by law. On 15 September 1893, the cabinet met with the new Prime Minister, Dr Alexander Wekerle, to discuss the general theme of the festivities. Wekerle was a rarity in Dualist Hungary, a politician of relatively humble bourgeois origins who had managed to overcome class barriers and rise to the top largely through his own efforts. He had made his mark as a financial expert in parliament and remained interested in economic problems throughout his long political career. Wekerle saw the planned millennial celebrations as a splendid opportunity to show the world the remarkable material progress the country had made during the thirty years since the Compromise of 1867. This is why he insisted that the millennial exhibition in Budapest should be national rather than international in character. He wanted it to be a showcase for Hungarian agriculture and industry with little competitive intrusion from abroad. But he believed the millennial celebrations could be useful in achieving important political objectives as well: by emphasizing the joyous reconciliation 'between nation and monarch', the festivities might help to obscure the unhappy and divisive memories of the War of Independence in 1848–49.[4]

The theme of Hungary's material progress was to be emphasized by a number of impressive public works projects in Budapest and elsewhere throughout the country. The capital was to receive a new Danube bridge to be named after Franz Joseph I. The grandiose new supreme court building was scheduled to be inaugurated in 1896 along with a new art exhibition hall and a new museum of applied arts. The royal palace, overlooking the Danube and the sprawling city of Pest beyond, was to be doubled in size. Continental Europe's first electric underground line would be rushed to completion. The government promised to construct 500 elementary state schools for the millennial year. Work was to proceed rapidly on the Iron Gates Canal on the Hungarian–Romanian–Serbian border. It was to be opened, as the final great ceremonial act of the year, by King

---

4   Geza A. von Geyr, *Sándor Wekerle 1848–1921: Die politische Biographie eines Ungarischen Staatsmannes der Donaumonarchie*, Munich, 1993, p. 167.

Franz Joseph accompanied by the rulers of Romania and Serbia, 'like some medieval Hungarian sovereign surrounded by his vassals'.[5]

Though Wekerle felt that the themes of progress and reconciliation should be emphasized throughout the festivities, he was equally convinced that pride of place had to be given to history.[6] The whole Hungarian political establishment, and beyond, was united in this. The millennial year was designed to present both Hungarians and foreigners alike with the spectacle of an ancient European state with a long, turbulent but continuous history celebrating a thousand years of existence. The tone was set by Count Géza Teleki, the president of the Hungarian Historical Association: 'We have been on this soil for a thousand years', said Teleki in 1893:

> and our one-thousand-year-old history has been a long chain of trial and struggle. Nor could it have been otherwise. Ever since Árpád founded this country, the state he established has been Europe's bastion against the enemies of Christian civilization, and it is this bastion which broke the power of those dreadful forces coming from Asia [...] which have, time and time again, threatened Western civilization with complete annihilation.[7]

The contradictions in this viewpoint are obvious. Árpád did not in any accepted sense of the word found a Hungarian state; that was to come much later. The Magyars themselves were, after all, semi-nomadic horsemen from the east and the terror-stricken inhabitants of Germany and France, subject to their raids, could be forgiven for regarding them as dreadful enemies bent on destroying the fragile civilization of the west. These contradictions were not altogether lost on the organizers, who eventually tried to emphasize the role of Hungary's first Christian king, St Stephen, in the festivities. But ultimately it was the image of Árpád which was to triumph.

That image was to a large extent the creation of a number of gifted and imaginative artists. The lead was taken by Michály Munkácsy, a Hungarian painter with something of a reputation in Paris, whose vast and often gloomy

---

5   The noted historian Gyula Szekfű, quoted in Éva Somogyi, 'Császári és királyi 'udvartartás': A Burg és a milleniumi ünnepségek', *Historia*, 18, 1996, 5–6, pp. 6–9.

6   von Geyr, *Sándor Wekerle*, p. 167.

7   Speech given by Count Géza Teleki to the general meeting of the Hungarian Historical Association on 13 February 1896, *Századok*, 1896, 3, p. 13.

canvases enjoyed a certain popularity with American millionaires. In 1893, the Hungarian government commissioned him to paint a scene from the Magyar conquest for the new parliament buildings currently being constructed on the banks of the Danube in Budapest. When finished, the vast (4.5 metres by 13.5 metres) painting showed Árpád, attired in a resplendent, vaguely Oriental costume and astride a richly caparisoned white horse, proudly accepting the submission of the newly conquered country's indigenous inhabitants.[8] The same theme was taken up with a vengeance by a lesser artist, Árpád Feszty, whose impressive diorama of the conquest was opened in 1894 and two years later became one of the most popular sights of the Millennial Exhibition.[9]

Árpád and the ancient Magyars were to figure prominently as well on a series of monuments which were to be erected throughout the country to mark the anniversary of the Conquest. Apparently these were the brainchild of the historian Kálmán Thaly, who also happened to be a member of parliament for the opposition Independence Party. Thaly's proposal for a series of millennial monuments had its supporters on the other side of the parliamentary benches as well. Prime Minister Wekerle himself was in favour, and even wrote a pamphlet in 1894 outlining his own suggestions for a millennial monument to be constructed in Budapest.[10] Eventually a parliamentary committee decided that a national millennial monument was to be erected at the far end of Andrássy Avenue in Budapest. The monument was to be a summation of a thousand years of Hungarian history in sculptural form, with Árpád and his chieftains occupying the central position.[11]

In the event, the monument was not begun until the millennial year was nearly over; construction was to last until 1905 and the final sculptural elements were not put in place until 1929. Two gigantic hemicycles surrounded a seventy-metre-high corinthian column topped by a statue of the Archangel Gabriel. The two hemicycles contained fourteen statues of Hungarian kings from St Stephen to

---

8   András Székely, *Mihály Munkácsy*, St Paul, 1981, p. 12, and Júlia Szabó, *A XIX. Század festészete Magyarországon*, Budapest, 1996, pp. 14–15.
9   Árpád Szűcs and Malgorzata Wojtowicz, *A Feszty körkép*, Budapest, 1996, pp. 14–15
10 von Geyr, *Sándor Wekerle*, pp. 167–68
11 János Pótó, '…Állj az időnek végezetéig! Az ezredévi emlékművek története', *Historia*, 18, 1896, 5–6, p. 17.

Franz Joseph I. By far the largest sculptural grouping showed the by now conventional representation of Árpád on horseback surrounded by his seven allied Magyar chieftains. This was put at the base of the column at the very centre of the monument, just as the parliamentary committee had recommended.

The Budapest monument was the largest and artistically the most satisfying among the many erected throughout the country that year or immediately after. Thaly had suggested that places which had an important connection with events of the conquest should also receive appropriate monuments. For a historical account of the conquest, Thaly relied largely on the celebrated *Gesta Hungarorum*, written by an anonymous late twelfth-century chronicler. Anonymous — as he is known to Hungarian historiography — wrote that Árpád and his chieftains and followers met at Pusztaszer on the great plain and established the laws and customs of the land. Naturally Pusztaszer — whose abbey and village virtually disappeared during Turkish times — was singled out for one of the first monuments. It was to be inaugurated with much ceremony on 5 July 1896 in the presence of delegations from both houses of parliament and amidst heady claims that here was the birthplace of the 'oldest constitution' in Hungary, at least, if not all Europe.[12]

Following the anonymous chronicler's somewhat romanticized account, another monument was destined for Nyitra (now Nitra in the Slovak Republic), where the Magyars defeated the forces of Svatopluk, prince of Greater Moravia. The abbey of Pannonhalma also received a monument, for it was here apparently that Árpád rested after the last battles of the conquest and 'saw the beauty of the land of Pannonia'.[13]

Four other monuments were erected on the northern, western, eastern and southern frontiers of the kingdom. The northern one at Munkács (Mukacheve, Ukraine) showed the eagle-like, mythical Turul bird of the ancient Magyars. A somewhat bellicose Turul bird was shown brandishing a scimitar in the direction of Belgrade on the southern monument at Zimony (Zemun, Serbia) on the Danube. The western monument at Dévény (Devín, Slovak Republic) featured a monumental column guarded by an ancient Magyar warrior, as did the eastern one at Brassó (Kronstadt, Braşov, Romania). These four monuments were intended to

---

12   Ibid., pp. 16–17, and 'Milleniumi történelmi ünneplések', *Századok*, 30, 1896, 7, pp. 667–68.
13   Ibid., p. 668.

symbolize the permanence of the Hungarian frontiers, the country's determination to defend them if necessary and, in the words of Thaly, 'to give a visual expression of the Hungarian state idea' in areas with large non-Magyar populations.[14] Needless to say, every one of these monuments was to be dismantled or destroyed once the frontiers changed following the First World War. Only those in Budapest, Pusztaszer and Pannonhalma have survived to this day.

Hungarians were far from being the only people in Europe with a weakness for ancient half-mythical ancestors. The nineteenth century was the heyday of the romanticization of history. The Hungarian Árpád cult had its French and German equivalents in those of Vercingetorix or Hermann. There were significant differences, however. Both Hermann and Vercingetorix were leaders who had resisted the conquering, imperialist Roman legions. They could be seen through the veil of romantic historical exaggeration as fighters for national independence. Árpád was different, of course. It was he who was the conqueror, and the descendants of the peoples he had conquered could scarcely be expected to celebrate what they saw as the subjugation of their ancestors. In homogeneous or pseudo-homogeneous states like France or Germany, it was relatively easy to create a sense of national solidarity around the figures of Vercingetorix or Hermann. But Hungary was not a homogeneous national state. Less than half the population in 1896 was Magyar-speaking. The Germans, Slovaks, Romanians, Serbs and Ruthenians of Hungary could not identify with the conquest. Moreover, the cult of Árpád among the Magyars now faced rival cults among the nationalities: Svatopluk, the wise ruler of ephemeral Greater Moravia, was a hero to Slovak nationalists, while nationally conscious Romanians in Transylvania had their own powerful myth of Daco-Romanian continuity. Croatia, an associated kingdom under the crown of St Stephen, had never been conquered by Árpád but joined Hungary much later as the result of a dynastic alliance.

Croats, Slovaks, Romanians and Serbs were understandably less than enthusiastic about the millennial celebrations. The Croatian opposition in the

---

14 Pótó, '... Állj az időnek végezetéig!', pp. 15–16

Sabor — the Croatian parliament — suggested a total boycott.[15] In the end, more moderate voices prevailed and official Croatia decided to participate in the Budapest national exhibition. Croatia had several separate pavilions, each flying the red, white and blue Croatian flag as if to show the country's status as an autonomous kingdom within what was somewhat pompously called the 'Hungarian Empire' (*Magyar Birodalom*). There were Croatian pavilions devoted to art, history, industry and even forestry. To make it all a little more evocative and exotic, the streets of the Croatian section were paved with slabs of dolomite brought to Budapest all the way from the Adriatic coast.[16] Croatian parliamentarians were also eventually persuaded to join the Ban of Croatia at unveiling of the millennial monument at Zimony, which, despite some initial apprehension, apparently turned out to be a festive and fraternal affair.[17]

While official Croatia was generally won over, the same could not be said about national groups within Hungary proper. The 1895 Congress of Hungarian Nationalities, dominated by Romanian, Slovak and Serbian radical nationalists, sounded a note of intransigent hostility. Referring to the millennial celebrations, the Congress declared:

> We consider the coming celebrations as an attempt to deceive the public opinion of Europe. They are trying to present an image to the rest of Europe according to which the nations of Hungary live side by side in peace and harmony, whereas in fact the majority of the Hungarian population is deeply dissatisfied.[18]

The Congress added that its members would not participate in what it called 'insulting' celebrations designed to show them as 'conquered and enslaved nations.'

Here too there were moderate voices, however. The non-Magyar Uniate hierarchy, for instance, went out of its way to strike a conciliatory tone: 'We also owe gratitude as children of this dear motherland', wrote Julius Firczák, the

---

15 László Bíró, 'Tiltakozó nemzetiségek: Horvátország és a magyarországi szerbek a millenniumról', *Historia*, 18, 1896, 5–6, pp. 25–28.
16 Gelléri, *Führer*, p. 179.
17 Bíró, 'Tiltakozó nemzetiségek', p. 25.
18 Ibid, p. 26.

Uniate bishop of Munkács, in a pastoral letter to his diocese about the millennial year:

> 'For Hungary is our motherland. Our ancestors took an active part in the establishment of this homeland. Coming from Kiev, the Russians fought side by side with the conquering Hungarians and together with them forged a common homeland.

Here was an echo of the ancient Ruthenian attachment to the Hungarian kingdom. What is more, continued Firczák, Hungary stood for basic civic rights, constitutional rule and — in a veiled criticism of ecclesiastical conditions in neighbouring Russia — it guaranteed 'the free exercise of our eastern rite'.[19]

The Romanian Uniate hierarchy was somewhat cooler in its enthusiasm. Referring to the Minister of Education's decree urging villages to plant pines and solid hardwoods to commemorate the millennium, Mihai Pavel, the Uniate bishop of Nagyvárad (Oradea, Romania), suggested somewhat caustically that fruit trees would be 'more practical for our faithful'.[20]

The Hungarian government, Churches and patriotic associations did everything possible to make the non-Magyar nationalities feel included in the festivities. The Catholic hierarchy followed the Minister of Education's guidelines in determining how the millennium was to be celebrated in Catholic and Uniate schools. Apart from language, there was to be no difference in the ceremonies at Magyar and non-Magyar schools. On the designated day (9 May 1896), elementary-school rooms were to be decorated with flowers, pine branches and national flags. Pupils were to wear their best clothes for the occasion; girls were expected to wear garlands of flowers and decorate their dresses with ribbons in the Hungarian colours. Teachers, for their part, had to read a paper, prepared in advance, on the significance of the Conquest and the 'one-thousand-year-long life of the

---

19 *Ezeréves Magyarország. XIII. Leó pápa és a magyar katholikus főpásztorok ünneplő szava papjaik és híveikhez* [edited by the St Stephen Society, a publishing house of the Hungarian Roman Catholic Church], Budapest, 1896, p. 115, Pastoral Letter of Gyula Firczak, Greek-Catholic Bishop of Munkacs [=Mukachevo, Ukraine], Ungvár [= Uzhgorod, Ukraine], 13 April 1896.

20 Ibid., p. 201: Pastoral letter of Mihály Pavel, Greek-Catholic Bishop of Nagyvárad, Nagyvárad, 10 April 1896.

Hungarian nation'. This was to be followed by poems, children's speeches and patriotic songs, all in the language of the school concerned.[21]

Patriotic associations and high minded individuals also entered the fray to win over the non-Magyar masses. One good example of one such attempt is a pamphlet published in Nyitra in Hungarian, German and Slovak. The title was fairly self-explanatory: 'The Millennium, or Thousand-Year-Old Hungary: About the Many, Wonderful Things Which Happened in Hungary During the Past Thousand Years and Those Which Are About to Happen During this Coming Year, for the Instruction of Good, Honest Village People'.[22] The text, written in the style of farmers' almanacs, presented a charmingly naive version of Hungarian history: the Magyars, wrote the anonymous author about the aftermath of the Conquest, 'did not kill the Slovaks (Totokat) and other people they found here, but treated them humanely, became their brothers, allowed them to keep their property and enabled them to get ahead. Since that time Slovaks, Germans, Ruthenes and Romanians have lived here together. No one harms them in the least; on the contrary, Hungarians are happy to see so many contented people in Hungary.'[23] Naturally, Slovak or Romanian nationalists would have phrased this somewhat differently, to say the least.

The theme of the Nyitra pamphlet was taken up at the National Exhibition which opened in Budapest in May 1896. An entire section was set aside for ethnography and folklore. A reconstructed village displayed peasant architecture from every region of Hungary. Some statistical equity was maintained in its design: twelve of the houses on display represented Magyar architecture and folk art, while the remaining twelve were distributed among the various nationalities. On the village's 'street of nationalities' there were German peasant houses from Transylvania and upper Hungary, Slovak, Ruthenian and Slovene houses, as well as a lovely Romanian house from Hunyad county in Transylvania, which was

---

21 Ibid., pp. 244–48: Instructions of the Hungarian Catholic Hierarchy on celebrating the one-thousandth anniversary of the Hungarian Conquest.

22 *A Millennium, vagy az ezeresztendős Magyarország. Azokról a mindenféle szépséges és dicső dolgokról amik Magyarországon az elmult ezer esztendő alatt történtek, és azokról amik ebben az esztendőben történnek, a falubeli becsületes jó emberek okulására*, Nyitra, 1896.

23 Ibid., p. 6

apparently much admired by visitors. To make things complete, there was even a model of a Gypsy encampment on the outskirts of the village, put there on the insistence of Archduke Joseph, who was a notable Gypsy scholar. The illustrated photograph album of the millennial year describes the Romany encampment in patronizing, almost colonialist, style: 'Dirty, uncombed children in tattered dresses swarm around makeshift abodes, but in spite of the misery', writes the author, 'the spirit of liberty floats over these figures'.[24] This image of backward but happy natives would not have been out of place in a catalogue of any French or British imperial or colonial exhibition.

Though some non-Magyar political leaders boycotted the festivities, the boycott was not universally observed. The great march past the country's élite before the King on June 8, the *Bandérium*, of which more later — contained the odd non-Magyar. Szeben (Sibiu, Romania) county in Transylvania, still partly German-speaking and settled by Germans in the twelfth century, sent its representatives in distinctive Saxon national costume. According to contemporary accounts, the Saxons received more cheers than anyone in the procession except for the largely Italian delegation from the port city of Fiume (Rijeka, Croatia).[25] Multi-ethnic Torontál county in southern Hungary sent a number of Serbs and Bulgarians as its representatives alongside the Magyar majority.

If the Árpád image had a somewhat divisive effect in a multi-ethnic state, the same could not be said of the cult of St Stephen. The Catholic Church, whose membership cut across ethnic lines, found the image of Hungary's first apostolic king a more congenial one than that of the pagan warrior Árpád. In a special pastoral letter to the Hungarian nation, Pope Leo XIII encouraged the Hungarians to pay special homage to the memory of their first Christian king.[26] St Stephen was an eminently suitable hero for a whole host of contemporary political reasons: he was known to have been remarkably tolerant of linguistic diversity and urged his successor to welcome able foreigners into his kingdom. Moreover, St Stephen

---

24 Julius Laurencic, *The Millennium of Hungary and the National Exhibition: Hungary During the Millennium*, Budapest, 1896, p. 228.

25 *Az 1896. évi junius hó. 8-án megtartott millenniumi hódoló díszfelvonulás leírása*, Budapest, 1896, pp. 19–20.

26 *Ezeréves Magyarország*, pp. 6–7: Pastoral Letter of Pope Leo XIII to the bishops of Hungary, Rome, 1 May 1896.

was also a distant ancestor of Hungary's present sovereign (was there any medieval royal figure from whom the Habsburgs could not claim descent?), whose long and wise reign could now be associated with the golden age of Hungary's early history.

Hungarians had had an ambivalent relationship with the House of Habsburg for four centuries. Until 1686, the dynasty controlled only about a third of the kingdom in any case, and the largely Protestant princes of Transylvania acted as a rival centre of power in protecting the rights of Protestants and Hungarian constitutional liberties. It was not until 1711, with the defeat of Prince Francis Rákóczy II, that the Habsburgs can be said to have consolidated their rule over all of Hungary. Nearly 140 years later came the Hungarian Revolution of 1848, the dethronement of the Habsburgs and the crushing of the War of Independence by Habsburg and Romanov forces. This ushered in a period of ruthless repression. Memories of the execution of Hungary's first responsible prime minister and of thirteen generals of the Hungarian army were still deeply etched on the public memory.

The great problem for the millennium organizers was that all of this had been done in the name of the ruler who was still on the throne. Even more inconvenient was the nationalist cult which exalted the memory of Lajos Kossuth, Franz Joseph's greatest Hungarian enemy — the man who had dethroned him in 1849. Kossuth statues and Kossuth streets could be found in practically every Hungarian town. When the great exile died in Torino (Turin) just two years before the millennium, his body was brought back to Budapest and buried amidst scenes of unparalleled mass emotion.

Undaunted by the spectre of the dead Kossuth, the organizers made a valiant and largely successful effort to put the King and Queen at the centre of the celebrations. Several factors came to their aid in achieving this. For one, the Catholic Church continued its traditional support for the dynasty. The Pope himself urged Hungarians to rally around the King, whose ancestors, as he put it, had toiled for the welfare of the country for centuries.[27]

The passage of time also helped to erase some of the bitter memories of 1849. Almost half a century had passed since those events. Only those in their late fifties

---

27   Ibid., p. 18.

or early sixties would have had any real memories of 1848. The veterans of the War of Independence were now doddery old men in their seventies. Furthermore, the preceding forty years had been ones of quite remarkable social and economic development in most parts of the country. Budapest was growing into a large and attractive European metropolis. In 1867, the constitutional arrangements of the Habsburg Empire had been settled in Hungary's favour. Not since the days of Matthias Corvinus had Hungary been as secure and prosperous. It seemed as if the huge gap which had developed between Hungary and the West during the period of the Turkish wars was being bridged at long last. All of this was accomplished during the reign of the same King Franz Joseph who had ordered the execution of the Hungarian generals at Arad! By downplaying or ignoring the King's role in the latter events (and, to be fair, he was only nineteen at the time and manipulated by his advisors), it was possible to claim that Hungary's recent prosperity and progress was the direct result of his 'wise rule'. Public memory being what it is, all but the most recalcitrant of malcontents were prepared to accept this proposition.

Every conceivable attempt was made to identify the King with a thousand years of Hungarian history. His descent from the Árpád dynasty was constantly emphasized; the solemn reburial of Béla III in the Coronation Church in Budapest four years before provided a marvellous opportunity to emphasize that the present King was his direct descendant. On a more simplistic level, propaganda depicted Franz Joseph as another Árpád who would gloriously lead Hungary to greatness on the threshold of the country's second millennium. No opportunity was missed to associate the King with Árpád. The commemorative plaque at the Pass of Verecke, where Árpád entered Hungary, bore the inscription: '896 Árpád — 1896 Franz Joseph I'.[28] At the cornerstone laying ceremony for the millennial memorial at Pusztaszer, the elaborate tent occupied by dignitaries was decorated with pictures of Árpád and the seven Magyar chieftains, with Franz Joseph added on as the eighth.[29] At a somewhat more mundane level, a prize-winning meerschaum pipe at the National Exhibition manage to combine Árpád and his warriors with

---

28 'Milleniumi történelmi ünnepségek', p. 667.
29 Sinkó, 'A valóság története avagy a történelem valósága', p. 13.

finely carved portraits of the King and Queen crowned with the crown of St Stephen.[30]

In the historical section of the National Exhibition in Budapest, the role of the Habsburg dynasty in Hungarian history was emphasized. The grandest hall was devoted entirely to the Habsburg kings, whose portraits, brought from Vienna and various Hungarian country houses, covered the walls. Only Franz Joseph's portrait was absent; instead, he was represented by the throne on which he had sat when signing the Compromise agreement in 1867.

The theatre and opera collaborated in glorifying the dynasty and emphasizing its ties to Hungarian history. The gala performance of Erkel's *St Stephen*, in the presence of the King and Queen at the Royal Opera House in Budapest, ended with a stirring rendition of the national anthem while the stage showed an apotheosis of the royal couple surrounded by a garland of electric lights.[31] The National Theatre's special performance on the same day also managed to mix patriotism with dynastic loyalty, though this time without the presence of the royal couple. Jenő Rákosi, a popular nationalist man of letters, had been commissioned to write a play especially for the occasion. His 'Celebration of a Thousand Years, A Vision in One Act' presented a pageant of Hungarian history from the time of Árpád's grandmother — the mythical Emese — to the present day. The final lines struck a suitably loyal note: 'A thousand years look down upon us and see millions [...] bless the God of the Hungarians, [and] the King of the Hungarians.'[32]

The following day, it was the turn of the Church to proclaim the nation's loyalty to the dynasty. On May 3, 1896, the Prince Primate, Cardinal Vaszary, celebrated a festive *Te Deum* in the newly restored gothic Coronation Church in Buda. All the participants in the ceremony were required to wear Hungarian gala dress. The glorious music of Liszt's Coronation Mass could be heard where it was first performed for the coronation of Franz Joseph twenty-nine years before. At the high point of the ceremony, the Prince Primate addressed the royal couple:

---

30 Hungarian National Museum, Budapest, Permanent Exhibition.
31 Sinko, 'A valóság története avagy a történelem valósága', p. 13.
32 Jenő Rákosi, *Az ezredév ünnepe. Látomás egy felvonásban. Az 1896-ik évi ezredéves ünnep alkalmára*, Budapest, 1896, p. 28.

Majesty, Father of the Nation! Through the grace of God, you are destined to lead this nation into its second millennium, not with the sound of arms but with the light of your wisdom and the warmth of your love. May the King of Kings place His protective arms above your person and bestow upon Your Majesty the plenitude of His grace so that you might clearly see the needs of your nation and fulfil your royal duty with courage and success, with a deep sense of duty, with constitutional exactitude and with unflagging energy [...] My Nation! [...] under the rule of the best of sovereigns, you have at last been able to take your destiny into your own hands.

Turning to the queen, Vaszary said 'when you became the mother of our nation, you spoke to us in our dear mother tongue [...] and we remember how you wove the golden threads which now bind our beloved King indissolubly to the nation'.[33] This reference to Queen Elizabeth's enthusiasm for all things Hungarian and the undeniable role she played in paving the way for the Compromise could not have been lost on the Cardinal's listeners. The Queen had always been a much more popular figure in Hungary than her husband. Where Franz Joseph had become accepted and even respected, she was loved. Now, after the suicide of Crown Prince Rudolf, the slim, still beautiful woman, dressed perennially in black, was surrounded by a tremendous wave of sympathy and affection. The Queen's genuine popularity certainly made it a good deal easier to arouse affection for the dynasty even among those who were by conviction or tradition most predisposed to view it with hostility.[34]

This unexpected outpouring of loyalty to the crown was to be duly rewarded. Four years before the millennium, Budapest had been raised to the rank of capital and royal residence (*Haupt- und Residenzstadt*), thus making it, in theory at least, the equal of Vienna. Proposals were also made in parliament to establish a separate royal Hungarian court at Budapest, though in the end this old Hungarian ambition was never to be completely realized. On the other hand, the King and the royal family made a special effort to spend as much time as possible in Budapest during the millennial year. King Franz Joseph visited the National Exhibition on

---

33 *Ezeréves Magyarország*, pp. 38–39: Sermon given by Cardinal Dr Kolos Vaszary at the Millennial Service of Thanksgiving, 3 May 1896.
34 András Gerő, 'A Hungarian Cult, Queen Elizabeth' in K. Foldy-Dozsa (ed.), *Elizabeth, Queen of Hungary*, Hungarian National Museum, Budapest, 1992.

twelve separate occasions and spent as much as four hours at a time there visiting various pavilions and conversing with officials, delegations and exhibitors. As a special gesture intended to flatter Hungarian vanity, the diplomatic corps moved to Budapest for the summer months and the popular press could exult that the Hungarian capital had now truly become the capital of the entire monarchy. The King took special pains to appear at public functions in the uniform of a Hungarian cavalry general, while the ladies of the family (except, paradoxically enough, the Queen herself) were almost invariably seen wearing Hungarian noblewomen's gala costumes on these occasions. Copies of Julius Benczúr's splendid portrait of the King in his Hungarian uniform, painted during the 1896 festivities, eventually decorated schools and public buildings and could be found on the walls of bourgeois homes and on humble postcards. It must have seemed to the Hungarian on the street as if their King was indeed 'the first Hungarian gentleman', as the popular press was fond of repeating.

On 2 May 1896, King Franz Joseph, accompanied by twenty-nine members of the royal family, opened the National Millennial Exhibition in the presence of foreign ambassadors, the joint Ministers of War, Finance and Foreign Affairs and a special delegation representing the Austrian government and parliament. The exhibition was destined to unite the three major themes of the celebrations: patriotism, progress and loyalty to the dynasty.

This was not the first national exhibition to be held in Budapest; the 1885 exhibition had already aroused a great deal of interest both at home and abroad. The man behind both exhibitions was a remarkable aristocrat with unusually far-ranging interests: Count Jenő Zichy was best known as a zealous apostle of Hungarian industrial development, a cause he promoted with considerable energy as president of the Hungarian Industrial association. The National Millennial Exhibition was largely his idea for he believed, as did Wekerle, that it would make an ideal showcase for Hungary's undeniable economic progress during the previous quarter of a century.

Zichy's other interests — Hungarian history and pre-history — coincided nicely with the other themes promoted by the millennial-year organizers. In 1895, he had financed and led an expedition to the Caucasus and central Asia in an attempt to make contact with peoples he believed were related to the ancient Magyars. The expedition got as far as Bukhara and Samarkand, gathering costumes, jewellery, weapons and other artefacts on the way. The decoration of these objects often showed an uncanny resemblance to designs used by Magyar peasants in contemporary Hungary. Count Zichy's rich collection eventually became the principal attraction of the ethnographic section of the Millennial Exhibition.[35]

The highlight of the exhibition was to be an unprecedented display of objects relating to ten centuries of Hungarian history. The organizing committee wanted this to be housed in a building which would show the development of architectural styles in the country. The building was not to be 'theatrical' but was meant to be picturesque enough to arouse the interest of visitors by its external appearance.[36] Perhaps taking the word picturesque somewhat too literally, Ignác Alpár — the architect selected for the job — first produced a neo-Moorish monstrosity which was fortunately rejected. A subsequent design, however, met with general approval. Popularly called Vajdahunyad Castle, after its most characteristic element, the exhibition building still stands at the edge of Budapest's city park. Alpár managed to produce a skilful amalgam of some of Hungary's best known architectural monuments. Vajdahunyad Castle in Transylvania was reproduced in somewhat reduced and slightly altered form for the main facade, while the rest of the building was made up of facades copied from burgher's houses in northern Hungary and architectural elements borrowed from the romanesque abbey church at Ják in western Hungary. The great medieval clock tower from Segesvár (Sighişoara, Romania), tacked on to the rear facade, served to counterbalance the turrets of Vajdahunyad in the front.

The interior, made up of a long suite of great halls, was the site of the historical exhibition. No effort or expense was spared to make the latter as impressive as possible. Foreign and domestic museums lent prize items from their collections while the great historic noble families competed to display their treasures. Particularly striking was the number and quality of the sixteenth and seventeenth century gold and silver objects, textiles, arms and historic portraits lent by the Esterházy, Batthyány, Erdődy, Bánffy and Teleki families, among many others. Some of these rare and valuable objects had never been seen by the general public

---

35 Gelléri, *Führer*, pp. 276–77.
36 Ibid., p. 141.

before. Where historically significant objects could not be transported to Budapest, excellent plaster copies were made, as in the case of the sixteenth-century tomb of Queen Isabella in the Cathedral of Gyulafehérvár (Alba Iulia, Romania) or the splendid late fifteenth-century monument to Palatine István Zápolyai. Rare medieval frescoes or carved ceilings lurking in remote Transylvanian churches were also faithfully copied and the copies brought to Budapest and installed in the appropriate section of the exhibition. Foreign aristocrats with Hungarian connections were glad to help by lending their prize objects; Count Wilczek, for instance, lent pieces from his collection to furnish the Hungarian medieval chamber.

The exhibition was divided into eight sections, each devoted to a period of Hungarian history from the conquest to 'the re-establishment of parliamentary rule in 1867'. Touchy subjects were not avoided. Thus there was a section on 'the national revival' and on the events of 1848–49, with a display of the arms and uniforms of the 'rebel' forces.[37] One can only guess the King's feelings as he passed through that particular exhibit. He was likely to have been better pleased with the final hall which, as we saw earlier, was devoted to the glories of the House of Habsburg and to Hungary's progress under the wise rule of its present sovereign. Though the nationalities were hardly represented, a few Romanian icons and the gold crowns and vestments of Serbian Orthodox bishops on display did hint, ever so slightly, at the multi-ethnic nature of the Hungarian kingdom.[38]

A special exhibition dealing specifically with Hungarian military history was attached to the main historical exhibition. The first room here featured a life-size sculptural group showing Árpád and the seven associated chieftains taking possession of the land — a theme now familiar from Munkácsy's and Feszty's vast canvases. As if to drive home the point that this was to be the image engraved on every schoolchild's mind, Munkácsy's sketches for the 'Conquest' were prominently displayed on the walls. The costumes, weapons and ornaments worn by the figures were based on architectural finds and inspired by contemporary

---

37 János Szendrei (ed.), *Magyar hadtörténelmi emlékek az ezredéves országos kiállításon*, Budapest, 1896, p. 12.
38 Béla Czobor and Imre Szalay (eds), *Magyarország történeti emlékei az 1896. évi ezredéves országos kiállításon*, 2 vols, Budapest and Vienna, 1897–1901.

accounts of the ancient Magyars by the Byzantine Emperor Leo.[39] Indeed, the highly didactic nature of the whole historical exhibition was made clear in the foreword to the splendidly illustrated two-volume catalogue which was eventually published in both Vienna and Budapest. The editors suggested that it be made available to every secondary school and university library. Furthermore, 'certain appropriate illustrated pages from it should hang on the walls of every kindergarten and elementary school in the country in order to instruct pupils about the outstanding events in the history of our thousand-year old state'.[40]

Though history might have been the focal point of the exhibition, it was by no means its dominant feature. That was given over to the theme of progress. Innumerable pavilions displayed the products of Hungarian agriculture, industry and craftsmanship. Pride of place must go to the great machinery hall, whose gigantic iron construction was apparently exceeded in size only by that of the great railway station in Frankfurt.[41] It was designed to be dismantled after the exhibition and re-erected as a railway station. Displays in the hall included Hungarian-made milling machinery, machinery used in shipbuilding and munition-making, as well as a large selection of agricultural machinery. The nearby Great Hall of Industry, left over from the 1885 exhibition, displayed various Hungarian-manufactured products, while the Hall of the Milling Industry showed how and why Budapest had risen to become the milling capital of the world. Private companies, both domestic and foreign, had their own elaborate pavilions. The Salgótarján Coal Company showed its products in a mock medieval castle, while the Viennese Thonet firm of furniture-makers and Gerbeaud's, the Budapest confectioners, among many others, all had their own elaborate individual pavilions. The great landowners often had pavilions of their own: a many-turreted half-timbered edifice of indeterminate style housed a display of agricultural products from Archduke Joseph's estates.

There was a pavilion devoted to public health, while the Ministry of Education displayed the progress Hungary had made in the field of elementary, secondary and higher education. There was a Bosnian pavilion complete with 'a typical

---

39 Szendrei (ed.), *Magyar hadtörténeti emlékek*, pp. 4–5.
40 Czobor and Szalay (eds), *Magyarország történeti emlékei*, p. 3.
41 Gelléri, *Führer*, pp. 215–16.

Bosnian house' and a Bosnian coffee-house on display, perhaps to remind the public that the province was jointly administered by both halves of the monarchy. One of the most popular displays was in the Kineskop Pavilion, where Edison's recently invented 'living pictures' were regularly shown to suitably amazed audiences.[42]

Though the manifold displays of the National Exhibition were undeniably impressive, they were to be overshadowed by what turned out to be the high point of the celebrations for Hungarians and foreign observers alike. One 8 June 1898, the twenty-ninth anniversary of Franz Joseph's coronation as King of Hungary, the country's official élite marched in solemn procession to render homage to the sovereign. This was the famous 'Banderium', an echo of the distant days when each county was required to send a certain number of armed knights to aid the king in time of war. Now the knights were as likely as not civil servants, landowners and even industrialists, but clad in the historic garb of the Hungarian nobility they were a suitably picturesque sight.

At first something entirely different had been planned for that day. The art historian Flóris Rómer had written extensively on the role played by historic pageants in raising national consciousness. This inspired Count Jenő Zichy to propose the holding of a gigantic costumed pageant to represent major episodes from Hungarian history. Pál Vágó, an artist, duly volunteered to provide 200 sketches for a vast march of over 2,000 participants in historic costume. The first float in his proposal showed 'Hungaria' seated on a gilded throne decorated with ancient Hungarian designs and symbols. This was to be followed by another female figure representing 'Hungarian virtues', accompanied by youths in the historic costume of the nobility and peasants in regional Hungarian costumes as well as others in the costume of Hungary's various nationalities. Next came twelve *tableaux vivants* depicting various scenes from Hungarian history. The final float was to be an allegory of the Compromise of 1867: 'a lavishly decorated chariot bearing a portrait bust of His Majesty surrounded by portrait medallions representing the ministers of the first responsible government in 1867'.[43] In the

---

42   Ibid., p. 196.
43   Sinkó, 'A valóság története avagy a történelem valósága', p. 15.

end, however, this ambitious project was abandoned because of the high cost involved.

Instead, it was decided that delegations from every county, the capital, the royal free cities, both houses of parliament and representatives of the Churches, as well as other official bodies, would parade before the King in front of the royal palace. The procession would then move on to escort the Holy Crown to parliament, where the solemn enactment of the law commemorating Hungary's 1,000 years of existence would take place. Following this, members of both houses of parliament, accompanied by high officials of the court, Church and state, would return to the palace to hear a loyal address.

In the end, all went according to plan and even the weather was accommodating, for 8 June was a beautiful, warm, sunny day. Nine hundred and ninety-five horsemen gathered at dawn on the great field below the Buda façade of the royal palace. Each member of the procession wore the historic Hungarian noble gala dress. Some of these were made of ancient brocades and velvets handed down from the seventeenth and eighteenth centuries. The buttons, clasps and auguillettes were often masterpieces of the jeweller's art; some of them were worth a small fortune. The horses, magnificently caparisoned, occasionally outshone their riders. One did not of course have to be of ancient noble lineage to wear a nobleman's costume. A clever Budapest tailor could whip one up in no time at all for those who had but recently entered the charmed circle of the élite. The ostentation of these newly minted historic costumes, with their surfeit of lace, brocade, fur and plumage, occasionally verged on the ridiculous. But everyone who could afford one wore one: the former Prime Minister, Wekerle, of good German burgher stock, was so clothed, as was the president of the Hungarian Credit Bank, Baron Maurice Kornfeld, one of the country's leading Jewish citizens, among countless lesser lights similarly attired.

The usually quiet streets of Buda were thronged with spectators as the colourful procession wound its way up the hill to the royal palace. Heralds with silver trumpets preceded the procession followed by the Minister of the Interior, Dezső Perczel — whose uncle, the revolutionary general Mor Perczel, had been condemned to death by Franz Joseph in 1848. Perczel, clad in blue velvet decorated with gold thread and precious stones, carried a splendid ancient mace which he raised high, 'according to ancient custom, when passing before His

Majesty'.[44] Then came representatives of Budapest, the county of Abaúj (now partly in the Slovak Republic), the royal free city of Kassa (Kaschau, Košice, Slovak Republic) the county of Alsó-Fehér in Transylvania, and so forth. The county delegations varied in size, but most included members of old county families in historic dress accompanied by retainers in the garb of medieval pages, eighteenth-century footmen or seventeenth-century warriors. Each county carried its ancient banner — that of Nyitra county, for example, dated from 1660 — and tried to be distinctive in its dress. The delegates from Pozsony county were dressed largely in white silk; pale blue dominated the ranks of Pest county; while Esztergom's representatives were accompanied by knights in seventeenth-century chain-mail.

The county delegations were followed by noblemen carrying the flags of Hungary, Croatia, Transylvania and former vassal states of the medieval Hungarian Kingdom, including some, like Lodomeria and Cumania, which had long since disappeared from the map. The historic flags of Rama (Bosnia) and Dalmatia might have irritated Hungary's Austrian partner, since Dalmatia was now an Austrian province, but it was the presence of the ancient Serbian banner in the procession which aroused the hypersensitive nationalism of the neighbouring Balkan state. The Serbian government was quick to launch an official protest.[45]

Next came representatives of parliament led by magnate members of the House of Lords, followed by the gilded coaches carrying the Prince Primate and the new Prime Minister, Baron Dezső Banffy. Cabinet ministers had their own coaches, as did the Ban of Croatia, Count Khuen-Hédervary, the Lord Treasurer, Count Zichy, and the Deputy Speaker of the House of Lords, Count Tibor Károlyi.

By a quarter to nine, members of the royal family started to gather on the balcony facing the great courtyard of the royal palace. Archduchess Stephanie, dressed in resplendent Hungarian costume, was the first to appear, with her daughter Archduchess Elizabeth. Soon the balcony was filled. There were archduchesses in Hungarian costume — Isabella and Augusta — archdukes in military uniform, archdukes bearing archaic titles, like Ferdinand, the Grand Duke of vanished Tuscany. At last, the King appeared in a Hungarian general's uniform,

---

44 *Az 1896. évi junius hó 8*, p. 7.
45 Sinkó, 'A valóság története avagy a történelem valósága', p. 15.

followed by the Queen dressed entirely in black and adorned only with the diamond insignia of the Order of the Starred Cross. Facing the balcony stood an elaborately decorated tribune for ambassadors, visiting dignitaries, selected foreign journalists and wives of those riding in the procession.

> For over an hour the nobles passed in dazzling, glittering groups [wrote the American journalist, Richard Harding Davis, who witnessed the spectacle] each rivalling the next, and making one long line of colour that wound around the shady streets [...] like a many-coloured scarf of silk and gold [...]. The Englishmen who had seen the Queen's Jubilee procession in 1887, said that the Banderium was much finer and those who had witnessed the entry of the Czar into Moscow found it, if not so impressive, at least as beautiful [...]. The Banderium was a moving panorama, an illustration of the history of Hungary by some of the men themselves who helped to make it or by their sons, or grandsons.[46]

After the almost 1,000 riders had passed before the royal balcony, the Holy Crown was placed in a glass carriage and escorted by the Banderium to the new Houses of Parliament on the other side of the Danube. There, in the great domed hall of the still uncompleted building, the Millennial Law was officially enacted with great ceremony. The text was simple and straightforward. It thanked Providence for maintaining the Hungarian state for a thousand years and then rendered homage to the King, 'under whose glorious reign, the constitutional liberties and untroubled development of the country are secure'.[47] The text of the law was to be read publicly in every town and village.

Afterwards, the Banderium moved down Andrássy Avenue to the exhibition grounds, while a delegation from both houses of parliament, accompanied by the great officers of state, crossed the Danube once again to the royal palace. Dezső Szilágyi, the speaker of the lower house, gave the loyal address to the King in the throne room filled with parliamentarians, courtiers, clerics and assembled members of the royal family. Szilágyi's speech was an eloquent restatement of late nineteenth-century liberal nationalism. Though he rejoiced in the reconciliation between the King and nation, Szilágyi reminded the sovereign of the Hungarian passion for liberty and constitutional rule. Hungarians, he said,

---

46 Richard Harding Davis, *A Year from a Reporter's Notebook*, New York, 1903, pp. 86–89.
47 Gelléri, *Führer*, p. 6.

were determined to maintain the unity of the state while respecting individual rights and rejecting any form of discrimination based on religion or ethnic origin.[48] This terse summary does not do justice to the effect produced by Szilagyi's words. 'No man ever represented the spirit of a nation with greater dignity than did he at that moment', wrote the novelist and playwright Ferenc Herczeg, 'through his lips a thousand-year-old nation, which had endured so much, [...] spoke to the bearer of the crown. The King himself seemed moved by what he heard and everyone who was present felt that ruler and nation had at long last found one another and that henceforth nothing would be able to divide them.'[49]

Replying, the King urged Hungarians to remember their neighbours who had come to their aid while they were struggling to free themselves during more than a century of foreign rule. 'The wisdom of my ancestors had associated this country [with these neighbours] [...] thereby creating the monarchy whose existence here is a European necessity and whose maintenance and transfer to my successors in its integrity is not only my sacred duty but is also in the interests of both states.'[50]

Although other events were to follow during what remained of the year, this was undoubtedly the high point of the festivities. A tremendous amount of ingenuity, organization and expenditure of money had gone into making the millennial year a success. Had it achieved its aims? On the whole, one would have to say yes. The country was swept by a wave of patriotic fervour. Even the nationalist non-Magyar leaders failed to disrupt the proceedings. The country was dotted with permanent souvenirs of the year. Not all of them were bombastic statues, but rather useful things like schools, railway stations and theatres.

The face of Budapest was changed as a result of the gigantic building programme undertaken there. Foreign observers were certainly impressed. Richard Harding Davis called it 'the most modern city in Europe, more modern than Paris, better paved and better lighted; with better facilities for rapid transit than New York', and then, the supreme accolade, 'Pest is the Yankee city of the Old World,

---

48 Sándor Szilágyi (ed.), *A magyar nemzet története*, 10 vols, Budapest, 1898, X, pp. 830–32.
49 Ferenc Herczeg, *Emlékezései, A gótikus ház*, Budapest, 1985, p. 297.
50 Szilágyi (ed.), *A magyar nemzet története*, p. 832.

just as the Hungarians are called the Americans of Europe.'[51] Wekerle, Zichy and others who wanted to show Hungary's progressive face to the world must have been gratified by Davis's words.

The millennial year certainly succeeded in making the King more popular. Though he was not loved, he was honoured and respected and, what is more, his person became firmly associated with all the achievements of the past quarter-century and with those which were yet to come. Though hostility to the Habsburgs lingered on, especially on the benches of the Independence Party, the general public adopted a far more favourable attitude to the dynasty. Violent anti-Habsburg feelings were not to revive until the last disastrous days of the Dual Monarchy; even then they were partly artificial, fomented for political purposes.

Today, the millennial year looks like the apogee of a golden age, especially for older Hungarians. Though the period was beset with problems, for one year these were banished to the background during a round of festivities for which it is hard to find a parallel in modern history.

---

51 Davis, *A Year from a Reporter's Notebook*, pp. 71–72

PROVINCE VERSUS METROPOLIS: THE INSTRUMENTALIZED MYTH OF ARCHDUKE JOHN OF STYRIA (1782–1859)

Dieter A. Binder

On 8 September 1878, the larger-than-life bronze statue of Archduke John was unveiled on the main square of Graz.[1] The original plans of 1863 envisioned it being located in the Joanneum Garden, which at that time was still rather large.[2] In 1870, the foundation-stone was laid at what is today the square of the Eiserne Tor. In 1874, it was decided to place the statue in the very centre of the city, directly facing the city hall. In order to appreciate the implied value judgement of this decision, one needs to take into consideration the site of the monument to

---

I would like to thank Professor Walter Gründzweig for his kind help with this chapter.

1 The statue, designed and cast by Franz Pönninger, is a fountain rich with iconographic decoration; allegorical bronze reliefs point to agriculture and mining, industry, hunting, forestry, viticulture, and health resorts, whereas the actual figures at the fountain symbolize the four main rivers of what was then Styria: Mur, Enns, Drau (Drava) and Sann (Sava). The central base cites as John's central achievements science, agriculture, mining, the train line from Vienna to Graz across the Semmering mountain; his larger-than-life-size figure towers above it: see *Grazer Zeitung*, 8 September 1878, pp. 1–3 and 9 September 1878, pp. 2ff.

2 *Joanneum* is the name of the Museum of Styria in Graz. R. Baravalle, 'Das Erzherzog-Johann-Denkmal' in Baravalle, *Blätter für Heimatkunde*, Graz, 1968, pp. 85–96; H. Schweigert, *Graz. Dehio-Handbuch*, Graz and Vienna, 1979, p. 109.

John's imperial brother: On 19 August 1841 the statue of Emperor Franz I was placed on today's Freiheitsplatz in the immediate vicinity of the Burg, the cathedral, the theatre and the site of the old university.[3] It is still located on the margins of the old city in the area of imperial Graz. While Emperor Ferdinand was present for the unveiling of the monument to his father, Emperor Franz Joseph unveiled the statue of his great-uncle at the time of the fourth Styrian choir festival.[4] Contemporary political cartoons clearly interpreted the ceremony of 1878, which was shaped by court etiquette, as an unsuccessful attempt to return John, the Styrian, to his imperial world.[5] The design of the monument was quoted as iron proof of John's actual attitude: he was not depicted in a general's uniform, as demanded by several groups, but in plain civilian clothing. Only the Leopold Order and the Golden Fleece emphasized his imperial origin. The inscription on the central base praises the Archduke as patron of progress and as a friend of the people. The Dehio art guide ascribes the text to Robert Hamerling,[6] but the catalogue to the Styrian exhibition on Archduke John calls it the work of another liberal author, Anastasius Grün.[7] Altogether, the iconography of the monument has been interpreted as the self-stylization of the liberal bourgeoisie, who viewed Archduke John as a counter-figure to the head of the dynasty and to the authority of the state, even though Josephine attitudes towards liberalism always remained distant and sceptical.[8]

Already during the Napoleonic wars, Archduke John's reputation was associated with separatism and dynastic criticism, epitomized in the images of an 'Alpine Federation' and the 'King of the Alps'. The controversy over John's plan

---

3 See *Grazer Zeitung*, 19 August 1841, p. 1, and 21 August 1841, p. 1. The larger-than-life bronze statue was cast by Luigi Manfredini and Giovanni Battista Viscard according to a model by Pompeo Marchesi: Schweigert, *Graz. Dehio-Handbuch*, p. 110.
4 See G. Klingenstein and P. Cordes (eds), *Erzherzog Johann von Österreich*, 2 vols, Graz, 1982, I, p. 557, and II, p. 438.
5 See *Steirer-Seppl*, 18, 1878, p. 25; A. Legat, 'Johannes Nachleben in den Künsten' in Klingenstein and Cordes (eds), *Erzherzog Johann von Österreich*, II, p. 441.
6 See Schweigert, *Graz. Dehio-Handbuch*, p. 109.
7 See Klingenstein and Cordes (eds), *Erzherzog Johann von Österreich*, I, p. 556.
8 B. Sutter, 'Erzherzog Johanns Kritik an Österreich, *Mitteilungen des Österreichischen Staatsarchives*, 1982, pp. 172.

of 1813 for an insurrection of the Alpine lands following Napoleon's defeat in Russia concerned both the fight over the political orientation represented by Metternich and the question of the political authority of a talented son of the crown who had no scope for action of his own. Grete Klingenstein focuses on the basic dilemma:

> It seems, however, that the person of Archduke John revealed a problem of state politics which went to the very foundations of Habsburg rule: the declining role of the dynasty in the modern state. [...] Which role should the sons of Leopold, who had a talent for governing, perform in a state whose cohesion had for a long time been safeguarded by a highly diversified bureaucracy?[9]

Three major themes have long dominated the research on Archduke John. The first relates to the Archuke's own journalistic writings covering the period 1806–16,[10] and is dealt with especially in the studies by Franz Joseph Adolph Schneidawand, Franz Ritter von Krones and Hans von Zwiedineck-Südenhorst.[11] The second, centring on the Regency, comprises contemporary journalism and early biographical works.[12] The third, involving John's work in Styria, is

---

9   G. Klingenstein, 'Joanneische Skizzen' in Klingenstein and Cordes (eds), *Erzherzog Johann von Österreich*, II, p. 13.

10 Regarding the significance of the material, see D. A. Binder, 'Die politisch-historische Instrumentalisierung des Erzherzog Johann-Mythos' in *Österreich in Geschichte und Literatur* (forthcoming).

11 F. J. A. Schneidawand, *Das Leben des Erzherzog Johanns von Österreich*, Schaffhausen, 1849; F. Krones, *Tirol 1812–1816 und Erzherzog Johann von Österreich*, Innsbruck, 1890; idem, *Aus dem Tagebuch Erzherzog Johann's von Österreich 1810–1815*, Innsbruck, 1891; idem, *Aus Österreichs stillen und bewegten Tagen*, Innsbruck, 1892; H. Zwiedineck-Südenhorst, 'Das Gefecht bei St. Michael und die Operationen des Erzherzogs Johann in Steiermark 1809, *Mitteilungen des Instituts für Österreichische Geschichtsforschung*, 1891; idem, *Zur Geschichte des Krieges von 1809 in der Steiermark*, Graz, 1892; and idem, *Erzherzog Johann von Österreich im Feldzuge von 1809*, Graz, 1892.

12 J. P. Lyser, *Erzherzog Johann, der Freund des Volkes*, Vienna, 1849; A. Frey, *Kurzer Lebensabriß des Reichsverwesers Erzherzog Johann von Österreich*, Nuremberg, 1848; F. Althaus, *Das Buch vom Erzherzog Johann*, Leipzig, 1848; K. A. Schimmer, *Das Leben und Wirken des Erzherzog Johann von Österreich*, Mainz, 1849; and Erzherzog Johann von Österreich, *Achtundvierzig Briefe ... Johann von Müller*, Schaffhausen, 1848 (hereafter *Achtundvierzig Briefe*).

dominated by Styrian historians. Although there are numerous studies on individual questions, editions of sources[13] and several popular monographs,[14] there is as yet no comprehensive academically researched biography of the Archduke[15]. Although a wealth of editions of sources shed light on partial aspects, there is no complete edition of those diaries which have not been destroyed by war and of John's autobiographical *Denkwürdigkeiten*. Nor is there any systematic access to John's extensive correspondence. However, historians have employed the wealth of existing sources to interpret John's significance for various political and ideological objectives.[16] Given the haphazard selections from this material, the historiographical usefulness of these studies can be likened to a placebo. If this research was regional in orientation, it always took account of the fact that John's work transcended Styrian borders despite the fact that some aspects, such as his criticism of Vienna and the centralist agencies of the Metternichian system, have occasionally been overstated.

Twentieth-century Styrian research on John has undergone occasional surges in popularity due to the use of the object of research for nationalistically inclined folklore studies (*Volkskunde*) and the pleasure Styria took in stylizing anniversaries. Styria's natural resources provide an identity-shaping frame. In spite of their much-changed social and economic significance, iron ore, wood and the peasantry retain critical importance and have become canonized elements of

---

13 For example, studies by Franz Ilwof and Anton Schlossar: see A. L. Schuller, 'Bibliographie der Erzherzog-Johann-Literatur (Auswahl)' in O. Pickl (ed.), *Erzherzog Johann von Österreich*, Graz, 1982. In addition to the authors, it is also necessary to look up the key word 'Erzherzog Johann'.

14 A. Schlossar, *Erzherzog Johann von Österreich*, Graz, 1902; V. Theiß, *Erherzog Johann. Der steirische Prinz*, Graz, 1950; and H. Wiesflecker, *Erzherzog Johann*, Graz, 1959.

15 Three instalments (vol. 1, parts 1 and 2, vol. 2, part 1) were published of Viktor Theiß, *Leben und Wirken Erzherzog Johanns*, Graz, 1960–69, bringing the work up to c. 1811. This attempt at a biography, which was disrupted by the death of the author, was probably also condemned to failure for reasons of approach: see G. Klingenstein, 'Zur Einführung' in V. Theiß, *Erzherzog Johann. Der steirische Prinz*, 2nd edn, Graz, 1981, pp. 11–19.

16 E. Staudinger, 'Wandel der Denkmäler', *Sterz*, 1982, pp. 3–5.

Styrian state exhibitions. The cult surrounding Archduke John is located on this very foundation.[17]

In 1911, Viktor von Geramb's article on John's 'significance to Styrian *Volkskunde*', in a *Festschrift* on the centennial celebrating the foundation of the Joanneum, immediately followed the introductory appreciation by Anton Mell, who surveyed John's life's achievement as a whole.[18] Initially, Geramb links the Archduke and his activities with the 'founders of the academic discipline of *Volkskunde*', the Grimm brothers, and defines the Archduke's interest in demography as modern ethnographic research.[19] The statistical record-keeping encouraged by John found special recognition, and the significance of these records as sources for *Volkskunde* found as much praise as the activities of the painters and musical institutions which were commissioned by John. The positioning of the article in second position in the book, preceding Arnold Luschin von Ebengreuth's contribution on the history of the Joanneum between 1811 and 1911 and, more remarkably, the individual articles relating to the various sections of the museum, suggest that Geramb wanted to legitimize his call for a special *Volkskunde* department by 'proving' that his field had already been promoted by Archduke John in the founding period of the Joanneum.

In Graz, academically orientated *Volkskunde* was first undertaken by Karl Weinhold, a professor of German, who professed to adhere to a '*Volkskunde* and *Altertumskunde* influenced by the Romantics' in the Grimm tradition.[20] In 1873,

---

17 This can be illustrated by examples of state exhibition themes. 'Archduke John. Commemorative Exhibition' (1959); 'The Styrian Farmer: Achievement and Destiny from the Stone Age through the Present' (1966); 'Miners and Foundrymen: Designers of Styria' (1968); 'Styrian Craft' (1970). 'Archduke John of Austria' (1982); 'Ore and Iron in Green Styria' (1984); and 'Glass and Coal' (1988). More culturally orientated exhibitions, such as those on musical life, the Gothic period and literature, were always limited to Styria; only one exhibition, 'Witches and Magicians', went beyond this local frame.
18 V. Geramb, 'Erzherzog Johanns Bedeutung für die steirische Volkskunde' and A. Mell, 'Erzherzog Johann und sein Wirken in der Steiermark', both in Mell (ed.), *Das steiermärkische Landesmuseum Joanneum und seine Sammlungen*, Graz, 1911, pp. 37–66 and 1–35, respectively.
19 Geramb, 'Erzherzog Johanns Bedeutung für die steirische Volkskunde', p. 40.
20 H. Eberhart, 'Zu den Anfängen der Volkskunde in Graz' in W. Jacobeit, H. Lixfeld and O. Bockhorn (eds), *Völkische Wissenschaft*, Vienna, 1994, p. 403.

another Germanist, Anton Emanuel Schönbach, joined the Graz faculty. Harking back to Weinhold, he too frequently offered lectures in *Volkskunde*. The chair for Sanskrit and comparative linguistics was filled by Rudolf Mehringer, who was called the founder of the 'Graz school of *Sach-Volkskunde*', a version of material culture studies. Mehringer decisively influenced Geramb. It was under his guidance that Geramb completed his *Habilitation* in 'Deutsche *Volkskunde*'.[21] Following his great model, German ethnologist Wilhelm Heinrich Riehl, Geramb advocated a kind of ethnography which would serve the myth of a 'German nation'. Geramb's interpretation of the life of Archduke John was significantly shaped by the notion of a 'German' archduke.[22] At first this mode of reception was but a stage setting. His actual fascination with the Archduke proceeded from John's specialized collections: John's stock-taking in the area of *Volkskunde* and regional culture, preserved in the Styrian state archive as *Göth'sche Serie*,[23] the great watercolours of native costumes by the court painters, especially by Karl Ruß, were used time and again for Geramb's later work on regional architectural design and native costumes, especially for his comprehensive book on Styrian costumes.[24] While he did not refer to John in his academic work of the 1920s and 1930s, he did connect his activities in popular education, especially his *Heimatwerk*, closely with the person of the 'Styrian prince', who served as a metaphor to popularize his work.[25]

A close consultant of Governor Karl Maria Stepan, Geramb definitely influenced cultural politics in Styria during the period of the Austrian corporate state, although as an old-school German nationalist he harboured great

---

21 H. Eberhart, 'Nationalgedanke und Heimatpflege' in Jacobeit, Lixfield and Bockhorn (eds), *Völkische Wissenschaft*, p. 430.

22 V. Geramb, *Ein Leben für die Anderen*, Vienna, 1959, p. 11.

23 J. F. Knaffl, *Die Knaffl-Handschrift. Eine obersteirische Volkskunde aus dem Jahre 1813*, Berlin, 1928.

24 Regarding the significance of the material see Jacobeit, Lixfeld and Bockhorn (eds), *Völkische Wissenschaft*, pp. 653–54. V. Geramb and K. Mautner, *Steirisches Trachtenbuch*, Graz, 1932–35.

25 H. Koren, 'Vorwort' in Viktor Geramb, *Ein Leben für die Anderen. Erzherzog Johann und die Steiermark. Aus dem nachgelassenen Manuskript bearbeitet von Oskar Müllern*, Vienna, 1959, pp. 5–6.

reservations about the system as such. The author Paula Grogger, working within the framework of the festival culture of the corporate state, which was informed by the ideal of popular education, wrote *Die Hochzeit* (The Wedding), a play for amateur actors, whose dramatic plot is based on the historically documented attendance of John and Anna Plochl at a wedding:[26] 'Thematically, Paula Grogger's play was a natural part of the Archduke John renaissance initiated by Governor Stepan between 1934 and 1938. Moreover, her work also corresponded to the notion of literature held by the corporate state according to which popularity [...] had been raised to a criterion for true art'.[27] Grogger, who kept her distance from both the *Vaterländische Front* of the corporate state and the Nazi party, did manage, as reported by Ferdinand Tremel, to unite 'actors of all camps in one common cultural project', so that the 'church square in Öblarn' could become an 'island of peace', 'where monarchists, Nazis and Social Democrats could close their ranks behind a black-and-yellow flag, and where the audience rose from their seats when the imperial anthem was played, regardless of their political points of view'.[28] The combination of an accepted popular author and a subject matter which was generally seen in a positive light made this feasible. Grogger's play was revived in the two important years of 1959 and 1982 when John was commemorated.

During the Nazi period, the Joanneum and also the person of Archduke John remained exempted from the general *damnatio memoriae* regarding all cultural achievements of the Habsburgs. John, the 'Alpine King', was recognized as a clever forerunner of the idea of the unification of all German-speaking territories, and through his position as Regent he was placed in an all-German context. It was, however, left to historians after 1945 to emphasize his loyalty to the imperial house and to Austria. In fact, one author was able to entertain both ideas. To Hans Pirchegger, John was the 'standard-bearer of the German idea' in 1934, but the

---

26 C. H. Binder, *Paula Grogger*, Trautenfels, 1985.
27 A. Spreitzhofer, *Grundzüge der steirischen Kulturpolitik von 1934 bis 1938*, Graz, 1989, p. 79.
28 F. Tremel, 'Landeshauptmann Karl Maria Stepan', *Blätter für Heimatkunde*, 1972, pp. 121–22.

guarantor of the interests of Austria in 1949.[29] Whereas the 'German' Archduke had already been lovingly admired by the German-nationalist bourgeoisie of the nineteenth century, conservative Catholics regarded him much more as a symbol of integration of the bilingual population of Styria.[30] In 1940, in the first volume of a new series entitled *The Joanneum: Contributions on Nature Study, History, Art, and Economy in the Eastern Alpine Region*,[31] Graz historian Oskar Meister acknowledged the 'Styrian professional meetings prior to 1848' for their significance for the idea of German unity. He praised the participation of Styrian scholars in events such as the 1843 millennium of German unity (Treaty of Verdun) invented by the Prussian King Friedrich Wilhelm IV. 'At that time the Styrian Historical Association [Historischer Verein für Steiermark] was founded as a birthday gift to one-thousand-year-old Mother Germania'.[32] Explicitly, Meister emphasized the close relationship of the founders of the Association to Archduke John, whose toast to the 'German Fatherland' on the occasion of the commemorative celebration of the building of the Cologne Cathedral in 1842 was praised as much as his addresses at the all-German meetings in 1843 and 1846, the Twenty-first Assembly of German Natural Scientists and Physicians and the Tenth Assembly of German Farmers and Foresters. Already in 1882, Zwiedineck

---

29 'Police pressure was the reason why the national idea was never truly expressed in public by Germans in Austria up to 1835. Already at that time, Styrians were asked to feel and think as Austrians and not to look beyond the black-and-yellow border posts. After the death of Emperor Franz, however, the pressure lessened somewhat and Archduke John was recognized as a standard-bearer of the German idea not only in Styria and in Austria but also in the rest of Germany': H. Pirchegger, *Geschichte der Steiermark 1740–1919*, Graz, 1934, p. 369. The words 'already at that time' suggest an analogy, to be made explicit by the reader, to the current political scenario, the corporate state. See also idem, *Geschichte der Steiermark*, Graz, 1949, pp. 256–58.

30 Staudinger, 'Wandel der Denkmäler', p. 3.

31 The Introduction to the first volume of the series comments: 'The name of honour "Joanneum" was chosen in order to demonstrate the conscious position to build on the cultural creations of Archduke John, the German Regent of 1848, one of the most popular men most deeply rooted in the life of Styria': see W. Teppner, 'Dem Joanneum zum Geleit' in J. Papesch (ed.), *Das Joanneum. Beiträge zur Naturkunde, Geschichte, Kunst und Wirtschaft des Ostalpenraums*, Graz, 1940, p. 6.

32 O. Meister, 'Der deutsche Einheitsgerdanke auf steirischen Berufstagungen vor 1848' in Papesch, *Das Joanneum*, pp. 175–83.

stressed John's 'truly German conviction' in accordance with his own German-nationalist world view: 'Archduke John was Austrian and German, a true servant of his master and an equally true servant to his nation. He so much loved all things German that he never put the interests of his own dynasty above those of the shared fatherland'.[33]

With the end of the Nazi period, the paradigm that guided the reception of Archduke John shifted. John's patronage of the revolutionary *Vormärz* was reinterpreted to support Austrian post-war reconstruction; the 'German Prince' re-emerged as the 'Styrian Prince'. This change can be documented most radically in the works of Richard Walzel. In 1941, Walzel published a history of the Leoben University of Mining and Metallurgy in a *Festschrift* for armament minister Fritz Todt. In a grand-scale, self-stylizing volume, *Styria: The Land, Its People, Its Achievements*, published in 1971, this essay was brought up to date but otherwise published essentially unchanged: the epithet 'German', however, was replaced by 'Styrian'.[34] The case of Viktor Theiß was very similar. Originally an ethnographer, he had taken over the directorship of the *Volkskunde* museum in 1938 after the Nazis had virtually banned Viktor von Geramb from the museum grounds. In 1945, he was removed and transferred to work in the Styrian provincial archives. Thus, Theiß started to 'deal with Archduke John', according to Grete Klingenstein, in the 'context of a ruined ideology and a ruined Reich'.[35] Poet Hans Gustl Kernmayr also turned to John in the wake of de-Nazification; he focused on the relationship between John and his lover Anna Plochl.[36] A similar picture emerges from the work of Robert Bravalle, a specialist on Styrian castles, who in 1949 published a volume entitled *Archduke John: The Man, His Life and Work* with the Archduke Johann publishing firm using the pseudonym Hermann Burg.[37] In contrast to Viktor Theiß, Bravalle kept his distance from the sources. The intention behind this work was in line with the policy of political re-education. Regarding John's work,

---

33 Staudinger, 'Wandel der Denkmäler', p. 4.
34 R. Walzel, 'Montanistische Hochschule Leoben' in *Die deutschen Technischen Hochschulen*, Munich, 1941, reprinted in *Die Steiermark. Land, Leute, Leistungen*, Graz, 1971.
35 Klingenstein, 'Zur Einführung', p. 16; Theiß, *Erzherzog Johann. Der steirische Prinz*.
36 H. G. Kernmayr, *Erzherzog Johanns große Liebe*, Gmunden, 1949.
37 H. Burg [R. Bravalle], *Erzherzog Johann. Der Mensch, sein Leben und Wirken*, Graz, 1949.

one would be justified in using the poet's beautiful words: 'One grand example inspires emulators and provides higher laws for judgement'. If each Styrian of our present time, observing this line, will stop and think about the work of Archduke John and use it as a guiding principle for his own actions, our country will not fail to blossom forth anew from poverty and ruins.[38]

In the Styrian memorial year of 1959, Governor Josef Krainer, Senior, praised post-war reconstruction in the programme listing the commemorative events taking place throughout the year and provided an account of the country's achievements.[39] The use of the Archduke as a symbol of reconstruction had a grand tradition in Styria. Karl Maria Stepan, who had a portrait of the Archduke hung in the state parliament, postulated the goal of an economic and cultural revival[40] 'in the spirit of Archduke John'.[41] The intellectual and spiritual reconstruction of the country announced by Stepan was expressed by Viktor von Geramb and Hanns Koren as 'enthusiasm for and deeper understanding of [...] native customs and culture' which were said to have been concealed by foreign fashion trends.[42] The passionate support for native customs was intended to level political, social and ideological differences. Visually, this was to be symbolized by the national costume, the grey coat of the Archduke: 'Our Styrian costume, our Styrian traditions, our customs, are expressions of our being, of our character, of our particular nature. They have sprung forth from the soil of the native land and are as holy as the soil itself.'[43]

Hanns Koren, Geramb's student and collaborator prior to 1938, continued this idea after the war when working in Styrian cultural politics:

> [Archduke John] again puts on his grey coat, which he himself has raised to the position of honour in order to provide an example of plainness of customs; this coat that he elevated to be the honoured garment; standing for all that is better in the province and which he has left us as one of the dearest heirlooms. The grey coat has remained our shared inheritance up to

---

38 Ibid., p. 7.
39 J. Krainer, 'Die Steiermark heute', *Steirische Berichte*, 1959, p. 37.
40 W. Semetkowski, 'Landeshauptmann Stepan und unsere Heimat', *Steirische Volks- und Trachtenzeitung*, 1936, p. 1.
41 Spreitzhofer, *Grundzüge der steirischen Kulturpolitik*, p. 44.
42 *Grazer Volksblatt*, 16 February 1936, p. 6.
43 Semetkowski, 'Landeshauptmann Stepan und unsere Heimat', p. 2.

the present day. It is not the badge of a religious denomination or of a party; it belongs to the young as well as to the old, to the inhabitants of the city as well as to the dwellers of the countryside, it is a symbol for what we have shared through all quarrel and natural oppositions, and that has remained common to all of us. This both delights and obliges us: our homeland.[44]

In 1959, Philipp Meran, a descendant of Archduke John, praised the grey coat, referring specifically to hunting, as a symbol of equality among all hunters, as this coat 'also forges together poor and rich in the art of hunting'.[45]

The notion of the homeland which, according to Stepan, 'cannot be defined academically',[46] emerged as a tautology, namely that 'Styrian-ness' is whatever is Styrian. One of the rituals of Styrian domestic politics is the expression of regional opposition. The epithet of such oppositional behaviour is the definition of the Styrian in contrast to the capital, Vienna. This is certainly a version of the controversy between countryside and metropolis whose historical dimension Adam Wandruszka has demonstrated, using the example of 1848:

> The isolation of the petty-bourgeois-proletarian 'democratic' October revolution from the surrounding country shows this developmental difference in sharp focus. It would live on in the history of the whole First Austrian Republic as the opposition between 'Red Vienna' and the 'bourgeois-anti-Marxist' *Länder*.[47]

Stepan defined this as follows:

> One major change I want to point to characterizes the new *Land* policy towards the federal government. We endeavour, one might say using a slogan, to take as our example the work of Archduke John, who was a 'loyal subject of the emperor' but nevertheless led Styria in an absolutely autonomous manner. In other words: We do want to work together with Vienna, but in doing so we emphasize our own character.[48]

Again, Hanns Koren affirms this statement years later, after the Second World War:

---

44 Koren, *Reden*, p. 63.
45 P. Meran, 'Erzherzhog Johann und die Jagd', *Steirische Berichte*, 1959, p. 92.
46 *Grazer Volksblatt*, 16 February 1936, p. 6.
47 A. Wandruzska, 'Österreichs politische Struktur' in Heinrich Benedikt (ed.), *Geschichte des Republik Österreich*, Vienna, 1954, pp. 423–24.
48 Spreitzhofer, *Grundzüge der steirischen Kulturpolitik*, p. 44.

There is a Styrian patriotism. Nevertheless, a true Styrian will never hesitate to express his allegiance to our common Austrian fatherland and to confirm it in deed. But he will express it in his inherited dialect, which can easily be understood on the shores of the Danube as well. And in realizing the genius and vital laws planted into this land and its people, he is convinced he is making his contribution to the common fatherland and doing justice to his Austrian mission. We belong to Austria. The allegiance to the federal constitution of the republic has a special and authentic ring in the voice of Styria. Without Styria, there is no Austria. The spirit permitting us to speak thus is that of the Styrian Prince. In this spirit, we are entering the second century after his passing.[49]

The Styrian government declared 1959, the one-hundredth anniversary of the Archduke's death, a Styrian year of commemoration, during which a series of state-wide and local events between 11 May, the anniversary of John's death, and 26 November, the foundation day of the Joanneum, were dedicated to the memory of Archduke John. For reasons of domestic Austrian politics, Styria received attention as a special force within Austria. The staging and liturgy corresponded to historical models in many details and were designed to mobilize the masses.[50] In 1956, the emphasis on autonomy had led to a separation of the Styrian elections from the Austrian national elections. The very pronounced first electoral success of Josef Krainer, Senior, in 1957 had confirmed this position and had increasingly led the Styrian People's Party to adopt an oppositional role within the Austrian People's Party. In January 1959, Krainer initiated the controversy by questioning the workings of the Grand Coalition between the People's Party and the Social Democrats. In April he called for an enhanced status of the *Bundesrat*, which would be transformed into a true chamber of the *Länder*, and in October he proclaimed the leadership of the *Länder* as a political goal.[51] At the end of the

---

49 Koren, *Reden*, p. 67.
50 George L. Mosse, *Die Nationalisierung der Massen. Politische Symbolik und Massenbewegungen in Deutschland von den napoleonischen Kriegen bis zum Dritten Reich*, trans. Otto Weith, Berlin, 1976 [original English edition, *The Nationalization of the Masses: Political Symbolism and Mass Movements in Germany from the Napoleonic Wars through the Third Reich*, New York, 1975], Berlin, 1976.
51 D. A. Binder, 'Steirische oder Österreichische Volkspartei' in *Volkspartei. Anspruch und Realität*, Vienna, 1995 (= *Schriftenreihe des Forschungsinstitutes für politisch-historische Studien der Dr.-Wilfried-Hauslauer-Bibliothek, Salzburg*, 2), p. 589.

Styrian commemorative year Hanns Koren re-emphasized this mobilization by quoting one of the leaders of the reformers within the party, the Governor of Salzburg, Josef Klaus: 'In a survey asking prominent Austrians about their hopes for the New Year, the Governor of Salzburg replied: "A strengthening of the national consciousness of Salzburg. 1959 has been a year of the Tyrolians and the Styrians; 1960 should be a year of the Salzburgers"'.[52] Thus was proclaimed the front of the reformers of the *Länder* within the People's Party, which made Klaus, a messianic conservative of Alpine bent, their leader.

Apart from this political dimension, which boosted the self-consciousness of the *Länder*, there is the question of the scientific-scholarly basis upon which the memorial year rested. The central exhibition organized by Berthold Sutter and his junior staff traced and visualized John's life and emphasized specifically those institutions whose origin and patronage were closely connected to the Archduke.[53] One of these collaborators, Oskar Müllern, a former Nazi, edited a collection of essays by Geramb entitled *Ein Leben für die Anderen* (A Life for the Others). In 1958, Hermann Wiesflecker presented a major lecture to introduce the members of the Styrian government and the Styrian district commissioners to John's historical dimension; an enlarged version of this lecture was published in 1959. The provincial historical commission announced publication of a study by Viktor Theiß which, according to the original publication schedule, was to document 'Childhood and Youth of Archduke John (1782–1805)', 'Years of Apprenticeship (1806–21)', 'Years of Success (1822–47)' and the 'Turning Point in History (1848–59)' in four instalments and two volumes. The Neue Galerie, directed by Walter Koschatzky, devoted an exhibition to one specific topic, namely the 'court painters of the Archduke'.[54] The completion of the restoration of various sites such as the ironworks of Radwerk IV in Vordernberg addressed specialized aspects of the work of John's life.

Measures to enhance popular education, which Hanns Koren employed and supported systematically, played a significant role in popularizing the topic.

---

52 Koren, *Reden*, p. 93.
53 Erzherzog Johann, *Achtundvierzig Briefe*.
54 W. Koschatzky, *Die Kammermaler um Erzherzog Johann*, Graz, 1959, and idem, 'Kunstwerke als Dokumente des Geites', *Steirische Berichte*, 1959.

Persons who had contributed to the formation of an instrumentalized myth about Archduke John since the 1930s played key roles in this undertaking: Franz Maria Kapfhammer, the federal official responsible for popular education, and author Paul Anton Keller. They all came from the St Martin Volksbildungswerk, directed by Josef Steinberger and Viktor von Geramb, and ensured that the continuity of the myth would not be disrupted by political changes. Thus it is not surprising that a significant part of the Styrian memorial year of 1959 corresponded to the conception designed by Stepan for the celebratory *Volkstage* of the corporate state. One paradigmatic example for this continuity is a speech on the Archduke's relationship to the peasantry given by Steinberger in 1936 and published in 1958.[55] Surprisingly, as pointed out by Staudinger, even the Styrian Social Democrats utilized the myth by interpreting John's work, which had been celebrated as supporting the bourgeoisie and the peasants in the nineteenth century, as a way to speak up for the social interests of the working class:

> The recourse to John skips over the change from a monarchical to a republican-democratic organization of the state, two painful world wars, the highly controversial First Republic, four years of an authoritarian corporate state, seven years of loss of national sovereignty and Nazi rule as well as ten years of allied occupation and reconstruction. These disruptions in the historical development of our country are within the experiential horizon of one single generation. History as common experience does not function as an integrative factor of a society and even leads to disintegration. Is this the reason for an evasion to a more distant and therefore less problematical past which allows for consensus? Is it possible to escape concrete historical positioning along with its social and cultural background and its threatening global framework by emphasizing Archduke John as the 'prototypical Styrian'?[56]

In 1982, the Social Democratic Party remained strangely non-partisan and non-political in its relationship to the mysteries of Archduke John brought forth by the People's Party. The haphazard quality of the myth facilitated the integration of Social-Democratic strategy. The historical consciousness of this party was so exclusively focused on the 'history of the labour movement' that it lacked safe instruments for dealing with bourgeois historical clichés and quotations.

---

55 J. Steinberger, 'Erzherzog Johann und der Bauernstand', *Steirische Berichte*, 1958, p. 52.
56 Staudinger, 'Wandel der Denkmäler', pp. 4–5.

The Archduke was marketed as historical evidence for current political needs in an interplay between politicians and historians, who furnished the required material. The myth consists of a reinterpretation of historical research for the benefit of day-to-day politics, provides the stage setting for the myth which in itself cannot be corrected by research:

> Attempts to establish thematically appropriate concrete analogies between the present and John's time, dominated by slogans such as 'historical turning point' or 'tension between tradition and innovation', are designed to provide seemingly objective motivations and reasons for occupying oneself with John in a legitimate and useful manner. The fact that today's sociopolitical systems and structures which condition public and private actions are basically different, and that claims, values and objectives are new, is mentioned in general terms but not examined in detail. Such superficial analogies simplify and distort both the present and the past and therefore conflict with a sound historiographical position.[57]

By appealing to the myth of Archduke John, it was possible both to accommodate former Nazi cultural officials and to promote avant-garde art. This is not meant to reduce the theoretical debate to a simplistic juxtaposition of preservation versus progress, but to emphasize the haphazardness of historical analogies.

In the Styrian memorial year of 1982, the Forschungsgesellschaft Joanneum (Joanneum Research Society) organized a top-level symposium (entitled 'Archduke John 2000') in order to discuss the 'crisis of progress' in an interdisciplinary forum. Grete Klingenstein, the academic director of the large Styrian state exhibition 'Archduke John of Austria', provided an analysis of John's objectives and ideas. Stressing John's significance as the founder and initiator of bourgeois clubs and associations, she concluded:

> [...] associations, as his American contemporary Alexis de Tocqueville put it in 1835, provide an opportunity for human beings to build a protective wall against the tyrannical will of individuals and against the tyrannical majority of parties. These, too, were concerns of Archduke John in the Austria of his time in which the first seemed destined to become even more threatening, and the second could already be observed in the cliques and

---

57   Ibid., p. 5.

parties at the court. Should we, in our time, not want to listen closely to these messages?[58]

The state exhibition was designed to present John in the context of his time:

> But with some exceptions, research dealing with provincial history is not yet prepared to tackle the era of Archduke John and the transition from agrarian-feudal to bourgeois-industrial conditions. Starting with the corporate system and feudalism, state administration and bureaucracy, the bourgeoisie in regional cities and in the capital, all the way up to John's Joanneum and other associations, there is a lack of basic research. What interest us are questions regarding the conditions of historical progress and its structures.[59]

This claim is to some extent redeemed by the visual dimension of the exhibition and the various contributions in the volume accompanying it. But this publication is not fundamentally different from the *Festschrift* of the Styrian Historical Commission, which also deals with 'structural history'.[60] A focus on the history of individuals and institutions predominates. This is also noted by Berthold Sutter in his biographical appreciation in the same volume:

> The danger for historians dealing with Archduke John is that biography mutates to a history of institutions that were founded by the Archduke and in which he still lives on. However, this means narrowing his image. To do justice to his personality requires also doing justice to what he has done for Austria as a whole, without concealing — due to a wrong notion of modernity — what the traditions and customs of the people meant to him, the great significance he attached to native customs and tradition, and the attempts he undertook to preserve them. In them he saw the natural prerequisites for the state's continuing development.[61]

During the 1982 memorial year, just as in 1959, Styria mobilized for the festive event; this found its expression — among other things — in the introduction of standardized maypoles throughout the land.[62] Similarly to 1959, there was

---

58 G. Klingenstein, 'Die Botschaften Erzherzog Johanns' in Klingenstein (ed.), *Krise des Fortschritts*, Vienna, 1984, pp. 157–58.
59 Klingenstein and Cordes (eds), *Erzherzog Johann von Österreich*, II, p. 452.
60 Pickl (ed.), *Erzherzog Johann von Österreich*, p. 9.
61 B. Sutter, 'Erzherzog Johann von Österreich. Sein Wirken in seiner Zeit' in ibid., p. 34.
62 J. Mayr, 'Erzählend ausstellen' in Klingenstein and Cordes (eds), *Erzherzog Johann von Österreich*, I, pp. 25–26.

emphasis on creating analogies between John and the Governor, now Josef Krainer, Junior, who had been elected in 1980. Similarly to Karl Maria Stepan, Krainer was to be turned into a new version of the Archduke:

> If one reads between the lines, a concept emerges which attempts to construct the profile of a personality that is providing new leadership with great power, initiative and innovative vigour. Such a concept, which stresses a federalist Styrian attitude largely detached from centralist Vienna, can more or less distinctly merge with an image of John which has already lived in the public consciousness, and which points out parallels between the then and now, and thus offers a possibility of creating an identity [of past and present Styrian leaders]. In this way it is hoped and expected that individuals themselves engage in a purely emotional and implicit process of identification where something of the received popularity and authority of old John would be transferred to the analogous personality. In a generally acceptable and understandable way, John is referred to as the 'founder and initiator of modern Styria' and thus, as the architect of the first model for the *Land*, a 'prototype Styrian', a 'progressive innovator and supporter in a difficult period who sought to attract the best advisors and staff', a 'popular uncrowned Alpine king with broadly based support among the people', an 'active human being with a social consciousness full of affection for the people', a 'personality of moral integrity', an 'unbureaucratic person' and thus an acceptable authority.[63]

The process of identification and construction of analogies was often enhanced by the fact that significant events to which the 'Governor of all Styrians' played host were frequently held in Stainz, where John had been mayor and a landholder. Such a 'strategic instrumentalization', comparable to references to Franz Joseph employed in the later Kreisky era, assiduously ignores the fact that such an assessment and sanctification of an individual personality is ideologically disturbing:

> In the strictly authoritarian, reactionary system of the *Vormärz*, impulses for progressive activities and foundations as well as their actual implementation could only emanate from leading figures and élites. This is John's achievement in his time. A society that compels its members to adopt democratic values follows different guidelines.[64]

---

63 Staudinger, 'Wandel der Denkmäler', p. 5.
64 Ibid.

The historian's activity was used to construct a stage for the politicians. This process assumed a dramatic quality in 1984 on the occasion of the Styrian state exhibition 'Ore and Iron'. Herbert Boeckl's characteristically shining painting of the Styrian Erzberg adorned the catalogue[65] and advertised the exhibition on large posters throughout Styria. At the same time it served as background for equally large election posters with the portrait of Governor Krainer, Junior.

At the symposium 'Archduke John 2000', Thomas Nipperdey spoke of history as 'the actual dominating power in European life for more than a century', as 'both an academic discipline and an ideology'.[66] John served history as an academic discipline through the collection of historical sources which he himself edited or which were inspired by him. He also used history to serve his own ideological ends. The same is true of the profession: John became an object of research and an instrument for the promotion of ideological objectives. In this way, it was only logical that politics would instrumentalize the myth and employ the academic discipline as a stage setting. To what degree individual researchers, through a lack of self-awareness regarding their own function, assisted these political ends or aided in their design will have to be determined in each individual case.

---

65 P. W. Roth (ed.), *Erz und Eisen in der grünen Mark*, Graz, 1984.
66 T. Nipperdey, 'Geschichte und Orientierung' in Klingenstein (ed.), *Krise des Fortschritts*, pp. 12–13.

PART III
MILITARY, NATIONAL AND PATRIOTIC FESTIVALS

EARLY MODERN TOURNAMENTS AND THEIR RELATIONSHIP TO WARFARE: FRANCE AND THE EMPIRE COMPARED

Helen Watanabe O'Kelly

When I first began to work on tournaments in the 1980s,[1] it was a standard assumption that the tournament of the early modern period was pure spectacle and that it had no relevance for practical warfare whatsoever.[2] Having examined a large number of tournaments at courts in the Holy Roman Empire, I did not find that the facts bore this out. It took me some time to realize that if a scholar worked on English material, his or her view was dominated by the Elizabethan tournament which was so exclusively involved in the cult of Elizabeth I and so divorced from developments in the rest of Europe that it was indeed merely a theatrical version of the medieval tournament and as such pure show.

If the same scholar then moved on to examine the tournament in France, a set of specific factors there could confirm this view and obscure his or her view of developments in other countries. There are four factors which decisively influenced

---

1   For a book entitled *Triumphall Shews: Tournaments at German-Speaking Courts 1580–1730*, Berlin, 1992.
2   See, for instance, Richard Barber and Juliter Barker, *Tournaments: Jousts, Chivalry and Pageants in the Middle Ages*, Woodbridge, 1989, and Sydney Anglo, 'Le Déclin du spectacle chevaleresque' in *Arts du spectacle et histoire des idées: Recueil offert en hommage à Jean Jacquot*, Tours, 1982, pp. 21–35 (p. 26).

the French development. The first is the death of Henri II in 1559 in a tilt. This led to a ban on jousting and tilting with sharp weapons, if not, as sometimes claimed, to a ban on all jousting and tilting, and to a corresponding emphasis on the tournament as theatrical display. This bears fruit in the extraordinary series of dramatic tournaments or *tournois à theme* staged at the Valois court and in the distinction the French make between what they call the *carrousel* and the tournament, the *carrousel* being a staged theatrical contest which has little to do with the medieval tournament. The French are the only nation to make such a consistent distinction. The second is the fact that it is at the French court in 1581 that we have the first documented horse ballet.[3] Both it and the *ballet de cour*, also performed for the first time at the same festival, the wedding of Anne, Duc de Joyeuse, and Marguérite de Vaudémont, were influenced by Antoine de Baïf's Académie de Poésie et de Musique and were thought of as re-creations of the riding and the dance of antiquity respectively. The horse ballet formed part of a larger festival which included a dramatic tournament and a running at the ring, but the inclusion of such an artificial form as the horse ballet moves the whole thing away from the battlefield. The choreographer of this first horse ballet is in all probability Antoine de Pluvinel, the famous riding master and author of the riding manual *Le Maneige royal* (1623), who served under Henri III, Henri IV and Louis XIII. Pluvinel is the third important factor to be considered when looking at the development of the tournament in France. Pluvinel, in contrast to his teachers and colleagues, moves riding away from the stables and into the court, places the emphasis not on the horse but on the rider and so imparts to the tournament exercises which he teaches his young pupil Louis XIII, as chronicled in *Le Maneige royal*, the atmosphere of an elegant courtly pastime, as far removed from the stench of the battlefield as from the whiff of the stables.

The fourth peculiarly French factor is that during the seventeenth century tournaments were few and far between in France. During the reign of Louis XIV, for instance, there were only two on such a scale as to be thought worthy by Louis to be recorded in official publications. These were the *Grand Carrousel* staged in Paris in 1662 to mark the birth of an heir and the small-scale running at the ring

---

[3] See Helen Watanabe-O'Kelly, 'The Equestrian Ballet in Seventeenth-Century Europe: Origin, Description, Development', *German Life and Letters*, 36, 1983, pp. 198–212.

put on in Versailles in 1664 as part of the larger festival in honour of Louise de la Vallière known as *Les Plaisirs de l'isle enchantée*. Only during the 1680s, when the Dauphin staged four tournaments at Versailles — two small-scale ones in 1682 and two of greater magnificence (the *Carrousel des Galans Maures de Grenade* in June 1685 and the *carrousel* of Thalestris and Alexander in May 1896) — do we see any great tournament activity again at the French court. If one worked exclusively on French material, therefore, one would consider the tournament as of little importance in the sum of festive culture — certainly of lesser importance than the *ballet de cour* and the opera — and one would fail to connect it in any way with the battlefield.

Matters look very different when we consider tournaments in the Empire. Before discussing German tournaments, however, let me summarize developments on the battlefield in the early modern period.[4]

On the medieval battlefield, as in the medieval tournament, the knight at arms covered in a suit of armour and wielding a lance was the dominant figure. This human projectile rode straight forward at another similar human projectile. Once pikemen and crossbowmen became increasingly successful on the field of battle from the fourteenth century on, and once firearms were sufficiently advanced to make them a practicable proposition in ordinary combat, the knight in armour diminished in importance. It is thought that he was at his most efficient around 1450, that he continued to be important until at least 1500 and that he was only driven from the battlefield during the last quarter of the sixteenth century. Of course we are talking here about the knight in armour. The cavalryman in general remained important in all European armies until the twentieth century, though his role and the qualities needed to carry it out changed.

Meanwhile, from the end of the fourteenth century, the handgun continues to be developed, so that by the middle of the sixteenth century the pistol in particular was becoming an indispensable part of the cavalryman's equipment.[5] The heavy cavalryman thus gradually gave way to a different type of mounted soldier — one

---

4   I have discussed some of this material before in 'Tournaments and their Relevance for Warfare in the Early Modern Period', *European History Quarterly*, 20, 1990, pp. 451–63.

5   See Jaroslaw Lugs, *Handfeuerwaffen Systematischer Ueberblick über die Handfeuerwaffen und ihre Geschichte*, 2 vols, Berlin, 1979, I, p. 22.

who could ride down quickly on a pikeman, shoot him and then ride off again, instead of charging slowly at him. The cavalryman now also tended to be used much more as a scout, messenger and raider. Speed, mobility, accuracy of aim and quickness of eye were now more important than sheer strength and endurance. As well as his pistol, the cavalryman was armed with a sword. But the lance remained in use at least until the beginning of the Thirty Years War; it fell out of fashion in the latter half of the seventeenth century, but never died out completely, undergoing a remarkable revival in Napoleon's army, for instance, and only becoming abolished in the British and German armies after the First World War.

At the same time the infantry grew in importance throughout the sixteenth century.[6] Its weapons were principally the pike and the sword, the musket and the pistol. Towards the end of the sixteenth century the introduction of military drill by Maurice of Nassau and his cousins Wilhelm Ludwig and Johann Wilhelm of Nassau-Siegen revolutionized the behaviour of the army on the battlefield, but especially that of the infantry, turning it into a disciplined body of men acting in unison.

Thus, by the end of the sixteenth century, most European armies consisted of pikemen and musketeers on foot as well as of cavalry. The latter had to be able to ride well and fast and to use a number of different weapons in quick succession — sword, pistol and sometimes lance — and both infantrymen and cavalrymen had to able to fight as members of a team, with the infantry in particular becoming more numerous and more professional.

If the tournament bears any relationship to actual warfare, one would expect to see the joust or tilt with lance and sword still being practised up to the Thirty Years War but gradually giving way to exercises which relate to the new skills needed by the modern cavalryman: the ability to ride well and fast on a lighter, better-trained horse, to use a handgun alongside more traditional weapons, the discipline to fight as part of a group, to be sure of aim and quick of eye. The tournament would also have to accommodate the infantry as well as the cavalry.

Equally, once the army begins to be professionalized from the middle of the seventeenth century on and standing armies displace the previous practice of

---

6   This has been documented in detail by Geoffrey Parker, *The Military Revolution: Military Innovation and the Rise of the West, 1500–1800*, Cambridge, 1988, pp. 16ff.

assembling an *ad hoc* force, the officer can no longer be an amateur practising at court the fighting skills he will need on the battlefield. He must instead learn his trade in the cadet school and on the parade ground. At this point, tournament and warfare must part company.

This is exactly the development which we see taking place in the Empire. There were jousts and tilts in Munich in 1568 to celebrate the wedding of Renée of Lorraine to Wilhelm V of Bavaria, in Kassel in 1596 and 1600 for the christenings of Elizabeth and Moritz of Hessen-Kassel, respectively, in Breslau in 1611 for the arrival of the Emperor Matthias, in Heidelberg in 1613 for the arrival of Elizabeth, the English bride of Friedrich of the Palatinate, and for the wedding of Wolfgang Wilhelm of Pfalz-Neuburg to Magdalena of Bavaria in Munich, also in 1613, and the tilt was still to be found sporadically up to the middle of the seventeenth century.

At the same time, the element of theatrical display in sixteenth-century tournaments in the Empire is much less than one might find in France or Italy. The only tournament at a German-speaking court in this century which exhibits an overall design and in which all the participants are costumed according to the dictates of a planned mythological framework was held in Vienna in 1571 and was designed by the Italian Mannerist Giuseppe Arcimboldo. This all-embracing framework which unites the participants into one spectacle would be highly unusual in the German-speaking world for many decades to come. By contrast, such a lavish and well-publicized tournament as that held in Munich in 1568 for the wedding of Wilhelm of Bavaria and Renée of Lorraine uses very little costume of any kind. Equally, I know of only one dramatic tournament or *tournoi à theme* in the Empire, the so-called *Ebentheuer* organized in Kassel in 1596 by Moritz of Hessen-Kassel for the christening of his daughter Elisabeth, and this bears witness to the close political and cultural links between Kassel and France at this date.[7] German tournaments up to the Thirty Years War remain much more focused on the actual contests, whether on foot or on horseback, contests which, unlike the theatrical *carrousel*, had no pre-ordained outcome.

---

7   See Gerhard Menk, 'Die Beziehungen zwischen König Heinrich IV von Frankreich und Landgraf Moritz' in *Moritz der Gelehrte. Ein Renaissancefürst in Europa*, exhibition catalogue, Eurasburg, 1997.

During the same period, that is, during the second half of the sixteenth century, we see a great increase in the frequency and popularity of other equestrian exercises which gradually displaced the joust and tilt. These exercises are running at the ring, at the quintain and at the head. The first two are of medieval origin. Running at the ring involved galloping down a predetermined course towards a ring hung up between two posts, usually rather above shoulder height. The ring was usually divided into various fields and the score depended on exactly where the lance pierced the ring, the aim being to carry it off on the point of the lance — not an easy undertaking while guiding the horse with one hand. Running at the ring, with its combination of riding skill, speed and accuracy of aim, was the single most widespread form of equestrian exercise, to be found at virtually all European courts, except the English one, for about 200 years from the mid-sixteenth to the mid-eighteenth century. It is still possible today in many court cities to see the arena in which this exercise was practised with the ring suspended from two pillars at the far end. The Stallhof in the Electoral Palace in Dresden is an example. Running at the quintain involved striking the solid static wooden figure of a Turk or Moor while dashing past at full gallop, shattering one's lance in the process.

These two types of contest became more and more popular at the same time as the tilt between two riders fell out of favour. The lance which was used in running at the ring and the quintain was not the heavy, sharp battle-lance attached to the breastplate, but a long, light, wooden pole, and it is arguable that the purpose of both of these exercises was not so much to learn to manipulate the lance itself as a weapon but to train those abilities which would be useful in general, namely, sureness of aim, mobility and speed.

It was in the Empire that the only new exercise to be devised in the seventeenth century had its inception. This is the running at the head which developed out of the quintain. The first mention of it occurs in Georg Engelhard von Loehneyss's riding manual of 1609, *Della Cavalleria*. Loehneyss still calls it running at the quintain, but it corresponds exactly to what later became universally known as the running at the head or 'Kopfrennen'. In the running at the head three or four Moors' or Turks' heads were fixed down the lists, each at a different height. The rider galloped past them, using a different weapon against each one. In Loehneyss, three weapons are envisaged: lance, pistol and axe. In the first festivals at which we find the form in practice — at Heidelberg in 1613 for the Palatine wedding, at Dessau in 1614 for the wedding of Georg Rudolf of Liegnitz-Brieg and Sophia Elisabeth of Anhalt and at Halle in 1616 for the christening of Sophie Elisabeth of Brandenburg — the pistol is not yet used, the three weapons being sword, lance and javelin.

From about the 1630s, however, the records of pistols being used become commoner and the pistol is almost invariably employed during the next 100 years, when running at the head becomes extremely popular all over Europe. Significantly, therefore, the only tournament form to be invented in the seventeenth century tested versatility in a range of weapons, prominent among them the handgun.

Another equestrian exercise was also being practised at German courts in the early seventeenth century, that is, the so-called *carisell*. The name is clearly related to the French term 'carousel' but is a quite different type of event. The German *carisell* is an equestrian game in which two teams line up at either end of the arena. A member of one team dashes out into the centre, protecting himself with a large shield, while a member of the opposing team bombards him with earthenware balls. The first rider then has to regain his ranks while a member of his team dashes out in his turn to bombard the first assailant. Escape, pursuit and sureness of aim are the main elements of this exercise. We find the *carisell* at the great wedding in Stuttgart in 1609 between Johann Friedrich of Württemberg and Barbara Sophia of Brandenburg, at Jägerndorf in 1610 for the wedding of their sister and brother, respectively, and again in Stuttgart in 1617 for the joint wedding of Johann Friedrich's brother and the christening of his son, and in Halle in 1616 for the christening of Sophie Elisabeth of Brandenburg. Those familiar with Spanish tournaments will recognize this exercise as the popular Spanish *juego de alcancías*, which corresponds exactly to the description given above. It probably came from Spain to Italy together with the Arab horses which Spain exported to Naples (in Italy the form was called the *giuoco de' cariselli*) and went from there North of the Alps. From the Empire the *carisell* went to Scandinavia, predominantly to Denmark where it is known as the *karusseløb*.[8]

---

8 A comparative overview of tournaments throughout Europe is provided in Helen Watanabe-O'Kelly, 'Tournaments in Europe' in Pierre Béhar and Helen Watanabe-O'Kelly (eds),

As well as these mounted exercises, however, the tournament on foot or *Fußturnier* becomes a frequent, indeed almost invariable, element of any large-scale event. This foot combat should not be confused with the one-to-one sword combat of jousters and tilters once they have been unhorsed. The earliest example of the true foot tournament known to this author anywhere in Europe was held in Vienna in 1560, the next in Ferrara in 1561 and the third in Munich in 1568. The weapons used are those employed by the infantryman on the battlefield, namely, pike and sword. The participants march in rank and file onto the arena, as a regiment would onto the battlefield. They are divided into at least two groups or teams, but sometimes as many as six, distinguished by their costumes. They usually fight over a low wooden barrier, at first one-to-one and then team against team. Musketeers and arquebusiers usually march on with the teams and often let off their firearms at the end, as in the christening festivities in Kassel in 1596. From this date on, the foot combat is at least as common as running at the quintain, and its importance is attested by the fact that by the early seventeenth century it appears for the first time in the theoretical literature on tournaments, in such works as Bartolomeo Sereno's *Dell'uso della lancia a cavallo. Del combattere a piede Alla Sbarra. Et dell'Imprese, Et inventioni cavalieresche* (1610) and Bonaventura Pistofilo's *Il torneo* (1627), which in spite of its title deals exclusively with the tournament on foot. Pistofilo explains why the foot tournament is important enough to be dealt with in a work such as his. This is not only because it is a noble, knightly and scientific exercise but because it 'resembles war'. He goes on to explain that this is because the same weapons are used as in war, that is, pike, battleaxe, halberd and sword, as well as the recent additions of firearms, muskets, arquebusses and so on, and because in the foot combat the drummers play all those drum calls which are usual in battle and the participants fight in the same battle-order as in war. Throughout his treatise, in fact, Pistofilo treats the tournament and actual warfare as two aspects of the same thing.

Spectaculum Europaeum: Manuel de l'histoire du spectacle en Europe de la fin du XVIe au milieu du XVIIIe siècle / Spectaculum Europaeum: Theatre and Spectacle in Europe from the End of the Sixteenth to the Middle of the Eighteenth Centuries — A Handbook, Wiesbaden, 1998, pp. 591–639.

Early Modern Tournaments and their Relationship to Warfare 241

The German military literature of the early modern period is also convinced of the relevance of the tournament. Wilhelm Dilich, court poet of Maurice the Learned of Hessen-Kassel and well-known military writer, tells us in his account of the tournament held in Kassel in 1596 that tournaments and knightly exercises are 'a very useful and indeed necessary practice in peacetime'.[9] He develops this idea in a military treatise called *Kriegss-buch/darin die Alte und Newe Militia eigentlich beschreiben* (1608), explaining that lancers have to be taught how to lower their lance and hit home with it and how, once their lance is broken, they should take up their musket, the best training for this being the tilt, the running at the ring and the quintain. These exercises teach precision of aim at a series of targets in succession.[10]

A year later, Johann Oettinger, court poet at Stuttgart, in describing the *carisell* held there in 1609, again emphasizes the useful training such an exercise affords, for it not only teaches quickness of aim and attack but the ability to regain one's battle-order afterwards.[11]

The military writer and soldier Johann Jacobi von Wallhausen also discusses the running at the ring. In his *Ritter-Kunst* (1616) he emphasizes the practical usefulness of this exercise.[12] In Chapter 6, for instance, he shows how the use of the lance on the battlefield can be practised by running at the ring, for the various heights at which the ring can be hung correspond to the visor and the head of one's opponent and to the horse's chest. In his treatise on cavalry combat of the same year, *Kriegskunst zu Pferdt*, he again emphasizes both the range of weapons the cavalryman needed to be able to use and the tournament as a useful setting in

---

9   Wilhelm Dilich, *Beschreibung und Abriss dero Ritterspiel/so der durchleuchtige Moritz/Landgraff zu Hessen/auff die Fürstl Kindtauffen Frewlein Elisabethen/.zu Cassel angeordnet und halten lassen*, Kassel, 1601, p. 7.

10 Wilhelm Dilich, *Kriegss-buch/darin die Alte und Newe Militia eigentlich beschrieben*, Kassel, 1608, pp. 73–74.

11 Johann Oettinger, *Warhaffte Historische Beschreibung Der Fürstl Hochziet/...So Der Durchleuchtig Hochgeborn Fürst unnd Herr/Herr Johann Friderich Hertzog zu Würtemberg und Teck ... mit ... Barbara Sophia Marggrävin zu Brandenburg ... anno 1609 ... celebriert und gehalten hat*, Stuttgart, 1610, p. 251.

12 Johann Jacobi von Wallhausen, *Ritterkunst Darinnen begriffen/I Ein trewhertziges Warnung [= Schreiben wegen dess Betrübten Zustands jetziger Christenheit II Underricht aller Handgriffen so ein jeder Cavallirer hochnötig zu wissen bedarff]*, Frankfurt am Main, 1616.

which to practise these skills. We might remember that Wallhausen was the first director of the military academy founded by Johann von Nassau-Siegen in Siegen, and we can therefore assume him to be *au fait* with modern military developments.

What I have called 'the tournaments of the Protestant Union' exemplify this close connection between military need and courtly tournament.[13] These are tournaments staged at Protestant courts in the run-up to the Thirty Years War, in which various members of the Protestant coalition celebrate events such as weddings or christenings which cement relationships between them, in which they articulate a specifically German Protestant political programme and which they use as occasions on which to hold summit conferences. Stuttgart, with its tournaments staged in 1605, 1609, 1616, 1617 and 1618, is by far the most important of these courts, but the tournaments held in Jägerndorf in 1610, in Heidelberg in 1613, in Dessau in 1613 and 1615 and in Halle in 1616 form part of the same group. While the costumes and floats put across a clear political message, once the processions have taken place on the first day, the participants take off their elaborate head-dresses and costumes and get down to the contests, which take up far more time. One gets the impression that these provided a welcome opportunity for allies to train together and to review each other's troops without anyone being able to say that they were arming for war. It is here that we see the running at the head for the first time in Europe; it is at these tournaments that we see the *Carisell* in practice; and it is here that we have the full range of mounted and foot contests described above.

This outburst of tournament activity was cut short by the Thirty Years War. The great courts such as Dresden and Vienna kept a relatively sporadic festival culture going during the war years. The tournaments in Dresden in 1620, 1622, 1630, 1638 and 1644, and those in Vienna in 1631, 1633 and 1636, are examples. They all comprise at least a running at the ring and sometimes also at the head, in

---

13 See Helen Watanabe-O'Kelly, 'The Iconography of German Protestant Tournaments in the Years before the Thirty Years' War' in Pierre Béhar (ed.), *Images et Spectacles: Actes du XXIIe Colloque D'Études Humanistes du Centre d'Etudes Supérieures de la Renaissance*, Chloe Beihefte zum Daphnis vol 15, Amsterdam 1991, pp. 47–64.

Early Modern Tournaments and their Relationship to Warfare   243

which costumed participants and festival cars of varying elaborateness are to be seen.

In Vienna and Munich, however, we begin to see the German tournament being brought into line with Italian practice. In Vienna in 1631 the horse ballet is introduced on the Florentine model. In Munich after the war we have the staging of three great tournament operas on the Italian model — in 1654, 1658 and 1662. The pre-war tournament has now given way to a grand dynastic show in which the ruler is presenting himself, his family and his own function within the state.

Even at the court of the Saxon Electors in Dresden, with its more continuous and German tradition, we see the tournament losing its connection with warfare. Tournaments become less and less related to military reality, not because they are Italianate but because the military reality is elsewhere. Once the standing army becomes the norm and the cadet school rather than the *manège* becomes the training ground for the officer corps, the tournament turns into a combination of sporting fixture and entertainment. In Dresden, for instance, the entertainment element can be seen in the way the tournament, still consisting of either a running at the ring or at the head, grows in scale, so that by the 1690s it is common to have double or even quadruple contests, in which several participants compete simultaneously, riding parallel to each other. It can also be seen in the fact that ladies are allowed to take part in the so-called *Damenringrennen*.[14] The tournament as sporting fixture can be seen in the many small, relatively informal contests in which the prince and his courtiers simply ran at the ring in the *manège* in the Electoral Palace in Dresden, for example, in 1656, 1662, 1663, 1669, 1683, 1685, 1686, 1695, 1697, 1708, and many more. This is a tradition which carries on well into the eighteenth century. Archival records in Dresden show that running at the ring in the *manège* uncostumed against a few courtiers was a particularly popular pastime for the Electoral Prince Friedrich August II between 1724 and 1731. In these seven years he participated in at least forty-six such informal contests. Karl Albrecht, as Electoral Prince and then Elector of Bavaria, took part in the same type of informal small-scale running at the ring in Munich in

---

14   See Helen Watanabe-O'Kelly, 'Das Damenringrennen — eine sächsische Erfindung?', *Dresdner Hefte*, 22, 1991, pp. 307–12.

the 1720s and 1730s. This is the tournament as substitute for the round of golf or game of squash or polo with a group of friends.

Dresden also demonstrates another tendency, namely, the re-staging of obsolete tournament forms. August the Strong staged foot tournaments in 1709 and 1714, and a joust and foot tournament in 1719, using armour and weapons taken from the extensive store in the Electoral Palace.[15] The score-sheets in the Dresden archive demonstrate that the courtiers and army cadets using these outmoded accoutrements no longer knew how to use them. Once the tournament has really died after the middle of the eighteenth century, it is only ever again staged as such a historical reconstruction.

It is no coincidence that the last great courtly shows in the reign of both Louis XIV, King of France, and August the Strong (Friedrich August I, Elector of Saxony, as August II, King of Poland), should be military manoeuvres at Compiègne and Zeithain, respectively, grand shows which provided both training for a professional army and a demonstration of its competence to friend and foe alike.

---

15 See Helen Watanabe-O'Kelly, 'Joseph und seine Brüder. Johann Georg II von Sachsen und seine Feste (1660–1679)', *Dresdner Hefte*, 8, 1990, 1, pp. 29–38, where this is discussed.

NATIONS IN ARMS: MILITARY AND COMMEMORATIVE FESTIVALS IN GERMANY AND FRANCE, 1871–1914

Jakob Vogel

Historians have long recognized the military's role in the formation of European nations. The nationalizing effect of compulsory military service is often cited: for the male population the army was in a double sense a 'school of the nation'.[1] But the army's role was not limited to a mere socialization of the nation; it also helped construct the nation culturally. In this chapter I will show how from the 1870s until the First World War military festivals in Germany and in France established themselves as a central component in the cult of the nation.[2] In opposition to

---

A first version of this chapter was presented in May 1994 at a conference organized by the European Forum, Florence. I would like to thank my friend Adam Tooze for his comments which helped me to revise the text for this publication. I am also indebted to Kevin McAleer who translated this chapter into English.

1 See, among others, Reinhard Höhn, *Die Armee als Erziehungsschule der Nation. Das Ende einer Idee*, Bad Harzburg, 1963; Eugen Weber, *Peasants into Frenchmen: The Modernization of Rural France, 1870–1914*, Stanford, CA, 1976, and Maurice Agulhon, 'La Fabrication de la France: Problèmes et controverses' in M. Segalen (ed.), *L'Autre et le Semblable: Regards sur l'ethnologie des sociétés contemporaines*, Paris, 1989, pp. 109–20.

2 This chapter is based on research for my book, Jakob Vogel, *Nationen im Gleichschritt. Der Kult der 'Nation in Waffen' in Deutschland und Frankreich 1871–1914*, Göttingen, 1997. For a more extensive analysis of military festivals in Germany and France (especially for the

George Mosse's thesis that the military ceremonial and the official staging of military festivals stood in contradiction to a dissemination of the cult of the nation,[3] I will argue that, as regular rituals of the 'nation in arms', these occasions in fact nourished and hastened the spread of the national cult.[4]

In examining the military ceremonies, our leading question will be what sort of influence, in comparison to other institutions and social groups, did the state and its élites exert in constructing the 'nation in arms'. In this connection it will be discussed whether the process of the social construction of the nation can be understood as a 'collective discourse' between the various societal actors, or rather as mainly formed by the state and its élites, who possessed an organizational monopoly on military ceremonies as well as other official national festivals. Naturally, in its programming of national festivals, the state did not operate in a vacuum independent of other social groups, whose wishes had to be at least partially met; but nevertheless, the state disposed of great latitude in orchestrating an official version of the cult of the nation.

---

commemorations of the Franco-Prussian war and other wars of the eighteenth and nineteenth centuries in both societies), it may be useful to study the original text in German.

3   George L. Mosse, *Die Nationalisierung der Massen. Politische Symbolik und Massenbewegungen in Deutschland von den napoleonischen Kriegen bis zum Dritten Reich*, trans. Otto Weith, Berlin, 1976 [original English edition, *The Nationalization of the Masses: Political Symbolism and Mass Movements in Germany from the Napoleonic Wars through the Third Reich*, New York, 1975], pp. 103, 110ff.

4   This assertion is based on the concept of the 'political cult', which, relying on Emile Durkheim's theory of religious cults and rituals (Durkheim, *Les Formes élémentaires de la vie réligieuse: Le système totémique en Australie*, 4th edn, Paris, 1960), has been elaborated by the political scientist Murray Edelman (Edelman, *The Symbolic Uses of Politics*, Urbana, IL, 1964) and the sociologist Steven Lukes (Lukes, 'Political Ritual and Social Integration', *Sociology*, 9, 1989, pp. 289–308). See also David Kerzer, *Ritual, Politics and Power*, New Haven, CT, 1988, and my own text, Jakob Vogel, 'La legittimazione rituale della "nazione in armi"'. Esercito, Stato e società civile nelle manifestazioni militari in Germania e Francia (1871–1914)', *Quaderni storici*, 94, 1997, pp. 105–20.

The Cult of the Nation and the Rise of French and German Military Festivals

The establishment of the military festival within the framework of the national cult in Germany and France was linked to the 'nationalization' of the army, its elevation to a key symbol of the nation. This process would not have been possible in Germany before the founding of the German Empire in 1871, for it was only then that the military emerged as a national institution around which a national cult might develop. Even if the troops of the individual German states had entered the field against France under their own particularistic banners, the Franco-Prussian War (1870–71) evoked proud national memories.[5] The war had helped forge the German nation, and so the army obtained a central place in the official mythology of the founding of the empire — a mythology promoted by a Prussian leadership that found its most ardent supporters in the 'national'-minded bourgeoisie.[6] During the first decades of the *Kaiserreich* it was in particular the annual Sedan commemoration that helped to glorify the so-called 'military unification of the empire'.[7]

---

5   Annette Maas, 'Der Kult der toten Krieger. Frankreich und Deutschland nach 1870/71', in: Etienne François, Hannes Siegrist and Jakob Vogel (eds), *Nation und Emotion. Deutschland und Frankreich im Vergleich. 19. und 20. Jahrhundert*, Göttingen, 1995, pp. 215–31; Ute Schneider, *Politische Festkultur im 19. Jahrhundert. Die Rheinprovinz von der französischen Zeit bis zum Ende des Ersten Weltkrieges, 1806–1918*, Essen, 1995.

6   This theme is evidenced in the works propagated by Anton von Werner and other painters. See Ekkehard Mai, 'Nationale Kunst — Historienmalerei vor und nach 1870: Von der Romantik der Geschichte zu geschichtlicher Wirklichkeit', pp. 19–32, and Jörn Grabowski, 'Leitbilder einer Nation. Zur Präsentation von Historien- und Schlachtengemälden in der Nationalgalerie' both in Dominik Bartmann (ed.), *Anton von Werner: Geschichte in Bildern*, Munich, 1993, pp. 91–100.

7   Fritz Schellack, *Nationalfeiertage in Deutschland von 1871 bis 1945*, Frankfurt am Main, 1990. It should be noted that Schellack's historical sketch of the development of the Sedan commemoration up until the First World War does not take into account the ceremonial changes that began to take place with the accession of Wilhelm II. Contrary to what Schellack describes as the expanding importance of the Sedan commemoration, a gradual diminution in its significance is discernible after 1888: see Vogel, *Nationen im Gleichschritt*, pp. 144–62. A very lively, but sometimes problematic (especially for its later periods in the 1890s) description of the Sedan Day commemorations in Württemberg is given by Alon Confino, *The Nation as a Local Metaphor: Württemberg, Imperial Germany, and National Memory, 1871–1918*, Chapel Hill, CT, 1997, pp. 27–93.

The ceremonial military parades which the Kaiser began to hold outside of Prussia in the various federal states, starting in 1876, soon numbered among the most important national celebrations. Of all the regularly held national rituals of the pre-war era, the Kaiser parades were the only ones whose basic ritual would remain a constant and which would be performed throughout the whole of Germany. Not even the Kaiser's birthday generated comparable mass appeal, as it never developed a uniform national ceremonial and never obtained official status, for instance, in Bavaria.[8]

The occasions for the Kaiser parades were the annual autumn manoeuvres. Since 1876 the Kaiser held these manoeuvres every year in from two to four different regions of the empire where, in his capacity of *Oberster Kriegsherr*, he controlled the troops' training, which had been standardized in the German army following the wars of 1866 and 1870–71.[9] In this fashion, a tradition of the Prussian regency was adopted by the empire with minimal changes. The Kaiser parades retained a strong martial flavour through their integration with the training of the troops, although from the very start they assumed the character of a public spectacle through their ritualized programme and extravagant staging for a general civilian audience.

The parade ceremonial adopted from the Prussian army was changed slightly to accord with the federal constitution of the German army. In order to conspicuously highlight his continued recognition of princely sovereignty, the Kaiser would inspect his troops at the side of the respective potentate.[10] In addition, the custom practised by both Wilhelm I and his grandson Wilhelm II, of wearing the decorations and the uniforms of the federal state's regiments on the occasion of parades, was an expression of the Kaiser's esteem for the federal order of the German national state.[11] The Kaiser parades throughout Germany not only

---

8   Schellack, *Nationalfeiertage*, pp. 23–25, 48, 49.
9   Wilhelm Deist, 'Kaiser Wilhelm II. als Oberster Kriegsherr' in J. C. G. Röhl (ed.), *Der Ort Kaiser Wilhelms II. in der deutschen Geschichte*, Munich, 1991, pp. 25–42 (pp. 26, 27).
10 This had already taken place at the first parade, when on 6 September 1876 in Leipzig Kaiser Wilhelm I reviewed troops together with the King of Saxony: see *Leipziger Nachrichten*, 7 September 1876.
11 Ibid., and *Leipziger Neueste Nachrichten*, 6 September 1903.

reinforced the Kaiser's claim as sovereign head of the nation, but simultaneously confirmed symbolically the federal structure of the empire.[12]

The sole exception to the Kaiser parades was Bavaria, whose two army corps were until 1888 normally inspected by the King of Bavaria accompanied by the Prussian Crown Prince and heir to the throne, Friedrich Wilhelm. The absence of the Kaiser from these Bavarian military festivals did not contradict the cult of the national army. Because of the Crown Prince's close affiliation with the Bavarian Army through his command of Bavarian troops in the Franco-Prussian War, Friedrich Wilhelm's participation was rather the Hohenzollern's special recognition of Bavaria's role in the German unification of 1871. Following the death of his father, Wilhelm II henceforth included both Bavarian army corps in the series of Kaiser parades so that the Kaiser's claim as sovereign head of the nation could also be visibly extended to the Bavarian Army.[13] A further exception in the national cult of the army were the parades of the Prussian Guards, which took place annually toward the end of May and at the beginning of September in Berlin and Potsdam, in a demonstration of the close relationship of the Guards with the House of Hohenzollern.[14]

The manoeuvre parades, to which the Kaiser travelled every year in his extended *Kaiserreisen*, were able to showcase the level of training and combat strength of the troops — symbolic of the collective nation — before only a limited regional audience. It was only over the years that the national cult of the army was constituted around the person of the *Oberster Kriegsherr*, who eventually visited all the regions of the empire on his manoeuvre trips. In 1876 the *Norddeutsche Allgemeine Zeitung* described the nationalizing effect of these visits:

> If the Kaiser is simply being greeted in the Prussian provinces by the revival of a time-honoured devotion grown more ardent owing to a recent glorious past, then the reception which meets him in the other German federal states

---

12 This is roughly the argument of Werner K. Blessing, 'Der monarchische Kult, politische Loyalität und die Arbeiterbewegung im deutschen Kaiserreich' in Gerhard A. Ritter (ed.), *Arbeiterkultur*, Königstein, 1979, pp. 185–208 (p. 190).

13 Ibid.

14 The Guards Regiments served not only as the traditional seat for the military education of Prussian princes, they also assumed manifold social duties in the sphere of the dynastic cult of the Hohenzollerns.

has the partial character of tribute to the German Empire's newly gained unity and its hope-filled future.[15]

The national military festivals presented the monarchy side by side with the army as the unifying bond of the German national state, thus simultaneously enabling the population in the individual regions to identify with 'their' regiments and 'their' princely houses. The regional distribution of the empire was thereby interpreted not as antagonistic to but rather as the natural foundation of German national unity, personified by the Kaiser and his ruling house.

Unlike in Germany, in France before 1870 there already existed a national cult of the army. This failed, however, to develop any stable form as a result of the country's frequently changing political constitution. The strongest influence was exerted by the Napoleonic army cult, which had been developed at the beginning of the century for the imperial army of Napoleon I.[16] Successive regimes attempted to remould this cult of the army in their own image through symbolic reinterpretations and other slighter modifications.[17] Apart from France's chronic political instability and the conservative and Bonapartist orientation of large parts of its corps of officers, it was the recruiting of soldiers from the lower-class peasantry, their relatively shabby outfit and the army's frequent deployment against the civilian populace that hindered any showcasing of the army as a symbol of French national unity.[18] As late as 1870, Ernest Renan could assert that only in Prussia did the 'identité de l'armée et de la nation' exist, since it was only

---

15 *Norddeutsche Allgemeine Zeitung*, 7 September 1876. See also the *Leipziger Nachrichten*, 6 September 1876, and the *Dresdner Journal*, 15 September 1882.

16 The Napoleonic tradition's decisive impact reveals itself in the fact that King Louis Philippe, the Second Republic and Napoleon III all copied Napoleon I's ceremonial conferring of new standards (*aigles*) on Paris's Field of Mars, first staged on 5 December 1804: see *Le Figaro*, 13 July 1880.

17 Rosemond Sanson, 'Le 15 août: Fête nationale du Second Empire' in Alain Corbin et. al. (eds), *Les Usages politiques des fêtes au XIX–XXe siècles*, Paris 1994, pp. 117–36; Françoise Wacquet, *Les Fêtes royales sous la Restauration ou l'Ancien Régime retrouvé*, Paris, 1981.

18 Raoul Girardet, *La Société militaire dans la France contemporaine (1815–1939)*, Paris, 1953, pp. 175ff.; Bernard Schnapper, *Le Remplacement militaire en France: Quelques aspects politiques, économiques et sociaux du recrutement au XIXe siècle*, Paris, 1968, pp. 280–88; William Serman, *Les Officiers français dans la Nation (1814–1914)*, Paris, 1982, pp. 65–73.

here that the population took part in the national defence as a result of compulsory military service.[19] Following the Franco-Prussian War many politicians, like Renan, saw the institution of compulsory military duty as an essential step towards the nationalization of the French army.[20] It was first through the tying together of the national idea and that of national defence that the concept of a general and compulsory military service could be realized, enabling the army to propagate itself as a true 'national' institution, as the embodiment of the *nation en armes*, a symbolic status which the state leadership of the Third Republic often undertook to emphasize on the occasion of military festivals. Accordingly, in an address of 1894, Minister-President Casimir Périer presented the troops as an *image de la nation*, while his predecessor captioned the picture of the compulsory service army with: 'Cette vaillante armée qui est la nation même dans sa virile jeunesse'.[21]

The national cult of the army in the Third Republic flourished every year on the national holiday of 14 July, which had been dutifully observed by all the garrisons throughout the land with military parades.[22] Of course, military parades had already been an integral part of the cult of the state before 1870, but the Third Republic expanded their meaning by placing the army ceremonies in the centre of the official stagings, where they now served annually as the 'high-point' of the 14 July festivities. Moreover, the important parade of the Paris Garrison at the Longchamps racetrack was the only official ceremonial among all the other public

---

19 Ernest Renan, 'La Guerre entre la France et l'Allemagne', *Revue des Deux Mondes*, 15 September 1870, as cited in Renan, *Qu'est-ce qu'une nation? et autres essais politiques*, ed. Joel Roman, Paris, 1992, pp. 80–106 (p. 104).

20 For the introduction of compulsory military service in France, see Francis Choisel, 'Du tirage au sort au service universel', in *Revue Historique de l'Armée*, 1981, 2, pp. 43–60. The efforts undertaken by the Third Republic to make military service more 'attractive' and its 'positive' effects on the army's public image are described in Michel Auvray, *Objecteurs, insoumis, déserteurs: Histoire des réfractaires en France*, Paris, 1983, pp. 113ff.

21 *La France militaire*, 26 September 1893, 21 September 1894; see also *Le Figaro*, 21 June 1876.

22 Rosemond Sanson, 'La Célébration de la Fête nationale sous la Troisième République', Sorbonne doctoral dissertation, Paris, 1970; Christian Amalvi, 'Le 14-Juillet' in Pierre Nora (ed.), *Les Lieux de mémoire*, 3 vols, Paris, 1984–92, I, pp. 421–72; Jean-Pierre Bois, *Histoire des 14 Juillet: 1789–1919*, Rennes, 1991.

festivals and popular amusements observing the national holiday in which the Republic's entire state élite took part. The army thereby acquired a prominent place in the national cult of the Third Republic — a place it had never possessed under the previous regimes, since up until 1870 the military parades had always played a subordinate role to other official events such as special religious services and banquets.[23]

Incorporation of the army into the new republican cult of the nation occasioned no essential change in the military ceremonials as they were traditionally carried out pre-1870. Already in 1880, with the first military parade celebrating Bastille Day, the republican state leadership fell back upon a ceremonial that derived from the formal awarding of regimental standards as staged by Napoleon I in 1804.[24] In a conscious distancing from the Napoleonic cult of the army, however, the ceremonial was recast as a festival of the *armée vraiment nationale* by embedding it in the national holiday celebrations and — through some insignificant changes — adapting it to the changed political situation.[25]

Already by the time of this first celebration in 1880, French national military festivals were manifesting their characteristic centralized construction. Their centrepiece was the Paris Garrison parade, whose participants included the President of the Republic, members of the government and both houses of parliament. The local parades in France's various garrison towns simply reproduced the Parisian model by having the troops defile past the mayor or some other 'high-ranking' state official such as the prefect. As a result, Bastille Day, with the help of these identically patterned parades, was able to disseminate a unified ritual of the armed nation throughout all France. This combination of centralism and localism in the French military festivals enabled the spread of the cult of the army throughout France as part of republican folklore.[26]

Although the national military festivals in Germany and France had clearly differing styles, there remain crucial similarities which underline the important

---

23 Archives Municipales de Dijon, 1I, 1/46; Archives Départementale de Dijon, 20 M, 1304/2.
24 For the programme of the 14 July ceremony in Paris, see Archives de la Préfecture de Police, Paris, BA 1, no. 471.
25 *Le Figaro*, 15 July 1880. In general, see also Jérome Hélie, 'Les Armes' in Nora (ed.), *Les Lieux de mémoire*, III, pp. 236–83 (pp. 243–46).
26 See Maurice Agulhon (ed.), *Cultures et folklores républicaines*, Paris, 1995.

place occupied by the army in the cult of the nation. The military festivals on either side of the Vosges were the sole events to propagate an identical model of the cult of the nation to the collective populace. Each respective ritual presented the army as an allegory for the manly, ordered and obedient fighting community of the nation, whose metaphors were the *Volk in Waffen* and the *nation en armes*.[27] The military festivals were stagings that can be understood in the sense of Emile Durkheim's religious concept of a *rite représentatif*, which periodically revives central elements in the collective consciousness in order to strengthen the feeling of national unity and general military preparedness.[28] The stereotypical repetition of the military ceremonials in both countries did not therefore have a numbing effect on 'the dynamic of the cult of the nation', as depicted by George Mosse, who focused his analysis only on the non-official celebrations of the German national movement.[29] Rather, the official military festivals furthered this cult, which was elevated to a central place in the periodic reinforcement of national society in Germany and France.

Military Festivals as Rituals of the National State and its Élites

When one analyses more closely the staging of military festivals in Germany and France, what becomes apparent is the enormous weight of the state and its élites in the external representation of the 'nation in arms', for the shows presented not only the army but also the heads of state before a broad public, and in this way identified the nation as a state constituted society.

Forming the hub of the Kaiser parades in Germany were the Kaiser and the sovereign princes of the federal states and their entourages, while in France it was the president and a collection of other representatives of the republican state who, next to the troops, composed the chief figures of the ceremonial. Here, however,

---

27   Illustrative of how closely allied was the concept of the '*Volk in Waffen*' with the official discourse regarding compulsory military service, is the text of a document from 1863 concerning the introduction of universal conscription in which Wilhelm I recalled the 'Prussian uprising' against Napoleon: see Geheimes Staatsarchiv Merseburg, OHMA, 1616, Bl. 19-21.
28   Durkheim, *Les Formes élémentaires*, p. 536.
29   Mosse, *Die Nationalisierung der Massen*, pp. 103, 110ff.

was a striking contrast with the German parades, since until the turn of the century the French president — as a civilian — functioned only as a passive spectator of the staged military proceedings. This strict division between the 'civil' sphere of the state and that of the military began to blur only gradually after 1900, at which time the president began to enjoy a more active role in the ceremonial, opening it by reviewing the arrayed troops from a coach and conferring medals upon high-ranking officers in front of the presidential bleacher.[30] Although such changes in the ceremonial can be regarded as harmless details, they embodied the army's symbolic subordination to the civil political power, a situation delayed by more than twenty years but one which finally determined the army's political-institutional position within the republican state. At the same time, these innovations indicate the ascent of the civilian state élite of the Third Republic, which now placed them squarely in the centre of its national public image. The laggardly process of adaptation to the existing political structures underlines how slowly ceremonial rules of the cult of the nation changed. In similar fashion to other spheres of societal life, the state's ceremonial self-representation was apparently governed by a logic of its own which made it at least partially independent of developments in other areas, such as politics.[31]

Although the military festivals reflected essential features of the respective national structures, it should be noted that in neither country did the military festivals convey a complete picture of the institutional and social order. The exclusion of certain social groups and institutions is partly explicable in light of the ceremonial's originally military function. The strong military orientation of the festivals in Germany, for example, dictated that the deputies of the *Reichstag* not be officially included in the ceremonial proceedings, even though they represented one of the most important national institutions of the German Empire. Their politically more potent French parliamentary counterparts, on the other hand, were from the very start given a prominent place in the stagings of the military festivals.

---

30 See, for example, *La France militaire*, 15 July 1905.
31 In his examination of the artistic design of German national monuments, Thomas Nipperdey has already shown the limited autonomy of representations of the nation in the public forum: see Nipperdey, 'Nationalidee und Nationaldenkmal in Deutschland im 19. Jahrhundert', *Historische Zeitschrift*, 1968, 206, pp. 529–85 (p. 531).

In their focus on the Kaiser and the princes, the German military festivals therefore appeared as pure military-monarchical shows with no reference at all to the constitutional system of the empire.

The wide latitude inherent in any staging of military festivals simultaneously afforded people the chance to be incorporated into the cult of the army who did not occupy an official position in the institutional structure of the state. Even existing official hierarchies could be circumvented so long as this was acceptable to the individual parties concerned.[32] This ceremonial flexibility was utilized in order to integrate into the representation of the state a number of persons who either through personal relations or through professional position were closely connected with the head of state. In Germany, in addition to the various regional monarchs, the imperial family, the court and court society were all included in the ceremonial of the Kaiser parades.[33] In France, the public nature of the ceremonials resulted in the president being surrounded by subalterns, personal friends and family members every 14 July. The outward composition of this circle was not unlike that of a monarchical court society, even if its size never attained the dimensions of Germany's imperial *Suite*.[34]

In both Germany and France, the prominent position enjoyed by the spouses and female adjuncts of the various state dignitaries was not constitutionally founded, but was rather a state tradition and the embodiment of the bourgeois family ideal. Yet, whereas the cult of the monarchy granted the female members of the princely families a more active role in the military ceremonial, as they were allowed to appear on the parade field along with their male kin in the Kaiser's

---

32 In certain specific cases, this could lead to abundant discussion as to whether or not the proposed ceremonial changes took into proper consideration the formal and informal degree of rank. Illustrative of this point is the example of Hamburg, where a squabble between the mayor and the citizenry took place over the issue of the appropriate civic representation in the parades: see Tobias von Elsner, *Kaisertage. Die Hamburger und das Wilhelminische Deutschland im Spiegel öffentlicher Festkultur*, Frankfurt am Main, 1991, pp. 408-12.

33 For just this reason, it was only first in the year 1905, with the erection of bleachers for spectators, that anyone other than members of court society, who followed the parade in carriages, were allowed on the parade field.

34 Under President Félix Faure this personal circle grew so large that in the press the president earned the nickname of '*Le Président soleil*': see Eric Lem, *La Présidence de Félix Faure, 1895–1899*, Chantonnay, 1979, p. 12.

entourage, the wife of the French president was restricted to a seat in the 'ladies' bleachers'.[35] Accordingly, the wives of the bourgeois-republican state leadership were relegated to a less significant role than their opposite numbers in the German monarchy, while still maintaining their place of privilege within the larger context of the mass public.

Summing up, one can say that the military festivals — in view of their relative openness and public nature — presented a picture of the armed and ready nation-state that bore only a vague resemblance to the constituted legal order. In Germany the national cult of the army remained entirely a domain of the monarchy, for none of the empire's remaining institutional agencies ever questioned the Kaiser's claim to sole representation of state and army. Therefore it was those élites aligned with the imperial and princely houses which dominated the military festivals. Yet even the Third Republic was unwilling in its military festivals to forgo showcasing the state leadership and personalizing the state in the figure of the president.

The State and the Social Composition of the 'Nation in Arms'

The *mise en scène* of the military festivals was not solely limited to profiling the state representatives and their dependants. They also attempted in multifarious ways to integrate the broader public into the ceremonial. In this respect, the celebratory ritual propagated a specific societal concept that bound certain groups of the nation especially closely to the army and its cult — for example, in the structuring of the onlookers, which effected a distribution of coach space or bleacher seats (to the state representatives and to those in high society) and standing room (to the broad mass of the public) in such a way as to denote the different ranks of society. While a limited circle of persons — through personal relationships with members of the military or the state élite, or by dint of their wealth — could follow the military ceremonials from the vantage point of the bleachers, in both France and Germany the general public could only follow the

---

35 In its report of the Bastille Day parade in 1895, *Le Figaro* wrote that 'naturally' Mme. Faure presided over the 'ladies' bleachers', which were reserved for the wives of ministers and high officials: *Le Figaro*, 15 July 1895.

Military Festivals in Germany and France (1871–1914) 257

proceedings from a distance, at the edge of the parade field.[36] Similar to many religious rituals, in this way the military festivals defined a specific terrain only accessible to a select group of *initiés*.[37]

The division of the social élite from the general population had similar effects in both Germany and France, although the distribution of the bleacher seats in both countries was organized differently: while the bulk of the bleacher tickets for the French parades were distributed free of charge to selected members of 'better society',[38] these tickets in Germany were sold at high prices by private bleacher entrepreneurs.[39] Pre-circulated price lists and discounted prices, however, did allow military personnel, state bureaucrats and members of public institutions to acquire preferred bleacher seating for the Kaiser parades and other military festivals.[40] This financial selection and privileging of certain circles meant that German bleacher spectators hardly differed from their French counterparts: reserve officers, high officials, members of the bourgeois upper-crust holding public positions, many with their families, as well as the family members of the performing soldiers — these populated the bleachers in both countries.[41] Despite

---

36 The contemporary sources do not give exact figures for the number of spectators at the parades. The figures for the Kaiser parade in Leipzig in 1876 range anywhere from 50,000 to 80,000 persons (*Leipziger Nachrichten*, 8 September 1876; *Kreuzzeitung*, 8 September 1876), and for the military celebrations on Bastille Day, anywhere from 100,000 in 1900 (*La France militaire*, 16 July 1905) to between 300,000 and 400,000 in 1895 (*Le Figaro*, 14 July 1895). The number of bleacher seats was given as 4,500 for Leipzig in 1876 (*Leipziger Nachrichten*, 1 September 1876). Thus, less than 10 per cent of the population could follow the action from the bleachers.

37 See Durkheim, *Les Formes élémentaires*, pp. 50ff., 543.

38 The distribution of tickets in Paris was organized by the Bureau of the President and the Ministry of War. Some blocks of tickets were handed out to representatives in the Chamber of Deputies and the Senate, which they would then distribute among their electorate (*Le Figaro*, 13 July 1907 and 12 July 1911).

39 For example, the going rates for bleacher tickets at the 1907 Kaiser parade in Münster were between three and ten Marks (Staatsarchiv Münster, OP, 1294, *passim*).

40 Ibid., and Sächsisches Haupt-Staatsarchiv Dresden, Sächsisches Kriegsarchiv (D), 25338, Bl; Ibid., Generalkommando XII. Korps, 8545.

41 As a rule, the sources do not allow any exact figures concerning the social composition of the bleacher patrons and the remaining public. Therefore, in order to obtain a more accurate

the methods of ticket distribution, in both countries it was the social élites of the state and those in public life who constituted the larger part of the privileged public at the military festivals.

This crude differentiation of the military festival public notwithstanding, there were indeed certain social groups at these celebrations which were clearly distinguished from the remainder, being portrayed as a link between army and nation. From the very beginning of the *Kaiserreich*, the veterans' associations were integrated into the national cult of the army. Delegations from the respective regions were permitted to take part in the Kaiser parades, where they would be placed near the troops.[42] Their admittance to the military festivals was supposed to demonstrate the close relationship that should bind the former soldier, even many years after completion of service, with *Kaiser und Vaterland*.[43] The veterans' associations, for their part, strove to be included in the official ceremonial of the military festivals, because they regarded it as a form of social upgrading and as a recognition of their solidarity with the Kaiser. Moreover, the distinction that was theirs, by dint of the special honour conferred on participants in the cult of the nation, helped in their mobilization of often inactive members, as well as in their recruitment of new ones. The Prussian authorities utilized this interest of the veterans' associations to extend their political influence to the associations and suppress so-called 'anti-imperial tendencies' by regulating access to the military festivals. The political observation of the civil and military authorities led in 1891 to seventeen veterans' associations of the Military Association of Reuss being excluded from the Kaiser parade in Erfurt, because according to the official assessment they had displayed a 'particularistic

---

picture of the public frequenting the military festivals, I have availed myself of general indicators in newspaper accounts and official police files.

42 See, for example, the reports on the Kaiser parades in Breslau in 1875 (*Norddeutsche Allgemeine Zeitung*, 12 September 1875); in Leipzig in 1876 (ibid., 7 September 1876); in Merseburg in 1876 (ibid., 10 September 1876); and in Kassel in 1878 (ibid., 22 September 1878).

43 See also the speech of Kaiser Wilhelm II on 19 August 1895 before the collective Berlin veterans associations, as cited in *Vossische Zeitung*, 20 August 1895. See also Schacht, 'Die Mitgift des Reservisten', *Militärwochenblatt*, 96, 1911, 1, pp. 1122–24.

attitude'.[44] On the other hand, the example of the 1907 Kaiser parade in Münster shows that in particular instances the state authorities did not always succeed in implementing their regulation policies against the resistance of local officials.[45] Along with the veterans' associations and their volunteer medical columns,[46] after the turn of the century student and youth groups, especially of the Jungdeutschland-Bund (founded in 1911), were permitted to take part in the military festivals. As a brochure of the Jungdeutschland-Bund declared, the stagings should assist 'all male youth in developing into strong, patriotic and morally pure men'.[47]

In a similar fashion, as of 1910 the French authorities also exploited the national cult of the army in the interest of the patriotic education of male youth, by allowing several '*sociétes de préparation militaire*' to send delegations to the Bastille Day parades.[48] The apparent intention here was to strengthen the republican-styled societies, which stood in competition with the Catholic youth organizations.[49] The French soldiers and veterans associations remained excluded from the national celebrations up until shortly before the First World War — although they constantly pressed for inclusion by pointing to the privileges of the German veterans' associations.[50] The reason for the state's denial probably lay in the fact of the associations' ideological proximity to nationalistic activists of the Right, whose Bonapartist orientation many of the former soldiers shared.

The particular prominence of soldiers past and future in the ritual of the military festivals symbolized in both countries the all-embracing claims of

---

44 Bundsarchiv Potsdam, 09.01, *AA*, no. 28976, *passim*.
45 Staatsarchiv Münster, *OP*, 1297, vol. 2, 109.
46 See Jakob Vogel, 'Samariter und Schwestern. Geschlechterbilder und -beziehungen im "Deutschen Roten Kreuz" vor dem Ersten Weltkrieg' in Karen Hagemann and Ralf Pröve (eds), *Landsknechte, Soldatenfrauen und Nationalkrieger. Militär, Krieg und Geschlechterordnung im historischen Wandel*, Frankfurt am Main, 1998, pp. 322–44.
47 Jungdeutschland Gruppe Gross-Berlin (ed.), *Jungdeutschland-Bote für das Jahr 1914*, Berlin, 1913, p. 149.
48 *La France militaire*, 9 July 1910 and 11 July 1911.
49 Archives Nationales, Paris, F 1cI, 201.
50 *Le Vétéran*, 20 March 1912. Until 1912, the exceptions were the Paris parades of 1880 and 1886, in which, in addition to veterans groups, other 'patriotic' associations were included.

military allegiance which the state and the nation placed on the (male) citizen.[51] From youth until old age, he should be attached to the army, serving the nation. The festivals were in this respect more than just a showcase for the active troops. Alongside the nation-state and its heads, all of the army-affiliated groups should also be celebrated so as to invoke the unity of the armed and ready nation. With the inclusion of male youth and former soldiers, and with the army as rallying point, the nation-state sketched a social picture of the 'nation in arms' that was characterized by manliness, order and fealty to the state leadership. In both countries, the government reserved the right to restrict participation in the festivals to those groups of society that conformed to an ideal vision of the 'nation in arms'. Not least, this careful selection of participants disclosed the more or less hidden political character of the military festivals which, although claiming to transcend party politics by representing the national community, must still be viewed as a narrow expression of the state leadership's conception of the military nation.

Military Ritual and National Enthusiasm

Similar to most religious ceremonies — and above and beyond the mere military ceremonial — the military festivals were animated through a whole series of elements that also allowed the public participants to participate emotionally in the ritual, thus stoking their enthusiasm for army and nation.[52] This was necessary, since without an inner participation of the public the staging of the national cult would have been an empty form. The sounds and the rhythms of martial music, the colourful uniforms of the soldiers, the well-rehearsed entrance of the military and state dignitaries, the precise choreography of the innumerable marching troops — all this called into life the atmosphere of a mass theatrical production that the participants apparently found hard to resist. This impression is strengthened by

---

51 Jakob Vogel, 'Stramme Gardisten, temperamentvolle Tirailleurs und anmutige Damen. Geschlechterbilder im deutschen und französischen Kult der "Nation in Waffen"' in Ute Frevert (ed.), *Militär und Gesellschaft im 19. und 20. Jahrhundert*, Stuttgart, 1997, pp. 245–62.
52 See Durkheim, *Les Formes élémentaires*, p. 547.

contemporary reports, which usually describe the military festivals as an 'imposing military theatre', as a 'martial spectacle'.[53]

The theatricality was partly a spin-off from military training, which had been developed in similar form in eighteenth-century European armies.[54] In the national cult of the army, however, the ceremonial was expanded through a whole series of representative elements and national symbols that were thrown into relief as visible tokens of the festival's national dimension. Accordingly, military bands would set the marching soldiers in rhythm with the national anthem or other symbolic military music, while a forest of national flags adorned the parade ground and the bleachers. Spectators and participants were thereby enveloped in an atmosphere steeped in military and national symbols.

In order to keep the fairly repetitive festivals attractive to the general public, in both countries the theatrical effects were intensified over the years so as to avoid ossification into a lifeless ritual, although the changes remained limited so as not to endanger the ritualistic character of the festivals. In Germany, in an attempt to instrumentalize the military festivals for the cult of the Kaiser, Wilhelm II would often personally initiate such theatrical innovations. For example, he decisively changed the ceremonial by habitually riding into the city at the head of his troops following the official parade. Contemporary impressions regularly depicted this as a 'genuine triumphal procession' of the Kaiser, who was enthusiastically greeted by the massed public along the parade route.[55] The theatrical effects of French military festivals were no less surcharged. Since the centennial of 1889, a special attraction of the Paris parades was the *charge finale* of the cavalry, in which the horsemen would charge the bleachers in close order and then come to an abrupt halt directly before them.[56] Such innovations made the 1889 parade '*exceptionellement attrayante*' for the reporter from *Figaro*.[57] In the same way,

---

53   See, for example, *Vossische Zeitung*, 10 September 1888, 13 August 1889 and 22 August 1891; and *Le Figaro*, 15 July 1888, 15 July 1889 and 15 July 1990.

54   See *Le Figaro*, 15 July 1909. See also, more generally, Hans-Peter Stein, *Symbole und Zeremoniell in deutschen Streitkräften vom 18. bis zum 20. Jahrhundert*, Herford, 1984.

55   See *Vossische Zeitung*, 1 September 1888, 10 September 1888 and 22 May 1889.

56   *Le Figaro*, 15 July 1889.

57   Ibid. See also *La France militaire*, 16 July 1911: 'Ce merveilleux spectacle déchaine, une fois de plus, l'enthousiasme des spectateurs.'

the re-transfer in 1886 of the Paris Bastille Day parade to the Longchamps flatland by the French Minister of War, General Boulanger, was a reaction to general complaints about the poor view afforded the public at the Champs Elysées parades during the two previous years.[58]

In the charged atmosphere of the military-national spectacles, the public was no passive recipient. It cheered the passing soldiers and applauded the especially well-managed manoeuvres of the troops. Next to the army, the state head was the most important object of general enthusiasm, 'boisterous hurrahs' greeting the arrival of the Kaiser on the parade field, and shouts of *'Vive le Président!'* welcoming the same in the Paris spectacles.[59] The Social Democratic press in Germany spoke disparagingly of *'Hurrahpatrioten'* who cheered the *'militärischen Klimbim'* of the Kaiser parades, and denounced the French *'Kanaille'* that went into raptures over the *'Tschintara der Militärmusik und den bunten Uniformen'*.[60] Neither the German Kaiser nor the French President could resist the emotionally suffused atmosphere. In a letter to his friend Philipp Eulenburg, Wilhelm II raved about the 'great day' in Berlin on which he first reviewed the 'magnificent parade' of the Guards,[61] while the French Minister-President Périer gushed after an 1894 manoeuvres parade: 'Le spectacle que je viens d'admirer était plus qu'une fête pour les yeux, c'était une joie pour les coeurs. Je remercie tous ceux auxquels je dois cette réconfortante émotion.'[62]

On the basis of such enthusiasm, the military festivals became emotionally charged rituals of national unity and military strength. With the public and the participants regularly confirming their membership in the armed and ready nation, the festivals assumed a communal-sacramental function, analogous to those

---

58 *Le Gaulois*, 15 July 1886; and *Le Temps*, 15 July 1884 and 14 July 1885.
59 *Berliner Tageblatt*, 1 September 1900; *Vossische Zeitung*, 1 September 1900; *Le Figaro*, 15 July 1888, 15 July 1895 and 15 July 1900. See also the extensive police reports on the Paris parades in the Parisian Archives de la Préfecture de Police.
60 *Vorwärts*, 4 September 1907 and 21 March 1912. In spite of such verbal attacks by *Vorwärts*, Social Democratic workers did take part in the parades, as indicated by a memorandum of the Dresden police in their report on the Kaiser parade of 1882 (Sächsisches Haupt-Staatsarchiv Dresden, Polizeidir. Dresden, no. 899, p. 22).
61 J. C. G. Röhl (ed.), *Philipp Eulenburgs politische Korrespondenz*, Boppard, 1976, p. 311.
62 *La France militaire*, 21 September 1894.

religious rites described by Emile Durkheim.[63] In the military parades, the 'nation in arms' always to some degree constructed itself as an experiential community mediating between the army and the civilian public. Even if the symbolism and content of the military ceremonial possibly remained hidden to many spectators,[64] its emotional, nationalizing effect remained undisputed among contemporaries. As early as 1873, in a talk before the Paris Academy, Henri Baudrillart therefore proposed that the military parades should form the centre of the cult of the nation:

> Seule la revue militaire [...] offre un imposant spectacle, auquel toute grandeur ne manque pas; ce n'est pas seulement l'éclat des armes et des uniformes, et l'art prodigieux de mettre en mouvement de pareilles masses; quelque chose de plus grand encore nous émut à notre insu, l'idée de courage, du dévouement, de l'ordre, d'une force morale qui au dedans s'appelle la discipline, au dehors l'indépendance, la puissance, l'unité armée de la patrie.[65]

Final Thoughts

The elaborate staging of the military festivals in the national cults of Germany and of France exhibits the enormous role that the state leadership in both countries ascribed to the army as motor of a cultural nationalization of society. On the basis of their peculiar effect on the masses, the military festivals became a central element in the nationalization 'from above', what Benedict Anderson has characterized as the 'official nationalism' of the European nation-state at the end of the nineteenth century.[66] The 'European-wide militarization process', which Gerhard Ritter has identified as the aftermath of the wars of 1866 and 1870–71,[67]

---

63   Durkheim, *Les Formes élémentaires*, 553.
64   As Paul Veyne correctly noted: see Veyne, 'Propagande expression roi, image idole oracle', *L'Homme*, 114, 1990, pp. 7–26 (pp. 12, 21–22).
65   Henri Baudrillart, *Les Fêtes publiques*, Paris, 1873.
66   Benedict Anderson, *Imagined Communities: Reflections on the Origin and Spread of Nationalism*, London and New York, 1983, pp. 80–103.
67   Gerhard Ritter, *Staatskunst und Kriegshandwerk. Das Problem des Militarismus in Deutschland. 2, Die Hauptmächte Europas und das wilhelminische Reich, 1890–1914*, Munich, 1960, p. 115; Laurence Cole, 'Vom Glanz der Montur. Zum dynastischen Kult der Habsburger und seiner Vermittlung durch militärische Vorbilder im 19. Jahrhundert. Ein Bericht über ein "work in progress"', *Österreichische Zeitschrift für*

assumed at the cultural level in both Germany and France the form of an increasing nationalization that was dramatized in the concept of the 'nation in arms'. In this connection, the state military cult served both in France and Germany simultaneously to disseminate an official concept of the nation and to serve as the 'natural' framework for its presentation.

What sort of a dynamic the state's cult of the nation could generate with regard to the cultural nationalization of the European societies is especially obvious in the German case, where, naturally, it was only with the founding of the nation-state that a cult of the nation could in fact be propagated by the state. As official state functions, the national celebrations of the *Kaiserreich*, particularly the annual 'Kaiser parades', demonstrate that a far larger segment of the German population could thus be mobilized than was the case before 1870 in the political-opposition festivals of the German national movement, which have been given ample attention by historians.[68] The newly founded nation-state — through the defining and staging power of the 'official' cult of the nation, as well as on the basis of the extraordinary resources at its disposal — had a distinct advantage over the liberal-national movement. So it was with relative ease that it was able to disseminate its monarchical interpretation of the nation to the German public. For their part, the republican élite of the Third Republic profited in a similar fashion from the state resources of power so as to suppress the memory of the Napoleonic Empire and to impress the republican cult of the nation on French society.

Admittedly, in order to have an effect, the officially propagated national image had to correspond at least in rough outline to the general expectations of the people. In this regard, the state productions had to take into account certain social groupings — such as the veterans' associations — which served as important mediators of the cult of the nation. This naturally limited the state's staging options. Yet it still possessed a considerable power advantage over other social groups and institutions, which thus reduced the 'construction' of the publicly propagated image of the nation to a relatively one-sided act.

Geschichtswissenschaften, 1996, 7, pp. 554–91; Ilaria Porchiani, *La festa nazionale nell'Italia unita. Rappresentazione dello stato et spazi sociali*, Bologna, 1997.

68 For further particulars, see Dieter Düding (ed.), *Öffentliche Festkultur. Politische in Deutschland von der Aufklärung bis zum Ersten Weltkrieg*, Reinbeck, 1988.

WAR IN MIND: CELEBRATIONS AND WAR ENTHUSIASM IN THE RHINELAND, 1913

Ute Schneider

I

'The idea, openly propagated from many sides in public and in private circles, to celebrate the ever recurring anniversary of the Battle of Leipzig as a sacred national holiday, is so worthy and fine that I am compelled to wish and hope for the participation of the *Generalgouvernement* in its realization.'[1] With these words Staatsrat Sack, the Governor of the department Nieder- und Mittelrhein (later part of the Prussian Rhine Province) on 11 October 1814 called on his subordinate officials to support the celebrations of 18 October. One year earlier,

---

I am grateful to Cora Molloy for the translation of an earlier version of this chapter, my colleagues and friends in Darmstadt, Düsseldorf and Victoria for frequent discussions about the topic, and Prof. Dr. Nathalie Fryde, who helped me with the finishing touches.

[1] 'Die von vielen Seiten her öffentlich vor dem Publikum, wie in Privatzirkeln, schon ausgesprochene Idee, den wiederkehrenden Jahrestag der Leipziger Schlacht als einen heiligen National Festtag im ganzen Umkreis deutscher Zunge und deutschen Sinnes zu bewillkommen, ist so würdig und so schön, daß ich wünschen muß, für ihre Ausführung im diesseitigen Generalgouvernement beigetragen zu sehen, was ohne öffentliche Aufforderung, wozu es an Veranlassung von oben her ganz fehlt, irgend in unseren Kräften steht': Generalgouverneur Staatsrat Sack to Gouvernementskommissar Bölling, 11 October 1814, Nordrhein-Westfälisches Hauptstaatsarchiv Düsseldorf (NWHStAD), Nieder- und Mittelrhein 1405.

the 'Battle of the Nations' at Leipzig had resulted in the liberation of the territories on the eastern bank of the river Rhine from French rule and in the defeat and retreat of Napoleon. The anniversary of this event was celebrated by many towns and communities throughout the German territories between 1814 and 1819.[2] A hundred years later, the centenary celebrations were held with even greater extravagance in the German Empire.

In contrast to the period directly after 1814, the celebrations in 1913 no longer concentrated solely on 18 October, but the Wars of Liberation were commemorated in a cycle of celebrations throughout the year, crowned by two royal celebrations. Contemporaries remarked upon the frequency of celebrations and were aware of their political importance and function.

During recent years much has been said about popular festivals as an important part of political culture and nationalism. Historians are fascinated by new questions and answers, as well as by the discovery of new sources, yet occasionally they simply forget that not all sources mirror reality in the way they assume. The question of sources is one of two aspects upon which this chapter will focus.

In common with people in all other German regions, the people of the Rhineland commemorated the Wars of Liberation in several festivals in 1913. But both the collective memory of the events and the tradition of the festivals were constructs, as participants and organizers traced a period of history in which they had not actually participated. As most parts of the later Rhine Province had belonged to the French state or one of her German allies, they had participated in the Wars of Liberation on the losing, French, side. But as early as 1814, intellectuals, priests and politicians like Staatsrat Sack tried hard to bridge the gap between defeat and victory. The successful invention of tradition connected with the 18 October festivals, and its subsequent promotion throughout the course of the nineteenth century, made it, especially after 1900, an integral part of the

---

2   Dieter Düding, 'Das deutsche Nationalfest von 1814. Matrix der deutschen Nationalfeste im 19. Jahrhundert' in Dieter Düding, Peter Friedemann and Paul Münch (eds), *Öffentliche Festkultur*, Reinebek, 1988, pp. 67–88; Stefan-Ludwig Hoffmann, 'Mythos und Geschichte. Leipziger Gedenkfeiern der Völkerschlacht im 19. und frühen 20. Jahrhundert' in Étienne François, Hannes Siegrist and Jakob Vogel (eds), *Nation und Emotion*, Göttingen, 1995, pp. 111–32.

national collective memory. The events of 1813 were mythologized as a unique moment in the nation's history when, forgetting social, political or religious differences, the whole nation had acted together. By 1913, the historical reality was either forgotten or distorted.

During the various festivals which the Germans celebrated throughout 1913, they constantly referred to the time of the Wars of Liberation. The revival of symbols, poems and so on, together with shifts in military policy and the public discourse about war — which will be my second line of enquiry — supported the existing militarism in two respects: on the one hand, the idea of war was romanticized; and, on the other, a mental preparation was set in motion for a possible future war.[3]

II

Between 1814 and 1819 the programme of festivities was similar everywhere; variations derived only from local circumstances and possibilities. Roughly speaking, the celebration was arranged as follows. Throughout the land the day began with bell-ringing followed by a church service. All denominations, including the Jewish communities, took part, in some cases even in ecumenical form. Some of the services even had to be held in the open air for lack of space.[4] Sermons played a central role in these services, as the priests used suitable biblical words to focus on the liberation and the connection between religious and national unity.[5] After the services, local dignitaries met for banquets, while the population enjoyed itself with various entertainments and competitions. The highlight of and conclusion to the day was a combined procession of all inhabitants to a central place, preferably a hill, where the participants lit bonfires and fireworks. At the

---

3 Thomas Rohkrämer, 'August 1914 — Kriegsmentalität und ihre Voraussetzungen' in Wolfgang Michalka (ed.), *Der Erste Weltkrieg*, Munich, 1994, pp. 759–77.
4 Ute Schneider, *Politische Festkultur im 19. Jahrhundert. Die Rheinprovinz von der französischen Zeit bis zum Ende des Ersten Weltkrieges (1806–1918)*, Essen, 1995, pp. 52ff.
5 Graf Gerhard, *Gottesbild und Politik. Eine Studie zur Frömmigkeit in Preußen während der Befreiungskriege 1813–1815*, Göttingen, 1993; Ute Schneider, 'Die Feiern der Leipziger Schlacht am 18. Oktober 1814 — Eine intellektuelle Konstruktion?', in *Blätter für deutsche Landesgeschichte*, 133, 1997, pp. 219–38.

same time, towns and major buildings, such as the dome of Cologne Cathedral, were illuminated: 'The fires from the hills illuminated the Rhine Valley in celebration, as if to proclaim the joy of the people at Germany's liberation.'[6] At a time when street-lighting was still scarce, these bonfires impressed all participants, visually and emotionally. It was not only the religious-national symbolic meaning of fire as such but also the integrative power of bonfires, as they visually presented a unifying bond between the participants in all German territories.[7]

The organization of the festival day on the local level lay mainly in the hands of officials, mayors, teachers and priests, who staged the festivities with the active help of local dignitaries such as merchants and doctors. The mobilizing power of the celebrations was, according to the major sources,[8] exceedingly high in 1814 and 1815, although the population had to carry the financial and material burden itself. Regardless of social, political and religious differences, men, women and children of all ages participated in the festivities.

But the celebrations of 18 October were by no means the product of spontaneous joy, as they are still often presented in modern historiography. Certainly they no longer took place merely by royal command, as had been the case under Napoleon, but the celebrations at that time had also been promoted by writers and patriots, as explicitly stated in Staatsrat Sack's statement quoted above.

In the course of 1814, a circle around Ernst Moritz Arndt and the 'father of gymnastics', Friedrich Ludwig Jahn, applied their own ideas of German national festivals to the festival of 18 October. As the result of close social connections between the nationally orientated circles and their access to a variety of newspaper editors, they disseminated their idea of a general celebration on 18 October and, at the same time, transmitted their precise concept of what form the festivities should take. In some places this was taken up, especially by the above-mentioned

---

6 NWHStAD, Regierung Düsseldorf 128, pp. 31–32.
7 Schneider, *Politische Festkultur*, pp. 55–56.
8 Besides newspapers, memoirs and so on, our main sources of these festivals are a collection of festival reports, published immediately after the first festivals in 1814: Karl Hoffmann (ed.), *Des Teutschen Volkes feuriger Dank- und Ehrentempel*, Offenbach, 1815.

group of local organizers, with the result that the festivities took on an almost stereotypical form.[9] In other places the local élites were — by official order — not allowed to organize or even to participate in the festivities. The reason was obvious: some German territories and parts of the Rhineland had been French allies or under French rule in 1813, and for them 18 October represented in political terms a day of defeat.[10] But as some of the local élites were closely related to the German patriots mentioned above, they used the regular church services and private meetings to celebrate the anniversary. Both groups wrote reports about their celebrations, and these were brought into line with the published and widely disseminated official version. These reports draw a picture of very similar celebrations, not only in the organization of events but also in their choice of words, and especially in the terminology employed for the participation of the population. Certain expressions were used that can be traced back to the French Revolution and are also found in newspaper appeals and the writings of literary personages. In this way, terms such as *Gesinnungsbegriffe*, *Volk* and *Brüder* were applied with a mixture of religious and national meaning, purporting to represent the whole nation without discrimination.[11] The public use of these words also had the specific function of bridging the gap between the *Brüder* in the case of the Rhine Province, the Prussians and the former French subjects.[12] The political implications, however, were far from being intended by the initiators and local organizers of the celebrations, as their active participation was only approved of on the margins of the official programme.[13]

---

9   Schneider, 'Die Feiern der Leipziger Schlacht', p. 224.
10 Wolfram Siemann, *Vom Staatenbund zum Nationalstaat*, Munich, 1995, pp. 23ff.
11 According to most reports even gender differences were of no importance on this day: ' Alt und Jung, Greise, Jünglinge, Mädchen und Kinder alles nahm Anteil am Zuge': NWHStAD, Nieder- und Mittelrhein 1448.
12 'Vergegenwärtigt auch die edelmütigen Aufopferungen unserer Deutschen Brüder und besonders der Preußen, die sie vorher dargebracht haben und auch jetzt für die gute Sache zur Stürzung des Kriegs-Ungeheuers des Bonaparts, und zur Erringung eines allgemeinen und dauerhaften Friedens so gerne beweisen wollen! Laßt uns von gleichem Geiste beseelt uns als Brüder an sie anschließen, für Vaterland unseren König leben, Opfer bringen, und den Frieden helfen erkämpfen!': NWHStAD, Nieder- und Mittelrhein 47
13 In reality, most activities were limited to a small group of notables and officials, who sometimes went to great effort and expense to underline their new loyalty. Later they

In Prussia, and consequently also in the Rhineland, the tradition of publicly celebrating 18 October ended with the execution of the Carlsbad Decrees in 1819.[14] Only in schools did it remain a date for celebration. Political interest-groups failed to adopt 18 October for various reasons. First of all, it was only a short period of celebration; secondly, politicization and diversification were only slowly beginning; and, thirdly, it was not a publicly celebrated national festival in the former French and some territories of the 'Third Germany',.[15] Finally, the memory of the Wars of Liberation and 18 October even in Prussia — and the Rhineland had belonged to Prussia from 1815 — was not undisputed, and the date was, outside the schools, of minor importance in the Rhineland during the nineteenth century.[16] In 1863, the fiftieth anniversary had been boycotted by many Rhineland towns due to the constitutional conflict in Prussia.[17] But through their ostensibly uniform character and the social openness expressed in the collected reports, these festivals had started to conform with officially accepted festivals of the German nation.[18]

Gradually, during the second half of the nineteenth century, history was brought into line. By means of memoirs, literature, schoolbooks and historiography, a monarchist interpretation of the Wars of Liberation was disseminated. One of the central and soon widespread slogans was 'Der König rief und alle, alle kamen' ('The King called and everyone followed'); others dwelt on the *Opferbereitschaft* of the Germans, who financed the war through private donations.[19]

---

    sometimes had problems paying the debts thus incurred: NWHStAD, Regierung Düsseldorf 128, p. 54ff.

14 Thomas Nipperdey, *Deutsche Geschichte*, Munich, 1991, pp. 282ff; Schneider, *Politische Festkultur*, pp. 63ff.
15 Schneider, 'Die Feiern der Leipziger Schlacht'.
16 Christopher Clark, 'The Wars of Liberation in Prussian Memory: Reflections on the Memorialization of War in Early Nineteenth-Century Germany', *Journal of Modern History*, 68, 1996, pp. 550–76.
17 Schneider, *Politische Festkultur*, pp. 166ff.
18 Düding, 'Das deutsche Nationalfest', p. 85.
19 Clark, 'The Wars of Liberation', pp. 552f.

Despite German unification in 1871, the Wars of Liberation and the date of 18 October did not gain a central place in the official national 'memory'. Wilhelm I decided against a national holiday, and in many regions the *Sedantag* (2 September) came into existence in the German Empire on the initiative of Protestant middle-class groups. It was not until after 1880 and the end of the *Kulturkampf* that this holiday gained roots in the Rhineland. Thanks to a new generation and increasing historicization, the Sedan festivals became less important under Wilhelm II. As the result of the *Sammlungspolitik*, the Wars of Liberation provided a better focus for the cult of national memory, especially as 1913 was to be the centenary of the battle and the erection of a memorial, the *Völkerschlachtdenkmal*, was being projected.[20]

Contemporaries noticed the sharp increase in celebrations between 1913 and January 1914. Erich Mühsam summed up the preceding year as 'a year of pleasure, in which sweet tones and joyful celebrations seemed to know no end. There were celebrations everywhere, meetings, serenades and speeches, speeches upon speeches. It was very uplifting'.[21] Apart from numerous local and regional anniversaries and town festivals, the empire, including the Rhineland, held four national celebrations in 1913.[22]

III

The cycle of festivals began in January, with the Emperor's birthday, which was staged particularly pompously in Berlin but did not go beyond the usual display of parades, banquets and associated festivities in the Rhine Province. Six weeks later, on 10 March, the anniversary of the foundation of the 'Iron Cross', the nation commemorated the Wars of Liberation and the birthday of Queen Luise.

---

20 Schneider, *Politische Festkultur*, pp. 191ff; Jakob Vogel, *Nationen im Gleichschritt*, Göttingen, 1997, pp. 170ff.

21 'Dort war 1913 ein Jahr der Lust, in dem liebliches Geläute und fröhliches Festefeiern keine Grenzen hatte. [...] Da gab es allüberall Spezialfeiern, Kommerse, Serenaden und Reden, Reden, Reden. Es war sehr erhebend': Erich Mühsam, 'Bilanz 1913' in Mühsam, *Ausgewählte Werke*, 2 vols, Berlin, 1978, II, p. 161.

22 Wolfram Siemann, 'Krieg und Frieden in historischen Gedenkfeiern des Jahres 1913' in Düding, Friedemann and Münch (eds.), *Öffentliche Festkultur*, pp. 298–320.

This tight schedule resulted from the need to avoid Easter week, which began on 17 March. Wilhelm II was also keen to emphasize the royal role in events, and the dates in March were particularly appropriate for this. This royal element is also clear in the Emperor's decision not to hold a special reception for the Veterans of 1870–71, although otherwise the war of those years was publicly regarded as a repetition of 1813.[23] At the same time, in March, the preparations for the twenty-fifth anniversary of Wilhelm II's reign (on 16 June), began on a local level. This celebration, initiated by the state, is most remarkable since Wilhelm II's predecessors, as he himself also did in 1898, had celebrated anniversaries of this kind rather quietly and in private. A single exception was the anniversary of Wilhelm I's rule in 1886, which had become a bigger event in the Rhineland mainly through the initiative of the people, largely out of a desire to express loyalty to the monarchy after the *Kulturkampf*.[24] Even after this third festivity, the local organizations still could not rest: immediately they began preparations for the one-hundredth anniversary of the 'Battle of the Nations' at Leipzig on 18 October, now transformed in the public awareness into the most original and most popular celebration of the Wars of Liberation.

At first glance, this concentration of national celebrations in the year 1913 does not seem extraordinary, as two of them were commemoration days for the Wars of Liberation. Certainly one cannot see this as an active preparation for war, as Golo Mann has suggested in his memoirs.[25] Nevertheless, the festivities must be seen in connection with the empire's military policy, which welcomed public discourse on the Wars of Liberation and on war in general. Furthermore, the permanent debate about the Wars of Liberation, related to the national celebrations, created a mental receptivity and readiness for war that supported the existing militarism to a greater extent than all previous festivals had, despite their historical dimension.[26]

---

23 Schneider, *Politische Festkultur*, pp. 320ff; Vogel, *Nationen im Gleichschritt*, p. 176.
24 Landeshauptarchiv Koblenz, 403/7043, p. 493; NWHStAD, Regierung Düsseldorf Präsidialbüro 31 and 372; Schneider, *Politische Festkultur*, pp. 326ff.
25 Golo Mann, *Erinnerungen und Gedanken*, Frankfurt, 1986, pp. 15, 31.
26 Jakob Vogel calls it 'Folkloremilitarismus'. I am not sure that this concept is suitable for 1913, because the military impact of the festivals covered greater parts of the population than in all previous festivals: Vogel, *Nationen im Gleichschritt*, pp. 275ff.

The official promotion of such festivals in 1913 had its origin in a monarchical shift towards a public commemoration of the Wars of Liberation[27] and was the product of domestic politics. There were plans that year to increase spending on the army, which necessitated an unparalleled increase in the defence budget.[28] Following initial rumours, these intentions had been announced in mid-January and were to be debated in the Reichstag from the beginning of April until the end of June.[29] Most of the festivities were concentrated precisely around that time. For the imperial government they offered a suitable means of manipulating opinion and mentally preparing the people who, after all, had to swallow further expenditure on armaments and carry the resulting financial burden in the form of a wealth tax. The calculation paid off. Two weeks after the Emperor's anniversary the Army Bill was passed by parliament — even the Social Democrats voted for it.[30]

But the celebrations and their substance had evoked much deeper emotional and mental processes in the population. The central topic of 'war' dominated the minds of the general public during the whole year, not only thanks to the historical dimension of the festivities, but also due to the Balkan wars of 1912–13, the fear of the threat from Britain and France — who increased her military service requirement to three years — and to the Army Bill.[31]

---

27   Ibid., pp. 177 ff. Wilhelm II and the Staatsministerium had already decided in January 1912 that, from January 1913, the Wars of Liberation should be the main topic in all subjects and schools: Bundesarchiv Potsdam, Reichskanzlei 1364, pp. 49–51.
28   Hans-Ulrich Wehler, *Deutsche Gesellschaftsgeschichte. III, 1849–1914*, Munich, 1995, pp. 1110ff.
29   *Düsseldorfer Tageblatt* 16 January 1913; Michael Geyer, *Deutsche Rüstungspolitik 1860–1980*, Frankfurt, 1984, pp. 83ff.
30   Wehler, *Deutsche Gesellschaftsgeschichte*, p. 1113.
31   Wolfgang J. Mommsen, 'The Topos of Inevitable War in Germany in the Decade before 1914' in Volker R. Berghahn and Martin Kitchen (eds), *Germany in the Age of Total War: Essays in Honour of Francis Carsten*, London, 1981, pp. 23–45.

IV

In the Rhine Province the memorial celebrations and the government anniversary took their usual form. The organization and arrangement of the day lay chiefly in the hands of the *Kriegervereine*. For them it was, on the one hand, the occasion that corresponded most with their interests and commitments; on the other, their high degree of national connections and organization allowed them to prepare the festivities on a grander scale. Furthermore, their internal structures allowed them easy access to their members, who were obliged to participate in national celebrations.[32]

Everywhere the festival day began with services of all denominations, in which mainly officials, schools and associations participated. The services were followed by parades of the *Kriegervereine*, which also lent the day a visually military character. After that, the association members, separately from the officials, met for banquets in restaurants. In some places the richer inhabitants participated. In the schools, as well as in the universities, special celebrations took place, consisting of speeches and singing. In March, the most diligent pupils received books in commemoration of 1813 or, as in Aachen, a reproduction of the picture of the 'Speech of General Yorck to the Estates on 5 February 1813' for the classroom, while in June the school prizes consisted of pictures of the Emperor.[33] In October, some smaller communities, according to a tradition of the Wars of Liberation, treated their schoolchildren to special delicacies financed by the community budget.

The evening programme was again addressed to a larger audience, as all four days were normal working days for the majority of the population. Only in June did some factory-owners close for the festivities, which was very unusual but certainly reflected their worries about their workers simply skipping work for a long weekend.[34]

---

32 Thomas Rohkrämer, *Der Militarismus der 'kleinen Leute'. Die Kriegervereine im Deutschen Kaiserreich 1871–1914*, Munich, 1990; Schneider, *Politische Festkultur*, p. 324; Vogel, *Nationen im Gleichschritt*, p. 156.

33 Schneider, *Politische Festkultur*, p. 322.

34 The fact that all these festivals were not officially declared national holidays caused a great deal of debate and differences in practice during the nineteenth century. Again and again

So far, the arrangements corresponded to a traditional, and over the years only slightly modified, scenario. Yet the population did introduce new features: they brought in festival elements going back to the Wars of Liberation, partly spontaneously, partly stimulated by the initiative of the state and the associations. The decisive factor was that for months the period of 1813–15 had been discussed, historicized, and at the same time made publicly relevant. This historical interest by no means took into account military and technical innovations, but was still wedded to romanticized notions of war.[35] An important factor of this process was the renaissance of heroes of the Wars of Liberation. One particular example was Theodor Körner, the *Freiheitssänger*, who quickly became the most popular poet in schools, newspapers and among the public. Parallel to the celebrations many reprints and facsimile editions of his poetry collection 'Leyer und Schwert' were published. The warmth of the reception of these poems was expressed in the spontaneous popular planting of oak trees on 10 March. For Theodor Körner the oak was the symbol of freedom and loyalty, and in 1814 Ernst Moritz Arndt had declared oak leaves the sign of 18 October.[36]

Furthermore, the evening programmes employed a festival element also dating back to the Wars of Liberation: torchlit processions and bonfires. The former had become rare in the course of the nineteenth century as festivities had more often taken the form of processions in honour of outstanding local personalities. Bonfires and illuminations had become antiquated, mainly because of electrification, and in addition restrictions had been imposed by the fire authorities. Now with official blessing they enjoyed a comeback. Directed by the *Kriegervereine*, the population arranged torchlit processions, often in historical costumes (or what they thought to be such) and ended the day with bonfires and illuminations. These processions not only served as reminders of 1813–15, they

---

political groups demanded a national holiday or the common celebration of national holidays on a Sunday: *Deutsche Nationalfeste. Mittheilungen und Schriften des Ausschusses*, Heft 1, 1.April 1897.

35 Certainly the growing conflicts between the War Ministry and the general staff mirror this attitude. Only when these conflicts were settled during the First World War was the change-over to a modern army possible: Geyer, *Deutsche Rüstungspolitik 1860–1980*, p. 92ff.

36 Ernst Moritz Arndt, *Noch ein Wort über die Franzosen und über uns*, Frankfurt am Main, 1814, p. 37; NWHStAD, Landratsamt Essen 103, p. 280.

also pointed up a mythologized picture of popular political consent and national unity during those years. The high-point of the popular-national unity this myth proclaimed was the victory celebration of 18 October 1813, a day which, as reflected in many lectures of the time, was seen as a turning-point for nineteenth-century Germany.[37] These historic lectures and speeches, as well as the collections of contemporary festival reports, were now used as a mirror of reality, as a blueprint for the festivities of 1913.[38] Seen against the background of the socio-political situation in the empire in 1913, this mythologized memory of national unity contained an anachronism which could only partially hide existing tensions.[39]

The inhabitants of Düsseldorf arranged a torchlight procession which ended on the meadows near the Rhine with illuminations and the burning of a sacrificial tower, the *Opferturm*. The word *Opfer* (sacrifice) and its various compounds became the catchword of the year. Newspapers wrote of the '*Opferjahr* 1913', and different institutions urged the population to show their '*Opfergeist*'. The first such entreaty, relating to the anniversary of the Emperor's coronation, was made by the two Christian Churches in March, with their launch of an appeal for national donations to support missions in the German colonies. Donations and financial contributions on such occasions had been customary since the early nineteenth century, but in June 1913 contributions far exceeded the usual amount.[40] In addition to large cash donations, there were also donations in the form of hospitals, sports-fields and so on, which not only benefited the public but also reflected the donors' social commitment. Albeit expressly against the Kaiser's wishes, some local authorities also gave donations to veterans, thereby creating a link between past and present, and especially relating to the events of 1870–71.[41]

---

37   NWHStAD, Regierung Aachen Präsidialbüro 995; Vogel, *Nationen im Gleichschritt*, p. 177.
38   In 1863, the local organizers explicitly wanted to celebrate the festivals when they had been called off due to the constitutional conflict. And already in 1863 the organizers had made use of the festival reports written by Arndt, Sack and other patriots: Landeshauptarchiv Koblenz 403/9524, pp. 317ff; NWHStAD, Regierung Düsseldorf Präsidialbüro, p. 333.
39   Wehler, *Deutsche Gesellschaftsgeschichte*, pp. 889ff.
40   Schneider, *Politische Festkultur*, pp. 330ff.
41   NWHStAD, Landratsamt Düsseldorf 520.

The *Opferfreudigkeit* seized large parts of the population, who, as in 1813, could give vent to their national feelings. At that time, the population's *Opferbereitschaft* (willingness to sacrifice) had contributed significantly to the financing of the war and, through literary works and schoolbooks, had become mythologized ('Gold gab ich für Eisen' — 'I gave gold for iron'). In 1913, the same topos gained new currency and was put to service in domestic affairs: the 1913 Army Bill again demanded popular financial sacrifice, and the theme was reiterated time and again.

Another striking point about the 1913 festivities was the increased emphasis on physical exercise, sports events and sports-field openings. On the occasion of the anniversary of the Battle of Leipzig on 18 October, gymnasts arranged a so-called *Eilbotenläufe* ('messenger relays') to Leipzig, with itineraries across historically important regions and sites, past monuments and the places of birth and death of famous men connected to the Wars of Liberation and the war of 1870–71.[42] Besides the main event, several minor runs took place, so that every region and every larger town was included. Every 200–500 metres a new stage began, where, instead of a relay baton, the runner handed over a case wreathed in oak-leaves and containing a document about the relays. The run lasted day and night so as to keep to the strict schedule, guaranteeing that the last runners would arrive in Leipzig in time, on October 18, for the opening of the monument of the Battle of the Nations. Altogether there were 43,000 active participants: from the northern Rhine Province approximately 2,000 men of military-service age took part. In addition, many others had functions as organizers, stage controllers and escort teams. It was an event which literally 'moved the masses' and, since it concerned the whole of the empire at the same time, was heavy with national-unity symbolism. Furthermore, the event was not simply decoration for the monument's opening ceremony: it had more the character of a *levée en masse*. The army and gymnastic societies were closely linked, since the latter played an important role in preparing men for the army, and gymnastic events were regarded as *turnerische Heerschau*, with an unmistakably military character. One obvious visual aspect of this was the pace of the exercises which, at 120 steps per minute, was identical to the pace of a

---

42   Siemann, 'Krieg und Frieden', pp. 305ff.

military march.[43] In 1913 the gymnasts proved publicly their physical and psychological preparedness to 'get on the move' for the nation.

V

All the celebratory elements of 1913 so far mentioned show that the theme of war, in both its historical and current dimensions, was omnipresent. Even a person as keen on self-presentation as Wilhelm II was neglected on the anniversary of his government, as popular celebrations focused on the Wars of Liberation. In contrast to the Prussian festivities of 1863, however, the monarchy did provide the context and background to the celebrations. Wilhelm II referred to this in a speech on 16 June 1913, which made no reference to the Wars of Liberation but played up the 'glowing beams of the sun of peace' which had shone on the empire since 1870–71.[44]

Imperial Germany thus returned to a strong emphasis on francophobia, which was disseminated by newspapers and taken up by national associations and societies. This shift was a result of the empire's current military policy, which with the Army Bill of 1913 had switched its naval emphasis to a land-based defence strategy, with obvious implications for France. Thus there was a central historical dimension to the celebrations in 1913.[45]

Warning voices or protests were rare on a local level. The firmness of the consensus is illustrated by the fact that on the Rhine not even in the Carnival did the participants poke fun at the militarist message of the celebrations. Nationally, the youth movement organized a huge counter-demonstration, the festival on the Hohen Meißner, from 11–13 October. The pool of participation was similar to the

---

43 *Deutsche Turnzeitung*, 25 September 1913, p. 743; Geyer, *Deutsche Rüstungspolitik 1860–1980*, p. 90; Vogel, *Nationen im Gleichschritt*, p. 81.

44 BA Potsdam, Reichskanzlei 809, p.67; Vogel, *Nationen im Gleichscritt*, p. 173.

45 This change is remarkable as after 1871 the *Sedantag*, especially, emphasized national unity and became much less francophobe. Jakob Vogel points out that the call for national unity was not directed against France until the beginning of the First World War: Vogel, *Nationen im Gleichschritt*, p. 178. See also *Deutsche Turnzeitung*, 25 September 1913, pp. 743ff; *Düsseldorfer Tageblatt*, 27 February 1913; *Neue Preußische Zeitung (Kreuzzeitung)*, 9 May, 10 May, 31 May, 28 June and 2 July 1913.

2,000 *Eilbotenläufer* in the northern Rhine Province, which underlines the minority nature of the event.[46]

On a national level there was some protest from the Social Democratic Party. But as the years 1813–15 had an outstanding significance, even to Social Democrats, they challenged militarism but not the collective commemoration, although they did emphasize different aspects.[47] In general the significance of the date remained undisputed among the various German political, social and religious groups. No one mentioned the real political situation of 1813 and the fact that the Rhineland, as well as some other German territories, had been on the 'wrong side' at the time. Although it was far from the historical truth, the idea of national unity was employed, not only against external enemies, but also in the socially integrative concept of the *Volk*, which was deeply rooted in German national memory. The actual historical breach of 1813, between those Germans who had participated in the Wars of Liberation on the winning side and those who had been on the losing side, was successfully bridged by a consciously constructed collective national memory, a construct we also see in the festival 'tradition'. With regard to the past, all Germans were seen as part of a united *Volk*, which had participated in the Wars of Liberation as one body; as far as present and future were concerned, all festival participants in 1913 sought to affirm the ideal of unity, regardless of their existing social, political and religious differences.[48]

The cycle of festivals in 1913 peaked in a celebration of national unanimity, but the festal themes and contents lived on. The fusion of the current and historical dimensions of war during the 1913 celebrations created not only a strongly romanticized popular image of war, but also a mental disposition towards it. In the Rhineland the festivities, instrumentalized for domestic political aims, developed a populist dynamic of their own. The build-up of popular emotions and expectations found an outlet in August 1914, in the spontaneous enthusiasm, especially among the younger generation, for war.[49] In the light of what forms

---

46 Siemann, 'Krieg und Frieden', pp. 314ff.; Winfried Mogge and Jürgen Reulecke, (eds), *Der Erste Freideutsche Jugendtag in Dokumenten, Deutungen und Bildern*, Cologne, 1988.
47 Schneider, *Politische Festkultur*, p. 325; Siemann, 'Krieg und Frieden', p. 314.
48 Schneider, 'Die Feiern der Leipziger Schlacht', pp. 233.
49 Rohrkrämer, 'August 1914', pp. 767ff.

mobilization took in 1913, it is no wonder that young Germans regarded the outbreak of the war, as Thomas Mann expressed it, as an 'uplifting, historical elation, joy at change, throwing off everyday dreariness, freedom from a worldwide stagnation which had to end, an enthusiastic embracing of the future, an appeal to duty and masculinity, in short, a heroic festival'.[50]

---

50 'Erhebung, historisches Hochgefühl, Aufbruchsfreude, Abwerfen des Alltags, Befreiung aus einer Welt-Stagnation, mit der es so nicht weiter hatte gehen können, als Zukunftsbegeisterung, Appell an Pflicht und Mannheit, kurz, als heroische Festivität': Thomas Mann, *Dr. Faustus*, Frankfurt am Main 1960, p. 399 (English translation here by Nathalie Fryde).

CELEBRATING THE REPUBLIC WITHOUT REPUBLICANS: THE *REICHSVERFASSUNGSTAG* IN BERLIN, 1929–32

Pamela E. Swett

In countries throughout the world, national holidays have been created to provide popular symbolic support for the foundation myth of the state, two classical examples being those celebrated by the French on Bastille Day and by the Americans on Independence Day. The foundation myth gives coherence to a state's past and builds consensus about a state's guiding principles.[1] In the Weimar Republic the official state holiday was 11 August, the date on which the Constitution came into effect. The implementation of the Constitution, which amounted to a bureaucratic formality, could never engender the same popular enthusiasm as the storming of the Bastille; the *Verfassungstag* (Constitution Day) was a compromise among political interests, and even then the holiday was never ratified by the Reichstag. From the early 1920s, organizers saw the opportunity to

---

1 As Alon Confino argues in his recently published monograph on the German concept of *Heimat*, 'Every society sets up imagined pasts. But to make a difference in a society, it is not enough for a certain past to be selected. It must steer emotions, motivate people to act, be received; in short, it must become a sociocultural mode of action' (p. 11). For further analysis of collective memory and Sedan Day in particular, see Alon Confino, *The Nation as a Local Metaphor: Württemberg, Imperial Germany, and National Memory, 1871–1918*, Chapel Hill, NC, 1997.

honour the freedoms embodied in the Constitution through speeches and song, but as the decade passed they grew more conscious of the need to transform the occasion from a mundane official assembly to a participatory event which celebrated republican achievements.

An examination of the *Verfassungstag* is useful to the historian of Weimar, because in many ways its fate mirrors that of the Republic. In the early 1920s, the debate surrounding the naming of a national holiday illustrates the lack of consensus about how to represent the Republic. In the mid-1920s the *Verfassungstag* was a quiet, even cautious, affair. During these years Republicans tried slowly to extend the scope of the holiday. The celebration in 1928 was buoyed by the success of the republican parties in that year's elections. With the naming of a Social Democratic Chancellor, it finally appeared possible to flaunt the stability of the Republic and seek mass participation in the holiday. The *Verfassungstag* of 1929 was a turning-point. The tenth anniversary celebration demonstrated the conscious attempts made by republican leaders to compete aggressively with Nazi and Communist counter-myths and to showcase the advantages of republican life. However, analysis of the holiday rituals in the capital, Berlin, in 1929 and thereafter also makes clearer the structural and ideological difficulties faced by those who supported the Republic. The shortcomings and inconsistencies of this annual celebration demonstrate how difficult, and ultimately impossible, it was to create and popularize a foundation myth for the Weimar Republic.

The Weimar Republic and Political Holidays before 1929

The process of selecting a national holiday did not come easily for Weimar Germany. Throughout the life of the Republic, debates raged as to which past achievements and future aims should be given official recognition. Each political party had its own version of the correct way to represent the state publicly, and each region had its own political traditions and interests to uphold. The controversy, which was discussed at length in the Reichstag and covered extensively by the press, surrounded four holiday options: 18 January, the founding day of a united German state in 1871; 1 May, the traditional international workers' holiday; 9 November, the abdication of Wilhelm II and the declaration of the Republic in 1918; and 11 August, the enactment date of the Weimar Constitution in 1919. Perhaps the greatest advantage of creating a holiday on 11 August was that it fell within the German summer vacation period.

As a handful of scholars have shown, the conflict and paralysis which resulted from these debates was another example of the inability of those who held political power in Germany to come to agreement about the goals of their state.[2] The lack of consensus at the top was mirrored in Weimar's fragmented society, which was divided along regional, cultural and political lines. On the eve of the Republic's collapse, all four holidays continued to be celebrated with varying degrees of popular and official participation. Although the parliamentary debates about giving one of these days preference over the others are not the focus of this chapter, a quick synopsis will be helpful.[3] The early discussion, in the spring of 1919, centred around making 1 May the official state holiday of the new German Reich. Immediately the 1 May Bill ran into problems in the Reichstag. The left-wing USPD faction wanted to establish 9 November alongside 1 May as an official holiday. In the centre, the Democratic Party (DDP) wanted to shift the focus away from the day's traditional connections with the workers' movement and towards a more bourgeois agenda. They suggested an amendment which would define the 1 May holiday as a 'people's rally for political and social progress, for a fair peace, for immediate release of prisoners of war, for the evacuation of the occupied regions and for equality in the League of Nations'.[4] On the right, the DNVP believed it to be inappropriate to inaugurate any type of celebration so soon after the war. In the end, a compromise was reached which satisfied no one and only served to put the question of a national holiday off for a

---

[2] With respect to the problem of holidays and the divisiveness of Weimar's socio-political milieux, see Detlef Lehnert and Klaus Megerle (eds.), *Politische Identität und nationale Gedenktage. Zur politischen Kultur in der Weimarer Republik*, Opladen, 1989.

[3] Although state holidays and memorials continue to be of interest to historians, little work has been done on Weimar's political holidays. For a more complete description of the debates surrounding these holidays, see Fritz Schellack, *Nationalfeiertage in Deutschland von 1871–1945*, Frankfurt am Main, 1990. For a short analysis of the potential of each of the possible political holidays, see Dietmar Schirmer, *Mythos — Heilshoffnung — Modernität. Politisch-kulturelle Deutungscodes in der Weimarer Republik*, Opladen, 1992, pp. 108–12.

[4] Steno. Berichte, Bd. 335, Drucksachen, Nr. 275, Abänderungsantrag der DDP vom 14. April 1919, as quoted in Schellack, *Nationalfeiertage in Deutschland*, p. 137.

year. The date 1 May was accepted as an official state holiday, for 1919 only, under the broader definition outlined by the DDP. The SPD faction was compromised most by this decision, because it had to vote against the inclusion of 9 November, which was seen as a day of victory by SPD supporters and was already a legal holiday in the SPD-led states of Prussia and Saxony.[5]

Although there was some discussion in 1919 and 1920 about a celebration of the Constitution, the aftermath of the war and questionable support for the young Republic kept any official pronouncements from being made. Finally, in 1921 Reich Chancellor Joseph Wirth and President Friedrich Ebert decided that a celebration of the Constitution and the new republican state was in order. The planning, however, faced problems from the start. Recent elections had brought large numbers of anti-republican representatives into the Reichstag, and their lukewarm reaction to the decision was echoed in the organizers' inability to find anyone willing to give the keynote speech for the holiday festivities at the State Opera in Berlin.[6] The mild success of the day did not measure up to the grand goals set out by Wirth and his advisors in the Interior Ministry, who dreamed that the *Verfassungstag* would immediately create more respect, understanding and pride for the Republic. Nevertheless, Wirth was pleased with the potential of the holiday and declared after the 1922 festivities that 11 August would be recognized annually as a national holiday, beginning the following year. From 1922 onwards the basic structure of the official celebration of the Constitution remained the same. The day began with a morning commemoration in the Reichstag, which was closed to all but members of the government and their guests. Afterwards there was a small military parade outside the Reichstag. In the evening there was another official gala held at the State Opera, comprised of musical selections and speeches by dignitaries. Early organizers of the *Verfassungstag* realized they needed to address two problems if the holiday was ever to achieve the republican

---

[5] Schellack, *Nationalfeiertage in Deutschland*, p. 136–42.

[6] Ibid., pp. 182–93. In the end, Chancellor Wirth was left to give the speech. Reichskunstwart Edwin Redslob's account of the festivities highlight the tension between republicans and conservatives. It was 'unbearable' for those still mourning the passing of the monarchy to see the black-red-gold republican decorations in the opera house, and many guests refused to stand as Reich Chancellor Wirth entered the theatre: Edwin Redslob, *Bekenntnis zu Berlin. Reden und Aufsätze*, Berlin, 1964, p. 12.

significance they hoped for. The first was the need to transform the celebration from an official bureaucratic event for members of the government into one which would welcome citizen participation. The second was even more daunting: how to develop an explicitly pro-*republican* celebration, which would build a better image of Germany's future at home and abroad without provoking the enemies of the state.

These problems were addressed in numerous ways between 1923 and 1929. In 1923, for example, the *Verfassungstag* was combined with a day of remembrance for the victims of the continued occupation of the Rhine and Ruhr areas in western Germany. Regional officials were brought to the Reichstag for the festivities in an attempt to unite the country both geographically and politically around this national cause. Unfortunately, the planned events were cut short because of a strike and additional unrest, casting a shadow over the optimistic atmosphere of the day's celebrations. Following the death of President Friedrich Ebert (SPD) in 1925, the holiday was made more politically palatable to the right by the participation of Ebert's successor President Paul von Hindenburg. In 1926, the organizers introduced sports competitions to the day's events as a way to build popular enthusiasm. Sports clubs competed for plaques marking the occasion. In 1927 civil servants were finally given the day off so they could participate in the festivities. The following year the Reichszentrale für Heimatdienst issued poems, music and other writings on the Constitution, with the aim that such materials would aid citizens and village officials in planning their own local celebrations to honour the Constitution and the Republic.[7]

This 1928 publication promoted the ideal recipe for a successful *Verfassungstag*: local initiative combined with educational pro-republican reflection, tempered by a modicum of state control. Those in the government knew, however, that many Germans still lacked an emotional connection to the holiday. Emboldened by the victory of republican parties in the May election, they requested that private employers make 11 August a non-working or shorter

---

[7] Schellack, *Nationalfeiertage in Deutschland*, pp. 217–18. These pamphlets should also be seen as early evidence of the state's belief that a republican style of ritual could be created and that this style could win over the minds and hearts of German citizens: see, for example, Reichszentrale für Heimatdienst, *Zum Verfassungstag, Eine Materialsammlung*, Berlin, 1928.

working day and suggested that pub-owners hold their own parties to appeal to workers. Each August the combined celebrations in Berlin of the national, Prussian and city authorities had grown in scale and pageantry. Despite the fact that far less enthusiasm accompanied the holiday in some other regions, the authorities in Berlin were looking forward to 1929. They were confident that this tenth anniversary celebration of the Republic would be the breakthrough year, completing the transformation of the *Verfassungstag* from an obligatory official spectacle to a celebration of popular support for republicanism.

Verfassungstag *1929: Images of a Stable Republic?*

The relative calm, and even optimism, among republican supporters during 1928 began to dissipate in Berlin by early 1929. A new government led by the Centre Party's Heinrich Brüning had replaced that of the Social Democrat Wilhelm Marx at the end of March, and stricter regulations on political demonstrations soon followed. Despite the Berlin Police Chief Zörgiebel's (SPD) ban on street demonstrations for 1 May, the KPD continued to advocate the annual workers' marches throughout the city. Apprehension for what the day would bring mounted as both sides refused to compromise in the last days of April. In the aftermath of what became known among members of the radical left as 'Blood-May', both sides were held accountable for the death of over thirty workers. But because many of the dead were not KPD radicals, and not one policeman died in the three days of street battles, it was the image of the SPD-controlled police and the state which suffered the most. The black eye caused by the violence, and the immediate ban on the KPD paramilitary organizations (Roter Frontkämpferbund and Rote Jungfront), was not an auspicious start to the summer months. The rift between the parties of the left was insurmountable, and the May violence was likely still on the minds of organizers as they prepared for 11 August.[8]

---

[8] A secondary goal for the celebrations, especially from 1929 onwards, was to make a good impression for the foreign press. Positive reports in European and American newspapers would pacify worried statesmen and investors alike. Because there were no major disturbances surrounding the festivities, Germany's international image slowly recovered from the May Day chaos. The *New York Times* covered the events in a front-page story, 'Germans Reaffirm Faith in Republic'. The article stressed the desire of the government to

Nevertheless, special preparations for the 1929 *Verfassungstag*, beyond the annual morning ceremony in the Reichstag and evening celebration for state dignitaries at the State Opera, had been underway for months. Commemorative stamps, postcards and a special edition of the Constitution itself were printed and made available to the public. The day's festivities also received widespread radio coverage.[9] The bronze and iron medals previously given to winning athletes in the sporting competitions were replaced with ones made of silver and bronze.[10] An afternoon celebration in the Berlin Stadium, however, was the greatest addition to the festivities and represented the first officially organized jubilee for the 'masses'.

Most of the planning for the afternoon celebration was carried out by the office of the Reichskunstwart, Edwin Redslob.[11] The thousands of participants included children, students, singers from workers' music clubs, gymnasts and members of the army and Reichsbanner. The most honoured members of the audience (among the 30,000 expected) included President Hindenburg and other members of the government. The theme for the show was unity. After official greetings and two musical selections, hundreds of workmen entered the stadium with gold rods and worked to connect them. Next the chorus spoke the following lines, which were repeated in an echo fashion:

> Brother on another shore listen,
> We are one people, we are creating a work — the living Reich,
> Ancient inheritance from ancestors and fathers handed down to us,
> In the errors of life, in the confusion of our ways, continued hope.
> Steadfast goal,
> Come to us.
> The bridges are broken

    Integrate workers into the new Republic and continue Germany's peaceful role on the world stage: *New York Times*, 12 August 1929.

9   Schellack, *Nationalfeiertage in Deutschland*, p. 221.

10   Bundesarchiv, R32, Nr. 422, Letter from Prussian Interior Minister Carl Severing to the Deutscher Reichsausschuss für Leibesübungen, 6 May 1929, p. 85. The same memo was sent to the Zentralkommission für Arbeitersport und Körperpflege, in which it was added 'that only with the participation of the broadest sections of the population can the *Verfassungstag* achieve the character of a real people's festival': ibid.

11   For information on Redslob or the office of the Reichskunstwart, see Annegret Heffen, *Der Reichskunstwart — Kunstpolitik in den Jahren 1920–1933*, Essen, 1986.

The staves are splintered
The work is in vain.

With their efforts in vain, they called on the 'purity' and 'triumphant strength' of youth to bring the work to completion. Young men entered, half of them carrying the colours of the federal states and the other half the Reich colours, and declared: 'We want to build a golden bridge'. Once this was completed, those carrying the black, red and gold colours of the Republic moved about the stadium as a 'living flag'. After more singing and the raising of the actual flag of the Republic, the spectacle was brought to a close with all present singing the national anthem, 'Deutschland, Deutschland über alles'.[12]

The desire to create a united front against regionalism and political radicalism was the obvious intent of the show, and the emphasis on youth as the saviour of the dream demonstrates the willingness of republicans to compete with the NSDAP and KPD for the political energy of the younger generation. What makes this state-organized spectacle unique, however, is its explicit dramatization of the negative. Although the climax of the show was the successful creation of republican unity, the event begins with an admission of failure. As a description of the celebration explained, 'the working people of the Reich work at the task of reconnecting the broken bridge to a *Volksgemeinschaft*'.[13] After ten years of a republican state, this was not a positive analysis of the situation. In fact, as a visual representation of a republican foundation myth, it is counter-productive. Instead of envisioning the accomplishments, the birth of the Republic and codification of its values within the Constitution, the stadium show highlighted the work that still needed to be done.

The writings of Redslob and others in this period express a belief that theatrical displays, such as the one described above, could be used in a democratic state to embody a 'mass expression'. Public spectacle should appeal to the individual experience but inspire a collective experience. 'The *social* play', wrote those directing the stadium show in Wiesbaden, 'meets the necessary requirements of

---

12 Bundesarchiv, R32, Nr. 430, Reichskunstwart's description of the Berlin Stadium celebration on 11 August 1929, pp. 84-86.

13 Bundesarchiv, R32, Nr. 430, Reichskunstwart's narrative description of the Berlin Stadium celebration on 11 August 1929, p. 93.

our times; a play that, as a general expression of the common experience of problems, characterizes the individual, independent of national or religious ties, as a member of the whole.'[14] The goal was symbolically to represent the work still needed to build a viable state, to demonstrate it was possible, and to create enthusiasm for the task. This collective sentiment was to be embodied not only in the actions of the participants, but also in the totalizing art work that was the stadium show. 'Poets, architects, directors and musicians' all made contributions to the effort.[15] The final element was the audience. They were not to sit idly by as in traditional theatre. Rather, 'this theatrical form knows no separation between audience and actor, it knows no presentation of the individual will, only the order of all factors into the expression of the totalized will [*Gesamtausdruckswillen*]'.[16] It has been argued that Redslob's desire to create a feeling of community in 1930 was an attempt to reconstitute an earlier festival culture which had been rejected by the imperial style of the *Kaiserreich*.[17] While some of the rituals and visual imagery used in the stadium shows was taken from earlier religious and *volkstümlich* symbolism, the objective of inventing a new republican theatrical form which would represent the emotional connection between a state and sovereign people should not be underestimated. The sombre self-criticism of the show in 1929 was a product of the Redslob administration's desire to foster the growth of a rational political sphere in the form of theatre. The new form, as imagined by Redslob, would strip public occasions of the pomp which had separated the population from their leaders during the Wilhelmine period. However, reflection on the shortcomings of the present system (political and regional conflict) did not have to forego the emotional energy present in Nazi and Communist spectacles.

---

14 Bundesarchiv, R32, Nr 273, from the essay by Dr. C. B. Kniffler and A. J. Wenk, 'Versuch eine Festspiel Theorie (Anläßlich des Befreiungsfestspiels "Deutschlands Strom" von Edwin Redslob)', p. 65.
15 Ibid.
16 Ibid, p. 67.
17 Schellack, *Nationalfeiertage in Deutschland*, pp. 226–27. Schellack argues on p. 252 that in the 1930s there was a concerted effort to create a new republican cultural form, but he is most interested in analysing it as an art form.

The organizers of the festivities faced many problems. In addition to the financial shortcomings that worsened as time progressed, those such as Redslob who favoured a strong show of republican pride had to manoeuvre among those interests they hoped to win over with the celebration. At the administrative level, pro-republican forces risked provoking more conservative state governments, which could result in their complete refusal to observe the holiday in their regions. At the local level, it was feared that any show of republican confidence would be met with brash rebellion by Communist and Nazi forces. A second set of problems, however, was more fundamental to the success or failure of the holiday. The organizers were faced with the difficulty of coming up with a coherent vision of the Republic, its past and future. They had to create a message which would sell the Republic to a largely unconvinced — if not outright hostile — population. Though much had been written about the importance of the new form of theatre as a tool in creating a cohesive society, and therefore a more stable Republic, it was unclear what sort of society was imagined. In comparison to the previous years, therefore, the symbolic importance of the tenth anniversary did not provide any new conceptual ideas. The mass spectacle of the stadium celebration was a new form for representation of the state, but the creation of 'the living flag' left few lasting impressions on the population as to the sort of society it represented.[18]

The vision of the Republic presented in the annual *Verfassungsrede* (Constitution speech) by one of its staunchest supporters, Reich Interior Minister Carl Severing (SPD), was also a mixed bag of cautious optimism, reverence for the past and nationalist melodrama. He began by comparing the crisis faced by Germany in 1929 to that of the inflation disaster of 1923, and expressed his hopes that those leaders meeting in The Hague would construct an agreement that would

---

18   The symbolic value of the flag was debated throughout the Weimar era. The republican defence organization, Das Reichsbanner Schwarz-Rot-Gold, took its colours into its title, but those on the left wanted the red flag of revolution. Those on the right never honoured it and ridiculed it as black, red and yellow (instead of gold). As Sabine Behrenbeck rightly points out in her chapter in this volume, the republican flag was an especially bad symbol for use in state holidays, because it was at the root of the divisive political conflicts which these commemorative days were trying to overcome. The very lack of acceptance of the republican flag demonstrates, therefore, the fundamental instability of the state. On flags and other political symbols, see Dietmar Petzina (ed.), *Fahnen, Fäuste, Körper. Symbolik und Kultur der Arbeiterbewegung*, Essen, 1986.

'finally wind up the war'. He complained that 'it is not at all easy for the Republic to celebrate holidays. On her scales stands no splendour, no golden abundance, rather the most bitter need, the hardest privation.'[19] Severing described how Weimar democracy was part of a longer tradition, which was not only manifested in the work of the 1848 Frankfurt Assembly but also in the political achievements (for example, voting rights) of the Wilhelmine period. In response to the Republic's detractors, Severing responded that the Republic had achieved much since 1919. He stressed that republican accomplishments were not limited to 'saving the country from the fall into bolshevism' but included the continued unity of the Reich (*Reichseinheit*) and the belief among workers 'that the new state is their state'. He concluded that the Republic had always been stunted by external and internal enemies, but would continue to fight for a state based on 'the solidarity of all social ranks [*Stände*]'.[20]

While the public image portrayed by Severing and others in the capital was hopeful, if also cautious, a great deal was being done behind the scenes to ensure that things ran smoothly. As early as 13 June 1929, Redslob wrote to the Police Chief in Berlin requesting police support and protection against 'malicious disruptions' at the practice sessions of the 9,000 singing and dancing children, which were to take place at sports fields around the city during the two weeks leading up to Constitution Day.[21] Another memo to the city's *Schutzpolizei* stressed the importance of positive press reports and photographic coverage of the festivities, and the police were reminded to assist the reporters where possible and make sure that the festivities were 'under no circumstances' marred in any way.[22] The police were also called on to protect the estimated 100,000 Reichsbanner men arriving from around the country. Extra trains were scheduled, and the police

---

19 'Severings Festrede', *Vorwärts*, 12 August 1929. I am very grateful to Sebastian Simsch for locating a copy of the speech for this article. For the texts of the preceeding years' speeches, see *10 Jahre Weimarer Verfassung. Die Verfassungsreden bei den Verfassungsfeiern der Reichsregierung*, Berlin, 1929.
20 'Severings Festrede'.
21 Brandenburgisches Landeshauptarchiv (hereafter Blha) Rep 30, Bln C, Tit 90, Nr. 7531, Reichskunstwart memo to Polizeipräsident, 13 June 1929, p. 156.
22 Ibid., Memo from the Kommando der Schutzpolizei, July 1929, p. 172.

insisted on knowing each regional group's arrival time so as to schedule protection at the train stations.[23]

The Reichsbanner, the multi-party republican defence organization, was probably the most enthusiastic participant in the annual *Verfassungstag* celebrations. It was their day to demonstrate their strength in numbers, their patriotic loyalty and their close relationship with the state authorities. For the 1929 festivities the Reichsbanner planned two days of events. On 10 August the Reichsbanner leadership was greeted upon arrival with music and a triumphal accompaniment to its hotel, and in the evening the leadership rubbed shoulders with state ministers, including Severing, Wirth and Berlin Mayor Gustav Böß, in the State Opera House. The night came to an end with musical numbers on the Platz der Republik and a 'Demonstration for State Unity' in front of the Reichstag. On the following day the various Reichsbanner troops, who were housed by their Berlin comrades, marched from all corners of the city to the Lustgarten Park, where they listened to the words of their commander, Otto Hörsing. This speech was followed by a march down Unter den Linden and dispersal, to be followed by *Volksfeste*, people's festivals, in the neighborhoods.[24] The significance of the Reichsbanner's plan was that they intended to take over the streets of Berlin, in a way which mimicked the tactics of anti-republican forces. Large numbers of disciplined 'soldiers' would mobilize in all areas of the city before 'taking control' of the Lustgarten (the prized spot for large political demonstrations) and marching down Unter den Linden, the main boulevard of the capital's governmental quarter.[25]

The Reichsbanner's appearance in the administrative section of Berlin was a special privilege. The *Bannmeile*, which prohibited unofficial political demonstrations within a prescribed area surrounding official buildings, was not a result of the heightened radicalism at the end of the 1920s. The law protecting the

---

23 Ibid., Correspondence between the Reichsbanner Berlin-Brandenburg and the Polizeipräsident Abteilung II, August 1929, pp. 297, 318.
24 Ibid., Reichsbanner programme for the Bundesverfassungsfeier, 1929, p. 277.
25 See Thomas Lindenberger, *Straßenpolitik. Zur Sozialgeschichte der öffentlichen Ordnung in Berlin 1900 bis 1914*, Bonn, 1995. Lindenberger analyses the political significance afforded to public spaces and the increasing competition between the population, state authorities and political groups for control of these politically charged areas.

area around the Reichstag dated from 1920 and was changed little before 1933. The *Bannmeile* was taken quite seriously, and permission to traverse its boundaries in close formation required approval from a number of high-ranking officials, including the Reich Chancellor, Prussian Interior Minister and Reich Interior Minister. Although the Reichsbanner was not the only organization which was given such permission for the Constitution Day celebrations in 1929, it was by far the largest and most important. Permission was granted on a case-by-case basis, and the applicant had to convince the authorities that the proposed parade was 'private' or 'apolitical'. Security may have been the official priority for the strict control of the *Bannmeile*, but it is clear that those who determined access also used their powers selectively to create an image of a powerful, stable state.[26] Thanks to this secondary consideration, the political Reichsbanner was given permission to march on 11 August 1929. The political right took great offence at the decision, declaring it 'an example of state corruption of legal rights'. Reichsbanner access, charged a conservative newspaper, amounted to preferential treatment which belied the Constitution's fundamental principle of 'equal rights for all'; it should be seen as a 'provocation to all citizens' and was an example of 'how a state is not to be governed'.[27]

Nor was the importance of creating a powerful public image lost on the Reichsbanner leadership. In preparation for the trip to Berlin for the festivities in 1929, a brochure was issued to members with tips, maps and regulations to make the visit of RB-men from around the country more pleasant and more controlled. A list of 'ten commands for RB men in Berlin' began with the suggestion of seeing the tourist attractions of the city. This idea was followed by the more earnest command to 'practise discipline' so as to make an orderly impression on the 'critical Berliners' and foreigners in the city. The visitors were also warned of

---

[26] In one case, the police requested the denial of permission for a *Verfassungstag* parade by a national society which promoted horse-breeding. There may have been a fear that this organization did not fulfil the goal of portraying a modern industrial state. The Prussian Interior Minister suggested to the Reich Interior Minister that the organization might be persuaded to hold their parade in the highly populated, but less politically charged, shopping district: see Bundesarchiv, R15.01, Nr. 25681/2, pp. 110–11.

[27] 'Reichsbanner und Bannmeile', *Der Tag*, 19 June 1929; also in Bundesarchiv, R15.01, Nr 25681/2, p. 109.

the possibility of provocation by their opponents. 'Do not discuss politics with the misled. [...] However, do not put up with insults to the Republic, your emblems or leaders'. Finally, the Reichsbanner leadership insisted that their men abstain from over-indulgence in alcohol, refrain from complaining within the listening range of others, and steer clear from 'nightly adventures', all of which 'damaged the image of the Reichsbanner'.[28]

Throughout the 1920s, the major opponents of the Republic, the KPD and NSDAP, made little concerted effort to organize any large-scale resistance on the 11 August holiday. Both parties took an official stance against the celebration, but perhaps because they knew most people would want to enjoy the holiday they did little to dissuade them. Berlin's Communists did try to mount campaigns against the observation of the day in Berlin schools. The party tried to convince parents to protest against nationalist as well as religious teachings in schools under the banner 'proletarian school fight against the nationalist constitution-bustle'. They urged parents to hold their children back from school-sponsored parades and festivities.[29] Police detachments were posted at targeted schools, and patrolmen accompanied children on their parades to ward off any rabble-rousing.[30] There were small counter-parades and concerts sponsored by the KPD around the city on 10 August, but their request to stage a larger protest on the eleventh at their traditional gathering place — Bülowplatz, site of the Karl Liebknecht House and KPD headquarters — was denied because the Reichsbanner had cunningly reserved the area with the police as one of many gathering-spots for their large assembly.[31]

The extent of the police surveillance of the KPD demonstrates that there was a much greater fear that the KPD, and not the NSDAP, would orchestrate attempts to disrupt the proceedings. Police spies reported discussions that detailed plans for

---

28 SAPMO, SgY2/V/DF/VII/58, 'Orientierungsplan fur die Reichsbannerkameraden zur Bundesverfassungsfeier des Reichsbanner Schwarz Rot Gold am 11. August 1929 in Berlin', p. 9.
29 *Rote Fahne*, morning edition, 6 August 1929.
30 BLha, Rep30, Bln C, Tit 90, Nr. 7531, memo by the Schutzpolizei Kommando, 8 August 1929, p. 273.
31 Ibid., letter from the Polizeipräsident IA to the KPD Berlin-Brandenburg, 7 August 1929, p. 391.

KPD Reichstag and City Assembly representatives to convince the Reichsbanner men gathered in the Lustgarten to join the more radical party. Another police spy suspected that members of the Communist-led youth groups, the KJVD and the Rote Jugend, were to 'greet warmly' the arriving Reichsbanner men. The following day they were to receive postings along the parade routes and at the Lustgarten assembly in order to pelt marchers with stones and steal their flags. Perhaps sensing a continued solidarity between SPD and KPD rank-and-file, or understanding the desire among Communists for a day off from confrontations with police, the spy conceded, 'it remains questionable whether these commands will be followed'.[32] In the end the day's events ran quite smoothly, and the Chief of Police was so pleased that he granted two days vacation to all those who had served under his command.[33] Berlin police-station diary entries provide a thumbnail sketch of the problems which arose on the weekend of the anniversary celebration. There were at least fifty-seven fights and attacks which were ruled political; none led to serious injuries or deaths but many arrests were made. There were three incidents deemed 'acts of sabotage' by the KPD, which in reality were nothing more than anti-*Verfassungstag* propaganda activities.[34]

The Decline of the Verfassungstag *in the Early 1930s*

The optimism which had accompanied the 1929 Constitution celebration had faded considerably by the following year. The economic crisis had worsened and representatives of the Berlin, Prussian and Reich governments argued over how to limit the *Verfassungstag* budget, which had ballooned to RM 102,000 for the 1929 festivities in the capital. There were thoughts of cutting out the 'popular national' afternoon stadium show, but because the recent evacuation of the

---

32 Ibid., see both the memo from the Abteilung IA to the Kommando der Schutzpolizei, 9 August 1929, p. 392, and the spy report from Inspektion Neukölln of a KPD meeting on 9 August 1929, p. 395.
33 Ibid., Memo from the Kommando der Schutzpolizei, 13 August 1929, p. 411.
34 Ibid. These tallies were gathered from the short notes taken down by police for internal records of police activities. None of these numbers should be seen as completely accurate totals, but they provide a measure of what the police believed to be a smooth weekend in Berlin.

Rhineland by French troops provided the organizers with a theme suitable for uniting all political interests, it was decided to eliminate the evening gala at the opera instead.[35] The afternoon events, therefore, were once again topped off by a stadium show, entitled 'Deutschlands Strom', in which the nation's rivers were represented by young people. The chorus representing the Rhine appeared in chains. The climax was the freeing of the Rhine, accompanied by music and shouts of 'freedom'.

The *Verfassungsrede* of 1930 was delivered by Centre Party member and Reich Interior Minister Wirth, who had fought as Reich Chancellor in 1921 and 1922 to make 11 August an official holiday. He began his speech with references to international developments: the end of French occupation in the Rhineland and the new reparations settlement were seen as positive developments, but the Versailles Treaty as a whole 'still digs like a spike in German flesh'. On this note Minister Wirth described the difficulties facing the Republic. The growing economic crisis had created a 'rich harvest for political radicalism', and given reason 'to worry about the form of the state itself'. It was clearly not to be an optimistic speech when he finished his opening comments with the question, 'What is the right, the helpful, the saving word for this difficult hour?'[36] He then criticized the divisiveness of the Reichstag, and stressed the danger of a parliament which cannot build majority coalitions. Wirth challenged the parties of the political centre: 'Only where the push toward responsibility has not yet been tested, in the opposition of both extremes, is there party dogmatism at any price'.[37] With this declaration he hoped to stress the necessity of compromise in order to maintain the coalition which still 'tolerated' the Chancellorship of Centre Party member Brüning. In the Reichstag election which followed one month after this speech, the KPD garnered four-and-a-half million votes and the NSDAP tallied over six million.

The larger implications of Wirth's speech, however, went beyond voting and coalitions. He also spoke about his desire to see the development of a 'political individual'. Wirth exclaimed that the citizens of Weimar were perhaps 'the freest

---

35 *Vossische Zeitung*, morning edition, July 1, 1930.
36 Bundesarchiv, R32, Nr 527, 'Verfassungsrede gehalten von Reichsminister des Innern, Dr. Wirth', 11 August 1930, p. 83.
37 Ibid, p. 87.

people on the Earth', thanks to the liberal Constitution, 'but one has not yet been made free: the political individual!' The system, explained Wirth, was still controlled by political parties and interest groups, which made it difficult for those who were capable to find solutions to the crisis. 'The freedom, the inner political freedom, which has been bestowed upon us through democracy, remains a very formal one. It has not yet achieved the effect which it should: to smooth the way for the politically talented, those called to politics [*dem zur Politik Berufenen*]'.[38] It was this fact which, in Wirth's estimation, provided the seedbed for the persistent growth of radicalism. The radicalism of youth which plagued the Republic was not just the 'psycho-physical' radicalism which appeared in all eras, it was a time-specific radicalism affecting the political centre as well as the extremes. Young people were not given channels in which to move ahead or enough room to fight these limitations, resulting in 'a radicalism of bitterness [...] a radicalism out of political necessity'.[39] Wirth's argument is intriguing, because unlike most contemporaries he does not place the blame for radicalism squarely on economic despair or the hypnotic power of charismatic leaders. Rather he implies, in this speech meant to honour the republican Constitution, that the fault lay in the republican political culture itself. The lack of compromise and the distraction of political extremism had halted the development of the Republic. Professional politicians were hindered from carrying out their duties. As time went on and the Republic faced political and economic difficulties, vast sections of the population had grown ever more resentful that the practical application of the Constitution did not correspond to the will — or wills — of the people. Even those who had supported the Republic as a first step toward a more democratic and socially just state lost faith in its transforming power. Wirth's analysis was therefore more troubling than other positions of the day, many of which maintained that republicanism could survive if radicalism could just be contained until the economic forecast began to brighten. This view, on the eleventh anniversary of the Constitution, was a more pessimistic one, placing the blame for radicalism on an embittering political culture and offering little in the way of solutions. Wirth ended his speech with the simple plea 'not to make the coming

---

38 Ibid, p. 88.
39 Ibid, p. 88.

Reichstag unable to carry out its tasks with your hate, with your radicalism. [...] The building of German democracy is there for all who have good will. And when the entrance appears still to be locked or difficult to move, [...] that is where help is needed. But be present, because we must finally become one people, a political people.'[40] Wirth, a long-time supporter of the holiday, seems no longer convinced that the Republic's political structures allow the leaders to lead.

Despite the sombre tone of the speech, the 1930 *Verfassungstag* was not marred by violence. The Reichsbanner was able to hold its annual large-scale march through the government quarter. The extent of rebellion reported by the Communist daily *Die Rote Fahne* was that children in secular schools shouted out the 'The Internationale' when asked to sing 'Deutschland, Deutschland über alles' during the 'forced celebration'.[41] The following day the newspaper *8 Uhr Abendblatt* seemed to sigh with relief in the headline: 'Police balance sheet for 11 August: very good! Never before have mass demonstrations run so smoothly as yesterday'.[42] Although the article reported that twenty-seven people were detained by police, the majority of whom were National Socialists, the police records show no evidence that special precautions were taken to contain the activities of Nazi supporters.

The same can be said for the Berlin celebrations of 1931, during which drunkenness was the main cause of disturbance. A central police report written on the evening remarked only that 'heightened attention' would be given until the pubs closed down, especially to those pubs most frequented by Communists and Nazis. Though incidents of violence had increased dramatically by 1931, especially during the hot summer months, grave problems never developed on the *Verfassungstag*. A number of reasons for the calm have already been proposed: heightened police patrols, the unwillingness by opponents of the Republic to appear in the minority when confronting an influx of Reichsbanner and other supporters of the Republic, and the need by all for a day of rest. By 1931, however, another factor may also have played an important role. The increasingly negative atmosphere surrounding the 'holiday' meant that there was very little to

---

40   Ibid, p. 91.
41   *Rote Fahne*, morning edition, 12 August 1930.
42   *8 Uhr Abendblatt*, 12 August 1930.

protest against. Interestingly, this pessimism toward the Republic and its Constitution did not come from the opposition but from the republican pillars of society. Even leaders of the Reichsbanner, the most loyal of republican organizations, thought the Republic and its Constitution needed some tinkering. A holiday speech printed in the organization's main newspaper illustrated the move the Reichsbanner had taken towards the left, as the SPD rank-and-file lost patience with their party's policies of tolerance toward the government, and the Centre Party's members slowly lost their place within the organization. Speaking for his comrades, the author declared that support for the Republic was still strong, but that they 'desired a purer, more clear and decisive' Republic and Constitution. He called for an end to the 'rival governments' in the Republic and pointed specifically to the powerful industrial interests. Their remaining hope for democracy seemed no longer to lie with the Republic as it was, because 'freedom will first be secured when the terrible conflict between capital and labor has been fought to an end'.[43]

It was a tradition for the Berlin police to have their own brief ceremony early in the day on the eleventh, at which the Chief of Police would review his men and give a speech marking the day. The Social Democrat Albert Grzesinski spoke in a plainly pessimistic tone to the Berlin police force in 1931: 'under these circumstances there is no celebratory feeling [on this Constitution Day] and many of our brothers [*Volksgenossen*] ask themselves, how long can these conditions last'.[44] He referred to the Constitution celebrations of 1923, and insisted that, now as then, panic was the worst possible reaction to the crisis. Rather, 'public discipline, patience, steady will and clear volition' were called for. Grzesinski did not believe that these virtues were entirely enough, nor did he press for the solidarity hoped for by Redslob or the top-down political compromise advocated by Wirth. Instead he insisted on a strong state as a necessity to right Germany's path 'The state cannot act, carry out the laws and decrees which reach deep into the life of the nation without a strong, united executive, which sets forth with life

---

43 Bundesarchiv, R15.01, Nr 25966; see Theodor Haubach, '"Nun erst recht — es lebe die Republik!" Ein Ansprache zur Verfassungsfeier', *Das Reichsbanner*, 8 August 1931.

44 BLha, Rep 30, Bln C, Tit 90, Nr. 7532, Ansprache des Herrn Polizeipräsident Grzesinski vor der Berliner Polizei, 11 August 1931, p. 338.

and limb for the strength and security of the state.'[45] He then thanked his men for their contributions in these efforts, and closed with a moment of silence for those policemen who had fallen in service. Here we see a different analysis of the crisis, representing yet another critical vision of the Republic.

By August 1932 the political situation had changed dramatically in Berlin. On July 21 the Prussian government had been replaced by an 'overseer' appointed by presidential decree. Along with the newly appointed administration came severe limitations on political freedoms, suspending the last remnants of Weimar democracy. Although some of the harshest prohibitions of the state of emergency were lifted a week later, when it became apparent that no armed rebellion would be staged by the left, the city was still reeling from the coup in August. Two days before the holiday, yet another decree made the death penalty applicable in cases of politically motivated murder.[46] As in 1931, the evening festivities were eliminated and expenditures were cut to RM 40,000. Even the Reichsbanner was prohibited from holding its annual march through the restricted area; a July decree banning all public political assemblies and parades forced them to celebrate inside. The liberal newspaper *Berliner Tageblatt* tried to present a festive image of Berlin decked out in republican flags, but rumors of a Nazi putsch reported to the daily by phone-calls from citizens were also investigated. In the end the paper surmised that the rumours were for the most part 'a product of the fantasies of overly nervous people'.[47] Because of the prohibition on political speeches, uniforms, certain decorations and political assemblies, the resulting holiday took on a mostly apolitical character. Instead of protesting against the curtailment of political activities, the Reichsbanner announced that it would go along with these new conditions because many area branches of the organization had already invested funds for their own small-scale parties. What had once been thought of as a unifying day to celebrate democracy had effectively turned into a seasonal holiday, devoid of any national significance. *Vorwärts* joined other newspapers in announcing the 'Summer festivals instead of Constitutional celebration'.[48] The

---

45 Ibid, p. 339.
46 Reichsgesetzblatt, Teil I, 9 August 1932, Nr. 54. 'Verordnung des Reichspräsidenten gegen politischen Terror'.
47 BLha, Rep 30, Bln C, Tit 90, Nr. 7533; *Berliner Tageblatt*, 11 August 1932.
48 '"Sommerfeste" statt Verfassungsfeiern', *Vorwärts*, 12 August 1932.

New York Times, however, was most perceptive in its description of the atmosphere at the morning Reichstag ceremony as that of 'a funeral rather than birthday party'. The American reporter paraphrased Interior Minister Wilhelm von Gayl's *Verfassungsrede* description of the Constitution as 'woefully inadequate. It cramps everybody, and worse. Instead of making a happy family it "severs mind from mind", and it must be rebuilt.' Typically of the authoritarian Papen administration, the speeches by von Gayl and Chancellor Franz von Papen which followed did not include one utterance of the word 'republic'.[49]

Conclusion

There is much we can learn from the debates surrounding the celebration of the Weimar Constitution. The first point is that significant efforts were taken to create a foundation myth which could unite the political culture of the young Republic. The Constitution was not set on a pedestal, and its supporters did not demand that citizens feel loyalty to it in some purely rational way. Rather this chapter has tried to show that republican officials believed that celebration of the state was a necessary and positive way to build the confidence and enthusiasm which could overcome social and political division. Secondly, we see the importance of a monopoly on political space in the creation of a legitimate state. The selective guarding of the *Bannmeile* and the prestige which came in crossing this invisible boundary was apparent in Hitler's decision to mark his rise to Chancellor with a parade similar to the Reichsbanner's annual march on 11 August. Thirdly, we can see some continuity in the ritual. The military parades and marches down Unter den Linden had their roots in the pre-1918 monarchy. Finally, it becomes clear that republicans were more united in their efforts to maintain order than in their vision of a successful Republic. Statements by the press, police, republican supporters and government officials illustrate an uneasiness about the direction of the state. Attacks by those who never accepted republicanism in Germany were not Weimar's only hurdle. Those who favoured republicanism also had the task of creating a definitive public image of the state which could compete with the bombastic style of the past and the energetic audacity of those who were fighting

---

49 'Republic is ignored on Reich Fete Day', *New York Times*, 12 August 1932.

in the wings for power. Through the celebration of the *Verfassungstag*, we see how hope for democratic participation in 1928–29 soon turned to pessimism, division and reliance on the state to establish order. The failure of the *Verfassungstag* was, therefore, a failure to present symbols of the Republic's achievements or a convincing blueprint for the Republic's future. Without such images, the majority of Germans found it impossible to maintain faith or interest in republicanism during a crisis which demanded a confident and united strategy.

THE NATION HONOURS THE DEAD: REMEMBRANCE DAYS FOR THE FALLEN IN THE WEIMAR REPUBLIC AND THE THIRD REICH

Sabine Behrenbeck

I

In a retrospective view on the Third Reich, one development seems to be particularly characteristic of the Nazi practice of power: the extent of public ceremonies and rituals. These events, full of emotional pictures and effective symbolic actions, contributed substantially to the success of the Nazi regime by creating the illusion of mass-participation in the political process.

Historians frequently blame the democratic politicians of the Weimar Republic for misinterpreting the psychological needs of the masses. By displaying public modesty, they failed to have the people identify with the state. They left the field of symbolic actions without struggle to the right. Lothar Kettenacker concludes:

> After defeat and revolution there was no substitute for the pomp the Germans were used to in the Empire [...]. The government thought it unnecessary to pay special attention to national self-representation [...]. From one day to the other and without regard to its political culture, German society was expected to have an extremely rational understanding of

politics. The political showbusiness was left to the subversive parties from left and right.[1]

I will consider the validity of this reproach by comparing the ceremonies of the Republic and the Third Reich and analysing the differences between the public commemoration of war dead in both systems. Then I will look for reasons why the National Socialist ritual was more attractive. Which means were used and on what traditions were they based? At whom were the celebrations addressed and how did they affect the participants? Which intentions and messages did the organizers try to transfer with the ritual forms, and were they successful?

I will compare two events marking similar occasions: the commemoration for the fallen on 3 August 1924 in front of the Reichstag in Berlin, and the inauguration of the 'Temples of Honour' in Munich on 9 November 1935. The first ceremony was planned by the government ten years after the outbreak of the First World War to remember the war victims of the whole German people; the second was celebrated by a political party to honour sixteen persons shot by the police in 1923 during a putsch-attempt by Adolf Hitler. Nevertheless, the Nazi organizers claimed their commemoration day as an important event for the whole people. The party-martyrs were called 'political soldiers of the Führer', having died for the resurrection of the fatherland.

Before describing the two events, I would like to make some methodical remarks on political rituals in general.[2]

As in a religious service, a political ceremony usually tries to convey a message by means of signs and symbolic actions. An anthropologist would refer to a ceremony consisting of myths, symbols and rituals. I will concentrate on the last

---

[1] Lothar Kettenacker, 'Sozialpsychologische Aspekte der Führer-Herrschaft' in Gerhard Hirschfeld and Lothar Kettenacker (eds), *Der 'Führerstaat': Mythos und Realität. Studien zur Struktur und Politik des Dritten Reiches*, Stuttgart 1981, pp. 98–130 (p. 115). See also Gerhard Paul, *Aufstand der Bilder. Die NS-Propaganda vor 1933*, Bonn, 1990, pp. 13, 117–18, 127; and Alois Friedel, *Deutsche Staatssymbole, Herkunft und Bedeutung der politischen Symbolik in Deutschland*, Frankfurt and Bonn, 1968, p. 20.

[2] The following remarks are based on Fritz Kramer, entry on 'Ritual' in Bernhard Streck (ed.), *Wörterbuch der Ethnologie*, Cologne, 1987, pp. 181–83; 'Ritual' in Walter Hirschberg and Marianne Fries (eds), *Neues Wörterbuch der Völkerkunde*, Berlin, 1988, pp. 406ff.; Alfons Kirchgässner: *Die mächtigen Zeichen. Ursprünge, Formen und Gesetze des Kultes*, Basel, Freiburg and Vienna, 1959, p. 281.

element and investigate how a message is transferred into action, whether the ceremony represents the occasion appropriately and comprehensibly to the spectators. Also important are the atmosphere and the psychological effects created by the ritual, because they largely constitute its appeal and the degree to which its message is accepted.

Normally it takes a long time for rites to grow and become embodied in a community. In the shaping of ceremonies, on the other hand, only a little innovation is called for, since every cultural system has a reservoir of symbolic actions at its disposal. Thus, any liturgy can be created from a combination of well-known rituals. The political function of rituals consists of offering orientation, meaning and identity. But rites do not always stabilize the system: they may serve to legitimate or de-legitimate existing conditions, cause integration into the community or mobilize forces against it.[3] By providing psychological relief, rituals fulfil fundamental human needs. But the very importance of satisfying those needs offers itself to political misuse.

Research in traditional civilizations has suggested strong links between a society's support for rituals and its moral system. The higher the value a group places on continuity (because everybody depends on the aid of the group), the higher is the esteem for formalized behaviour and fixed social positions. In the ideal society constructed by Nazi ideology, the so-called *Volksgemeinschaft*, social roles were to be clearly defined and behaviour was formalized according to social role. Uniforms and insignia were the outward symbols of this formalization.

The ideal of the Weimar democrats, however, was the emancipated and independent citizen. This ideal resulted in scepticism towards public rituals. This is an indication of the fact that a social system striving towards the creation of an autonomous individual will value ritual behaviour less highly than a political system that emphasizes the importance of social ties and group identity. Thus, ritual as a medium of symbolic politics is highly ambivalent: on the one hand, it is necessary for the stability of a community; on the other, ritual carries the risk of being instrumentalized for special interests.

---

3 Andreas Dörner, *Politischer Mythos und symbolische Politik. Der Hermannmythos: zur Entstehung des Nationalbewußtseins der Deutschen*, Reinbek, 1996, pp. 26ff.

II

Despite first impressions, the accusation that the Weimar governing parties neglected public ritual is completely unfounded. As early as 1919 the government established the office of Reichskunstwart in the Ministry of the Interior.[4] This office was responsible for all questions of art and representation of the state. Its duties included the arrangement of public ceremonies which would represent the idea of the Reich in popular forms and articulate the cultural intentions of democratic government. Festivities were meant to foster identification with the Republic, stabilize democracy and win broad sympathies for the state. From 1920 the office was led by the art historian Edwin Redslob, a politically independent man with many contacts with contemporary artists and poets.[5]

It was Redslob's task to develop a 'design of the Reich', that is, to illustrate the abstract term of the national state vividly and to counteract the particularism of individual states after the loss of the monarch as an integrating symbol.[6] Redslob wrote several memoranda on the festival style of the Weimar Republic. I quote from one of them:

> As a counterbalance to the atmosphere of sobriety and criticism which enters public life from parliament, there is a growing wish for form and self-representation of the state [...]. Within this scope of duties the problem of public ceremonies is particularly important[7]

The ceremonies of a democratic state, Redslob argued, should not degrade the people to mere spectators, as did the monarchy's ceremonies, but should be built

---

4   Annegret Heffen, *Der Reichskunstwart — Kunstpolitik in den Jahren 1920-1933. Zu den Bemühungen um eine offizielle Reichskunstpolitik in der Weimarer Republik*, Essen, 1986, pp. 22ff, 37 ff., 68 ff.
5   See his autobiography, Edwin Redslob, *Von Weimar nach Europa. Erlebtes und Durchdachtes*, Berlin. 1972, pp. 157ff.
6   Ibid., p. 173.
7   'Als Gegengewicht zu der auf Nüchternheit und Kritik gestimmten Atmosphäre, die von seiten des Parlamentes auf das Leben des Volkes eindringt [...], wird im Deutschen Reich immer mehr ein ausgleichendes Verlangen nach Form und repräsentativer Äußerung fühlbar... Innerhalb dieses Aufgabenkreises [...] nimmt die Frage der staatlichen Feiern eine besondere Stellung ein': Edwin Redslob, 'Die Staatsfeiern der Reichsregierung' in *Reichskalender 1924*, Bundesarchiv Koblenz, R 32/499, p. 449.

around the people. The arts, particularly music and poetry, should be the mediators between state and people. Artistic representation of transpersonal values was seen as the key to a solemn, yet popular, form of ceremonies.[8]

The Reichskunstwart devoted particular attention to the public commemoration of the fallen soldiers which — as in other nations — was of great importance to German national identity. As early as 1919, a party struggle began over the establishment of a common day of mourning for the fallen of the First World War.[9]

Numerous dates were proposed and intensively discussed, but there was no majority for one special historical reference. Finally, the Reichstag chose the tenth anniversary of the outbreak of war to hold a public commemoration. The choice was justified by the interpretation of the enthusiasm for war in August 1914 as an outpouring of popular feeling of the 'perfection of the German nation' (Max Scheler) and the 'internal unification of the Reich'. Nevertheless, the attempt to establish a foundation myth and to celebrate the integrating effects of unity failed. For no small part this was because the Reichswehr leadership blamed the 'home front' for the defeat of 1918 (the myth of the 'stab in the back'), and thus public commemoration of the war was not a suitable mechanism by which to unify the nation. The ceremony was celebrated only once, on 3 August 1924.

In preparing this ceremony, Redslob sought a form 'inviting contemplation and private communion with the fallen'[10]. He wanted to guide the people through their need and suffering as a consequence of the war to 'a rebirth by the means of spirit and sacrifice'. He called for a solemn remembrance of the 'living spirit of those who had fallen', remembering them through their works of art in music, poetry, painting and sculpture.[11] Thus the 'spirit of August 1914' as a popular symbol of

---

8   Edwin Redslob, 'Feste und Feiern des Volkes' in *Feste und Feiern*, Bundesarchiv Koblenz, R 32/499, pp. 366–67.

9   See File R 43/I-566 of the Reichskanzlei in Bundesarchiv Koblenz, and Fritz Schellack, *Nationalfeiertage in Deutschland von 1871 bis 1945*, Frankfurt am Main, 1990, pp. 148ff., 189ff., 204, 231ff., 242ff., 266ff; see also Pamela E. Swett's chapter in this volume.

10   Redslob's suggestion concerning the Ceremony for the Fallen of 1 January 1923: Bundesarchiv Koblenz, R 32/221, p. 77.

11   Redslob was thinking of artists who had served and died in the First World War, for example, Franz Marc and August Macke (painters), Rudi Stephan (musician), Georg Trakl (poet):

unity should be identified with the Republic to increase public support for the new system.

The atmosphere Redslob desired showed sacral characteristics.[12] The Reichskunstwart recognized the religious needs of his contemporaries and tried to satisfy them. To that purpose, he developed ritual forms with no denominational background, as the public ceremonies were meant to overcome the divisions in German society. The main aim of these events was to produce a feeling of community, a meaningful connection between government and people.[13] The remembrance of the fallen in particular should help to establish the spiritual unity of the people because members of all German ethnic groups, parties and confessions had equally contributed to the sacrifices of war. The dead would be the model for a *Volksgemeinschaft* that so far had eluded the living.[14]

But already the preparations of the ceremony were accompanied by public dispute. Jewish leaders complained that no rabbi had been invited to participate, pacifists found fault with the anti-democratic idea of militarism they saw in the ceremony, while Conservatives attacked the idea that the commemoration was to be staged under a Social Democrat President.[15] Nevertheless the Reichskunstwart went ahead. A press bulletin announced the celebration of the 3 August as follows:

> For Berlin it is planned that in the morning all public and if possible private buildings are to be flagged at half-mast, the soldiers' graves are to be decorated and all memorials are to be wreathed. Services will be held in the churches in the morning. Between 11 and 12 o'clock a public ceremony will be held in front of the Reichstag.[16]

Redslob to the Minister of the Interior, 12 December 1922, concerning the Ceremony for the Fallen, Bundesarchiv Koblenz, R 32/221, pp. 64–65; see also Schellack, *Nationalfeiertage in Deutschland*, pp. 189ff.

12 Redslob to the Minister of the Interior, 12 December 1922.
13 Redslob, 'Die Staatsfeiern der Reichsregierung, 1924', p. 449.
14 'Die Pflicht der Lebenden, Zur heutigen Gedenkfeier', *Berliner Tageblatt*, 3 August 1924.
15 Jeffrey Verhey, *The Myth of the Spirit of 1914 in Germany, 1914–1945*, ch. 8, forthcoming (1999).
16 Newspaper notice of 9 July 1924 for the ceremony on 3 August 1924, Bundesarchiv Koblenz, R 32/222, p. 38.

Remembrance Days in the Weimar Republic and the Third Reich 309

The offical programme[17] delivers more details of the celebration. It began with a march-past by the two companies of honour of the Reichswehr, as the President (Friedrich Ebert), the government and the guests of honour were arriving. The whole procedure was accompanied by funeral music. The speeches of the Protestant and Catholic military clergymen each concluded with choral songs, 'Heldenfeier', written by Max Bruch, and 'Vaterland', by Gustav Wohlgemuth, respectively.

Then followed a short speech by President Ebert, who did not, however, mention either the revolution or the Constitution, but only remembered the dead, the disabled and other war victims. He called for a monument to be erected to the fallen soldiers, not from bronze, but everlasting: in the form of a free Germany.[18]

> The symbolic centre of the celebration was when the Reichs President, after his speech, laid a wreath with the national colours on the altar-like sarcophagus constructed in front of the Reichstag. Then followed a mourning-parade playing a funeral march to the melody of 'Ich hatt' einen Kameraden'. At twelve o'clock sharp the music broke off and the sign was given for silent remembrance of the fallen, while everywhere in the streets and squares of Germany every sound and every movement stopped.[19]

Afterwards the flags were raised to the top of the flag-poles while the people sang the 'Niederländisches Dankgebet'.

In a newspaper this symbolic action was explained as follows. The two minutes of silence were to allow time to commemorate of the suffering of the war-victims, whereas the following hoisting of the flags was to be a sign of confidence and a promise of concord and loyalty to the German *Vaterland*.[20] The chorale[21] recalled the wars of liberation against Napoleon and expressed confidence in a change for the better.

---

17 Programm der Feier vor dem Reichtagsgebäude, Bundesarchiv Koblenz, R 32/222, p. 116.
18 Friedrich Ebert, quoted in Heffen, *Der Reichskunstwart*, pp. 235–36.
19 Edwin Redslob, 'Die staatlichen Feiern der Reichsregierung', Bundesarchiv Koblenz, R 32/222 p. 212.
20 Ibid., p. 105.
21 'Wir treten zum Beten vor Gott, den Gerechten;/ er waltet und haltet ein strenges Gericht./ Er läßt von den Schlechten die Guten nicht knechten,/ sein Name sei gelobt, er vergißt unser nicht'.

The silent commemoration as a sudden pause in all activity and a counterpart to the noise of everyday life had a special function. In a religious cult, silence is supposed to be 'a kind of abstention, when power is not expended but collected [...]. Silence is required at the climax of sacral action'[22]. The chorale sung afterwards was supposed to unload the tensions accumulated during the moments of silence and to produce an intensive experience of community.

The decoration of the Reichstag underlined the character of common mourning: black cloth covered the tympanum of the collonades, a banner was attached under the architrave, proclaiming the leitmotiv of the celebration: 'For the living spirit of our dead'. In the passages between the columns likewise hung mourning-bands. In the centre, above the speaker's desk, was suspended a large heraldic eagle. Flower arrangements decorated the ramps and window-sills of the facade.

One detail of the decoration could only further polarize an already divided public: the flag. It was the object of a protracted party quarrel[23] and not at all a symbol of unity and loyalty to the fatherland. The conservative parties preferred the old colours of the empire (black, white and red) and did not accept the new black, red and yellow-flag of the Republic. The decoration of the Reichstag tried to compromise but was doomed to failure: on one side of the building stood the flag of the new Republic, on the other side the old flag of the empire at half-mast. A press bulletin announced:

> The celebration has nothing to do with politics. The government hopes that the whole population [...] without regard to political and social differences will participate [...]. Therefore associations and federations willing and ready to participate are not allowed to carry their flags.[24]

It was characteristic of the political culture of the Republic, however, that right-wing and anti-democratic groups disturbed the celebration, especially at the end, when the flags were drawn up during national anthem. Disrupting the two

---

22 Kirchgässner, *Die mächtigen Zeichen*, p. 258.
23 Wolfgang Ribbe, 'Flaggenstreit und Heiliger Hain. Bemerkungen zur nationalen Symbolik in der Weimarer Republik' in Dietrich Kurze (ed.), *Aus Theorie und Praxis der Geschichtswissenschaft. Festschrift für Hans Herzfeld zum 80. Geburtstag*, Berlin and New York, 1972, pp. 175–88.
24 Newspaper notice of 9 July 1924, Bundesarchiv Koblenz, R 32/222, p. 38.

minutes' silence, Communists shouted 'down with war' and sang 'The Internationale'. Conservative patriots responded with the 'Wacht am Rhein'.[25]

Without those disturbances, the celebration would have been a dignified and impressive commemoration with meaningful gestures but without ostentatious exaggeration or false modesty. The civilian head of state as protagonist and main speaker gave the ceremony a civil character. Although in our perception the Reichswehr had a dominant role, the participation of the military corresponded to the festival customs contemporaries had been used to in the empire, particularly with regard to public commemorations of fallen soldiers.

But the commemoration could not cover the fact that the German people was divided, not united, over the meaning of the war experience. Whereas in the first years after the war the forces of the left staged massive anti-war demonstrations of over 500,000 people, this climate changed in 1923 through the French occupation of the Ruhr. Now the right began organizing pro-militarist demonstrations commemorating the outbreak of war.[26]

In a memorandum, Redslob formulated his idea of the ceremony as the 'rebirth of the people by means of spirit and sacrifice [...]. It should be a day of resurrection'[27]. But this was in no way the message of the ceremony. The military and civilian rites of mourning honoured the dead, but the ceremony did not give meaning to the death and sacrifices of war, nor did it serve to legitimize the new political order. Redslob did not attain his goal of identifying the revolution of 1918 with the spirit of 1914, or of describing the new Constitution as the beginning of a new unity among the people[28]. The rituals merely conjured up the experience of a community of fate, united in suffering, which was supposed to become the source of new confidence.

These shortcomings cannot be blamed on Redslob alone. His plans for the ceremony differed considerably from the final programme, in which the poems

---

25 Redslob, 'Die staatlichen Feiern der Reichsregierung', p. 212; see also Schellack, *Nationalfeiertage in Deutschland*, pp. 240–41.

26 I am grateful to Jeffrey Verhey for suggesting this to me.

27 Redslob to the Minister of the Interior, 6 June 1924, 'Über die Grundgedanken zur Feier für die Gefallenen des Deutschen Vaterlandes am 3. August 1924', Bundesarchiv Koblenz, R 32/221, p. 134.

28 Verhey, *The Myth of the Spirit of 1914*.

and music of fallen artists played no important part. Although Redlob's idea of the artistic heritage of the fallen can be called dignified and demanding, it was addressed more to a cultural and intellectual 'elite than to the broad mass of the people. A contemporary observer therefore criticized his plan: 'Always the people will be ready to celebrate with its whole heart [...] when it is given supporting symbols [...]. But our celebrations are much too rational. Nobody can identify with them.'[29]

Indeed the symbol of the flag was particularly unsuited to winning hearts because it called attention to the very political conflict the celebration sought to overcome. After all, the new flag was not the one under which soldiers had died in the First World War. Equally importantly, the protests of the anti-democratic forces did not stop even at an event like the commemoration of the fallen, thereby hampering its effect.

III

In comparison to this commemoration day, very different conditions existed for the National Socialist event that took place on 9 November 1935 in Munich. This was one of the large-scale ceremonies of the Third Reich, and the liturgy showed the character of National Socialism as a political religion. As such the Nazis disposed not only of an extensive system of symbols, but also developed a mythical interpretation of the German past. This myth announced the Third Reich as 'rebirth of the people' and *telos* of German history.

The celebration of 9 November took place annually at the historical site of the 1923 event, in the 'capital of the movement'. Between 1933 and 1939 it was celebrated with great pomp; during the war ceremonies took a more limited form. In 1935 the bodies of the first sixteen party-martyrs were exhumed and transferred to a common grave in the very centre of Munich, the Königsplatz.

In his annual commemorative address on the eve of 9 November, Hitler time and again explained the meaning of this day. Using Christian allusions, he interpreted the blood lost at the crushed uprising as 'baptismal water for the Third

---

[29] Fritz Herbert Lehr in *Deutsche Allgemeine Zeitung*, 28 November 1930.

Reich'[30]. Thus this festive day commemorated the 'Gethsemane and Golgotha of the movement'[31], followed by its resurrection ten years later. This was the central credo of the November celebrations, which were called 'divine service' in the *Völkischer Beobachter*.[32] The rituals of this day[33] were meant to symbolize the story of salvation and took the Christian liturgy of sacrifice as a model. Instead of the common meal another symbolic action was chosen to share the event of salvation: the common pageant.

The 'march of remembrance' should not be seen as a demonstration but as a 'National Socialist procession'.[34] The explicit hint at ecclesiastical tradition thrust aside the obvious example of the civic-national tradition of pageants in the nineteenth and early twentieth centuries. The well-established silent protest march of the organized working class on 1 May also served as a model, but was not mentioned.

The liturgy of the march presented the party as a 'movement' and therefore symbolized the character of the NSDAP. Marching at demonstrations had been characteristic of the party from its foundation onwards, and had become its typical means of self-representation in public. Already the march of 1923 pointed to a historical example: the 'march on Rome' by the Italian fascists one year before.

At the beginning all participants of the march assembled and moved silently in fixed order, and in historical costume, with their sign of salvation, the 'blood-flag'

---

30 Hitler in his memorial-speech of 8 November 1934, quoted in Max Domarus, *Hitler. Reden und Proklamationen 1932 bis 1945. Kommentiert von einem deutschen Zeitgenossen*, Munich, 1965, p. 458.

31 Hans-Joachim Gamm, *Der braune Kult. Das Dritte Reich und seine Ersatzreligion, Ein Beitrag zur politischen Bildung*, Hamburg, 1962, p. 142.

32 *Völkischer Beobachter*, 10 November 1935.

33 The following interpretation of the November-rituals is based on an evaluation of the newsreels and documentary-films in the film archive of the Bundesarchiv: newsreels DTW 98/1933, DTW 150/1934, DTW 202/1935, DTW 254/1936, UTW 428/1938, and films Nr. 781: 'Der 8. und 9. November 1935' (1935); Nr. 68: 'Ewige Wache' (1936); and Nr. 77: 'Für uns' (1937); the Nazi newspapers *Völkischer Beobachter* and *Minutenprogramme* of 1933, 1935 and 1936, Bundesarchiv Koblenz, NS 26/1291, NS 26/103, NS 10/124; and the ceremony-programmes, published every year in similar form: 'Zum 9. November 1937' (ed. Traditionsgau der NSDAP München/Oberbayern), Munich, 1937.

34 Bundesarchiv Koblenz, NS 10/124, p. 195.

of 1923, through the historic streets of the putsch attempt. This was more than an imitation: as a ritualized 'copy event', it invested the historical event with the meaning of renewal and redemption. The event of 1923 was to be understood as a halt during the 'way of the cross', because the seizure of power of 1933 transformed the death of the martyrs into a victory by. Thus 9 November was declared to be the beginning of a new era.[35]

First of all the 'way of the cross' had to be restaged in the ceremony, just as Good Friday is celebrated before Easter. The decoration of the streets[36] illustrated this idea. The streets of this 'movement's walk of sacrifice'[37] were lined by pillars symbolizing the dead heroes, fallen in the 'time of struggles'. 'Here it seems that they rise again in front of us in heroic transfiguration and form a silent lane of death', wrote the *Völkischer Beobachter* in 1935.[38]

The brown-red wrapped pillars carried in golden letters the inscription 'Zum Appell!' above the name of each party-martyr. On top there was a basin with the smouldering 'fire of sacrifice'. When the head of the march, carrying the blood-flag, and the Führer's group reached each pair of pillars, loud-speakers proclaimed the names of the martyrs like a litany of saints in Catholic processions. The 'Horst-Wessel-Song', played in solemn tempo from the loud-speakers, accompanied the march and reminded the participants that the invisible dead walked in the ranks of their companions.

The 'march of the old combatants' also symbolized the expansion of the NSDAP in Germany. Called the 'conquest of the street', the march was accompanied by bloody conflicts. The party referred the dissemination of its faith

---

35 '[...] er ist das größte Datum am Eingang einer neuen, großen Zeitepoche': 'Der große Marsch', *Morgen. Nationalsozialistische Jugendblätter*, November 1936, p. 1, Institut für Zeitgeschichte, Munich, db 44.20.

36 *Völkischer Beobachter*, 9 and 10 November 1933, see the photographs in the newspaper, collected in the Bildarchiv of the Bayerisches Hauptstaatsarchiv in Munich, Abt. Nachlässe, Stichwort: NS-Gedenkfeier 9. Nov. 1933/1, 1934, 1935/2 u. 3, 1936/1, 2, 3, 4 u. 5, 1937, Stichwort: NS-Gedenkstätte Feldherrnhalle/1 u. 3, Stichwort: NS-Gedenkstätte Ewige Wache.

37 The commentator in *Völkischer Beobachter*, 10 November 1933, referred to the march as a 'path of sacrifice'.

38 *Völkischer Beobachter*, 9 November 1935.

back to the first martyrs, because through their dying 'the seed of the movement was spread all over Germany with one beat', as Hitler said in 1935.[39]

Only because these sixteen men were willing to die for the idea of the Third Reich could enough fearless combatants later be mobilized to overcome the *Novembersystem*, as Hitler termed the Republic founded on 9 November 1918: 'All the following bloody sacrifices were inspired by the sacrifice of these first men.'[40] Therefore, 240 supporters who, it was claimed, also died for the NSDAP were integrated into the liturgy with their names written on the pillars. Passing the pillars, the procession transported the mythical power of the proclaimed heroes to the 'altar', as the Feldherrnhalle was called in liturgical poems.[41] The fallen heroes were, so to speak, the National Socialist community's sacrifice.

The ritual culminated in sixteen symbolic gunshots in front of the Feldherrnhalle. With the first shot the march stood still, the drums and music suddenly breaking off. Alone, Hitler walked up to the coffins in the Feldherrnhalle, placing wreaths as his offering and remaining for 'silent conversation' with the heroes. Thus only the Führer was linked closely to the fallen by commemoration — not the whole people, as in 1924. During the wreath-laying the melody of the 'Good Comrade' was played.

Here we see the fundamental difference from the Christian liturgy of sacrifice. The Christian ritual does not repeat the crucifixion of Christ. This remains the subject of passion plays, which are not holy services. In the celebration of the Last Supper, the priest repeats the symbolic act by which Jesus himself explained his self-sacrifice before his death. In the Nazi liturgy, Hitler, as 'surviving martyr', could offer such an interpretation only on behalf of his comrades and only after the fact. This explanation was not part of the liturgy of sacrifice but took place on the evening before, when the 'old guard' met in the Bürgerbräukeller.

---

39   Hitlers memorial-speech of 8 November 1935, quoted in Domarus, *Hitler*, p. 552.
40   Ibid., p. 554.
41   For example, the second verse of the poem 'Am 9. November vor der Feldherrnhalle zu München', by Baldur von Schirach (published in *Vorschläge der Reichspropagandaleitung zur nationalsozialistischen Feiergestaltung*, Juni 1935, 3/40, E 1, Bundesarchiv Koblenz, NSD 12/39): 'Dort, wo die Teufel rufen:/"Schwör ab, Hund, oder falle!"/Was sie auch Dome schufen/Altar sind uns die Stufen/der Feldherrnhalle.'

With the staging of the 'movement's walk of sacrifice', the liturgy of 9 November was not yet finished: it remained to represent the 'salvation'. This salvation was to consist of the people's redemption and the resurrection of the fallen heroes. Accordingly, the second part of the event was called the 'celebration of resurrection'. After honouring the dead at the Feldherrnhalle, the 'walk of sacrifice' turned into a 'triumphal procession',[42] leading through the triumphal arch (the Propyläen) and a 'forest of flags' (the symbols of victory) to the newly built temples at the Königsplatz dedicated to the victims of the putsch attempt. This part of the march was accompanied by the hymn 'Deutschland, Deutschland über alles' rising joyfully from the loud-speakers.

The continuation of the march up to the Königsplatz no longer bore a historical reference to 9 November 1923. Instead, this part of the ritual referred to the 'torchlit procession' of 30 January 1933 through the Brandenburg Gate in Berlin — another example of symbolic politics. Both these historical references demonstrated that the National Socialist 'salvation' consisted of two parts: the sacrifice of the martyrs was consummated in the assumption of power. Only the combination of these two incidents brought about salvation.

No longer bound to historic authenticity, the triumphal procession to the Königsplatz gave way to further rituals. The high-ranking military officers who joined the march at the Feldherrnhalle symbolized reconciliation with the former opponents of 1923.[43] The so-called 'perpetrators and traitors' of 1923 could participate in the victims' celebration, and were thereby offered forgiveness. Thus,

---

42 'Dieser Weg soll den Opfergang der nationalsozialistischen Bewegung veranschaulichen. Der Weg von der Feldherrnhalle zu den Ehrentempeln versinnbildlicht den Sieg und die Auferstehung der Gefallenen im Jahr der Freiheit 1935': *Völkischer Beobachter*, 29 October 1935. The 'year of freedom' referred to the new *Wehrfreiheit*, proclaimed in March 1935.

43 Hitler in a speech of 9 November 1933: 'Zehn Jahre sind vergangen, und es ist für mich an diesem Tag das höchste Glück, daß nunmehr die Hoffnung von einst in Erfüllung ging, daß wir nun zusammenstehen: Die Repräsentanten des Heeres und die Vertreter unseres Volkes, daß wir wieder eins geworden sind und daß diese Einheit niemals mehr in Deutschland zerbrechen wird. Damit hat erst dieses Blutopfer seinen Sinn erhalten und ist nicht vergeblich gewesen. Denn wofür wir schon damals marschierten, das war das, was jetzt Wirklichkeit geworden ist'; quoted in Domarus, *Hitler*, p. 328.

the celebration represented the unity of the new Germany, which rested on the expiatory sacrifice of the heroes.

Corresponding to the double structure of the salvational event, the ritual of sacrifice was repeated at the 'temples of honour', while the dead heroes were finally buried in sarcophagi of bronze in the two temples. As the *Völkischer Beobachter* maintained, with this ritual the resurrection of the heroes was complete.[44]

In Catholic liturgy, transubstantiation is followed by a prayer commemorating all the martyrs and saints and by asking the congregation to confess its faith. At the end of the Nazi liturgy, the community was also asked to identify with the heroes and answered by confirming its will to self-sacrifice. For these proceedings the Nazis had developed a ritual similar to the example of the Italian fascists: the 'last roll-call'. In military manner, the party representative called out the names of the sixteen dead heroes of 1923, and in symbolic substitution thousands of members of the Hitler-Youth answered 'here!'. These young persons were solemnly admitted to the *Sturmabteilung* and NSDAP on that very day. So the 'last roll-call' was part of their initiation ritual and demonstrated that they were expected to be heroes as well[45]. Thus, the liturgy illustrated the renewal effect of sacrifice: while the death of the martyrs was the birth-day of the new Reich, party and SA were rejuvenated by a new generation carrying their spirit.[46]

A similar liturgy was developed for the military. On 9 November, in front of the Feldherrnhalle, the recruits of the army and air force (and, late at night, those of the SS) were sworn in. Combining their vows with the sacrifice-liturgy, the regime used ritual as a means of integrating the *Wehrmacht* into the National Socialist state.

---

44   *Völkischer Beobachter*, 18 October 1935.
45   This is mentioned in numerous propaganda publications for the Hitler Youth, for example, *Morgen*, November 1935, in Institut für Zeitgeschichte, Munich, db 44.20.
46   *Völkischer Beobachter*, 29 October 1935 and 9 November 1935.

As at Christian martyrs' graves, the salutary power of the dead heroes was to be experienced at their burial-place, and the temples were at once declared to be a popular 'place of pilgrimage'.[47]

The organizers were convinced that this liturgy of 9 November was 'a solemn action deeply anchored in Germanic religious feeling', as a statement in one party publication demonstrates.[48] This 'religious feeling of the Nordic, Germanic man' found its modern articulation in an unusual assemblage of rituals originating in Christian, courtly, civilian and military ceremonies. The author of the statement also revealed strategic arguments for this transformation: being familiar from other contexts, the rituals should facilitate the adoption of Nazi ideology. And the rituals were meant to satisfy religious needs without denominational ties. The experience of the celebration was to prompt the conversion of those who stood politically apart and to help dissolve scepticism and critical distance.

IV

As the comparison of the two events shows, the republican politicians were much more reserved in applying rituals than the rulers of the Third Reich. They also spent less money — and perhaps used less imagination — on them. The democratic rituals were not clothed in religious vocabulary and did not use Christian liturgy as a model, but were rooted in the tradition of the civilian festival culture of the nineteenth century. That meant a framework of speeches and poems, framed by music and songs, completed by military rituals and civilian burial rites and the impressive national moment of silence.

One could criticize Reichskunstwart Redslob for creating ceremonies which neglected the festival customs of German society and assumed a higher degree of aesthetic education and enlightenment than existed. With hindsight, and in

---

47 The 'temples of honour' were also called 'shrine of the movement': *Völkischer Beobachter*, 3 November 1935. One headline talked of the 'pilgrimage to the Eternal Guard-House': *Völkischer Beobachter*, 11 November 1935.

48 Dagobert Dürr, 'Die Lage' in *Unser Wille und Weg. Die parteiamtliche Propagandazeitschrift für die politischen Leiter der NSDAP*. Monatsblätter der Reichspropagandaleitung, ed. Joseph Goebbels, Issue B, Munich, December 1935, pp. 399–400, Bundesarchiv Koblenz, NSD 12/3.

comparison to the Nazis' pomp and cleverness, Weimar events may look academic, dour and much too modest. But with regard to the developing crisis in the Weimar Republic, it must be conceded that Redslob realized the social functions of Remembrance Day and tried to use it as a means of stabilizing democracy. Nevertheless, the celebration of 1924 suffered from its inability to establish an emotional link between state and people in common mourning. And this shows the organizers' main failing: they chose the wrong event. For the participants the mass fatalities of 1914–18 must have evoked great pain without the consolation and confidence which would have arisen from a united community.

The Nazi celebrations were of a very different nature, which fact contributed to their success. The rulers of the Third Reich were anxious to produce clear-cut and confident feelings as well as controlled aggression; they carefully avoided any introspective contemplation by the masses, sadness or low spirits in their celebrations. The sixteen dead party members were not a source of mourning for the whole German people, as had been the 1.8 million fallen soldiers of the First World War. Perhaps this experience of violence and death was the heaviest burden the Republic had to bear.

Nazi liturgy served to translate the heroic myth into symbolic action. The message was that the self-sacrifice of the heroes caused the victory of the movement and its Führer. This triumph brought unity and rebirth to Reich and people alike. Remembrance of the dead, therefore, was not a time for gestures of sorrow and mourning, but symbolized a victory, which they had fought for with their lives. Since the liturgy of sacrifice — practised at many other occasions throughout the year — always ended with a gesture of triumph, it was suggested that in the end all struggles would be successful if only the members of the community were ready to die for the cause.

Yet, the common reproaches against the democrats of Weimar seem unfair in relation to the real effort made by the organizers of mass celebrations. Such criticism, based on hindsight, disregards the difficulties any political system which followed the pompous Hohenzollern monarchy would have had to face. Above all, the radical forces of opposition prevented the Republic from successfully establishing an annual event and a national day of mourning. The creeping erosion of the Republic was brought about less by the insufficient efforts of democrats to establish a system of symbols than by the impossibility of succeeding by democratic means. The Republic, its institutions and symbols, were disparaged by its opponents on the left and right. Against such attacks the Nazi regime defended its political religion with increasingly brutal methods. And the Nazis used religious rituals that addressed deeper and more unconscious emotions than any civil festival tradition in the nineteenth century.

A uniform and positive reception of the ceremonies in the Third Reich was further assured by control of the mass media: all newspapers carried enthusiastic descriptions of the celebrations. In comparison, the effect of the ceremonies in the 1920s was badly impaired by varied and inconsistent press reports and by the existence of a well-organized hostile section of public opinion. As a result, the public was offered different points of view, many of which derided the efforts of the young Republic. Focusing all attention on one symbol or integrating figure, such as a flag, an emperor or a Führer, was impossible in a democratic context. In this respect, the Nazi dictatorship had an advantage, and used it to attractive and seductive effect.

The National Socialist organizers had a good grasp of the emotional needs of broad bands of society. The desire for a fundamentally formalized way of life was the result of the deeply felt disorientation after the war and the fall of the monarchy. The National Socialist rulers had no scruples in satisfying such needs, whereas the intellectual democrats wanted to push forward the progress of enlightenment and civic emancipation, and therefore rather tended not to be interested in traditional forms. This was too demanding and overtaxing for most of their contemporaries. From a moral point of view, the democrats' efforts appear to have been guided by integrity and honesty, but compared with their unscrupulous followers they were weak and ineffective.

Last but not least, the forces supporting the democratic state of Weimar — above all the Social Democrats — rejected a historic-mythical justification of the present and wanted to legitimize the political order by rational, democratic means. But this very legitimation was rejected by political groupings on both the left and right: they all favoured the use of mythical images and explanations.[49] The

---

49 Dietmar Schirmer, 'Politisch-kulturelle Deutungsmuster. Vorstellungen von der Welt der Politik in der Weimarer Republik' in Detlef Lehnert and Klaus Megerle (eds), *Politische*

National Socialists in particular developed a religious form of mythopoeia, and their myths were staged through rituals and symbolic signs. The political religion of Nazi ideology, and the ritual which shaped it, was so powerful that the Republic of Weimar, a disintegrating and unloved democracy, could not compete.

Identität und nationale Gedenktage, Zur politischen Kultur in der Weimarer Republik, Opladen, 1989, pp. 31–60.

CELEBRATING CHRISTMAS IN THE THIRD REICH AND GDR: POLITICAL INSTRUMENTALIZATION AND CULTURAL CONTINUITY UNDER THE GERMAN DICTATORSHIPS

Corey Ross

Modern dictatorial regimes have generally laid great value on the staging of elaborate festivals and memorial rituals aimed at emotionalizing the 'masses' for their own political cause. Neither the Nazi 'Third Reich' nor the Communist German Democratic Republic (GDR) were an exception to this. In both regimes official festivals displaying popular unity and mass subordination to the ruling party and ideology occupied a central position in their propaganda efforts, and were an integral part of the annual rhythm of the official calendar.

Official celebrations in both regimes stretched across the whole of the year. In the Third Reich, the 'Day of the National Socialist Seizure of Power' on 30 January was followed by Hitler's birthday on 20 April, then the 'National Holiday of the German *Volk*' on 1 May, soon followed by the 'Day of the German Mother', the 'German Summer Solstice' in June, the 'German Harvest Thanksgiving' in the autumn, the 'Memorial Day for the Fallen of the Movement' on 9 November and finally the 'German Winter Solstice', shortly before Christmas. In the GDR, the festival calendar began with the anniversary of the murders of Rosa Luxemburg and Karl Liebknecht in January, followed by

'Women's Day' on 8 March, May Day, the 'Day of Liberation' a week later on 8 May, the 'Birthday of the Republic' on 7 October and the anniversary of the Russian Revolution on 7 November. But alongside these official calendars of events was, of course, an older set of festivals and holidays derived from centuries of Christian tradition which could not simply be forbidden. Though this placed certain constraints on Nazi and Communist attempts to achieve a completely new festival culture, it also offered opportunities to anchor the new celebration forms and anniversaries by latching on to older, predominantly Christian, festival traditions and holidays, adapting and instrumentalizing them to serve a new purpose.

Taking Christianity out of Christmas

The leadership of both the Nazi Party (NSDAP) and Socialist Unity Party (SED) viewed Christianity as a dangerous ideological threat, a formidable obstacle to their totalizing political ambitions. It was an explicit goal of both regimes to replace all major Christian festivals with their own. This included not only the Christian sacraments — baptism, confirmation, marriage, burial and so on — but also the various anniversaries of the Christian calendar. As one of the two most sacred days of this calendar, Christmas was a primary target, and provides a useful case-study for comparing and contrasting how both regimes attempted to transform and instrumentalize festival culture. Neither the Nazis nor the German Communists were willing to leave this most widely observed of the traditional festivals to the Church.

Under both regimes, then, there was a broad attempt to 'de-Christianize' the Christmas festival, at least in terms of how it was celebrated in public. Though certain changes were made immediately, it took a number of years for new forms of celebration to become canonized. At the beginning of their rule in 1933, the Nazis offered no special guidelines as to how Christmas should be celebrated. The 'Erste Weihnachtsfeier der Reichsbahndirektion Berlin' in 1933 was indeed lavishly staged and even recorded in documentary film, but at this time Nazi and Christian elements coexisted: the audience sang the 'Horst Wessel Lied' as well as 'O du fröhliche', and the Holy Family was accompanied by a troop of SA men on to the podium.[1] These hybrid celebrations containing elements of both Christian belief and a 'Germanic Christmas' were also characteristic of the proposals for celebrations in the Nazi brochures appearing regularly from 1934.

By 1937, however, *Die neue Gemeinschaft* (the official Nazi journal for leisure-time and celebration) advocated purely National Socialist celebrations: 'For the "*Volks*-Christmas" there is no reason for us to bother with angels, shepherds or other figures of Christian legend.'[2] Though intended to replace Christian customs, most such celebrations were strikingly similar to Christian worship services in form, from the rows of benches to the pulpit-like lectern to the icons of the Führer instead of Christ. The organization of a 1938 '*volksdeutsche* Christmas celebration for the schools', for instance, included catechism-like statements by individuals followed by answers from the group, the periodic use of music and singing, a sermon-like speech followed by a 'declaration of belief in the community' (*Bekenntnis an die Gemeinschaft*).[3] Though these guidelines were intended primarily for the holiday festivities of the party and its various organizations, and though there were not yet any specific guidelines as to how to organize private family Christmas celebrations at home, it was clearly hoped that the festival forms of the party organization would have an influence on members' private celebrations as well. As we will see below, this attempt to penetrate into the private sphere became increasingly apparent during the war.

In East Germany, the SED lost little time in trying to de-Christianize Christmas celebrations, especially for the young. Already in 1946 the Communist youth organization Free German Youth (FDJ) published booklets of secular Christmas carols and poems,[4] many inherited from the Socialist and especially Communist

---

[1] The text of the film is reprinted in Karl Reimers, 'Der Führer als völkische Erlösergestalt. Die Berliner NS-Weihnachtskundgebung 1933 im offiziellen Filmbericht', *Geschichte in Wissenschaft und Unterricht*, 19, 1968, pp. 164–75.

[2] *Die neue Gemeinschaft*, November 1937, p. 3004.

[3] From Hans-Jochen Gamm, *Der braune Kult. Das Dritte Reich und seine Ersatzreligion*, Hamburg, 1962, pp. 183–86.

[4] The following is an incomplete listing of the FDJ publications: *Und wieder wird es Weihnachten*, Weimar, 1946; *Winter und Weihnachten*, Weimar, 1947; Zentralrat der FDJ, *Weihnachten 1948: Heimabendmaterial*, Berlin, 1948; idem, *Wir feiern Weihnachten! Für*

organizations of Weimar Germany, which were intended to replace all Christian elements of the organization's Christmas celebrations. The German Cultural League, or Kulturbund, published similar pamphlets from the early 1950s,[5] and there were also occasional internal party directives describing how Christmas celebrations in the schools and factories should be organized and conducted. To offer an example, a 1955 SED directive on children's Christmas parties instructed that: '"O, du fröhliche", "Stille Nacht" and similar songs should not be sung [...]. Also, all other things which remind one of church celebrations such as angels, child in the manger, etc. should be left out.'[6] In their stead were recommended recitations by the Communist poet Johannes Becher, old folk-songs and, of course, the many 'new songs' in official publications.

Compared to the Nazi celebrations, official Christmas festivals and customs in the GDR tended to digress more from Christian models, at least from the formal services of worship, and had more in common with the rather informal pre-war Socialist *proletarische Feierstunden*, or 'proletarian ceremonies' intended to replace Sunday church services. There was little sense of a formal liturgy in the celebrations, no catechism-like readings or professions of belief, though communal singing was always a central feature and, especially in the 1940s and 1950s, icons of Communist leaders such as Stalin, Walther Ulbricht and Wilhelm Pieck often featured prominently. There was also, apart from the occasional reverence of Stalin, less a sense of 'leader' and 'followers'; they were more 'collective' celebrations, 'convivial get-togethers', in the words of the Kulturbund.[7]

Somewhat less obviously ideologized than the SED or FDJ celebration guidelines, the Christmas programmes proposed by the Kulturbund still offer an idea of what these officially sanctioned festivities were supposed to look like. The

---

Weihnachts- und Neujahrsfeiern, Berlin, 1951; idem, *Weihnachten 1952: Material zur Durchführung von Weihnachtsfeiern*, Berlin, 1952.

5 Kulturbund, *Zieh, Friede, ein in jedes Haus! Programmvorschläge für Weihnachtsfeiern*, Berlin, 1952; idem, *... daß endlich, endlich Friede sei! Ein Material zur Ausgestaltung von Weihnachtsfeiern*, Berlin, 1954.

6 Landesarchiv Berlin, Bezirksparteiarchiv (SED) (hereafter LAB-BPA), IV2/4/06/332, 'Agitation zu den Weihnachtsfeiern', 6 December 1955, p. 2.

7 Kulturbund, *Zieh, Friede, ein in jedes Haus!*, p. 11.

first programme suggested in the 1952 booklet 'Zieh, Friede, ein in jedes Haus!' features the rather typical format of simple group-singing and readings as well as the typical mixture of traditional folk-songs, Christian carols and new Socialist texts. Like most of the programmes, it begins with the more traditional material, which included songs such as 'O du fröhliche' and 'Stille Nacht, Heilige Nacht', as well as various readings from Pushkin ('Wir freuen uns deiner Herrlichkeit'), Adalbert Stifter ('Auf dem Gletscher') and Joseph von Eichendorff ('Weihnachten'). About halfway through, however, the readings and song-lyrics become more clearly political in content, ranging from Arnold Zweig's 'Es geschah in Bethlehem', a story of how the centuries-old Christian message of peace and justice for the oppressed had taken a new language and new forms in the era of Socialism, to downright iconoclastic Communist poems such as Louis Fürnberg's 'Legende vom Stern und Kind', in which the people redeem themselves, the legendary wise men and shepherds act as Socialist agitators and the Star of Bethlehem is replaced by the Soviet Red Star:

> Wir kommen aus einem schönen Land,
> dort haben die Menschen die Not verbannt,
> als sie sich selbst erlösten.
> Dort wachsen die Kinder auf im Licht,
> und Hunger und Elend gibt's dort nicht,
> weil's keinem an Dach und Brot gebricht.
> Die Kleinsten wurden die Größten.
>
> Ach, führt uns hin! sprach Josef darauf.
> Da ging ein Stern am Himmel auf
> in einem roten Lichte.
> Das ist der Stern von Kraft und Mut,
> der Herzen stählt und Wunder tut,
> und kennt Ihr ihn, dann lest Ihr gut
> die biblische Geschichte.[8]

These celebration programmes reflect the general hybrid tendencies in official Christmas celebrations in the GDR between the rather conventional Socialist celebrations of the pre-war years, where the emphasis was on pacifist readings and singing old folk-songs, and the more antagonistic, iconoclastic and

---

8   Ibid., pp. 26–27.

uncompromising Communist festivities, which eschewed all Christian allusions and tended to prefer revolutionary fighting songs to traditional carols.[9]

However these two different strands of working-class festival tradition were interwoven, together they formed the basis for the broad de-Christianization process of the East German Christmas. This process was by no means confined to the more heavy-handed and rigidly ideological 1940s and 1950s, but continued throughout the following decades, as the SED attempted to eliminate all specific religious allusions at Christmas-time, even in the very language of the season. 'Frohe Festtage' ('Happy Holidays') gradually replaced 'Frohe Weihnachten' ('Merry Christmas') as the standard greeting in the official media. The eradication of religious allusions at Christmas-time was so thorough and transparent that it eventually became the butt of a widely known joke in the GDR during the 1980s: even if the party could not get East Germans to stop decorating their Christmas trees with 'angels', it might at least rename them with the acceptably atheist term *Jahresendflügelfigur* ('year-end winged figure').

Christmas as a Reflection of Official Ideology

Divesting Christmas of its Christian elements was only the 'negative' half of the overall project of redefinition. The 'positive' task of constructing new customs and a new meaning for the Christmas festival was undoubtedly more difficult. Clearly, a festival as important as Christmas would have to offer a faithful reflection of the official *Weltanschauung* of the ruling party, its values, objectives and social vision. Equally clearly, however, neither regime could afford to make its transformation of Christmas too obvious. A complete break with the traditional Christmas message or an over-politicization of its ritual forms would too blatantly reveal the authoritarian and ideological motives behind the official celebrations and would most likely be politically counter-productive. How best to juggle these two conflicting imperatives? And what should be the new content of Christmas?

In the Third Reich, the aim was less to take Christianity out of Christmas than to take Christmas out of Christianity; that is, to claim it as a pre-Christian

---

9 Wilhelm Guttsman, *Workers' Culture in Weimar Germany: Between Tradition and Commitment*, New York, 1990, pp. 292–93.

Germanic festival which needed to be returned to its original form and meaning. This 'Germanification' approach offered the Nazis not only a sense of continuity with Christmas past, but also an ideal vehicle for inculcating their mythical, romantic notions of Germandom. Throughout the 1930s and 1940s, folklorists from various academic backgrounds — mostly working for or in close affiliation with the Propaganda Ministry and the so-called 'Amt Rosenberg', or 'Dienststelle des Beauftragten des Führers' — tried to show that the early Christian Church actually adopted what were originally Germanic traditions out of tactical considerations, thereafter skilfully manipulating them for its own purposes.[10] With the advent of National Socialism, they argued, it was high time to reverse this process: 'If foreign [*artfremde*] customs — even if they have lived for centuries in our *Volk* — are slowly displaced and eradicated, this does not constitute a forceful and reprehensible abrogation of something that has evolved historically, but rather an entirely natural, even indispensable rectification and rehabilitation for the future of our *Volk*.'[11]

A variety of *arteigene* Germanic customs were thus propagated as the original, unadulterated customs of Christmas-time. Instead of readings from the Christmas gospel there were 'German fairy-tales'. Instead of Saint Nicholas or the Christ-child as the bearer of gifts there was *Knecht Ruprecht*, who was also understood to represent the Germanic god Wotan. Mary was re-interpreted as the 'prototypical German mother' and the Christ-child re-named the 'child of light'. And as for decorations, the traditional angels and shepherds were to give way to various Germanic symbols — the swastika, the 'pretzel' symbol for blood and soil, the 'sun-wheel' and so on. One of the principal activities of the Nazi girls' organization, the Bund Deutscher Mädel, in the weeks before Christmas was the baking of such Germanic decorations, or *Sinnbildgebäck*, for hanging on the Christmas tree.[12]

---

10 See, generally, Esther Gajek, 'Weihnachten im Dritten Reich: Der Beitrag von Volkskundlern an den Veränderungen des Weihnachtsfestes', *Ethnologia Europaea*, 20, 1990, pp. 121–40.

11 Hans Strobel, *Bauernbrauch im Jahreslauf*, Leipzig, 1936, p. 22.

12 See, for example, Karl Haiding, 'Backwerk für den Weihnachtsbaum', in: *Die Spielschar. Zeitschrift für Feier- und Freizeitgestaltung*, 1938, pp. 426–28.

John Heartfield skilfully captured the absurdity of the Germanification-mania surrounding Christmas in an ironic photomontage for the Christmas edition of the *Arbeiter-Illustrierte-Zeitung* in 1934. Under the heading 'O Tannenbaum im deutschen Raum, wie krumm sind deine Äste' ('O Christmas Tree in Germany, how crooked are your branches', a word play on the nineteenth-century carol 'O Tannenbaum, O Tannenbaum, wie grün sind deine Blätter') stands a small Christmas tree on a swastika-shaped tree-stand, its few thin branches broken and twisted to form several swastikas. Adopting the biological language of the Nazi folklorists, the caption reads: 'According to a decree of the Reich Food Minister Darré, as of Christmas 1934 the propagation of the Christmas fir tree as *artfremden* intruder on German soil is forbidden. Hereafter only the brown "Unity fir tree DRGM" bred in Valhalla will be permitted'.[13]

Besides claiming Christmas as an essentially Germanic tradition, the Nazis also tried, as they did for every other significant festival occasion, to turn it into an expression of the unity and singular will of the German *Volk*, into a *Fest der Volksgemeinschaft*. They did this in a number of ways. After the First World War, the custom of setting up a large Christmas tree in a central square became increasingly common in European cities. This 'Christmas Tree for All' (*Weihnachtsbaum für alle*), as it was called in Germany, was retained by the Nazis, but re-interpreted as a symbol of the *Volksgemeinschaft* — a central reference point for all onlookers and a substitute tree for those who could not afford one. From 1933 onwards, a huge Christmas tree from a different area of Germany was set up every year before the Reich Propaganda Ministry. All across the Third Reich, the *Weihnachtsbaum für alle* became the stage for the Nazis' solidarity campaign at Christmas: beneath the communal tree the *Winterhilfswerk* badges were sold and official handing over of gifts to the poor took place.[14] Another custom intended to boost the sense of the *Volksgemeinschaft* at Christmas was the newly invented *Heimholung des Feuers*, or 'fetching home of the fire'. According to this custom the local populace, led by the SA, SS, Hitler

---

13 John Heartfield, *Krieg im Frieden. Fotomontagen zur Zeit 1930–1938*, Munich, 1972, p. 72. DRGM, or *Deutsches Reichs-Gebrauchsmuster*, designated a registered standard product or item.

14 Gajek, 'Weihnachten im Dritten Reich', p. 130.

Youth et al., was to start a festive fire on a central village or town square on 21 December in celebration of the winter solstice, then organize a round-the-clock watch for the fire until nightfall on Christmas Eve, when all the children were to come out of their houses with specially-made lanterns to 'fetch home the fire' for the candles on their Christmas trees at home. The high point of the celebration, whose purpose was to draw a connection between the winter solstice and Christmas as well as between the private family Christmas and National Socialist-inspired public ritual, consisted of everyone in the village or town singing around a central Christmas tree, which was supposed to generate a sense of community.[15]

The East German Communists made a similar ideology-driven attempt to de-Christianize and redefine Christmas in the GDR, but the form and content of official celebrations there also showed important differences. In fact, the party ideologues in the SED Abteilung Agitation, Education Ministry and FDJ Abteilung Kultur sought to redefine Christmas to a large extent in contradistinction to its romantic, nationalist meaning in Nazi ideology. Instead of an expression of some spurious Germanic essence or a *Fest der Volksgemeinschaft*, they viewed Christmas foremost as a 'festival of peace, joy and light'. Indeed, the traditional Christmas theme of light, symbolized in Christian tradition by the star over Bethlehem, featured prominently in all SED and FDJ conceptions of Christmas celebrations, where it symbolized instead moral and societal renewal after the darkness of National Socialism. This notion was expressed in a number of ways, including torchlit processions, which were one of the principal Christmas-time activities of the FDJ in many areas, in bright images of happy children around a glowing Christmas tree, as well as in numerous poems and songs which carefully integrated the notion of a new dawn at winter solstice with the advent of Socialism. As we have already seen, the Star of Bethlehem as a sign of hope and redemption was quite commonly replaced by the Soviet Red Star. Probably the most explicit example of this was the well-known Communist writer Erich Weinert's pre-war poem 'Der neue Stern', which featured in most of the SED, FDJ and Kulturbund booklets on Christmas celebrations:

---

15   See Thilo Scheller, 'Die Heimholung des Feuers. Ein neues Weihnachtsbrauchtum', *Deutsche Volkskunde*, 1939, pp. 293–96.

Über dem Hof, in der eisigen Nacht
ist ein neuer, leuchtender Stern erwacht.
Er steht überm Fenster des armen Mannes
in blutrotem Glanz;
und seine fünf Zacken strahlen weit
in Elend, Hunger und Dunkelheit.
Er leuchtet überall auf Erden
wo arme Kinder geboren werden.
Denn nicht ein Erlöser ist uns erstanden,
Millionen Erlöser in allen Landen![16]

The Red Star was thus the symbol of hope and redemption for the masses by the masses, and official Christmas in the GDR was thus not about celebrating one redeemer in the form of the Christ-child, but a million redeemers in the form of the international Communist movement. Yet for a decade or so after the war, one redeemer none the less towered above all others. Until the mid-1950s, Christmas celebrations in the SBZ/GDR curiously intermingled with the celebration of Stalin's birthday on 21 December. The saviour-cult status of Stalin in official East German culture was clearly reflected in the ritual forms of Christmas celebrations organized for children. 'What do we do for the Christmas festival?' asks a 1949 FDJ booklet on Christmas celebrations. Answer: 'A few days before Christmas, on 21 December, all progressive, democratic people in the world celebrate the birthday of their great teacher [*Lehrmeister*] Stalin. He stands at the head of the peoples of the Soviet Union, to whom we are indebted for the fact that we can once again celebrate Christmas without fascist barbarity and air-raid sirens. For this reason all youth groups prepare beautiful, lovingly decorated birthday cards to Joseph Stalin in the time leading up to Christmas.'[17] The pervasive Stalin-veneration was by far the most quasi-religious element of official Christmas celebrations in the GDR, and can quite justifiably be compared to the careful positing of Hitler as a Christ-like figure of redemption under the Nazis. In a celebration ritual repeated thousands of times in schools across the GDR, the 1952 Christmas party at the 'Wilhelm Pieck Day Nursery' in Berlin featured children singing songs of peace while reverently decorating Stalin's portrait and

---

16 Zentralrat der FDJ, *Wir feiern Weihnachten!*, p. 10.
17 Zentralrat der FDJ, Abteilung Kultur, *Weihnachten 1949: Heimabendmaterial*, Berlin, 1949, p. 16.

surrounding it with candles, treating it, at least outwardly, much as altar-boys would a Christian icon or Hitler Youth a bust of the Führer.[18]

All purely ideological concerns aside, it was the practicalities of the Christmas season that presented the greatest challenge to the SED. The party was always very sensitive to problems in the provision of consumer goods, but this concern was at its annual height during the season of gift-giving. Because of the increase in consumption around Christmas, shortages of a range of highly sought-after goods were extremely common in the 1940s and 1950s, and only gradually improved during the following decades. A December 1958 report from Frankfurt an der Oder district offers a flavour of some of the problems. It complains of 'serious shortages' of certain foods (eggs, meat, chocolate and sparkling wine, which the local retail shops, or HOs, were forced to buy from other administrative districts), consumer goods (including shoes, winter clothing and electrical goods) and even packaging material. This 'great bottleneck' in packaging material was of special concern, as reports had already filtered in about goods being wrapped in old newspapers obtained from paper collection points, some of which came from the West (such as *Der Spiegel* and *Der Telegraf*).[19]

These problems of course had far-reaching political ramifications, not only in terms of simple material discontent, but also because they belied the official portrayal of the GDR as the German state that best provided for its workers. The SED thus tried its utmost to play down such problems and present the consumer situation in as positive a light as possible. An example of how this was done was a feature entitled 'A Christmas Story' in the Christmas 1951 edition of the official FDJ journal *Junge Welt*. It tells of 'Mother Fielitz's' Christmas shopping list, of what she wanted to buy for whom, how much it all cost and how she had just enough money saved up to buy it all. Having worked hard all year for her savings, she was surprised and delighted to find that prices had been reduced before the holidays: 'she saved DM 119.75 because of the eleventh price reduction of the HO [on 9 December 1951], which is a success of the Five-Year Plan [...].

---

18 *Junge Welt. Organ des Zentralrates der FDJ*, 20 December 1952, p. 2.
19 Stiftung Archiv der Parteien und Massenorganisationen der ehem. DDR im Bundesarchiv, IV2/5/665, 'Information, 13.12.58', SED-Kreisleitung Angermünde, Seelow to BL Frankfurt an der Oder.

Without a doubt, Mother Fielitz's Christmas table has never been as full as it is this year.'[20] Being the idealized East German mother she is, not a hint of cynicism about the timing of the price reduction enters her mind. This same message of a Christmas windfall was also a centrepiece of the main East German women's magazine, *Die Frau von Heute*, in the weeks running up to Christmas 1951. The 14 December edition praises the reduced prices and the rich selection of items to buy, contrasting this to the situation for poor West German families who are portrayed as having little to choose from and being forced to eat less in order to afford toys for the children.[21] The practice of painting a rather unrealistic picture of the consumer situation remained a standard propaganda feature around Christmas-time. A 1958 placard (see Figure 1) conveys a similar message. Beneath the image of a well-to-do couple loaded down with packages, the caption reads: 'Our rich array of goods is the result of our workers' hard work for the victory of Socialism!'.[22]

Unfortunately for East German Christmas shoppers, things were rather different in reality, especially in the early years. Ever concerned about the many continuing consumer shortages and production shortcomings in the economy, the SED always balanced its Yuletide panegyrics to the material progress of the GDR with admonishments for further increasing productivity and improving work discipline. The rather patriarchal message to workers at Christmas time presented a new twist to the old saying about 'who's naughty and who's nice'. As the SED *Kreisleitung* in Prenzlauer Berg put it in 1955: 'the size of your Christmas stocking [*Weihnachtsteller*] and those of your children depends on how you worked in your factory. If you helped in the struggle against material wastage, loafing and absenteeism, then you helped in adding to the stocking. If you have been thoughtless and superficial in your work, then you subtracted not only from your own stocking, but also those of other people'.[23] Despite significant improvements in consumer provision from the mid-1960s, in December 1975 the message in the women's magazine *Für Dich* was still much the same: 'Whoever

---

20 *Junge Welt*, 24 December 1951, p. 2.
21 *Die Frau von Heute*, 14 December 1951, pp. 4–5; ibid., 21 December 1951, p. 5.
22 Leipzig: VEB Graphische Werkstätten, 1958.
23 LAB-BPA IV2/4/06/332, 'Agitation zu den Weihnachtsfeiern', 6 December 1955, p. 2.

wants to buy good quality [...] must produce good quality.'[24] Even during the holiday season, the party's constant obsession with raising quality and work-productivity came through loud and clear in its Christmas wishes to workers.

'Peace on Earth ... '?

Of all the things for which Christmas stands, certainly the message 'peace on Earth' is central. However, both the Nazis and SED had their sworn enemies, and neither could incorporate this particular aspect of the Christmas message into their own conceptions of Christmas without some alterations. For the SED it was mainly a case of turning the peace message against the West German 'imperialists and warmongers' who were portrayed as a military threat. For the Nazis, who by 1939 at the latest had made their disregard for peace patently obvious, it was more a case of eliminating it altogether.

With the onset of the war in 1939, Goebbels's Propaganda Ministry systematically began trying to influence the private, family Christmas festival in such a way as to support the war effort. This growing interest in private Christmas had two principal causes. First, because of blackout conditions in most of the Reich, the Nazis' carefully staged public winter solstice bonfires could no longer take place. More importantly, it was precisely during the Christmas holidays that fallen husbands, sons, fathers and friends — as well as those still at the front — were most sorely missed. The Propaganda Ministry was acutely sensitive to the problem of war-weariness, as is clear in Goebbels's annual Christmas addresses heroicizing the fallen warriors and trying to soothe the pain of bereaved loved ones by glorifying soldiers' 'ultimate sacrifice' for the Fatherland — in the process also demanding further sacrifices. On Christmas Day 1942, as the fateful battle of Stalingrad was on most Germans' minds, Goebbels' message was one of pride in the loss of life, which itself was presented as a necessity for the future of Germany:

> This evening the soldier speaks of his fallen comrades [...] and today at home a mother, a father, a wife or children think of each dead hero in proud mourning. The mothers who mourn for their lost sons may be comforted. It

---

24 *Für Dich*, 1975, 52, p. 19

was not in vain that they have borne their children with pain and raised them with care. As men and heroes they led the proudest and bravest lives that a son of the Fatherland can lead, and crowned it with the most heroic conclusion with which one could ever bring it to an end: they sacrificed themselves so that we may stand in the light.[25]

Efforts were not confined to merely keeping a lid on war-weariness. From 1941 to 1944 the Propaganda Ministry also published an annual volume entitled *Deutsche Kriegsweihnacht*, which sought to go one step further by establishing a positive connection between Christmas and war through the propagation of new songs, visual images, poems and festival customs.[26] By far the most prominent among these new customs were the so-called *Heldengedenken*, or 'heroes' remembrances', whose aim was to honour and even, in a sense, conjure up the presence of the fallen soldiers at Christmas-time. In this custom, a portrait of the fallen was to occupy a prominent place of honour in the house, often beside or in front of the Christmas tree, and was to be decorated with greenery and flowers (see Figure 2).[27] In a similar vein, the Propaganda Ministry also published a range of visual images, poems and various readings intended to accompany the Christmas feast which also stylized the fallen soldiers as the eternal protectors of hearth, home and German Christmases to come. The purpose was to re-channel the pain of separation or lost loved ones into a more 'positive' sense of both the value and necessity of their absence at Christmas, the time when families should at least be together in spirit if not in body. A particularly egregious poem entitled 'Der toten Soldaten Heimkehr' ('The Dead Soldier's Homecoming'), whose title alone suggests that the sorely missed war-dead visit the living on this one night of the year, combines all of these elements into a callous glorification of war and loss of life:

Einmal im Jahr, in der Heiligen Nacht,
verlassen die toten Soldaten die Wacht,
die sie für Deutschlands Zukunft stehn.
Sie kommen nach Haus, nach Art und Ordnung zu sehn,
Schweigend treten sie ein in den festlichen Raum —

---

25 Goebbels's radio addresses were reprinted in the annual *Deutsche Kriegsweihnacht*: see note 26 below. This quotation is taken from the 1944 edition, p. 191.
26 Hermann Liese (ed.), *Deutsche Kriegsweihnacht*, Munich, 1941–44.
27 Reproduced from ibid., 1944, p. 123.

Celebrating Christmas in the Third Reich and GDR

[...]
Es brennt für sie eine rote Kerze am Tannenbaum,
es steht für sie ein Stuhl am gedeckten Tisch,
es glüht für sie im Glase dunkel der Wein.
[...]
Wenn dann die Kerzen am Lichtbaum zu Ende gebrannt,
legt der tote Soldat die erdverkrustete Hand
jedem der Kinder leise aufs junge Haupt:
'Wir starben für euch, weil wir an Deutschland geglaubt'.
Einmal im Jahr, nach der Heiligen Nacht,
beziehen die toten Soldaten wieder die ewige Wacht.[28]

In stark contrast to the Nazis' cynical justifications of war and death, official Christmas in the GDR was always dominated first and foremost by the peace message, albeit (especially in the early years) a rather militant message of peace, less in line with the New Testament than with Cold War views of 'peace through strength'. Although Christmas was always propagated as the festival of peace, the holiday season invariably witnessed a heightening, not diminishing, of the SED's anti-Western rhetoric and appeals for military vigilance. The Communist ideologues did not view this as at all paradoxical. Whether in their forewords, introductions or explanations of various programmes, few of the various party and FDJ booklets on Christmas celebrations failed at some point to cite Stalin's dictum that 'peace can only be preserved and strengthened if the peoples of the Earth take the matter into their own hands and defend it at all costs'.[29] This basic message of the necessity of vigilance was then re-conveyed in different ways throughout the media spectrum of the party and mass organizations. As one might expect, it was focused towards young people, whom from 1952 onwards the regime was trying to recruit into the growing armed forces. It was also, as one might expect, most clearly visible on those Christmases concurrent with major propaganda and recruitment drives for the military, namely, 1952 and 1955.[30]

---

28 First, second and final stanzas only, from *Deutsche Kriegsweihnacht*, 1944, p. 138. The folklorist Thilo Scheller authored the poem, which appeared in every edition of *Deutsche Kriegsweihnacht* from 1942 to 1944.

29 From Zentralrat der FDJ, *Wir feiern Weihnachten!*, p. 7.

30 The founding of the so-called *Kasernierte Volkspolizei*, or 'barracked police', in 1952 was followed by an intense recruitment campaign that lasted well into 1953. The campaign of spring and autumn 1955 was in anticipation of the official founding of the National People's Army in January 1956.

During these two holiday seasons even the most unimportant of events were used to infuse Christmas with the message of military vigilance. For instance, although the description of one FDJ group's Christmas party in the 20 December 1952 edition of *Junge Welt* showed little more than young people singing the usual carols around a Christmas tree, this did not keep the editors from featuring it under the rather awkward slogan 'Peace on Earth, if everyone fights for it!'.[31]

Apart from the issue of winning support for the armed forces, the official portrayal of the GDR as the peace-loving German state consisted for the most part of sniping at Christmas in the capitalist West. The West German government and business élite were constantly portrayed in official rhetoric as the primary enemies of the working-class and its struggle for peace, and therefore the very enemies of Christmas itself. As the SED *Kreisleitung* in Prenzlauer Berg put it in their guidelines for Christmas celebrations: 'The 150 multimillionaires, monopolists and militarists do not profit enough from the gifts that the workers have in their Christmas stockings. They need war, total war; that demands raw materials and brings the highest profits. [...] Pious carols, prayers and other nonsense in capitalism are tried and proven methods to divert the workers from realizing their own strength and struggling against privation and repression.'[32] The carols and poems propagated by the SED and FDJ were clearly intended to drive home the same message of capitalist exploitation at Christmas and ideological diversion via the 'false consciousness' of religious belief, for example in R. Raupach's 'Friede schafft der Mensch allein!':

> Leid ist dort, wo kalter Schnee
> dringt in Hütten ein,
> wo der Reiche mordet, raubt.
> Arm ist, wer an Wunder glaubt.
> Wunder schafft der Mensch allein.
>
> Freude sprüht, wo weicher Schnee
> flockt Fabriken ein,
> die dem Volk eigen sind.
> Froh schafft jeder, lernt das Kind.
> Friede schafft der Mensch allein.[33]

---

31   *Junge Welt*, 20 December 1952, p. 4.
32   LAB-BPA IV2/4/06/332, 'Agitation zu den Weihnachtsfeiern', 6 December 1955, p. 3.
33   From Zentralrat der FDJ, Wir *feiern Weihnachten!*, p. 20.

As militant and antagonistic as such rhetoric could be, it would be too simplistic to dismiss it all as no more than cynical propaganda gestures. After all, the promotion of peace was a decades-old aim of the German workers' movement and no doubt a sincere priority among most SED members all the way up to the party leadership. Moreover, it should also be noted that Christmas was used for propaganda purposes in the West as well, as a celebration of capitalism, Christianity and consumerism, and that in the context of German division the use of such counter-propaganda on the part of the SED is anything but surprising. But at the height of the Cold War, the SED leadership occasionally went to ridiculous lengths to present itself as the guarantor of peace at Christmas-time and the Federal Republic as a threat to it. For instance, a December 1952 feature article in *Junge Welt* claimed that the real motive behind the West German campaign to allow humanitarian 'Christmas packages' into the East was to supply US agents with weapons. The headline reads: 'Lethal weapons in "Christmas packets": New, monstrous crimes of the Kaiser Ministry uncovered'.[34] Like many others, this article managed to combine a number of propaganda themes, simultaneously denying Western goodwill, thus helping to drum up support for the growing East German armed forces, and invalidating the 'Christmas packages' as a symbol of Western wealth. In its Christmas greetings to the people of Stralsund, the local SED *Kreisleitung* rather unsubtly combined its anti-Western peace message with admonishments to improve work discipline:

> And today, after the Second World War, a new message has reached us, a new 'Fear ye not — but fight!', for peace, dear friends, does not lie like a present under the Christmas tree, but must be fought for and attained! [...] It all depends on your willingness to help with the faster construction of Socialism, to achieve the victory in the struggle between life and death. West German militarism and fascism, the arch-enemy of peace that has already raised its head in search of new murderous deeds, land theft and higher profits, must be suffocated by peace, for otherwise there will be war, atomic plague and mass death. [...] The peace of the world lies in our hands. Our Seven-Year Plan is a plan of peace, for which it is worthwhile studying, working and fighting. All-round fulfilment and over-fulfilment of

---

34 *Junge We*lt, 17 December 1952, p. 1.

the plan in 1960, that must be our goal, then the plague of war will be driven out of Germany and peace will triumph [...].[35]

In its tendency to politicize even the most quotidian aspects of life, the SED was not satisfied simply to wish East Germans a merry Christmas, but rather used the traditional message of peace and hope as an ideal opportunity to lambaste the West and call for greater work discipline and productivity in the year to come. Perhaps the low-point of SED Christmas propaganda came in 1961. Only several months after the erection of the Berlin Wall brutally separated tens of thousands of families, the party organ *Neues Deutschland*, in keeping with the official designation of the Wall as an 'anti-fascist protection wall' against an imminent Western attack, actually lauded it for having 'rescued peace at Christmas'.[36]

Conclusions: A Co-opted Christmas?

Both the Nazis and SED made use of the various media at their disposal to propagate their own specific Christmas messages and to introduce new, ideologically sound carols, rituals and other customs into the traditional Christian festival. In both regimes such customs were, despite their partial novelty, often based in either outward form or thematic selection on the Christian forerunners which they were intended to replace. Though there are striking similarities between the ways in and extent to which both regimes attempted to de-Christianize Christmas celebrations, there were important differences in both the form and content of these festival customs under the two dictatorships. The Nazis were not against religion *per se*, they merely wanted their own Germanic cult to prevail. Hence they tended to retain the mystical and liturgical forms of traditional Christian celebrations while filling them with a radically different message of national chauvinism and war. By contrast, the SED had less tolerance for the specifically religious elements of the Christian Christmas, but at the same time had little reason to discard the traditional message of peace and hope for humankind. Instead, it transformed this message into one of the need for military

---

35 SED-Kreisleitung Stralsund, Abt. Agitation, *Es sei gegrüsst die Weihnachtszeit!*, Stralsund, 1959, pp. 8–11.
36 *Neues Deutschland*, 24 December 1961, p. 1.

vigilance and higher productivity against the enemies of Socialism, held as the only system in which peace could truly be realized.

Both regimes were well aware that an over-politicization of traditional festival culture might prove counterproductive, and by and large stopped short of directly trying to transform Christmas celebrations outside of their own 'official' public festivities. It was only during the radical war-time phase of the Nazi dictatorship that the private, family Christmas became a target for political agitation, and the SED never made any great efforts in this regard. The extent to which either regime managed to influence private Christmas celebrations is difficult to judge. Certainly tens of thousands of National Socialist tree decorations were sold, and a number of changes the Nazis made to carols continued to be sung well into the 1950s.[37] According to internal SS reports, celebrations that centred around comforting those with absent loved ones and children with fallen fathers in particular had a 'good effect in terms of morale'.[38] But on the whole it seems that the influence of National Socialist ideology on the private family Christmas festival was negligible, and that of Marxism-Leninism even less. Participating in the 'new' Christmas festivals at work or in school was one thing, organizing them oneself at home was quite another. Although we are forced to rely heavily on anecdotal evidence, this overwhelmingly suggests that within the privacy of their own four walls, the vast majority of Germans in the Third Reich and GDR celebrated Christmas much as their parents and grandparents had, apart of course from changes in material circumstances.

For a number of reasons, the transformation of public Christmas, too, was only partially successful. Neither regime achieved a monopoly over it. The established Churches proved largely immune to the changes in festival culture that the Nazis and SED were trying to introduce, and still conducted Christmas masses and services much as they always had. The continuity they represented was an attractive alternative to the ideologized festivals that were being officially

---

37 See Angela Brown, 'Vom "germanischen Julfest" zum "Totenfest" — Weihnachten und Winterhilfswerk-Abzeichen im Nationalsozialismus', *Deutsches Historisches Museum Magazin*, 5, 1995, 14 (Winter), pp. 23–30; Ingeborg Weber-Kellermann, *Das Buch der Weihnachtslieder*, Mainz, 1982, pp. 226–37.

38 Heinz Boberach (ed.), *Meldungen aus dem Reich. Die geheimen Lageberichte des Sicherheitsdienstes der SS 1938–1945*, 17 vols, Herrsching, 1984, IX, p. 3140.

propagated, and the churches continued to draw relatively large crowds at Christmas. As a classified SS report put it in December 1941, the festivals put on by the Nazi party 'were unable to become the centrepiece for the populace, but in most localities were still overshadowed by the usual church Christmas celebrations'.[39] In the factories it was reported that the celebrations 'were most effective where they were conceived by the workers themselves'. And in the countryside, where only small handfuls of people reportedly participated or knew any of the new lyrics for carols, the Nazis seem to have been even less successful: 'the celebrations, which are in some ways very different from the usual Christmas celebrations of years past, are still finding it difficult to gain acceptance'.[40] Though the rather less ambitious SED leadership was basically satisfied with keeping pastors' Christmas sermons within acceptable limits, not even this modest aim was entirely achieved. Despite prior agreements with church leaders that pastors should keep strictly to the message 'peace on Earth', local functionaries none the less reported whole lists of pastors who ventured in their Christmas sermons into more politically explosive areas such as the remilitarization of the GDR and the incompatibility of materialist and Christian world-views.[41]

In the final analysis, it was the deep roots of Christmas festival customs in Germany, as well as — in many households, at least — the desire to uphold family traditions pertaining to private Christmas celebrations, that foiled the efforts of both regimes to bring about far-reaching changes in the meanings and rituals of Christmas outside of their own 'official' celebrations in the days leading up to 25 December. Though we are forced to speculate somewhat on the effects, it seems that in the annual rhythm of the calendar, Christmas, perhaps more than any other single day of the year, was a time for private authenticity over public conformity.

---

39 Ibid., pp. 3140–41.
40 Ibid., p. 3141.
41 For instance, Brandenburgisches Landeshauptarchiv Bezirk Potsdam Rep. 530, Nr. 2187, 'Betr.: Veranstaltungen in der Kirche an den Weihnachtsfeiertagen', 31 December 1953, bl. 213.

THE KING'S RIGHT HAND: A HUNGARIAN NATIONAL-RELIGIOUS HOLIDAY AND THE CONFLICT BETWEEN THE COMMUNIST PARTY AND THE CATHOLIC CHURCH (1945–48)

Árpád v. Klimó

Many in our times try to write, as they say, the true national history, using new historical world-views.[1]

This chapter focuses on the conflict between the Catholic Church and the Communist party in Hungary over the meanings of St Stephen's Day (20 August), one of the most important Hungarian national holidays, in the years between 1945 and 1948. In what follows I will analyse this conflict in three steps. First, I will introduce the major participants of the conflict and the context in which it broke out. In the second part of the chapter I will briefly sketch the historical background by reconstructing the history of St Stephen's Day from its medieval roots, through its 'invention' as a national holiday in the beginning of the nineteenth century to the inter-war period, when it became a part of the official

---

I would like to thank David Frey of Columbia University who kindly helped me with correcting the text.

1   István Farkas, *A mai magyar ifjúság nemzeti öntudata*, Sárospatak, 1937, p. 10.

ideology of the Horthy regime. In the last section I will examine the culmination of the conflict between 1946 and 1948.

The Setting of the Conflict: The Return of the 'Holy Right' by US Troops in 1945

In the summer of 1945 the Minister of Foreign Affairs of the Provisional National Government of Hungary sent a letter to Arthur Schoenfeld, the US Representative in Budapest:

> I wish to express once more my deepest gratitude to the Missions of the United States of America, both Political and Military, for their kind assistance in returning our sacred relic to the country. It was a most noble and moving gesture on the part of these Missions to have rendered it possible that the sacred Right of St Stephen, first holy King of Hungary, miraculously preserved during long centuries, was again in the country on our national holiday held in his commemoration. It was a deed worthy of the United States of America, standard-bearer of goodwill and understanding. In these times when the fate of nations is being forged anew, such a friendly and loyal gesture is of particular value and gives rise to a hope for achieving a higher ideal of peace and justice. Let me assure Your Excellency that the Hungarian nation is deeply grateful to the United States for this noble and touching action. You may have personally witnessed, Sir, the expressed response of this gratitude which found manifestation in the spontaneous cheers of the crowd in the streets: 'Long live America'. And all of us Hungarians wholeheartedly join in these exclamations![2]

The relic mentioned in the letter above was the 'Holy Right' of the first King of Hungary, Stephen (István I, *c.* 974–1038). The 'Holy Right' remains even today an object of Catholic veneration, national identification and dispute.[3] When the

---

[2] Magyar Országos Levéltár (Hungarian State Archive, hereafter MOL), XIX - J- 1- k, 10. doboz 4/b, 2o148/1945, 'Gyöngyösi külügyminiszter köszönő levele a Szent Jobb hazahozatala alkalmából', p. 5.

[3] English introductions to the topic can be found in Chris M. Hann, 'Socialism and King Stephen's Right Hand', *Religion in Communist Lands*, 18, 1990, 1, pp. 4–24; a broader perspective is offered by Katalin Sinkó, 'Árpád versus St István: Competing Heroes and Competing Interests in the Figurative Representation of Hungarian History' in Tamás Hofer (ed.), *Hungary between 'East' and 'West': Three Essays on National Myths and Symbols*, Budapest, 1994, pp. 9–26; and, from the perspective of history of the body, Árpád v. Klimó, 'Die Heilige Rechte des Königs. Eine Reliquie als Objekt der Zeitgeschichte' in *Geschichte*

Hungarian Communist Party, backed by the Red Army, tried to establish their domination over the country, the relic, and the national holiday associated with it, became a matter not only for national, but also for international politics.

Hungarian Foreign Minister Gyöngyösi, a member of the 'Smallholders' Party', a broad centre-left party which participated in the anti-fascist coalition government, addressed the US representative in a matter crucial to our argument: the return of the 'Holy Right' by a US military unit operating in Austria during summer 1945. The Hungarian national relic had been found by a CIC (Counter Intelligence Corps) unit in search of 'notorious Hungarian war criminals' and 'Hungarian fascists occupying high positions in the puppet Szálasi regime who had systematically looted the Jews of Hungary concurrent with the extermination of Jews by the Gestapo'.[4] These Hungarian soldiers, loyal to the fascist government allied to Germany, had taken the Hungarian crown jewels with them during their flight from the Red Army to Austria. The US soldiers were astonished when they found the relic in the small town of Mattsee, near Salzburg. They later composed a text called 'commemoration', in which they described their action with the following words:

> With the advent of Nazism, when *evil forces* disregarded the *sanctity of holy things*, the Holy Hand and the dedicated coronation robes of the Court of Hungary were *desecrated by impious hands* and carried in secret to foreign lands. The opportunity to restore these treasures to their rightful owners came through the collaboration of representatives of the Roman Catholic Church and of the liberating armies from the United States of America.[5]

The citation offers an interesting example of Christian, patriotic and anti-fascist sentiments. It seems as if the US troops regarded the Holy Right as a purely religious object, which had been stolen by anti-religious villains. Their standpoint was not shared by all actors in the event. The official stance of the Vatican and the hierarchy of the Roman Catholic Church, both in Hungary as well as in Austria, who pushed the Americans to restore the relic to Hungary before St Stephen's Day, was expressed in a letter to the Vatican by Archbishop Rohracher of

---

Macht Körper — Körper Macht Geschichte (proceedings of a conference held in Bielefeld, 15–17 December 1997), forthcoming (1999).

4   Konsistorialarchiv Salzburg (KAS), Fsz. 12/4 Rf2, Report by Captain Selke.
5   Ibid., 'Commemoration', my emphasis.

Salzburg, who played a major role in the action by using his good relationship with the US military representatives in Austria:

> On 19 June 1945 the famous relic of the right hand of St Stephen, the King of Hungary, was seized in Mattsee. The same had been taken along *by Hungarian refugees, obviously in order to rescue it from the Russians penetrating into Hungary.*[6]

The Archbishop thus described the Hungarian fascists and their action in a very different light than the US soldiers, who at that time were still allied to the Soviet army. But it was an opinion Hungarian Catholic officials would not have expressed in public. They preferred to use rich symbolic language to voice their sentiments. A procession, rooted in the tradition of a national holiday, offered an opportune occasion.

The relic was returned to Budapest on the evening before St Stephen's Day in 1945. The Hungarian Actio Catholica, usually responsible for the festivities, went to great lengths to organize the event. Already before the relic was found the Actio Catolica and the Catholic hierarchy agreed they would conduct the procession. In a letter of 26 June 1945, Archbishop Grősz of Kalocsa, the highest Catholic official of the time, agreed with the chief of the administration of Esztergom (where the primate of Hungary has his official seat) that the procession had to take place even without the relic, arguing that 'Besides everything else, we have to manifest our fidelity to St Stephen and to our millennial Christianity.'[7] At the end of June the head of the Dominican Order, Bertalan Badalik, agreed to deliver the sermon. In a letter Badalik asserted 'I will do my best to make an unpolitical speech.'[8]

The procession seems indeed to have proceeded as the organizers wished. Approximately 100,000 people gathered around the basilica of St Stephen in the centre of Budapest, where the event, displaying a seemingly unpolitical nature, took place.

---

6   Ibid., 'Sicherung der Reliquie des heiligen Stefan, König v. Ungarn', dated 29 September 1945, p. 1, my emphasis.
7   Esztergomi Primasi Leveltar (EPL) 1580/1945, 19 July 1945.
8   EPL 1838/1945, 6 August 1945.

Only afterwards did complications occur. Margit Slachta, the founder of the Order of the Social Sisters in Hungary, had organized a demonstration of believers in front of the American Military Mission to thank the US for its help in returning the Holy Right to the country. It was reported to the police that during the demonstrations anti-Russian slogans had been shouted. The leaders of the Actio Catolica were very upset about Sister Margit, because they had insisted that the festivities should have a purely religious character. Slachta, one of the major representatives of the Catholic women's movement, had been the first woman elected to the Hungarian parliament in 1920, but had then resigned from politics.[9] During the German occupation she rescued many Hungarian Jews. Her standpoint was consequently Catholic and anti-totalitarian and she seemed to be less politically sensitized than the Actio Catolica officials. One reason for their cautious behaviour may have been that one of the leading figures of the Hungarian Actio Catolica, Zsigmond Mihalovics, had been accused of promulgating nationalist and anti-Russian propaganda during the war.[10] Mihalovics, director of the newspaper *Katolikus Actió*, was responsible for an article published in August 1942 under the title 'In the Paths of the Holy King', containing the following lines:

> The commander of the Hungarian troops sent to Ukraine gave an order to erect the apostolic cross at every important street and at every village, everywhere, where triumph leads the Hungarian troops. These crosses should be the holy symbol of the Russian and Hungarian resurrection! Let us march in the path of the Holy King Stephen, as the bulwark of Christianity![11]

This demonstrates that it was not by accident that the Soviets had followed the events surrounding the national holiday in 1945. The Soviets had their reasons for harbouring a different opinion of the Catholic Church than the US soldiers. They

---

9   Ilona Mona, *Slachta Margit*, Budapest, 1997.
10 In 1948 he was sentenced to prison for 'war crimes' in a political trial, see Budapest Fővárosi Levéltára (City Archive of Budapest, hereafter BFL), Népbiróság, VII./5./e, Mihalovics Zsigmond, 3073/48. See also *Keresztény Magyar Közéleti Almanach*, 2 vols, Budapest, 1940, II, p. 699; Gyula Borbándi, *Magyar politikai pályaképek 1938–48*, Budapest 1997, pp. 297f.; and Ferenc Seres, *Mihalovics Zsigmond élete és művei*, Pilisszentlélek, 1993.
11 Ibid., pp. 6f.

regarded the Church as a political rather than a religious institution, an old enemy: the 'clerical reaction'. They particularly distrusted manifestations of the Catholic Church organized with the help of the United States. The same was true of the Hungarian Communist Party, the closest ally the Soviets had in the country. Rákosi, the Muscovite leader of the Communists who later became Hungary's Stalinist dictator, complained about the Americans not bringing back other valuables the Hungarian fascists had brought to Germany: 'They actually only gave back the Right [hand] of St Stephen, and this only for agitational goals.'[12]

Whether the US officials did indeed return the relic for propagandistic goals or not, what is more interesting is the fact that the Communists and the Soviets believed this to have been their intention. It is a fact that the most important non-Communist party, the Smallholders, to which the Foreign Minister also belonged, did profit from representing themselves (like the Catholic Church) as the 'heirs' of the holy King and thus of the whole 'millennial national tradition'. The semantic field of national history became a battlefield in the run-up to the first elections in November 1945, and the Smallholders seemed to have placed their ideological troops at a strategically important point on field: the procession of the Holy Right. The vice-mayor of Budapest in 1945, József Kővágó, a Smallholders politician, remembered the event forty years later and stressed its significance:

> I would like to say that the procession of St Stephen's Day was the real overture to the election campaign. We succeeded in this with American help, because they returned the Holy Right immediately before 20 August. When the relic arrived, the Soviet army of occupation finally gave permission to celebrate the procession. It was a wonderful feeling when we gathered there along with the miraculous relic. The people sensed that there was a God, that we were Hungarians, and that something good would happen to us. I saw Soviet soldiers of occupation at the procession who knelt down and made the sign of the cross. Perhaps they remembered the beautiful icons of their grandfathers when doing this. The fact that nearly the entire committee of the Smallholders' Party attended the procession of St

---

12 Mátyás Rákosi, *Visszaemlékezések 1940–1956*, ed. Feitl István et al., Budapest, 2 vols, 1997, I, p. 261.

Stephen produced a great effect, and this was the real beginning. The first meeting of the committee took place on the same day.[13]

Historians have to treat such memories very carefully, since they tend to simplify the complexity of the past and relate it in a very personal way. What we can learn from them, however, is that the main actors seemed to have consciously politicized the event. But this does not mean that they simply manipulated it without believing that they really represented the 'nation' and were defending her 'one-thousand-year-old' tradition.[14] Before I analyse the complex history of St Stephen's Day in the years between 1945 and 1948, I shall first go back to its history prior to the Second World War, working out the different meanings attributed to the relic, the procession and the national holiday.

The Background to the Conflict: The Cult of St Stephen in Hungary from its Origins to the End of the Second World War[15]

The cult of the first Hungarian King goes back to the eleventh century, a period of extreme political tension.[16] Religion played a major role in these conflicts, in part because Stephen and his successors had tried to strengthen their power with the help of the Church, using it as a source of legitimacy and as a framework for a modern administration.[17] The former nomadic structures were replaced by feudal institutions. After the death of King Stephen, who became king by appointment of Pope Sylvester in the year 1000, the conflicts between rival groups intensified.

---

13 Cited in Ferenc Virágh (ed.), *Balogh András [...] az Eckhardt Politikai Akadémián*, Budapest, 1995 (= A FKgP Tudománypolitikai Intézetének Kiadványa, 18), pp. 59–60. See also Ferenc Virágh, *A Kisgazdapárt rövid története (párttörténeti vázlat)*, Budapest, 1996, p. 47.

14 The complex relationship between nationalist language, ideology and interests is clearly decribed in Katherine Verdery, *National Ideology under Socialism: Identity and Cultural Politics in Ceausescu's Romania*, Berkeley, CA, 1992.

15 This section is a revised version of Árpád v. Klimó, 'St Stephen's Day: Politics and Religion in 20th Century Hungary', *East Central Europa/Europa Centrale Est*, 26. 1999, 2 (Fall).

16 A recent publication (with a reasonable bibliography) on the topic is Zoltán Magyar, *Szent István a magyar kultúrtörténetben*, Budapest, 1996.

17 Gábor Klaniczay, *The Uses of Supernatural Power: The Transformation of Popular Religion in Medieval and Early-Modern Europe*, Cambridge, 1990, pp. 79–81.

One of his successors, King László, substantiated his claim to the kingdom by the canonization of the house of Árpád. In this canonization programme Stephen, Bishop Gellért, his son Imre and two eremites were included. It took place in Székesfehérvár in the year 1083. The grave of Stephen, who had died in 1038, was opened on 20 August. According to the legend, the exhumed King's corpse was 'spreading a delicious odour of balms'.[18] This element of the legend aims to prove that the dead body of a saint, unlike a normal impure corpse, is as a perfect or ideal body not subject to ephemerality. The same is true for the right hand of the King, which was found after the ceremony and immediately became an object of veneration. The right hand, according to the *Reallexikon für Antike und Christentum*, 'represents the whole person, it is the physical manifestation of the spiritual intentions of the person'.[19] In his study of the 'pre-eminence of the right hand' written in 1909, the French sociologist Robert Hertz stated that the right hand belongs to the holy, pure part which, together with the evil, impure part, forms the universe of religious belief.[20] The right hand, according to Hertz, is not only a symbol of power and justice, but also of holiness. These qualities enabled the right hand of the state-building King to become a major source of political legitimacy in his country.

At the time, the elevation of a royal house was a common phenomenon in East-Central Europe. In the twelfth century the cult of St Stephen was transformed by new elements which changed its quality and function. This transformation could be described as the feminization of the cult; the same process was taking place all over Europe in the twelfth and thirteenth centuries. Some female members of the royal family, including Princess Margaret (St Margit), became canonized during this period, thus creating a royal holy family. But what is more important for our purpose is the way the legend of Stephen was adapted. On his deathbed the King offered St Mary the patronage of the whole country. This act assured the continuity of the institutions Stephen represented. At the same time Mary, as a female figure and a symbol for motherhood and female suffering, could together

---

18 Ibid., p. 87.
19 *Reallexikon für Antike und Christentum*, 13, 1986, p. 403.
20 Rodney Needham (ed.), *Right&Left: Essays on Dual Symbolic Classification*, Chicago, IL and London 1973.

with St Stephen be used as an identification screen for both sexes. Her involvement moderated the image of the cruel and pious King and offered the possibility of symbolizing the sexual division of religious labour.[21] This can also be observed in the modern iconography of the St Stephen cult, which often combines the Holy Right together with the holy body of St Mary.

During medieval times St Stephen's Day had been a day of royal justice. On 20 August every year the King assembled the body of the Hungarian aristocracy and held his annual justice day, arbitrating between nobles, the clergy and peasants. The Holy Right of St Stephen, simultaneously a symbol of power and justice, was the perfect symbol for this occasion. This tradition came to an end with the Turkish invasion of Hungary after the siege of Mohács in 1526. During the Turkish occupation Hungary became a centre of Protestantism.[22] This marked a dangerous threat to the cult of the relic, because both Calvin and Luther rejected the veneration of relics as a dangerous superstition interfering with the true creed. They emphasized the scholastic difference between *veneratio* of saints, which was seen as sanctioned practice, and *adoratio*, a practice only allowed with reference to God, thus transforming the pre-existing rule into a dogma, although believers often did not respect or comprehend this subtle differentiation. In practice, the veneration of saints and their relics became associated with Catholicism, whereas Protestant denominations intellectualized the concept of sainthood, to all intents and purposes purging their religion of (traditional) relics.[23] During this period, the Catholic Church also reconsidered the role of cults, adopting stricter controls over their use in ceremony. The final session of the Council of Trent (1563) laid down new principles in the *Decretum de invocatione, veneratione et reliquis Sanctorum et sacris imagibus*, insisting 'that the bodies of the Saints had been living

---

21 John Davis, 'The Sexual Division of (Religious) Labour in the Mediterranean' in Eric R. Wolf (ed.), *Religion, Power and Protest in Local Communities: The Northern Shore of the Mediterranean*, Berlin, 1984, pp. 17–50; see also Caroline Walker Bynum, et al. (eds), *Gender and Religion: On the Complexity of Symbols*, Boston, MA, 1986.
22 See Imre Revesz, *History of the Hungarian Reformed Church*, Washington, DC, 1956.
23 But they created new ones, like the images of the Protestant founders or the Bible.

members of Christ and temples of the Holy Spirit and will one day be resurrected to eternal life'.[24]

With the Habsburg reconqest of Hungary, at the end of the seventeenth century, Catholicism returned to the country. The Holy Right, which centuries earlier had been transferred to a monastery at Dubrovnik, was brought back to Hungary by order of Empress Maria Theresia in 1771. This action served different purposes: it strengthened baroque pious cults in the re-Catholicized country, and it legitimized Maria Theresia as Queen of Hungary and — analogous to St Mary — the protectress of St Stephen and his right hand. However, Maria Theresia's was only one claim to the legacy of St Stephen. Given the opposition of a substantial portion of the nobility to Habsburg rule and the religious division of Hungary into Catholic and Protestant camps, alternative uses of the symbols of Hungary's heritage were bound to emerge. This was precisely what happened; groups began to interpret St Stephen as a symbol of Hungary's splendid past and independence that could be used against the Habsburgs. The revolution of 1848–49 marked the culmination of this movement. After 1849, Austria's military government even suppressed the 20 August procession of the Holy Right, which had been introduced by Palatine Joseph in 1819.[25]

During the *Kulturkampf*, at the end of the nineteenth century, the Church, now in conflict with the national-liberal Hungarian government, tried to mobilize its believers against plans for the separation of Church and state. The Catholic Church had to find its place in a pluralistic society in which it could not, as in previous centuries, rely on state intervention. In a certain way the Church modernized itself during this defensive struggle, because it was forced to use modern means of political action. This was achieved by the mobilization of thousands of believers in lay organizations. Ultramontanism, a new cult of the Pope, was directed against liberalism and nationalism. This also led to the reinvention of traditional cults. St Stephen's procession thus gained increased

---

24 Karl Hausberger, 'III.-VII. Christliche Heiligenverehrung' in Gerhard Müller (ed.), *Theologische Realenzyklopaedie*, vol. 14, Berlin and New York, 1985, pp. 641–72 (p. 663).

25 Gábor Gyula, *A Szent István-napi ünnep története. Dr. Ripka Ferenc előszavával*, Budapest, 1927, p. 33.

notoriety due to the political climate and to Hungary's modernization. Catholics now came from outside of Buda, including growing numbers of peasants.

After the First World War, as well as having lost the war itself, Hungary had also lost two-thirds of its pre-war territory. Attempts to introduce a liberal parliamentary system failed, as did the experiment of a Bolshevik revolution. The French and other allied forces controlling the region would not tolerate either system. Eventually they backed the counter-revolutionary system under Admiral Horthy, a Protestant landowner loyal to the Habsburgs. The new political system of the Horthy regime constituted a mixture of Hungary's nineteenth-century liberal and aristocratic political system with elements of a modern charismatic dictatorship. It tried to suppress both the underground Communist Party and (to a lesser extent) the extreme right-wing parties which gained in strength during the 1930s. Horthy's foreign policy had just one goal: the restoration of the borders of the old kingdom by means of a revision of the Treaty of Trianon. This revisionist policy led to a dangerous and in the end catastrophic alliance with Germany. Against this background the figure of St Stephen became the symbol of the new, so-called 'Christian-national', course. This official ideology of the Horthy regime contained as one of its main elements the reconstruction of Greater Hungary, the so-called 'Szent István országa'. As evidence for the historical imperative behind this goal, the Horthy regime offered a new reading of the St Stephen myth, which stressed the 'Christian', that is the anti-Bolshevik, anti-Jewish, anti-liberal 'nature' of Hungary's past.

In 1938, 900 years after the King's death, the state and the Catholic Church organized hundreds of celebrations and major events in memory of St Stephen, whereas the Protestant Churches were only willing to celebrate 'King Stephen', not the Catholic saint and his relic.[26] In that year the King's right hand was exhibited all over the country, transported in a golden carriage. The organizers thereby wanted to stress the nation's will to reaffirm its unity after the lost war. The tiny old relic symbolized the eternal glory of the King as the founder of the

---

26 The critique of representatives of the Calvinist Church in Hungary, the second largest Church, representing a quarter of all Christian believers in the country, is treated in Árpád v. Klimó, 'Die gespaltene Vergangenheit. Die großen christlichen Kirchen im Kampf um die Nationalgeschichte Ungarns 1920–48', *Zeitschrift für Geschichtswissenschaft*, 47, 1999, 11.

state. The celebrations of St Stephen Year, in 1938, were combined with the Eucharistic World Congress in Budapest, organized by the Roman Catholic Church. This international assembly of the universal Church can be interpreted as an attempt to defend the restorative Horthy regime and Hungarian independence against the threats of social unrest and particularly of fascism, which in this period was already gaining ground all over Central and Southern Europe. On this occasion the Holy Right symbolized the independent Hungarian state based on its 'Christian' heritage. But the revisionist policy, which was continued, led to another lost war, the destruction of the country and the death of approximately one million people.

The Conflict: St Stephen's Day between 1945 and 1948.

In the months immediately after the war, all political parties and social institutions tried their best to subdue the aggressive propagation of their ideological stances. The higher Catholic clergy and the Communist Party leaders, who deeply distrusted each other, exhibited cautious behaviour on St Stephen's Day in 1945. The triumph of the Smallholders' Party at the elections in November and the appointment of Bishop József Mindszenty, an ardent anti-Communist, as Prince-Primate, changed the atmosphere and the tactics of the Communist leaders. They tried different ways of gaining legitimacy and fighting the enemies of a Communist take-over. One way was the appropriation of figures from the pantheon of Hungarian history and of Hungary's 'national' traditions, particularly its revolutionary legacies. The Hungarian Communists could trace the roots of this policy to the summer of 1936, when the coalition of the anti-fascist 'People's Front' gained the support of the VII Congress of the Communist International.[27] In 1944, Hungarian Communists had changed the name of the party, from 'Party of the Communists of the Country of Hungary' (Kommunisták magyarországi párt), which encompassed non-ethnic Hungarian citizens, to the ethnically 'purer' name 'Hungarian Communist Party' (Magyar kommunista párt), marking a shift from an internationalist to a more nationalist standpoint. This shift can also be

---

27 Hazafias Népfront Országos Tanácsa (ed.), *A Magyar Népfront története dokumentumok, 1935–76*, Budapest, 1977, p. 7.

observed in Italy and Germany, where the Communist parties similarly suffered from having been excluded from politics and labelled by the former regimes as 'national enemies'. Particularly after 1945, Communist parties tried to prove in fact that they were the only true representatives of the nation, a title they claimed fascists had usurped.

For example, in the first issue of the newly founded scientific journal of the Communist Party, *Társadalmi Szemle* (Social Review), Rákosi declared:

> The one-thousand-year-old history of the Hungarian nation shows that the Hungarian people has always been strong and honoured when it is in the vanguard of universal human progress. Therefore we should regard with good reason as our forerunners and relatives all those, from St Stephen, Rákóczi and Kossuth to the freshly buried martyrs, who like us fought simultaneously for the common cause of Hungariandom and humanity.[28]

Apart from genealogical appropriation[29] they also re-invented for their own propaganda existing folk traditions, another strategy they adopted from Stalin. To challenge the St Stephen's Day procession, the Communists created the 'Peasants' Day' festivals on 20 August. The Peasants' Days, which in fact lasted from 18 to 21 August to compete directly with St Stephen's Day, were related to the national- and class-liberation ideology of the anti-fascist coalition parties. The Communists utilized 'old Hungarian village traditions' such as folk songs and folk costumes. Additionally, instead of St Stephen's Day or Peasants' Day they would sometimes also speak of the 'Day of the New Bread', exploiting older village customs, particularly such as prevailed in the eastern, Protestant, parts of the country. In the years after 1945, the electoral success of the Smallholders' Party in the countryside enabled the wider implementation of this strategy. Another reason why the Communists focused their propaganda on the peasants was connected with the failure of the Soviet Republic in 1919. Hungary's first Communist revolution had failed to win the support of the peasants and remained a movement relatively restricted to the capital. In the immediate post-war years, the main party celebration took place in Kecskemét, a small town south-east of Budapest, where Rákosi gave a speech stressing that the Communists were the liberators of the nation, and that they regarded the peasants as a social class equally important as

---

28 Mátyás Rákosi, 'Feladataink az elmélet terén', *Társadalmi Szemle*, 1, 1946, 1, pp. 1–5.
29 I use the term as defined by Verdery, *National Ideology under Socialism*, pp. 138, 165.

the working class. He pointed to the land reform, carried out in spring 1945, to prove his assertion. After his speech the party secretary would usually kiss a child and receive the 'new bread' from a young girl, both dressed in a Hungarian folk costume — gestures that symbolized the emotional relationship between the leader and 'the people' and the recognition of 'his' efforts to care for a successful harvest. Before 1945 it had usually been the noble landowner who received the new bread on Stephen's Day. All over the country, the celebrations were planned in detail. As we can see from the documents of the 1946 Peasants' Day campaign, the Communist Party was still interested in creating a harmonious atmosphere, seeking co-operation with local representatives of other coalition parties as well as of local élites such as priests, doctors and teachers.[30] The script of the festivals went as follows: assemblies in the morning, public festivals in the afternoon. The cultural programme had to include folk songs and local songs, as well as songs about St Stephen. The propaganda department also stressed: 'It is possible that local processions or parades will be held. *Collisions of both programmes have to be prevented at any rate, in order that we cannot be blamed for anti-religious behaviour.*'[31]

A third way of altering the meaning of St Stephen's Day was the organization of popular performances, such as sporting events and 'high' cultural festivals. To accomplish this the Communists took over the organization of the non-religious aspects of the national holiday which had been introduced near the turn of the century. Sport was regarded by the Communists as an easy way to win access to large sectors of society. Mihály Farkas, a leading party official whose responsibilities included propaganda and sport, wrote that on 19–20 August the party organization units should try to promote sports events in every city, village and factory.[32] This reflects the Communists' idea of a total inclusion of the whole of society, especially the young. These Communist sporting events, as the writings

---

30 Politikatörténeti Intézet Levéltár (Archive of the Political History Institute, former Party Institute, hereafter PIL), Magyar Kommunista Párt, Központi vezetősége iratai, Propaganda Osztály, (274f./21cs.), 274f./21.cs./62.

31 Ibid., my emphasis.

32 PIL, Magyar Kommunista Párt, Központi vezetősége iratai, Sport Osztály, (274f./17cs.), 23, Paper 23, Letter of the National Sport department to all organizations of the HCP, 25 July 1945.

on youth policy emphasized, were focused on 'unity', symbolically represented in the processions of the clubs and teams during opening ceremonies. Another important aspect of sport was obviously the prospect it offered to take up an old proletarian tradition and extend it to the rest of society. During their speeches the Communist sport functionaries also stressed the liberating aspect of the new era and they argued that aristocratic sports like tennis and skiing should also be accessible to the working classes.

By trying to fill St Stephen's Day with new meanings and practices, the Communists went along with the National Peasants' Party, the Social Democrats and the left wing of the Smallholders. But they were always aware of Catholic competition, which was, as we have seen, successful in mobilizing large parts of society. The success of the 1945 procession and the election of the Smallholders by such a large majority shocked the left into taking legal — and illegal — measures to stunt this development. In the summer of 1946 the police dissolved nearly all Catholic lay organizations after they had been stigmatized as 'reactionary', 'fascist' or 'anti-democratic'. In a secret meeting on 16 August the same year, Rákosi agreed with Bán, the leader of the Social Democratic Party, that 'the St Stephen procession should not be allowed to be held outside of the inner city districts surrounding the St Stephen basilica'.[33] This seemingly innocuous decision set in motion a chain of events which within two years resulted in the effective elimination of the procession.

At the beginning of 1947, the Communists and their allies stepped up their campaign against the Catholic Church. In the field of public education, the Church still maintained a significant presence, a presence the left believed to be reactionary. The secularization of public education was a measure which in other countries, such as France and Italy, had largely been accomplished in the nineteenth century. From this perspective the Hungarian coalition parties argued persuasively that they simply aimed to 'modernize' the country. The religious

---

33 PTI 283/10/180, 16 August 1946: Sociáldem. Párt Főtitkarság: Összekötő Bizottság jegyzőkönyve (Meeting of the joined committee of the MKP and the Socialdemocratic Party), 4./Szent István körmenet, 'Az Összekötő Bizottság megállapodik abban, hogy a körmenet csak a belvárosban lehet utvonalat engedéyezni, a főutak kizárásával...' Rákosi, Bán.

higher schools, until 1947 representing about 40 per cent of all higher schools, had already been dependent on state subsidies, since large land-owning Churches had lost much of their property as a result of the 1945 land reform.[34] In the beginning of 1947, left-wing Smallholders proposed a law that would have made religion a non-compulsory school subject. The two largest Christian Churches, the Catholics and the Calvinists, began a campaign to mobilize hundreds of thousands of parents to protest against this proposal. This was the only time both Churches successfully co-operated in a political question. The government initiative was withdrawn. The overwhelming success of the campaign underlined the influence the Churches still had in Hungarian society.

The political polarization caused by the Communist campaign against 'inner enemies', 'reactionaries' and 'national traitors' had an important impact on the celebrations of 20 August 1947, a few weeks before the second parliamentary elections. Primate Cardinal Mindszenty had begun to mobilize Catholic believers to defend Catholic institutions. To this end he called for a year of celebrations dedicated to St Mary as patroness of Hungary. The procession on St Stephen's Day of 1947 was intended as the first big event of this festive year. Because of the St Mary's Year celebrations, the Actio Catolica won an exceptional permit from the Budapest police to hold the procession on Andrássy Boulevard and on Heroes' Square, one of the main stages for national celebrations. Never before had so many people taken part in the procession. The organizers spoke of half a million participants. The final celebration took place at Heroes' Square, emphasizing the national significance of the event. A huge crest of arms was raised in the middle of the square. St Mary was depicted as Patroness of Hungary, wearing the Holy Crown of Hungary on her head, while a burning cross at her back represented the fighting Church. This constituted the official coat of arms of St Mary's Year

---

34 Under Regent Horthy the Churches succeeded in enlarging not only their political influence, as important propagators of the 'National-Christian ideology', but also their property: see Mihály Bucsay, *Geschichte des Protestantismus in Ungarn*, Stuttgart, 1959, p. 198. Bucsay was a Lutheran Bishop who had studied theology in Germany during the 1930s. He and the Hungarian Lutheran Church as a whole fell after 1945 under the charge of 'fascism' because of their ties to Germany. Therefore they were the most willing to collaborate with the Stalinist state.

1947–48. In his sermon, the cardinal stressed the significance of St Stephen for Hungarian history:

> St Stephen is the best symbol of our one-thousand-year-old past. From him our nation received the greatest and eternal values: the holy mother Church, the veneration of St Mary and Christian education. Let us proudly protect the tradition of St Stephen in the family and in society, so that it will help us to resurrect the dying Hungary to new life.[35]

Mindszenty thus emphasized the 'eternal' and 'millennial' core of the Hungarian 'Christian' past as a source of inspiration for the present. The Cardinal used metaphors based on the human body ('dying Hungary') in order to describe the nation and its historical situation. Mindszenty reiterated what the Church had proclaimed in the St Stephen's Year of 1938, that the patron saint symbolized the independence of the country based on its Christian past.

The national holiday procession was surely the most successful anti-Communist demonstration since 1945. It may have been one cause of the relatively weak performance of the Communists in the elections some weeks later. The Communists, who used the police force against political enemies, manipulated voting lists and even stuffed ballot boxes, became the strongest party by gaining slightly more than 22 per cent of the votes. The coalition parties, however, with a split Smallholders Party reduced to a third of the votes it received in 1945, won the majority. The path towards a Stalinist dictatorship was now set. The anti-clerical campaign, culminating in show-trials against Mindszenty (1949) and Bishop of Kalocsa Károly Grősz (1951), led to the imprisonment of hundreds of priests, nuns and Catholic activists. Only for a short period between Stalin's death and 1956 and again after the 1960's did the policy of the ruling party towards the Catholic Church become more conciliatory.

In the years after 1947, when the open conflict with the Catholic Church escalated, 20 August increasingly fell under Communist control. In 1948 the authorities did their best to prevent another demonstration of the strength of the Catholic Church. When the Actio Catolica again applied for approval to hold the procession on Andrássy Boulevard, they were refused. The chief of the Budapest police force, a high-ranking Communist Party member, declared that this year the

---

35   EPL, 5583/1947, p. 3.

'festival of the New Bread' would take place in the central districts of the capital.[36] Shortly after that, the Police Chief even withdrew permission to organize a procession in the streets around the basilica. The Actio Catolica then decided to cancel the procession and organized a celebration inside the Church. Thereafter authorities denied access to the public space of Budapest for almost every celebration not organized by the Communist Party and its sister organizations. Only in 1988, when the legitimacy of the ruling party was already in jeopardy, could the St Stephen procession once more be celebrated in the streets of the capital.[37]

Unwilling to take any chances, the Communists found yet another means of altering the symbols and interpretations of St Stephen's Day. In 1949 the parliament adopted the new Constitution of the 'People's Republic of Hungary', to come into force on 20 August. With this act the Stalinist dictatorship effectively tried to extend its legitimacy over the whole '1,000 years' of Hungarian state history. The former St Stephen's Day was transformed into a national holiday, during which the Constitution, the 'New Bread' and King Stephen were simultaneously celebrated. This changed the character and meaning of 20 August, radically excluding all religious elements and emphasizing instead the state, the nation and the ruling party.

Conclusions

It is clear that both the Catholic and the Communist élites tried to embed their institutions into the reading of Hungarian national history. By portraying themselves as 'traditionalists', in other words by stressing the anachronistic aspects of historical myths, both the Catholic and Communist camps interpreted Hungarian history as linear and inevitably supporting their own viewpoint. Within the Catholic narrative, St Stephen was posited as the original figure of Hungarian history, as its starting-point and eternal symbol and its symbol of national independence. The Communists tried to establish a new national-liberation narrative of Hungarian history which was based on the mythical historical agent

---

36 MOL, M-KS-276-67/214, 17.
37 See Hann, 'Socialism and King Stephen's Right Hand'.

they called 'the people'. This second narrative transcended that of the Catholics, subsuming the anti-Habsburg and Protestant versions of Hungarian history as well as Stalinist nationalism. In this way the Communists could legitimize their own authority and de-legitimize the Catholic Church élites by questioning their loyalty to the Hungarian state and nation. However, aligning themselves with this national-liberation view of Hungarian history proved to be a double-edged sword, since it was easily appropriated by anti-Stalinists within the party and later by the participants in the uprising of 1956. Since Russia had been the power which helped to suppress the independence struggle of 1849, the historical precedence of Russia as occupier was already firmly installed in Hungary's collective memory when Soviet tanks suppressed the anti-Stalinist movement of 1956.[38]

The religious aspect of the St Stephen's Day holiday was especially important in the period after the war, when people were particularly receptive to religion after their long struggle for survival. The religious cult of the saints, offering as it did the hope of salvation to the believer, was particularly potent at this time. The Communists combated this problem on several different levels. First, they attempted to construct a myth of heroic Hungarian anti-fascism, a cult shared by all other countries liberated by the Red Army. It was no accident that the Red Army itself organized no fewer than three heroes' funerals in Budapest on 20 August 1945.[39] Again this demonstrates how the Communists, rather than totally abandoning religious traditions, appropriated them for their own ends. The second approach, which I have already mentioned, was the creation of National Peasants' Day, the celebration of the New Bread, which thrived on elements of traditional rural belief in the annual cycle of death followed by new life. And thirdly, the National Sports Day, related to the modern, secular, cult of the body. All these celebrations appeared to replace the religious meaning of the St Stephen day with alternative modern and ancient cults playing on the mortality of the individual.

All these different forms of celebrating St Stephen's Day shared the aim of representing the nation as a collective. The Catholics emphasized the integration

---

[38] Árpád v. Klimó, '1848/49 in der politischen Kultur Ungarns' in Helgard Fröhlich; Margarete Grandner and Michael Weinzierl (eds), *1848 im europäischen Kontext*, Vienna, 1999, pp. 204–22.

[39] See orders of the day of the Budapest police in the BFL.

of the country into the occidental cultural sphere, the *Abendland*, based on Latin Christianity. This represented one of the most difficult obstacles for the Communists, who had to justify the integration of Hungary into the Eastern Bloc. The Protestant, anti-Habsburg traditions, which they had used as a weapon against the Catholic Church, seem to have been too weak and too unpopular to win cultural hegemony over the country. While the Communists succeeded in preventing the Catholic Church from speaking for the whole nation, their strategies proved to be less integrative, more destructive and divisive.

INDEX

Aachen, 84, 89, 274
Abaúj, 208
Adrian, Patriarch, 151, 152, 154
Alba Iulia (Gyulafehérvár), 204
Albrecht V (Duke of Bavaria,
  r. 1550–79), 34
Aleksei Mikhailovich (Tsar,
  r. 1645–76), 151
Aleksei, Metropolitan of Moscow, 151
Alexander Monastery, 161, 163
Alexander Nevskii, St, 158, 161
Alexis (Tsarevich, son of Peter I), 157
Alpar, I., 203
Alsace, 109
Alsó-Fehér, 208
Altötting, 45, 62, 63, 133
Amberg, 41–42, 46, 48n, 51, 54, 56
America see USA
Amsterdam, 58, 62
Amt Rosenberg, 329
Anna (daughter of Peter I), 157
Anna Amalia (Duchess of Saxony-
  Weimar, Regent 1758–75), 173
Anne, Duc de Joyeuse, 234
Anton Ulrich (Duke of Brunswick,
  r. 1671–1714), 173, 175, 176
Antwerp, 58
Apraksin, F., Admiral, 159
Arad, 199
Arcimboldo, G., 126, 237
Army Bill (Germany, 1913), 13, 273, 277, 278
Arndt, E. M., 98, 101, 268, 275, 276n
Árpád, xii, 10, 187–204 *passim*, 350
Augsburg, 36–37, 55, 58, 61, 63–69
August Augusta (wife of Carl Wilhelm
  Ferdinand of Brunswick), 173, 174
August II see Friedrich August I
August III see Friedrich August II
Augustus, Duke of Brunswick
  (r. 1636–66), 176

Austria, xiii, 10, 12, 41, 123–35
  passim, 202, 208, 213–30 *passim*,
  345, 352
Austrian People's Party,
  224–26 *passim*
Austro-Hungarian Compromise
  (*Ausgleich*, 1867), 189, 200, 201, 206
Aventinus (Turmair, Bavarian court
  historian, 1477–1534), 33
Azov, 160

Bacon, F., 49, 50
Baden, 90, 103, 177
Baïf, A. de, 234
Balkan wars (1912–13), 273
Bamberg, 54
Bán, A., 357
Bánffy, Baron D., 208
Barbara Sophia of Brandenburg, 239
Bar-le-Duc, 140
Bastille Day, 252, 256n, 257n, 259, 262, 281
Battle of the Nations see Leipzig,
  Battle of (1813)
Baudrillart, H., 263
Bavaria, x, 5, 6, 12, 31–56 *passim*, 63,
  69, 70, 133, 248, 249; Bavarian
  Palatinate, 90; see also Upper
  Palatinate
Beaune, 112
Becher, J., 326
Béla III, 199
Belgium, 94; see also Netherlands
Belleau, R. (French poet, 1518–77),
  140–41, 148
Berlin, 12, 86, 97, 177, 249, 262,
  271, 281–300 *passim*, 304, 308,
  316, 340
Birken, S. von, 60
Blanchard, F., 179–80

Index

Bohemia, 63, 124, 129
Bolland, J. (Jesuit historiographer, 1569–1665), 36
Bolsheviks, 8, 10, 14
Bonn, 5, 84, 86, 87,
Bosio, A., 41
Bosnia, 205–06, 208
Böß, G. (Mayor of Berlin), 292
Boulanger, G. (French General, 1837–91), 262
Bourbon, Catherine de (wife of Henri, duc de Bar, sister of Henri IV of France), 141, 143, 146; *see also* Louis de Bourbon
Brandenburg Gate, 316
Bratislava *see* Pozsony
Braşov (Brassó, Kronstadt), 159, 192
Brecht, B., 99
Breslau (Wrocław) 93, 237
Britain, 169, 179, 197, 236, 273
Bruch, M. (composer), 309
Brüning, H. (German chancellor 1930–32), 286, 296
Brunswick, 9, 169–86 *passim*; *see also* Wolfenbüttel
Bruyn, C. de (Dutch painter), 155
Büchner, G. (German poet and dramatist), 171
Budapest, 9–10, 187–201 *passim*, 344–61 *passim*
Bulgaria, Bulgarians, 197
Burgundy, 5–6, 17–30 *passim*, 107–19 *passim*, 129, 142n
Buzhinskii, G., 160
Byzantium, 152

Calendar, Julian ('Old Style'), 153, 162, 163
Callot, J., 147
Calvin, J., 351
Campe, J. H. (journalist), 180–82, 185
Camphausen, L. (German liberal politician), 92
Carl Friedrich (Margrave of Baden), 177
Carl Georg August (Prince of Brunswick, son of Carl Wilhelm Ferdinand), 169, 170, 171
Carl I (Duke of Brunswick, 1735–80), 173, 176, 177, 185
Carl Wilhelm Ferdinand (Duke of Brunswick, son of Carl I), 169–86 *passim*
Carlsbad Decrees (1819), 74, 79, 270
catacomb saints, 32, 40–41, 52
Catherine I (Tsarina, r. 1725–27), 155, 157, 158, 163
Catherine de' Medici (wife of Henri II of France, Regent 1560–74), x, 139, 140
Catholic League (1609), 18, 28
Centre Party (Germany), 286, 296, 299
Châlon-sur-Saône, 112, 113
Champlitte, 109
Charles III (of Lorraine, r. 1563–1608), 138–48 *passim*
Charles V (Holy Roman Emperor, r. 1519–56), 64, 134
Charles VI (Holy Roman Emperor, r. 1711–40), 131
Charles IX (of France, r. 1564–74), 140
Château du Clos-de-Vougeot, 110
Cistercian order, 44, 45
Claude de France, 139, 146
Coblenz (Koblenz), 84, 86, 100
Coburg, 58, 60, 63–69 *passim*,
Cologne, 5, 75, 82–84, 88, 91, 93, 96–98, 100, 220, 268
Compiègne, 244
Constantine (the Great), 149n, 156
Corpus Christi festivals, 31–34, 46, 47–49, 66, 96, 133,–34
Côte d'Or, 109–12 *passim*
Croatia, 193–94, 208
Cumania, 208
Curio, J. C. D., 171n, 179, 180, 183

Index

D'Ester, C., 97
Dalmatia, 208
Danube, river, 189, 191, 209, 224
Darré, W. (Reich Food Minister), 330
DDP (German Democratic Party), 283
Denmark, 239
Dessau, 239, 242
Devín (Dévény), 192
Dickens, C., 88
Dijon, 18–30 *passim*, 112
Dilich, W. (poet), 241
Dillingen, 46
Dinkelsbühl, 69–71
DNVP (Deutsch-nationale Volkspartei, German National People's Party) 283
Donauwörth, 49, 57n
Donskoi Convent, 151, 158
Dresden, 238, 242, 243, 244
Dubrovnik, 352
Dürer, A., 75
Durkheim, E., 3, 246n, 253, 263
Düsseldorf, 84, 87–88, 89, 96, 102–103, 276

Ebert, F. (German President 1919–25), 284, 285, 309
Edict of Toleration (France, 1562), 24
Edison, T., 206
Eichendorff, J. von (poet), 327
Eichstätt, 37, 39, 40, 46–47
Elias, N., 124, 127, 131–32
Elisabeth Christine (of Brunswick, sister of Carl I), 173
Elizabeth (Empress, wife of Franz Joseph I), 200–02
Elizabeth (wife of Friedrich V of the Palatinate), 237
Elizabeth I (of England), 233
Elizabeth Marie (Archduchess, daughter of Crown Prince Rudolf), 208
Elizabeth of Hessen-Kassel, 237

England, 153, 173, 178
Eschenburg, J. J., 178
Esztergom, 208, 346
Eulenburg, P., 262
Eupen, 83

Fallersleben, H. von (poet), 88, 99
Farkas, M., 356
Faure, F. (French President 1895–99), 255n, 256
FDJ (Free German Youth), 325–26, 331–33, 337–38
Federal Republic of Germany (FRG), 339–40
Fedor (Tsar, r. 1676–82), 151, 153
Feofan Prokopovich, Archbishop, 149, 160–61
Ferdinand I (Austrian Emperor, r. 1835–48, d. 1875), 214
Ferdinand I (Holy Roman Emperor, r. 1558–64), 131
Ferdinand II (Archduke of Tyrol, 1529–95, brother of Maximilian II), 131
Ferdinand III (Holy Roman Emperor, r. 1636–57), 131
Ferdinand Maria (Elector of Bavaria 1651–79), 45, 50
Ferrara, 240
Feszty, Á., 191, 204
Filipp (Metropolitan of Moscow), 152
Firczák, J., 194
First World War, 12, 13, 193, 236, 245, 247, 259, 275n, 278n, 304, 307, 312, 319, 330, 353
Fiume *see* Rijeka
Florence, 146, 245
France, xi, 6, 8, 9, 12–13, 61, 73, 83, 138–48 *passim*, 170, 174, 178, 181, 188, 190, 193, 233–44 *passim*, 245–64 *passim*, 266, 269, 270, 273, 278, 296, 311, 357; *see also* Third Republic

François, Comte de Vaudémont, 140, 141, 146
Franconia, 62, 64
Frankenthal, 60
Frankfurt am Main, 13, 102, 180, 184, 205, 291
Frankfurt an der Oder, 333
Franz I (first Emperor of Austria, r. 1804–35), 214
Franz I (Holy Roman Emperor, husband of Maria Theresia, r. 1745–65), 184
Franz Joseph I (Emperor of Austria, r. 1848–1916), xii, 8, 10, 189–211 *passim*, 214, 229
Freiburg (Fribourg), 172
Freiburg im Breisgau, 63
Freiligrath, F. (poet), 88
Freising, 35, 46
French Revolution, xi, 6, 30, 60, 76, 182, 188, 269
Fribourg *see* Freiburg
Friederike Louise Wilhelmine (of Orange, daughter of William V), 169–71
Friedrich August I (Elector of Saxony, later August II, 'the Strong', King of Poland, r. 1697–1733), 244
Friedrich August II (Electoral Prince of Saxony, later August III, King of Poland, r. 1733–63), 243
Friedrich II (of Prussia, 'the Great'), 173, 177
Friedrich III (Emperor, 1888, as heir Friedrich Wilhelm), 249
Friedrich Wilhelm I, 173
Friedrich Wilhelm III (of Prussia), 86n
Friedrich Wilhelm IV (of Prussia), 96, 98, 101, 220
Fronde, 61
Füssen, 52

Gayl, W. von, 301
Gellért, Bishop, 350
Georg Rudolf of Liegnitz-Brieg, 239
Geramb, V. von (ethnologist), 217, 218, 221, 222, 225, 226
German Confederation (1815), 79, 80, 102
German Democratic Republic (GDR), xiii, 14, 323–42 *passim*
glasnost', 15
Glaßbrenner, A., 99–100
Goebbels, J., 335–36
Goethe, J. W. von, 99
Golden Fleece, Order of the, 35, 214
Golovkin, G., 149
Gonzaga, Margherita, 142, 146
Göppingen, 63
Gordon, P., 162
Grősz, Károly (Archbishop of Kalocsa), 346, 359
Graz, 10, 213, 214, 217–18, 220,
Great Northern War (1700–21), 159, 161
Grimm, J. and W. (brothers Grimm), 217
Grogger, P. (Austrian author), 219
Grün, A., 214
Guise family, 141
Gustavus Adolphus (King of Sweden, r. 1611–32), 70
Gutenberg, J., 75, 91
Gyöngyösi, J. (Hungarian Foreign Minister 1944–47), 345

Habsburg, house of, 10, 123–35 *passim*, 198–99, 204, 211, 215, 219, 352
Hague (The), 169, 180, 290
Halle, 239, 242
Hambach Fest, 75, 79, 93–94, 103–105
Hangut (Hangö), Battle of (1714), 159, 160
Hanover, 155, 176
Hansemann, D., 89

Harsdörffer, G. P., 60
Hausen, W. von (Bishop of Regensburg), 36
Heartfield, J., 330
Hecker, F., 98, 100
Heidelberg, 237, 239, 242
Heine, H., 99
Helmstedt, 170, 183
Henri de Navarre *see* Henri IV
Henri II (Duke of Lorraine, r. 1608–24), 139, 143, 148
Henri II (of France, r. 1547–59), 139, 140, 147, 234
Henri III (of France, r. 1574–89), 234
Henri IV (of France, r. 1589–1610), x, 18, 28–29, 141, 234
Henry the Lion (Duke of Bavaria and Saxony, 1142–80), 184
Herczeg, F. (novelist), 210
Hermannstadt *see* Sibiu
Hertz, R., 350
Hesse (Hessen), 73, 90
Heydt, A. von der, 92
Hindenburg, P. von, 285, 287
Hitler, A., xii, 14, 301, 312–17 *passim*, 323, 332, 333
Hitler putsch, 14, 304, 312–16, 319
Hitler Youth, 317, 330–31, 333
Hofer, A., 10
Hohenzollern (monarchy), 249, 319
Holy Roman Empire, 34, 49, 55, 59, 60–63, 69, 129, 233–39 *passim*
Horthy, N. von, 344, 353, 358n
Huguenots, 24
Hugues IV, Duke of Burgundy, 19
Huizinga, J., 125
Hungary, xii, xiii, 10, 14–15, 124, 129, 132, 187–211 *passim*, 343–62 *passim*; Hungarian Revolution (1848/49), 188, 189, 198, 199

Ioakhim, Patriarch, 151
Iov (Patriarch of Moscow, 1589), 152
Irmengard (Abbess of Freising), 36
Isabella (Queen of Hungary, r. 1519–59), 204
Italy, 129, 131, 197, 239, 243, 313, 355, 357
Ivan III (Tsar, r. 1462–1505), 159
Ivan IV (Tsar, 'the Terrible', r. 1533–84), 161n
Ivan V, (Tsar, r. 1682–89, brother of Peter I), 151, 152n, 153n, 158

Jägerndorf, 239, 242
Jahn, F. L., 268
Ják, 203
Jesuits, 8, 33, 35, 42, 48n, 52, 56, 133, 145–46
Jews, 102, 183, 267, 308, 345, 347
Johann Friedrich of Württemberg, 239
Johann III (Count of Nassau-Siegen, r. 1606–23), 242
Johann Wilhelm of Nassau-Siegen, 236
John (Archduke of Styria, 1782–1859), xiii, 10–12, 213–30 *passim*,
Joinville, 141
Jókai, M., 188
Joseph (Archduke, 1833–1905, son of Joseph Anton, Palatine of Hungary), 197, 205
Joseph Anton (Hungarian Palatine, 1776–1847), 352
Joseph II (Holy Roman Emperor, r. 1765–90), 177
Jungdeutschland-Bund, 259

Kővágó, J., 348
Kantorowicz, E. H., 17, 44, 144
Kapfhammer, F. M., 226
Karl Albrecht (Elector of Bavaria, r. 1726–45), 243
Karl II (Archduke of Inner Austria, 1540–90, son of Emperor Ferdinand I), 131
Karlsruhe, 84, 100

Károlyi, Count T., 208
Kassel, 237, 240, 241
Kecskemét, 355
Kemnath, 6, 31–32, 41–51 *passim*
Khuen-Héderváry, Count, 208
Kiev, 194
Kinkel, G., 89
Klaj, J., 60
Klaus, J. (Governor of Salzburg), 225
Klingenstein, G., 215, 221, 227
Košice (Kassa, Kaschau), 207
Koblenz *see* Coblenz
Königsberg, 90
Königsplatz (in Munich), 312, 316
Korb, J. (imperial secretary, Russia), 153–54
Koren, H., 222–24, 225
Körner, T., 98, 275
Kornfeld, M., 207
Kossuth, L., 198, 355
Kotzbue, A., 74
KPD (German Communist Party), 286, 288, 290, 294–95, 296
Krainer, J., Junior (Governor of Styria), 229, 230
Krainer, J., Senior (Governor of Styria), 222, 224
Kreisky, B. (Austrian Chancellor, 1970–83), 229
Kremlin, 151, 153, 155, 158
Kronstadt *see* Brașov
Kulturbund (German Cultural League), 326–27, 331
Kurakin, Prince Boris, 151

László I (King of Hungary, r. 1077–95), 350
League of Nations, 283
Leipzig, 102, 248n, 257n, 277
Leipzig, Battle of (1813), 7, 13, 265–66, 272, 277
Leo XIII, Pope, 197
Leoben, 221

Leopold II (Holy Roman Emperor, r. 1790–92, and Grand Duke of Tuscany), 10, 180, 215
Leopold, Order of, 214
Lesnaia, Battle of (1708), 159
Lessing, C. F., 103, 174
Lewenhaupt, A. (Swedish general of the Battle of Lesnaia), 159
Liebknecht, K., 294, 323
Lindau, 63
Liszt, F., 200
Lodomeria, 208
Loehneyss, G. E. von, 238
Longchamps racetrack, 251, 262
Lorraine, 8, 137–48 *passim*
Lorraine, Renée of, 237
Louis de Bourbon (Prince of Condé, 1621–86), 61
Louis de Guise (Baron d'Ancerville), 141, 147
Louis Phillipe (King of France, r. 1830–48), 250n
Louis XIII (of France, r. 1610–13), 18, 29, 234
Louis XIV (of France, r. 1661–1715), 18, 29, 61, 62, 138, 234, 244
Luther, M. , 39, 40, 64, 188, 351
Lützen, 70
Luxemburg, R., 323
Lyon, 25

Macke, A., 307n
Madrid, 134
Magdalena of Bavaria, 237
Mainz, 84, 100
Mann, G., 272
Mann, T., 280
Mannheim, 84
Maravall, J. A., 53
Marc, F., 307n
Maria Theresia (Empress of the Holy Roman Empire, r. 1740–80), 351
Mariazell, 133

Index

Marie Antoinette (Queen of France), 172
Marie de' Medici (mother of Louis XIII of France, Regent 1610–17), 29, 143
Marienburg (Castle), 7
Marx, W., 286
Matthias (Holy Roman Emperor, r. 1612–19), 237
Matthias Corvinus (King of Hungary, r. 1458–90), 199
Maurice of Nassau-Orange, 236
Maurice the Learned (of Hessen-Kassel), 241
Maximilian I (Duke [1597–] and Elector [1623–51] of Bavaria), 35, 39, 41, 57n
Maximilian I (Holy Roman Emperor, r. 1493–1519), 129, 130
Maximilian II (Holy Roman Emperor, r. 1564–76), 124, 131
Maximilian II Emanuel (Elector of Bavaria, r. 1597–1651), 50
Mazarin, Cardinal (as Regent for Louis XIV, r. 1643–61), 61
Mecklenburg, duchy of, 35
Medici see Catherine de'; Marie de'
Mehringer, R., 218
Meissen, 34
Meister, O. (historian), 220
Memmingen, 61
Menshikov, A., 158, 159, 162
Metternich, Prince Anton (1773–1859), 215, 216
Metz, 140, 141, 143
Mihalovics, Z., 347
Mikhail (Tsar, r. 1613–45), 153
Mindszenty, Bishop József (also Prince-Primate, Cardinal), 14, 354, 358–59
Mohács, 351
Montauban, 25
Moravia, 63, 192, 193

Moritz of Hessen-Kassel, 237
Moscow, 8, 149–68 passim, 209
Moskva, river, 155
Mosse, G., x, 246, 253
Mühsam, E., 271
Munkács (Mukacheve), 192, 194
Munkácsy, M., 190–91, 204
Münster, 58, 259
Murat Girei (Tatar Khan), 158

Nancy, 8, 139–48 passim
Naples, 239
Napoleon I (of France, Bonaparte, r. 1804–15), 12, 13, 76, 101, 102, 214, 215, 236, 250, 252, 253n, 264, 266, 268, 309
Napoleon III (of France, r. 1851–71), 150n
Nazi party (NSDAP), xii, 10, 11, 14, 219, 221, 225, 226, 227, 282, 288, 289, 290, 298, 300, 303–21 passim, 323–42 passim
Netherlands (as United Provinces), 58, 169, 170
Neva, river, 155
Nicholas II (Tsar, r. 1894–1917), 156
Niederaltaich, Benedictine abbey, 46
Nîmes, 25
Nitra (Nyitra), 192, 196, 208
Nördlingen, 71
Novgorod, 161
Novodevichii Convent, 151, 159
Nuremberg (Nürnberg), 54, 59–60, 62, 64, 70
Nyitra, see Nitra
Nymegen, Peace of (1679), 67
Nystadt, Treaty of (1721), 149, 161, 168

Oberammergau, 32
Oettinger, J., 241
Orange, house of, 59, 169; see also Maurice of Nassau-Orange

Orléans, 25
Osnabrück, 58, 67

Pannonhalma, 192, 193
Papen, F. von, 183, 301
Paris, 61, 62, 63, 172, 188, 190, 234, 250, 257n, 259n, 261, 262
Perczel, D., 207
Périer, Casimir Pierre (French Minister-President 1831–32), 251, 262
Pest *see* Budapest
Peter I (Tsar, 'the Great', r. 1682–1725), xiii, 7, 8–9, 13, 149–68 *passim*
Petr (Metropolitan of Moscow), 152
Philippine Charlotte (daughter of Friedrich Wilhelm I of Prussia), 173
Piccolomini, O. (imperial general, 1599–1656), 60, 62
Pieck, W., 326, 332
Pirchegger, H., 219, 220n
Pistofilo, B., 240
Plochl, A., 219, 221
Pluvinel, A. de, 234
Poland, 11
Polish Uprising (1831), 93, 97, 102, 103, 104
Poltava, Battle of (1709), 159, 160
Potsdam, 249
Pozsony (Bratislava, Pressburg), 207
Prague, 60, 63, 131, 132
Preobrazhenskii guards, 155
Preobrazhenskii Prikaz, 163
Pressburg *see* Pozsony
Prussia, 73–106 *passim*, 169, 173, 177, 247, 248, 249, 251, 270, 284, 286, 295, 300
Puligny-Montrachet, 107–19 *passim*
Pushkin, A. S., 327
Pusztaszer, 192, 193, 199
Pyrenees, Treaty of (1659), 61

Rákóczy, II (Prince Francis [Ferenc] of Transylvania, 1676–1735), 198
Rákosi, J. (Hungarian politician), 200
Rákosi, M. (Hungarian Communist leader, 1892–1971), 348, 355, 357
Rama (Bosnia), 208
Raveaux, F., 88, 89
Redslob, E., 284n, 287, 288–89, 291, 299, 306–11 *passim*, 318
Regensburg, 36, 39, 42, 49, 61
Reichsbanner, 287–301 *passim*
Reichskunstwart, 288, 291, 306–11 *passim*, 318
Reichstag (Diet of the Holy Roman Empire), 57n
Reichstag, 254, 281–300 *passim*, 304, 307–10 *passim*
Remiremont, 141, 142
Renan, E., 250
Reuss, 258
Rhine, river, 93, 276, 285, 296
Rhineland, xiii, 13, 265–80 *passim*, 82–106 *passim*, 296
Riehl, W. H., 218
Rijeka (Fiume), 197
Ritter, G., 263
Rohracher (Archbishop of Salzburg), 345
Romain, N., 140–41, 146, 148
Romania, 189, 193, 194
Romanov, house of, 198
Rome, 40–41, 313
Ronsard, P. de (French poet, 1524–85), 140
Rote Jungfront, 286
Roter Frontkämpferbund, 286
Rothenburg ob der Tauber, 71
Rouen, 25
Rousseau, J.-J., 2–3, 11, 181
Rubens, P. P., 134
Rudolf (Crown Prince of Austria–Hungary, 1858–89), 201

Rudolf I (Habsburg Emperor, r. 1273–91) 134
Rudolf II (Holy Roman Emperor, r. 1576–1612), 131
Ruhr, river, 285, 311
Russia, xiii, 8–9, 13, 149–68 *passim*, 195, 361; Russian Revolution (1917), 324

SA (*Sturmabteilung*), 317, 324, 330
Sack, G. (Staatsrat), 265, 266, 268, 276n
St Benedict, Order of, 36, 45, 46, 49
St Benno (Bishop of Meissen), 34
St Francis, Order of, 31
St Petersburg, 149–64 *passim*
St Ulrich (Bavaria), 36–38
Salzach, river, 45
Salzburg, 225, 345–46
Salzdahlum, 173
Sand, G., 88
Sand, K. L., 73–74, 98
Saumur, 109
Saxe-Coburg, duchy of, 64
Saxony, 58, 60–64, 197, 243, 244, 284
Scandinavia, 239
Scheler, M., 307
Schenkendorf, M. von, 98
Schiller, F. von, 75
Schinkel, K. F., 70
Schlüsselburg, 160
Schoenfeld, A., 344
Schönbach, A. E., 218
SED (Socialist Unity Party, GDR), 324–41 *passim*
Sedantag, 7, 12, 247, 271, 278n
Segesvár *see* Sighişoara
Serbia, Serbs, 189, 193, 194, 197, 204
Sereno, B., 240
Seven Years War (1756–63), 178
Severing, C. (Prussian Interior Minister, Weimar Republic), 287, 290–91, 292

Sibiu (Szeben, Hermannstadt), 197
Siebenpfeiffer, P. J., 103
Siegen, 242
Sighişoara (Segesvár), 203
Slachta, M., 347
Smolensk, 159
Social Democratic Party (Austria), 224, 226
Social Democratic Party (Germany), 13, 273, 279, 282–99 *passim*, 308, 320
Social Democratic Party (Hungary), 357
Sophia (Tsarina 1682–89), 151
Sophia Elisabeth of Anhalt, 239
Sophie Elisabeth of Brandenburg, 239
Spain, 56, 58, 61, 67, 127, 129, 239
SS (*Schutzstaffel*), 317, 330, 341, 342
Stahl, G. W., 71
Stainz, 229
Stalin, I. V., 326, 332, 337
Stalingrad, 335
Stepan, K. M., 218, 222, 223, 226, 229
Stephan, R. 307n
Stephanie (Hungarian Archduchess, 1864–1945, wife of Crown Prince Rudolf), 208
Stephen (István) I (of Hungary, c. 974–1038) 10, 190, 191, 193, 197–98, 200, 343–62 *passim*
Stifter, A., 327
Stralsund, 339
Stuttgart, 239, 241, 242
Styria, xiii, 10, 12, 213–30 *passim*
Svatopluk of Moravia, 192, 193
Svir, 163
Swabia, 58, 62
Swan, Order of the, 88
Sweden, 59, 60, 63, 70, 149, 154n, 161
Switzerland, 27, 41, 101
Sylvester, Pope, 349
Szálasi, F., 345
Szeben *see* Sibiu

Székesfehérvár, 349
Szilágyi, D., 209–10

Teleki, Count G., 190, 203
Teutonic Knights, 161
Thaly, K. (historian), 191, 193
Theiß, V., 216n, 221, 225
Third Reich, xiii, 303–21 *passim*, 323–41 *passim*
Third Republic (France), 12, 188, 251, 252, 254, 256, 264
Thirty Years War (1618–48), 5, 39, 40, 43, 53, 57, 58, 62, 63, 67–71, 236, 237, 242
Tiber, river, 45
Tocqueville, A. de, 227
Todt, F., 221
Torontál, 197
Toul, 140
Trakl, G., 307n
Transylvania, 193, 196, 197, 203, 208
Trent, Council of (1545–63), 33, 71, 135, 351
Trianon, Treaty of (1920), 353
Trier, 84, 87, 91, 95
Tschech, H. L., 98
Turin, 198
Tyrol, 10, 131

Ukraine, 347
Ulbricht, W., 326
Ultramontanism, 352
Upper Palatinate (Bavaria), 39, 40, 43, 52, 53
USA, 17, 114, 286n, 344, 345, 347, 348; American War of Independence, 170; Independence Day, 281
USPD (Independent Social Democratic Party, Germany, 1919–28), 283
USSR, 332, 345, 347–48

Vajdahunyad, Castle, 203

Valois, dynasty, 139–48 *passim*, 234; Marguerite de (wife of Henri IV of France), x
Vaszary, Cardinal (Prince Primate of Hungary), 200–01
Vatican, 41, 345
Vaudémont, Marguérite de, 234
Verdun, bishopric of, 140; Treaty of (843), 220
Verecke, Pass of, 187, 199
Versailles (court at), 174, 235; Treaty of (1919), 296
Vesalius, A. (anatomist) 52
Vienna, 10, 12, 63, 127, 129, 131, 172, 200, 201, 205, 223, 237, 240, 242, 243; siege of (1683), 50
Vischering, C. A. D. zu (Archbishop), 94,
Vormärz period (Germany), 5, 73–106 *passim*, 221, 229
Vosges, 142, 253

Waldsassen, abbey, 44
Wallhausen, J. J. von, 241–42
Walzel, R., 221
Wandruszka, A. (historian), 223
Wars of Liberation, German (1812–15), 98, 100, 266–79 *passim*
Wars of Religion, French (1562–1629), 18, 23, 26, 28
Wartburg (Festival, 1817), 75, 93
Weber, F. C., 155
Weber, M., 108n
Wedekind, F., 99
Weerth, G., 89
Weimar, 60; duchy of Saxony-Weimar, 173; Weimar Republic, 13, 14, 281–301 *passim*, 303–21 *passim*, 326
Weinert, E., 331
Weinhold, K., 217–18
Wekerle, A., 189–91, 202, 207, 211
Werner, A. von (painter), 247n

Index

Westphalia, Peace of (1648), 56, 57, 58, 59, 61–70 *passim*
White Mountain, Battle of the (1620), 63, 132
Wilhelm I (German Emperor, r. 1871–88), 248, 253n, 258, 261, 262, 271, 272
Wilhelm II (German Emperor, r. 1888–1918), 248–64 *passim*, 272, 271–72, 273n, 276, 278, 282
Wilhelm V of Bavaria, 237,
Wilhelm Ludwig of Nassau-Siegen, 236
William V (Dutch stadtholder), 169
Wirth, J. G., 103, 284, 292, 296, 299
Wittelsbach, dynasty, 34–35, 39, 45
Wohlgemuth, G., 309

Wolfenbüttel (ducal court of), 174, 176; *see also* Brunswick, duchy of
Wolff, J. W. G., 183, 186
Wolfgang Wilhelm of Pfalz-Neuburg, 237
Wotan, Germanic god, 329
Wrangel, C. G. (Swedish general), 59
Wrocław *see* Breslau
Württemberg, 62, 173

Zápolyai István (Hungarian Palatine), 204
Zemun *see* Zimony
Zichy, J., 202–03, 206, 208, 211
Zimony (Zemun), 192, 194
Ziwes, C., 172
Zweig, A., 327